Sun Web Server
The Essential Guide

Sun Web Server
The Essential Guide

William C. Nelson,
Arvind Srinivasan,
Murthy (CVR) Chintalapati

PRENTICE
HALL

Upper Saddle River, NJ • Boston • Indianapolis • San Francisco

New York • Toronto • Montreal • London • Munich • Paris • Madrid

Capetown • Sydney • Tokyo • Singapore • Mexico City

The publisher offers excellent discounts on this book when ordered in quantity for bulk purchases or special sales, which may include electronic versions and/or custom covers and content particular to your business, training goals, marketing focus, and branding interests. For more information, please contact:

U.S. Corporate and Government Sales
(800) 382-3419
corpsales@pearsontechgroup.com

For sales outside the United States please contact:

International Sales
international@pearson.com

Visit us on the Web: informit.com/ph

Library of Congress Cataloging-in-Publication Data:

Nelson, William C. (William Clayton)

  Sun Web server : the essential guide / William C. Nelson, Arvind Srinivasan, Murthy Chintalapati.

    p. cm.

  ISBN 978-0-13-712892-1 (pbk. : alk. paper) 1. Web servers. 2. Web sites[md]Design. I. Srinivasan, Arvind, 1968- II. Chintalapati, Murthy. III. Sun Microsystems. IV. Title.

  TK5105.888.N453 2009

  006.7—dc22

                    2009025812

ISBN-13: 978-0-13-712892-1
ISBN-10: 0-13-712892-4

Text printed in the United States on recycled paper at RR Donnelley, Crawfordsville, Indiana
First printing August 2009

We dedicate this book with heartfelt appreciation to our loving wives and family members, Rosella, William and Rachael Nelson, Tara and Nisha Abraham, and Sujatha Arundhati Chintalapati, for their unconditional love and encouragement.

Contents

Foreword

NETWORK computing is the heart and soul of Sun Microsystems. Always has been; always will be. If the World Wide Web (WWW) were to be one big telephone switch, Web Server would be the technology that reliably delivers the dial tone or the *web tone,* as we call it here at Sun. From massively scalable chip-based multi-core multi-threaded servers to the Solaris operating system to Java and the Web Server infrastructure software, Sun has the technology.

As our systems are built to last, the software components of a Web Server are designed to scale from a single core to hundreds of cores, from a few hundred to hundreds of thousands of user connections. Sun Web Server is no exception and is one of the key technologies that drive innovation across our systems and software stack. With its rock solid quality, superior scalability, and its unique architecture combining Java and native web dynamic web serving technologies, Sun Web Server is widely deployed by enterprises like Sun, Major League Baseball (MLB. com), and *The New York Times*, to name a few.

Even after a decade and a half since use of the web became widespread in the '90s, the world of Web Server software continues to evolve with significant innovations to meet the demands of the Internet. Web Server 7.0 release delivers outstanding innovations in many areas, including the following:

- Dramatic scalability improvements demanded by modern multi-core systems and the Web 2.0 era of richer web applications
- Manageability enhancements, with a brand new server management interface that drastically simplifies the system administrator's job of deploying and managing clusters of web servers
- Security feature updates to protect online properties from growing threats of web vulnerabilities
- Ease of developing and deploying heterogeneous dynamic web scripting technologies.

So I am very pleased to present the most authoritative technical guide on the Sun Web Server 7.0 release. I am proud of the authors who have brought years of experience developing, teaching, training, and supporting customers on Sun Web Server. With concrete examples and lucid explanations of complex concepts, the authors of this book have delivered a marvelous handy reference guide. Whether you happen to be a developer developing your web site or a server administrator responsible for managing and monitoring a large-scale web server farm, I hope that you will find the information in this book useful.

Thank you for choosing Sun and Sun Web Server as part of your web infrastructure solution.

Scott G. McNealy

Chairman, Sun Microsystems Inc.

Preface

"In summary, Sun Web Server is generally two times as fast as Apache. The Sun Web Server is fast, flexible, scalable, and a downright joy to run…if performance and ease of management are paramount, Web Server is the way to go."

—ServerWatch Review, April 2007.

T HE term *web server* broadly refers to the server computer and the software that hosts a web site and serves the site's content to the requesting user agents. At the very basic level, the web server software listens to the TCP/IP port for Hypertext Transport Protocol (HTTP) requests and serves the requested resource. Web servers are a critical part of the infrastructure that powers the public Internet, as well as the private intranets of institutions and corporations. Many web server software products are widely used in the market, namely Apache HTTP server, Microsoft Internet Information Server, Sun Java System Web Server, and newer servers such as lighttpd.

Sun Web Server (officially formerly known as Netscape Enterprise/SunONE/iPlanet Web Server) is the most secure web serving platform widely deployed by large-scale enterprises in the financial, telecommunications, government, travel, and sports worlds. The Sun Java System Web Server (also referred to as Sun Web Server) is a freely available, high-performance, feature-rich HTTP server that provides a simple, user-friendly administration interface. In addition to being a high-performance static-media delivery engine for items such as images and HTML documents, this versatile server supports a breadth of heterogeneous dynamic content technologies, including Java and popular non-Java native scripting technologies such as NSAPI (for Netscape Server Application Programming Interface), Java Servlets, JavaServer Pages (JSP), PHP, Perl, Python, Ruby On Rails, Active Server Pages (ASP), and Coldfusion. With support for hundreds of thousands of simultaneous connections, Sun Web Server demonstrates superior scalability and is the perfect choice for enterprises deploying Web 2.0 technologies, powered by multi-core systems and chip-based multi-threaded (CMT) architecture.

Sun Web Server's Scalability on CMT/Multi-core Systems Is the Industry Standard

A single 64-bit instance of Sun Web Server 7.0, on a Sun Fire T5220 CMT server running Solaris 10 Update 5 and JDK 1.6.0, set a world record SPECweb benchmark in April 2008. A few sample performance metrics showcase Web Server's superior scaling: over 250,000 simultaneous HTTP connections, 131,000 secure banking operations per second (which generated 1GB web server access log data per minute) and 1.4 terabytes of data over the HTTP interface.

With an in-depth discussion of its architecture, new features, administration, performance, and so forth, Sun's latest Web Server 7.0 release is the subject of this book. Gathering from their insights into the product's innovations and experience training the customers who use the product today in live productions, the authors have zeroed in on the most definitive technical information useful to administrators and architects, developers, and deployers alike.

Who This Book Is For

This book gives server administrators a handy guide for the day-to-day administrative tasks such as installation, configuration, cluster management, monitoring, and troubleshooting. You also get insights to developers and architects interested in understanding Sun Web Server internals and extending the server functionality with a variety of dynamic content technologies. Together with information to the deployers on sizing/tuning and reference configurations used in Web 2.0 style sites, this book is an essential guide for the users of the world's most scalable and versatile web infrastructure software.

This book is designed to help you—whether you are developing dynamic scripting technologies, deploying servers, or an administrator managing the server 24×7—get started quickly.

How This Book Is Organized

This book presents in-depth information that will help you build your product expertise gradually. First, Chapter 1 provides a bird's eye view of the product's new features. Then Chapter 2, "Web Server 7.0 Architecture," lays the foundation for your understanding of Sun Web Server's internals. Chapter 3 then explores various methods for performing initial installations or migrating from previous releases.

The following two chapters, Chapter 4, "Web Server 7.0 Administration," and Chapter 5, "Web Server 7.0 Configuration Files," provide the necessary foundation for the server administrator. Chapter 6 discusses how Web Server processes HTTP requests and is very handy when customizing Web Server, such as when you are adding a custom vanity URL rewrite rule. Chapter 7, "Monitoring Web Server 7.0," and Chapter 8, "Securing Web Server 7.0," both provide vital information to server administrators configuring and securing the web server and monitoring the server instances in live production for optimal performance. These chapters provide task-oriented hands-on examples of the administration interfaces and command-line examples—to the delight of server administrators, we hope. Chapters 9 and 10 turn to developers' needs, discussing how to build dynamic content through scripting languages and server-side Java based extensions.

Resolving the anomalies in the web server runtime behavior (such as those unexpected 500 Server Errors) rapidly could be very important for developers and deployers alike, so Chapter 11 is devoted to troubleshooting. The final chapter, Chapter 12, is devoted to building secure dynamic (Web 2.0/Enterprise 2.0 style) sites with Sun Web Server and explains why the product is ideal for building such sites with your dynamic content and database technologies of choice. This chapter also features a couple of Sun's own production deployments powered by Sun Web Server 7.0—namely, Sun Blogs and Sun Forums. Sun Blogs (http://blogs. sun.com) is an employee blogging site deployed with Sun Web Server 7.0, and the MySQL Sun Forums site (http://forums.sun.com) is a public forum for thousands of products and technologies deployed with Sun Web Server 7.0 and Oracle RDBMS.

Appendix A is a detailed reference guide to the main server configuration file, `server.xml`. Appendixes B and C provide sample reports of server runtime statistics, respectively in XML and plaintext format.

Getting the Most Out of This Book

There are many ways to get the most out of this book, whether you are starting to build a single server web site or managing a larger scale clustered web server deployment.

- Make sure you are using the latest version of Web Server because there may be security updates and bug fixes relevant to the job you like to accomplish. Links to official downloads and documentation can be found at this book's web site, http://www.sunwebserver.com/.

- Take advantage of the numerous command-line examples and the self-paced labs you will find throughout this book. Manageability is a major theme of the Sun Web Server 7.0 release, and its administration interfaces are designed to let you perform the common tasks with relative ease.

- This book is filled with numerous clear and concise how-to style examples, such as configuring a secure HTTP listener, a virtual server, a FastCGI interface, a reverse proxy front end, an LDAP authentication, or a data source such as MySQL database.

Conventions Used in This Book

It is our goal for you to get the most out of this book and get your job done efficiently. We have employed a few conventions to improve readability. Here are some conventions used in this book:

- The term "Sun Web Server" refers to all versions of the Web Server, whereas "Sun Web Server 7.0" refers to the specific version.

- The figures, tables, and examples are numbered consistently, using chapter number and a sequential number; for example, Figure 1.1, Table 6.1, and Example 6.2.

- A special font is used to distinguish configuration filenames (for example, obj.conf), variables, and snippets of command-line administration scripts from normal text.

- Special information is sometimes called out explicitly using notes like the following:

Note: Key themes behind the Sun Java System Web Server 7.0 release include manageability, security, interoperability, CMT scalability, ease of deployment via integrated support for dynamic scripting technologies, and proxy configurations.

- Most chapters end with a "Self-Paced Labs" section. These self-paced labs are designed to help validate your understanding of the concepts described in the respective chapters. The self-paced labs are modeled after Sun Web Server training and are designed by chief training instructor and one of the authors of this book, Bill Nelson. The answers to the self-paced exercises are available online at this book's ancillary web site, http://www.sunweb-server.com. At this site, you will also find FAQs, errata, discussions on the book, and links to more information on the Sun Web Server product, including its download locations and product forums. Please visit this web site and share your insights and impressions of our work.

Note: We make every effort to ensure accuracy of the information—content or examples—presented in this book. However, we do anticipate that there might be inadvertent errors in the book. So if you do find errors (whether it is a defective example or a typo) that need correction, we would like to hear from you. Please visit the SunWebServer.com web site, click the Errata link, and follow the instructions to submit the errors online.

Acknowledgments

WE would like to thank so many bright minds and subject matter experts who have helped shape this book. From the Sun Web Server product development team to product management to support team to field champions to enthusiastic customers (both inside Sun and outside), as well as our book reviewers and technical editors at Pearson Publishing, many people have played a critical role in our endeavor.

Technological innovations—namely, manageability, CMT systems scalability, and security—span many facets of the Web Server 7.0 release. Our motivation for this book is rooted in the product innovations. As such we want to thank the entire product development and quality engineering teams, including these current and past members—Chris Elving, Praveen Chandrasekharan, Jyri Virkki, Uma Sabada, Nelson Segura-Nunez, Tuan Tran (posthumously), Sriram Natarajan, Basant Kukreja, Meena Vyas, Isvaran Krishnamurthy, Irfan Ahmed, Yamini K.B., Rahul Nair, Srinivas Krishnan, Hamidul Haque, CV Padmanabhan, Anand Swaminathan, Manju Battula, V Premkumar, Megha Shivaprasad, Chandrashekar Arunachalam, Regi Augustine, Hariharasudhan Reghuraman, Partha Dey, Manoj Malhotra, Vinutha Nagaraju, Pallab Bhattacharya, Jackson Thompson and many more. These members of our extended product team have helped bring out the best quality product and helped review some of the administration samples presented in this book.

Our sincere appreciation also goes to the following members of the support team, who have helped review the content of the book and offered insightful comments and suggestions: Adilia Vallejo, Janice Hunt, Manish Kapur and Rodrigo Stumpf. Will Snow, Jed Michnowicz, John Renko, Ramachander Varadarajan, and Joe Mocker from Sun.com Common Web Platform engineering, for sharing their practical insight putting Sun Web Server in production deployments at Sun.com, Sun Blogs, and other online properties. Likewise, we thank Hal Stern for his keen architectural insights into MLB.com. Our sincere appreciation goes to our team at Pearson Education, Inc., for their outstanding support: Greg Doench, Michelle Housley, and technical editors Songlin Qiu and Christopher Steel. Our thanks to Myrna Rivera at Sun Microsystems Press, for her support in getting this project off the ground.

We acknowledge invaluable support we received from Joe McCabe, Chris Hogan, John Brock, Yvette Montiel, and John Shell, members of former Product Management and Marketing, for Sun's Web Tier products; Sun Web Server wouldn't exist today without some pioneering work done over the years by the brilliant engineering minds like Rob McCool, and enterprises worldwide who rely on the product for their mission-critical business. We appreciate their contributions and influence on the Web Server's evolution, some of which is captured in this book. We are also very grateful to Scott G. McNealy, chairman of Sun Microsystems, Inc., for graciously accepting our request for a foreword. We are so privileged to have it in this book. We appreciate Daniel Berthiaume in the chairman's office for his assistance with the foreword.

Finally, we would most graciously and lovingly like to acknowledge the patience and understanding of our families, who allowed us to feed our egos and become engrossed in a project that took way too much time away from them.

About the Authors

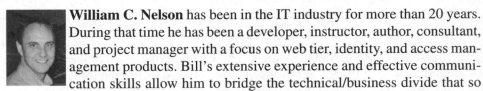

William C. Nelson has been in the IT industry for more than 20 years. During that time he has been a developer, instructor, author, consultant, and project manager with a focus on web tier, identity, and access management products. Bill's extensive experience and effective communication skills allow him to bridge the technical/business divide that so often prevents communication between the data center and the board room.

Bill has authored more than 10 courses for Sun Microsystems focused on the Java Enterprise System. He has been working with Sun's Directory, Web, and Identity products for several years and brings that experience to the courses, books, and articles he has written. Bill currently lives in Tampa, Florida, where he manages a professional services organization that specializes on identity and access management.

Arvind Srinivasan is one of three architects on the Sun Web Server development engineering team. Since joining Sun Microsystems in 2000, he has worked as an individual contributor and has been the technical lead for the Servlet/JSP container of Sun's Web Server and Application Server. Mass virtual hosting and the superior performance/scalability of the Servlet/JSP container are two of his key contributions to the Sun Java System Web Server. Arvind is also the co-author of *Java Networking and Awt Api Superbible: The Comprehensive Reference for the Java Programming Language* (ISBN: 157169031X).

Murthy (CVR) Chintalapati (who goes by CVR) is a development engineering leader responsible for Sun's web tier products, including Sun Web Server 7.0 and the OpenSolaris Web Stack (AMP). He specializes in infrastructure software products for enterprises deploying web 2.0 technologies, scalability on multi-core and chip-based multi-threaded (CMT) systems. CVR holds a masters degree in computer science and engineering from Indian Institute of Technology (IIT Mumbai), India. He has been awarded five U.S. patents and has received the Sun Microsystems Chairman's Award for Innovation.

Introduction to Sun Java System Web Server 7.0

What Is New in Sun Web Server 7.0?

"I'm quite happy with the changes from version 6.1 to 7. The Admin console is MUCH easier to work with. The server runs faster and takes up less resources. The INSTALLATION was 100x easier than with 6.1. Great job on this product!"

—Nathaniel Walker, Mellon Bank.

SUN Java System Web Server 7.0 (referred to as Sun Web Server 7.0, or simply Web Server 7.0 hereafter) is the most recent release of Sun's commercial web server, part of the Sun Java System branded family of software infrastructure products. The product family includes industry-leading infrastructure products such as Sun Java System Web Proxy Server, Application Server, Portal Server, and Directory Server Enterprise Edition (DSEE). Please note that the presence of "Java" in this family of products is primarily for branding purposes.

Sun Web Server 7.0 introduces a number of enhancements across the product and its constituent subsystems that make up the product. Extensive feedback from enterprise customers and the emergence of newer multi-core Chip Multi-threading (CMT) systems drove a number of these feature enhancements and scalability improvements. Throughput computing, powered by CMT technology, provides multiple threads of execution on a single chip. Sun's CMT systems, such as the Sun Fire T2000 Server and the Sun SPARC Enterprise T5120, offer substantial scaling and throughput benefits and architectural challenges to server applications such as Web Server.

As with any major revision of software, Web Server 7.0 incorporates brand new features, designed from the ground up, such as new administration UI, as well as incremental improvements, such as the conditional request processing aided by regular expression-based pattern matching. When designing new interfaces as part of a major revision of software products such as Web Server 7.0, compatibility with prior releases is an important design consideration. Although some incompatibility is inevitable with any major revision of software such as Web Server 7.0, care is taken to ensure backward compatibility to ease migration from prior releases.

After a brief introduction to earlier versions of Sun Web Server, we present a conceptual overview of Sun Web Server 7.0 technology, followed by various feature enhancements and improvements in the Web Server 7.0 release. You learn what is new and what changed in the 7.0 release relative to previous releases. Please make sure to refer to Chapter 2, "Web Server 7.0 Architecture," for more in-depth discussion of server subsystems such as the core, security, Java Servlet container, and administration.

1.1 Earlier Versions of Sun Web Server

Sun Java System Web Server, formerly known as Sun ONE Web Server, iPlanet Web Server, Netscape Enterprise Server, Netsite Communications Server, and Commerce Server, has a rich legacy of technological and branding evolution from the days of the rapid rise of the Internet in the mid-90s. The lineage leads to NCSA (National Center for Supercomputing Applications at University of Illinois at Urbana-Champaign) HTTPd, which was later known as Apache HTTP Server. In fact, these servers were developed by Rob McCool during his early days as a developer at Mosaic Communications Corp., which became Netscape Communications. The web servers originated from NCSA HTTPd, whereas Apache evolved in open source and Netscape continued commercial development, later by the Sun|Netscape Alliance. Table 1.1 shows a brief history of Sun Web Server.

Table 1.1 Earlier Versions of Sun Web Server

Web Server Version	Year	Major Features	Remarks
Netsite Communications Server 1.0, Commerce Server 1.0.	1994–95	HTTP/1.0, CGI, Server-side Includes (SSI), image maps, access logging and log rotation, additional document roots, UNIX home directories, HTTP-based Basic Authentication and DBM-based hashed file format used for "high-capacity" user databases. Commerce Server–supported RSA public key cryptography.	First commercial Internet server compatible with NCSA HTTPd server. Designed to make the conduct of electronic commerce transactions and exchange of sensitive documents over networks simple and secure.
Netscape SuiteSpot Server line—Netscape Enterprise Server (NES) 2.x–3.x; NES 4.0; Secure Socket Layer (SSL) ver. 3.0, HTTP Cookies specifications.	1996–98	Software virtual servers, integrated full text search engine (based on Verity), SNMP v1 and v2, one-button publish via HTTP PUT method, Access Control (ACL), Netscape Server Application Programmers Interface (NSAPI), client-certificate authentication and web-based remote graphical administration interface. NES 3.0/3.6–supported HTTP/1.1, multithreaded NSAPI, LDAP authentication, dynamic server-side JavaScript and Java (Web Application Interface, WAI); NES Pro–supported LiveWire Pro database connectivity, Objet-request Broker (ORB) and Internet Inter-ORB Protocol (IIOP).	NES 2.0 and 3.0 led a new era of innovation on the Internet and spurred the growth of the WWW and intranets—enabled by web publishing and electronic commerce technologies featuring shopping cart and secure transactions via HTTPS. SuiteSpot product line included Web Proxy, Directory, Media, Messaging, Calendar, News , Collaboration, and Certificate Servers. The SuiteSpot line won numerous awards—*PC Week*'s Best New Product of '96, Datamation and CNET Award for Best Web Server in '97.
Netscape Enterprise Server 4.0, iPlanet Web Server 4.1–6.0	1999–2001	Integrated Java runtime and J2EE-compliant Servlet container (which replaced WAI in iWS 4.1), removed ORB/IIOP support and thus provided a distinctive architecture relative to Apache HTTP server. iWS 6.0 incorporated scalable connection handling and enhanced virtual server support; it also improved quality and performance.	The iPlanet-branded iWS 4.1 was developed jointly by the Sun|Netscape Alliance. iWS 6.0 set a world record SPECweb99 benchmark and was touted as the fastest web server.
Sun ONE Web Server 6.1, also known as Sun Java System Web Server 6.1.	2003	A descendent of Sun ONE Application Server 7.0, which incorporated J2EE Reference Implementation and adopted open source Apache Tomcat in place of a proprietary servlet container. It's an integral part of Java Enterprise System from its inception.	Web Server 6.1 is probably the most deployed Sun Web Server version on the Web, powering some of the busiest sites such as MLB.com and NYTimes.com.

1.2 Sun Java System Web Server 7.0—A Conceptual Overview

Figure 1.1 provides a high-level conceptual overview of Sun Web Server 7.0. It contains information on how Web Server conceptually fits in a typical web site deployment where the web server is configured with a directory server or an identity service for single sign-on, a database server, or other data sources. In its most basic form, a web server responds to an HTTP request over a TCP/IP connection and serves the requested resource, identified by its Uniform Resource Locator (URL). The resources (also referred to as content) could be static media files (e.g. HTML, CSS files, flash files, etc.) or dynamically executed code or content such as NSAPI plug-ins, servlets, JavaServer Pages (.jsp), PHP pages (.php), and so on. The resource could be hosted on the same web server as the one on which the request was received or hosted elsewhere, in which case the web server could either redirect the user to its location or, acting as a proxy, fetch from its origin server, which could be another web server or application server. Web sites offer different services (e.g. MLB.com offers a scoreboard, stats, games schedule, tickets, etc.), each implemented by different web applications that comprise static and dynamically generated content. Security is critical to web sites, and web servers offer comprehensive security features, including support for SSL, authentication/ single sign-on, access control, and so on, as well as protection against common web vulnerabilities such as cross-site scripting attacks.

The diagram also highlights a few new features in the Web Server 7.0 release—for example, the FastCGI engine enables integration with scripting technologies such as PHP or Ruby On Rails; reverse proxy functionality helps to deploy Web Server in front of an origin web and application server for added security and load balancing; Administration Server provides secure infrastructure for cluster management and remote administration, via a web browser or a command-line interface.

New features in Sun Web Server 7.0 are discussed according to the following sections:

- Core server improvements including CMT scalability.
- Manageability enhancements.
- Security improvements.
- Web application features, ease of development, and deployment.
- Interoperability and protocol compliance.
- Internationalization and localization.

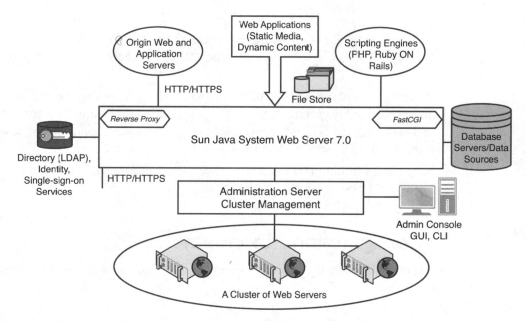

Figure 1.1 Sun Java System Web Server 7.0 Conceptual Overview

1.3 Core Web Server Improvements

As the name suggests, the Web Server core subsystem is the foundation on which the rest of the server subsystems are built, and it implements fundamental aspects of the server's configuration and runtime request processing. There have been a number of substantial improvements to the core subsystem in the 7.0 release.

With its native 64-bit support for the Solaris (as well as Linux) platform, Sun Web Server 7.0 incorporates several design improvements to scale well on CMT systems, as demonstrated by world record web server benchmark results. Before discussing improvements to the core in Web Server 7.0, we first outline a high-level overview of the core subsystem. A more detailed functional discussion of core and other subsystems can be found in Chapter 2.

1.3.1 Web Server Core Subsystem

Web Server core subsystem performs a central role in initializing, processing HTTP requests, and maintaining the runtime configuration and vital statistics. The following is a brief overview of the core subsystem's role in a functional Sun Web Server instance:

- Bootstrapping the server by reading the server configuration specified in `server.xml` and other files, thereby creating the runtime environment and loading and initializing subsystems such as the file cache and NSAPI plug-ins.

- Performing web serving functions such as handling incoming connections, encrypting and decrypting SSL communication as applicable, and parsing and servicing the HTTP requests. All aspects of request handling are customized using a series of directives in `obj.conf`.

- Responding to administrative actions such as monitoring the server runtime, changing the configuration on the fly, and so on.

1.3.2 Configuration Enhancements

Web Server 7.0 significantly enhances server configurability because of a number of improvements:

- XML Schema validation for server configuration—Providing ease of use (e.g., ordering of elements in server configuration is relaxed where it is appropriate), integrity checks for configuration elements and references (e.g., make sure the IP address specified in an HTTP listener is real or a reference to virtual server is valid), and apply robust type-checking for elements of server configuration.

- New server configuration (`server.xml`) syntax, which improves readability as it mirrors the conventions used in servlet deployment descriptors.

- Consolidated and delegated server configuration—Simplifying configuration by consolidating disparate configuration files and directives that existed in previous Web Server releases, such as `nsfc.conf` (file cache configuration), `password.conf`, `dbswitch.conf` (authentication database configuration), and so on, into `server.xml`. At the same time, the Web Server 7.0 release offers delegation by letting individual virtual servers have their own configuration.

1.3.3 Core Subsystem Improvements

This section introduces improvements to the core subsystem in Web Server 7.0:

- Conditional request processing, which offers a great deal of flexibility to service the request in certain ways when the incoming request matches with a set of expressions. For example, whenever a user requests a resource via a plain HTTP connection, you want to force the user to a secure HTTPS connection instead.

- Regular expression-based pattern matching, applicable throughout the configuration.

- URL rewriting, which enables you to rewrite a pretty URL (also referred to as a vanity URL) used externally into an ugly internal URL. This is similar to—if not more flexible and general purpose than—Apache web server's popular `mod_rewrite` module.

- URL redirects, which enable you to redirect requests from one URL to another. A sample use of URL redirects is when, say, the resource is moved to a different location and you want the server to redirect the user accordingly. Although this feature was available in prior releases, Web Server 7.0 enhances its ease of use and flexibility in that you can combine URL redirection with conditional processing and pattern matching.

- Integrated Reverse Proxy, which enables Web Server to be deployed as a secure HTTP front end to origin HTTP servers such as Application Servers. The reverse proxy supports rudimentary round-robin load balancing and sticky session requests routing.

- Integrated FastCGI engine, which enables Web Server to be integrated with dynamic scripting engines such as PHP and Ruby On Rails, which run out of process.

- Two new NSAPI request processing filters, one for input stage and another in the output stage, to enable administrators to manipulate the date sent to/ from Web Server using syntax used in the UNIX `sed` program. As you will see later, these filters would have numerous applications, such as detecting common forms of web vulnerability such as the cross-site scripting (XSS) attack.

1.4 Manageability Enhancements

Note: The term *manageability* generally refers to how easy it is for system/server administrators and end users to perform fairly routine tasks of configuring, deploying, monitoring, and customizing or extending one or more installations of Web Server, whether in a single machine development environment or in large-scale server farms.

Prior releases of Web Server included a browser-based interface that focused on configuring a single installation of Web Server and was simple in scope. However, the feedback from customers (administrators at major Internet sites deploying Sun Web Server) favored the interfaces to manage and monitor clustered Web Server installations across a server farm, a command-line interface for scripting routine tasks such as log aggregation or rolling upgrades that could be automated, and greater ease of use for commonly accessed tasks.

Manageability is one of the major themes of the Sun Web Server 7.0 release, and the new release incorporates a complete rewrite of the management infrastructure (also referred to as administrative framework) and the administrator interfaces. Ease of use with which an administrator would manage and monitor a single instance of Web Server or a set of clustered servers is key to manageability. From the technology perspective, manageability in Web Server 7.0 refers to several features, outlined in the following sections.

1.4.1 Web-Based Graphical Administrator Interface

The browser-based graphical administrator interface (also referred to as Administration Console) embodies very important manageability advancements in Web Server 7.0. Whether managing a single Web Server instance or a cluster of servers, the web-based interface provides a centralized console to configure the server, deploy the configuration to a server cluster, and manage and monitor the live servers. As you can see in Figure 1.2, the web-based interface offers greater navigation and ease of use with faster access to commonly performed administrator tasks such as requesting and installing server certificates, deploying web applications, tuning server settings, and starting and stopping the server.

1.4.2 Command-line Administrator Interface

Command-line interface (CLI) is essential for automating routine administrator tasks, many performed remotely, such as rolling a new application to a server farm, gathering access logs, or taking a subset or a cluster of production servers live or offline. Web Server 7.0's command-line management framework is comprehensive, secure, and scriptable.

Figure 1.2   Web-based Graphical Administration Console in Sun Web Server 7.0

Note: The `wadm` binary (or `wadm.bat` file in the Windows platform), located under the `bin/` subdirectory relative to the installation directory, implements the CLI in Web Server 7.0. One could choose to install just the CLI—not the entire server product—by selecting the custom install option in the Web Server installer.

Sun Web Server's CLI can be run as just a single command, in a shell mode to interactively run several commands, or in a batch mode where the commands can be input in a file. The CLI framew ork is designed to provide greater ease of use, with its embedded Java Command Language (JACL) shell with built-in TCL (Tool Command Language) interpreter offering richer scripting capabilities. The CLI also offers convenient auto-completion of commands. The management and monitoring functionality implemented in CLI is very comprehensive, including functionality for configuring the server and its subsystems, managing certificates, starting and stopping servers, monitoring the server, and so on.

Command-line (CLI) scripts can be run against remote servers. As Figure 1.3 shows, the `wadm` executed in Windows PC can securely access runtime performance information (via the `get-perfdump` subcommand of `wadm`) remotely from a Web Server running elsewhere.

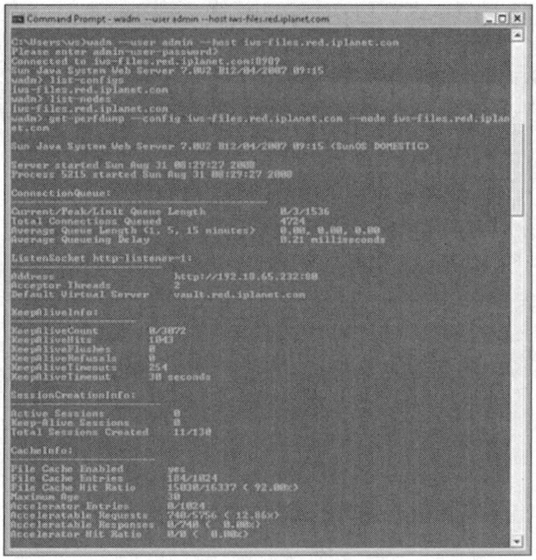

Figure 1.3   Remote Command-line Interface (CLI) in Sun Web Server 7.0

1.4.3 Cluster Management

Cluster Management refers to managing a set of web server instances, deployed across a set of nodes, via a single administration interface, web-based graphical interface, or CLI. As detailed in later chapters on administration, a node could be a single server box or a virtualized system. Cluster management is a key to manageability and is integral to the design of Sun Web Server 7.0 secure management infrastructure, which includes an Administration Server and an administrative agent per node in the cluster. An Administration Server serves both the web-based graphical administration console and the CLI via a secure HTTPS connection. As an administrator you would manage a set—actually, one or more sets—of server configuration files. As shown in Figure 1.4, the Administration Server maintains a central repository of server configuration files and helps manage them centrally by securely replicating them to the cluster of nodes that it manages. An installation of Web Server running in a node is termed a server instance, and all instances of a cluster employ the same configuration. The administration agents at each node also help centrally manage the life cycle of server instances and gather runtime statistics from those instances. Administration Server and the agents at each node also communicate via a secure HTTPS connection and together form the core cluster management infrastructure. Figure 1.4 shows the cluster management infrastructure in Web Server 7.0.

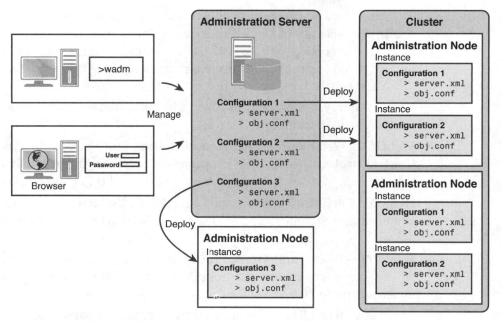

Figure 1.4   Cluster Management in Sun Web Server 7.0

1.5 Security Improvements

Security is as important a consideration for web application developers as it is to system and site administrators managing the web servers in live production. Having been deployed at secure deployments worldwide, security is a Sun Web Server's strength, as well as an important theme for improvements in Web Server 7.0. Here we introduce salient security features implemented in the 7.0 release, many of them requested by customers:

- **Elliptic Curve Cryptography (ECC) cipher suites**—Web Server 7.0 is one of the earliest adopters of ECC technology, which drastically improves efficiency of public key encryption by dramatically reducing the key sizes.

- **LDAP Authentication improvements**—Aimed to deliver more flexibility of configuring LDAP servers, Web Server 7.0 incorporates the following important changes.

  - Flexible configuration for searching and matching user and group and group membership information in an LDAP server. Web servers typically use attribute names and values in an LDAP entry to search and match for a desired value (such as userid or a group name, for example). In prior releases of Sun Web Server, the attribute name search patterns were hard coded. Web Server 7.0 removes this limitation and as a result it's much easier to authenticate against many LDAP servers, such as Microsoft Active Directory Server.

- LDAP server connection fail over, which lets administrators configure alternative backup LDAP servers.

- **WebDAV (Web-based Distributed Authoring and Versioning) Access Control protocol (RFC 3744) support**—Enables third-party authoring tools to set access control to the content via extended HTTP interface.

- **Dynamic Certification Revocation List (CRL) Refresh**—Allows server administrators to configure periodic live refresh of CRLs, without restarting the server.

- **Denial of Service (DoS) Attack Protection**—Offers a few defensive mechanisms to protect your web site from DoS attacks. Here are a few enhancements relative to Web Server 7.0 release:

  - Web Server 7.0 provides mechanisms to protect the web server and the resources it serves from overuse by potentially malicious clients. Administrators can configure how the web server would isolate those clients using various request time attributes (e.g. client IP address) and limit traffic from those clients up to certain thresholds (e.g. allowable requests per second or maximum simultaneous connections). In addition, one could specify that the traffic thresholds could be applied globally across servers, on a particular resource, on a set of resources matching a URL pattern, or by using more powerful conditional processing directives.

  - Another form of DoS attack could occur when a malicious client opens many connections (exceeding the maximum number of request processing worker threads) and trickles request data, thereby denying access to the server by legitimate clients. Prior releases of Web Server supported a limited form of protection against such attacks, limited to specifying timeout on how long a worker thread handing a CGI request would block on a connection waiting for request data. Web Server 7.0 broadens this to any HTTP request and enables administrators to apply timeouts on how long the server should wait on a connection to receive a request header or request body.

- **Cross-site Scripting (XSS) Attack Detection**—XSS attack is a common web security vulnerability that, unless detected and prevented, could compromise online security for unwitting users. The attack occurs whereby a malicious user posts a script into a vulnerable web site, such as an online bulletin board. When the site is viewed by an unsuspecting user in a browser, the embedded malicious script executes in the user's browser environment, which in turn can transmit personal information directly to the malicious user. Web Server 7.0's sed filters enable administrators to apply sed scripting to filter out malicious posts and prevent the vulnerability where it originates.

1.6 Web Application Ease of Development and Deployment

In addition to its native server extension API, namely NSAPI, with its integrated Java servlet container and support for native technologies, Sun Java System Web Server supports a broad spectrum of heterogeneous dynamic web application, scripting, and web services technologies, including JavaServer Pages (JSPs), JavaServer Faces (JSFs), PHP, Perl, Python, and Ruby, as well as traditional CGI scripting. Together with stronger security, scalability, and manageability, Web Server 7.0 is probably one of the most versatile web application development and deployment platforms. We explore some of the web application–related improvements in the 7.0 release and more recent update releases.

- **Java EE 5 web technologies**—Support for Servlet 2.5, JSP 2.1, JSTL (JSP Standard Tag Library) 1.2, Servlet response caching, and JSP caching tag library. The Java EE web container code in Web Server is actually shared with GlassFish Enterprise Server v2. Please note that while GlassFish is a collection of Java EE containers, one of which is a web container, Sun Web Server containers are just the web container. Sun Web Server also supports associated Java EE services; namely, Java Naming (JNDI) and Database connectivity (JDBC) and connection pooling. JNDI enables administrators to configure resources such as JDBC-based data sources so that the Java EE–compliant web applications can look up those in a portable way.

- **Java XML/SOAP Web Services**—Supported via Java Developer Pack (JWSDP) 2.0. This is a recent version of Java Web Services; namely, JWSDP 2.1, also known as the GlassFish Metro project. It works well with Web Server 7.0 Update 2 and later releases.

- **In-memory Session Replication**—Web Server saves session data to a backup web server so that in the event of a failure, the front-end load balancer can direct the traffic to the backup server, which provides the user session continuity, improving overall service availability.

- **PHP Support**—Available via PHP Add On and the Sun GlassFish Web Stack (formerly Cool Stack) product offering.
- **Support for Ruby**—Available via FastCGI interface with Sun GlassFish Web Stack. Please note that the Web Stack is a fully supported component of Sun GlassFish Portfolio—a complete web infrastructure stack comprising open source technologies; namely Apache web server, PHP, MySQL Community, Tomcat, and GlassFish application servers.
- **NetBeans 6.x IDE plug-in**—Capacity to develop, deploy, and debug Java web applications to Web Server 7.0.

1.7 Interoperability Improvements

Interoperability is an important consideration in any multi-tiered deployment architecture, and Sun Web Server 7.0 improves interoperability on many different fronts:

- **Solaris 10 platform interoperability**—Support for Solaris Crypto Framework (SCF) via PKCS#11 interface; Solaris Service Management Framework (SMF); Zones support.
- **Single SignOn**—Support for authentication across different services in a single web site or domain is provided using Sun Java System Access Manager/Federated Access Manager and its associated open source project, OpenSSO. Please note that the secure Web Services–based Federated Access Management provides the single sign-on capability spanning multiple web sites or domains. Sun Web Server 7.0 works well with OpenID, which is a lightweight decentralized authentication system that is used on the web. Commercial solutions are also available for single sign-on; namely, Computer Associates' Netegrity SiteMinder. In addition, as noted earlier, Sun Web Server 7.0 is easily interoperable with Microsoft Active Directory Server.
- **Web Services Interoperability (WS-I)**—Available through integrated JWSDP and Project Metro.
- **Application Server interoperability**—Enabled by the integrated reverse proxy.

- **Content/developer tool interoperability**—Tools such as Adobe Dreamweaver and WebDAV Access Control, which permits the use of DAV-based content management tools.

1.8 Internationalization (I18N) and Globalization (G11n) Support

With the global reach of Sun's products and technologies, I18N compliance is one of the big rules at Sun, and localization to many locales is a norm. Sun Web Server 7.0 is no exception, with its browser-based Administration GUI, server error messages, online Help, and Release Notes localized to seven languages, (French, German, Spanish, Japanese, Simplified Chinese, Traditional Chinese, and Korean). Figure 1.5 shows a snapshot of the Sun Web Server 7.0 web-based Administration Console in Japanese.

Figure 1.5   Sun Java System Web Server 7.0 Administration Console (Japanese)

1.9 Summary

Sun Web Server 7.0 is a major release in the evolution of one of the most widely deployed World Wide Web servers, driving some of the busiest and most secure web sites around the Internet, whose technological origins are rooted in Netscape Enterprise Server and NCSA HTTPd. Sun Web Server is a leading worldwide web server in the Fortune 100 and Global 250 companies spanning educational, e-commerce, financial, governmental, health care, information technology, media, military, retail, sports, telecommunications, and travel sectors world wide.

As a major release, Sun Web Server 7.0 incorporates improvements among several themes, namely manageability, security, updated Java standards compliance, and interoperability. Manageability improvements are made throughout the server, including how the server is configured, deployed, managed, and monitored in large clustered environments.

Cluster management is central to Web Server 7.0, which features a complete rewrite of management infrastructure, along with a newly designed web-based comprehensive graphical administration and secure, scriptable command-line interface. With support for modern Java EE web technologies and native scripting technologies enabled via FastCGI such as PHP and Ruby On Rails, Sun Web Server 7.0 represents the most comprehensive heterogeneous dynamic web serving platform. The core architectural enhancements include 64-bit (which helps larger file caches and Java heap sizes) multi-threaded architecture, pattern matching, URL rewriting, UNIX sed-based NSAPI filters (which can also be used to protect web sites from common web vulnerabilities such as XSS attacks), DoS attack awareness, and integrated reverse proxy, making Web Server 7.0 a robust, secure, and scalable deployment platform.

1.10 Self-Paced Labs

Use the information in this chapter to perform the following exercises. They will help validate your understanding of the concepts described in this chapter.

1. See how major sites have implemented Web Server by visiting any of the following URLs:

   www.sun.com

   forums.sun.com

   www.mlb.com

   www.nyl.com

   www.boeing.com

2. Visit the book's Web site (www.sunwebserver.com) and explore the additional information that can be found on that site.

3. Additional exercises:

   Research into building an OpenID-based federated Single SignOn infrastructure solution like OpenId At Work by reviewing the following article: www.sun.com/bigadmin/features/articles/openid_web_server.jsp.

   Find out how Sun Web Server scales to hundreds of thousands of simultaneous connections on modern 64-bit multicore chip-based multithreaded (CMT) system architectures by reviewing the following article: http://blogs.sun.com/webtier/entry/rise_of_cmt_systems_on.

Web Server 7.0 Architecture

WEB Server 7.0 is a fast, scalable, secure HTTP server that is easy to both install and manage. It is freely available for use on a variety of operating systems and is designed to work optimally on all platforms.

Understanding how the various components of Web Server 7.0 interact and what the underlying architecture looks like will help you administer and troubleshoot your Web Server 7.0 installation.

This chapter explains the overall architecture of Web Server and the relationship between the different components that comprise Web Server 7.0. Specifically, this chapter discusses the various processes that comprise Web Server, the different subsystems in the server, the support for hosting a variety of static and dynamic content, and the support in Web Server for threads and 64-bit architectures.

2.1 Server Processes

Multiple server processes run when you start your Web Server instance. Each of the processes plays a specific role in ensuring that your web site processes client HTTP requests and stays up and running. This section describes the different server processes that run when you start a Web Server 7.0 instance. The term *instance* refers to the environs of a Web Server daemon on a given node, including its configuration, log files, and other runtime artifacts such as lock databases, caches, and temporary files. For management purposes, an instance can be started/stopped/restarted or dynamically reconfigured.

As shown in Figure 2.1, three processes are created when a Web Server instance is started: the watchdog process, the primordial process, and the worker process.

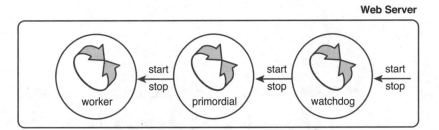

Figure 2.1   Web Server Processes

The watchdog process spawns the primordial process, which in turn spawns one or more worker processes. The worker process listens for HTTP requests on one or more ports and is responsible for processing requests received on those ports. The worker process is responsible for processing HTTP requests over secure and non-secure socket connections.

The sequence of creation of these processes (when you execute the `startserv` script to start your instance) is also shown in Figure 2.1 and is as follows:

1. Watchdog process
2. Primordial process
3. Worker process

The watchdog process and the primordial process provide a limited level of high availability within the server processes. If the worker process(es) crashes or terminates abnormally, the primordial process is responsible for restarting another worker process. If the primordial process itself terminates abnormally, then the watchdog restarts another primordial process.

On UNIX platforms, a Web Server instance has exactly one watchdog process, one primordial process, and one or more worker processes. On Windows platforms, each instance has exactly one watchdog process and one worker process. There is no separate primordial process on Windows and each instance cannot start more than one worker process.

Note: A single process could theoretically do the job of both the watchdog process and the primordial process. The reasons for their being separate processes (on UNIX platforms) are more historical than technical.

The primordial and worker processes are both named `webservd`. The name of the watchdog process is `webservd-wdog`.

On UNIX servers, these processes can be seen with the `ps -ef` command. The following example shows each of the processes for an instance running on Solaris:

```
# ps -ef | grep http

webservd 14857 14856  0  Jan 22 ?        33:12 webservd -d
/sun/webserver7/https-boulder.example.com/config -r /sun/webserver7

   root 14856 14855  0  Jan 22 ?         7:19 webservd -d
/sun/webserver7/https-boulder.example.com/config -r /sun/webserver7

   root 14855   1  0  Jan 22 ?          0:04 webservd-wdog -d
/sun/webserver7/https-boulder.example.com/config -r /sun/webse
```

Note: The `ps` command provides important information about the process owner, the process ID, the parent process ID, the date the process was started, the daemon process that is running, and the parameters that were passed to the process.

The first column specifies the process owner which, in this case, is `root` for the watchdog and primordial processes. This is required if your Web Server is listening to a port less than 1024 (a privileged port on UNIX). If the port is greater than 1024, the watchdog and primordial process can be a non-`root` user. The user for the child process owner is specified during the installation process. In this case the process owner is `webservd`, which is the default user.

The second column is the process ID of the running process, and the third column is the process ID of the parent process (or the process that started this process).

Looking at the entries from bottom to top, the following can be observed:

- Process 14855 is the watchdog process. It was started by the `init` process (which is indicated by a process ID of 1).
- Process 14856 is the primordial process. It was started by the watchdog process.
- Process 14857 is the child process. It was started by the primordial process.

There is a parent/child relationship between the various processes. You can use the UNIX `ptree` command on the watchdog process to determine this relationship as follows:

```
# ptree 14855
```

```
14855 webservd-wdog -d /sun/webserver7/https-boulder.example.com/config
  -r /sun/webse
```

```
14856 webservd -d /sun/webserver7/https-boulder.example.com/config -r
  /sun/webserver7
```

```
14857 webservd -d /sun/webserver7/https-boulder.example.com/config -r /
  sun/webserver7
```

2.2 Web Server Architecture

Web Server 7.0 is a multi-threaded, multi-process, highly scalable, and secure HTTP server. Of all the processes (watchdog, primordial, and worker) that are started for any Web Server instance, the worker process is the most interesting because it is the one that does the lion's share of work when it comes to processing HTTP requests.

Figure 2.2 shows some of the main components of the worker process.

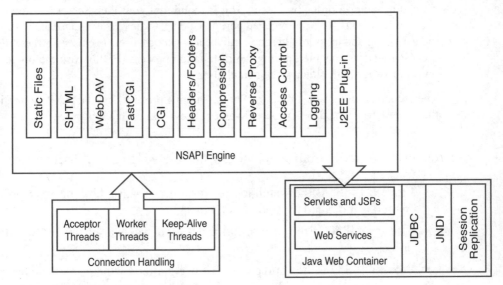

Figure 2.2   Worker Process Architecture

The following subsections describe the worker process in greater detail.

2.2.1 Connection Handling Threads

The web server receives HTTP requests and sends HTTP responses over network connections. Web Server supports HTTP over both secure and non-secure network connections. Web Server's connection handling subsystem comprises three distinct pools of threads that inter-operate to ensure connection scalability as well as efficient use of computing resources.

2.2.1.1 Acceptor Threads

A new incoming HTTP request will initially be handled by the acceptor threads. Acceptor threads are responsible for accepting the connection requests from clients and passing these connections on to one of the worker threads.

Figure 2.3 illustrates how incoming connections are first handled by one of the acceptor threads before being handed off to a worker thread for further processing. The Connection Queue is a thread-safe data structure that is used to pass incoming connections between acceptor and worker threads. When all worker threads are busy processing requests, new incoming connections wait in the Connection Queue until the next available worker thread picks them up. The capacity of the Connection Queue is typically configured to be many orders of magnitude greater than the number of worker threads.

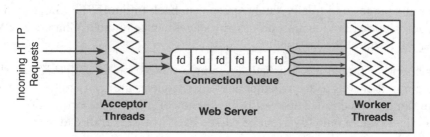

Figure 2.3   Connection Handling of Incoming HTTP Requests

You only need a few acceptor threads to handle large incoming connections because the work each thread does is not resource intensive. Typically, you would configure the number of acceptor threads to be the same as the number of processors on your computer.

2.2.1.2 Keep-Alive Threads

Keep-alive threads manage idle HTTP connections. An HTTP connection is deemed "idle" if the HTTP request data isn't readily available to be read by the server. Keep-alive threads periodically monitor all the idle connections for data. When data is detected on a connection, the keep-alive thread passes the connection onto a worker thread, which then processes the request.

Prior to persistent connections, an HTTP client would establish a separate TCP connection to fetch each URL. Establishing a new TCP connection for every URL is inefficient, increases the load on the web server, and causes congestion on the network. Using a persistent connection, HTTP clients can now send multiple HTTP requests on the same TCP connection, thereby opening and closing fewer TCP connections and reducing network congestion and latency. Persistent HTTP connections are also called Keep-Alive connections.

2.2.1.3 Worker Threads

Worker threads are the workhorses of the Web Server. Each worker thread processes one or more HTTP requests from an HTTP client. To process a request, a worker thread parses the HTTP request, and based on the information in the request headers, it sets up the virtual server environment for further processing of the request. The worker thread then runs the request through the various request processing stages and finally sends a response back to the HTTP client. A thorough description of the request processing stages can be found in Chapter 6, "Web Server 7.0 Request Processing."

After a worker thread has finished servicing a request on an HTTP Keep-Alive connection, it checks to see whether any other requests are ready to be processed on the same connection. This avoids the latency of passing the connection to the Keep-Alive system only to have it be passed back to a worker thread because data is available to be read on the connection.

If no request is readily available on a persistent connection, the worker thread deems the connection idle and passes the connection to the keep-alive threads for monitoring.

2.2.2 Server Application Functions

Server Application Functions (SAFs) are small functions written in the C Language. One or more SAFs are executed during each phase of request processing. The object configuration file (obj.conf) for a virtual server specifies the SAFs that are executed when a request is processed by that virtual server. SAFs can create, inspect, or change the values of variables that the server uses for request processing. Every SAF returns a result code that indicates whether it succeeded, failed, or took no action. Web Server examines the result code of each SAF that it executes, and this result code determines whether the next SAF should be executed. Web Server has numerous SAFs built in to the server. You can also write your own SAFs to extend and modify Web Server.

2.2.3 NSAPI Engine

Netscape Server Application Programming Interface (NSAPI) is a programmatic interface for Web Server specified in the C language. It was developed by Netscape Communications Corporation for use in Netscape's web and proxy server software. Microsoft's ISAPI and the Apache Software Foundation's Apache API are similar to NSAPI and were developed after Netscape developed NSAPI.

NSAPI also provides a set of C functions that provide the functionality necessary to implement Server Application Functions (SAFs). Applications that use NSAPI to extend the functionality of Web Server are referred to as NSAPI plug-ins. The set of NSAPI C functions included with Web Server 7.0 provide improved performance and platform independence and are thread-safe. The NSAPI Engine is the subsystem in the server that executes one or more SAFs at each stage in request processing.

2.2.4 Process Modes

Web Server 7.0 can be run in either single-process mode or in multi-process mode. The default mode is single-process mode. On Windows platforms, you cannot configure Web Server to run in multi-process mode.

Note: The terms *single-process* and *multi-process* refer to the number of worker processes that run and not to the overall number of processes (as shown in Figure 2.1) that run when you start a Web Server instance.

In single-process mode, a single worker process receives and processes all HTTP requests from web clients. Because the worker process itself is multi-threaded, multiple requests can be processed concurrently. All Server Application Functions (SAFs) written to run in a Web Server instance running in single-process mode must be thread-safe. All the SAFs and plug-ins provided with Web Server 7.0 are designed and implemented to provide high scalability and concurrency.

In multi-process mode, there are multiple worker processes (that can receive and process HTTP requests), each containing multiple threads. In this mode, Web Server does not distribute incoming connection requests among the various worker processes, but instead relies on the operating system to do so. This mode can be used for running legacy plug-ins or SAFs that are not thread-safe or thread-aware, as well as plug-ins that are thread-safe and thread-aware.

Note: The multi-process mode should not be used for running a Web Server that hosts Java web applications that use sessions to maintain state across requests.

2.2.5 Native Thread Pools

In the context of Web Server, a native thread is one that safely supports blocking calls. The native thread pool is a pool of such threads that the Web Server creates and uses for running NSAPI functions that require a native thread for execution.

Web Server uses Netscape Portable Runtime (NSPR), which is an underlying portability layer that provides a platform-neutral API for accessing operating system facilities and services such as threads, synchronization, time, I/O, network addresses, and memory management. Threads created using the NSPR API are not always the same as those created by the underlying operating system. This mainly applies to the NSPR implementation on Windows. On Windows platforms, Web Server internally uses threads from a pool of native threads to execute NSAPI functions that make blocking calls. NSPR threads have lower scheduling overheads (thereby contributing to improved performance) but are sensitive to blocking system calls to the operating system. NSAPI functions that make blocking system calls should not execute on a non-native thread because this can prevent the execution of all the other non-native threads.

By default, SAFs in a plug-in are scheduled to execute on a native thread. The NativeThread parameter to the load-modules function in magnus.conf is used to specify the threading model to use when executing the SAFs in a plug-in.

```
Init fn="load-modules" shlib="/plugins/test.so"
  funcs="ntrans_test,service_test" NativeThread="no"
```

2.2.6 Content Handling Subsystem

Using Web Server 7.0, you can host various types of static content (such as HTML, text, and image files) as well as dynamic content (such as CGI programs, Java Servlets, PHP, and so on) on your web site.

A high-performance web server must have an efficient and scalable subsystem to handle requests for a large amount of static content. Web Server 7.0's file cache enables the server to efficiently handle requests for static content by avoiding unnecessary disk accesses. The highly configurable file cache is also used to cache server-parsed HTML content. The server's file cache can be configured to use different kinds of efficient memory management techniques to cache static content based on parameters such as the size of the file. The file cache is known to be highly scalable and studies have shown it to be able to efficiently cache and serve requests for 32GB of static content!

Web Server 7.0 also supports HTTP content compression. With this feature, the server can be configured to either create precompressed versions of files in a directory or to dynamically compress data that it sends out. By reducing the amount of data sent, content compression reduces content download time and increases the rate at which pages are displayed.

2.2.7 Security and Access Control

Web Server 7.0 was one of the first products to support Elliptic Curve Cryptography (ECC). ECC is a next-generation security technology that uses shorter key sizes to provide the same level of security as traditional alternatives.

Web Server 7.0's innovative security features include throttling of Denial of Service attacks and detecting Cross-Site Scripting (XSS). A malicious user can prevent others from accessing the server by continuously sending requests to the server. Such attacks can be alleviated by configuring the server to detect such conditions and automatically either restrict the rate at which such requests are serviced or restrict the concurrency for such requests. sed is a popular UNIX/Linux utility that is used to transform lines of text using a simple command language. Web Server 7.0 includes new filters that incorporate sed's command syntax and can transform the content in either the request or the response. These filters can be used to neutralize cross-site scripting exploits. The following excerpt from the object configuration file (obj.conf) for a virtual server demonstrates a filter that replaces every occurrence of a web site's address in the response with another URL:

```
Output fn="insert-filter" type="text/html" filter="sed-response"
sed="s|http://internal.server/|http://external.server.com/|g"
```

The Access Control subsystem is used to restrict access to the entire server or to parts of it. Authentication, authorization, and access control are some of the mechanisms with which the server protects, restricts, and enforces access to its resources. Authentication is the process of verifying an identity, whereas authorization implies granting an identity access to a resource. Web Server 7.0's access control configuration is composed of a hierarchy of rules called Access Control Entries (ACEs). A collection of ACEs is called an Access Control List (ACL). ACLs can be configured for each virtual server, and if the server determines that ACLs apply for the request, then the server evaluates their ACEs to determine whether access should be granted.

The Access Control subsystem also contains an ACL user cache that is particularly useful when user-group authentication is performed with an external LDAP database. On a busy web site that contains ACL-protected resources, the ACL user cache helps improve overall performance by reducing the number of times an external LDAP database must be looked up.

Web Server 7.0 also supports access control using `.htaccess` files. The standard access control checks are always applied before any `.htaccess` access control.

2.2.8 Reverse Proxy

Unlike previous versions, Web Server 7.0 contains integrated reverse-proxy functionality. A reverse proxy server is one that appears to be the web server to clients, but in reality it forwards all requests that it receives to one or more origin servers that host the actual content. Web Server can be used for application load balancing by configuring it to reverse proxy requests to multiple origin servers. When configured as a reverse proxy, Web Server can be used to front-end any HTTP/1.1-compliant origin server. When used as a reverse proxy, the server periodically checks to ensure that the origin servers are online. When an origin server is found to be nonresponsive, it is marked offline and requests are not routed to it until it is deemed to be online again.

2.2.9 Dynamic Reconfiguration

A *configuration* refers to a set of meta-data that configures the runtime services of a Web Server. An example of a runtime service is that of serving of web pages (say HTML pages/images) from a given document root. The configuration meta-data is used by the server runtime to load built-in services and third party plug-ins and set up other server extensions such as database drivers, all of which help serve web pages and dynamic web applications.

Dynamic reconfiguration facilitates making changes to a running web server without having to stop and start the server process. Not having to restart the server process has benefits for web servers that are used in production as well as those that are used for development. For developers, dynamic reconfiguration reduces the time needed to deploy changes to the server. For administrators of live sites, dynamic reconfiguration enables them to safely make changes to the running server without interrupting the experience of users who might be actively browsing the site. This feature first debuted in the 6.0 version of Web Server (then called iPlanet Web Server 6.0) and has since been a highlight of Web Server.

The server is dynamically reconfigured when a change is deployed to the server through either the Administration Command Line Interface (wadm) or the graphical user interface. Executing the reconfig script that is found in each server instance's bin directory also triggers dynamic reconfiguration. Most of Web Server's configuration can be changed dynamically without a server restart. During dynamic reconfiguration, if the server detects that a server restart is required to effect a change, a warning message is logged to the server's error log. During startup, if configuration is rejected, the server does not start. Not all errors cause a configuration to be rejected; some just result in an error/warning message to be written to the server's error log. During dynamic reconfiguration, if the server detects an error in the configuration being deployed, an error message is logged and the server reverts to the previous known good configuration. This safeguard prevents a bad configuration from taking the server offline.

2.2.10 Pattern Matching

Web Server 7.0 includes a powerful new pattern matching subsystem that includes support for wildcards and regular expressions when specifying pattern matching expressions in configuration files. Web Server 7.0 also defines many variables such as $url, $cookie, $browser, and many more for use in request processing. Regular expressions and variable substitution can be used anywhere in request processing. Web Server 7.0 introduces a new expression grammar that uses a Perl-like syntax to specify complex request processing logic in configuration files.

The pattern-matching capabilities in Web Server can be used to implement complex URL rewriting and redirection logic in configuration files. The following is an excerpt from a virtual server's object configuration file (obj.conf) that demonstrates how to redirect a user who mistakenly enters the URL using uppercase alphabets to the correct resource name in lowercase (if the resource exists):

```
<If $code == 404 and not -U $uri and -U lc($uri)>
Error fn="redirect" url="$(lc($uri))"
</If>
```

Please refer to the appendixes titled "Using Variables, Expressions, and String Interpolation" and "Using Wildcard Patterns" in the *Sun Java System Web Server 7.0 Administrator's Configuration File Reference* for more information on the support for pattern matching, expressions, and variable interpolation included in Web Server 7.0.

2.3 Administration Server Architecture

The administration infrastructure in Web Server 7.0 includes a robust new command-line tool and a redesigned, task-based graphical interface that makes managing Web Server instances much easier than in previous versions.

A typical Web Server 7.0 installation creates a Web Server instance for your site and a specially configured Web Server instance (referred to henceforth as the Administration Server) that is used to administer your site(s). The Administration Server is a specially configured Web Server instance that is used only for administration purposes and on which administration applications are deployed. Using the Administration Server, you can create, delete, administer, and manage your Web Server instances.

During installation, you can optionally configure the administration instance to be an Administration Node. This is particularly useful when you are creating a farm/cluster of web servers. The term *node* (for our administration purposes) generally refers to servers or hosts in a network. A network of such nodes in a typical data center is referred to as a server farm. The Administration Node performs a limited number of actions upon receipt of commands from a designated Administration Server. Refer to Chapter 3, "Web Server 7.0 Installation and Migration," for the various ways in which you can customize your installation of Web Server 7.0.

The Administration Server manages the configuration information associated with each instance, and it can be accessed through a graphical or command-line interface. As such, the Administration instance listens on a particular listen socket for administrative commands.

Chapter 4, "Web Server 7.0 Administration," describes Web Server 7.0's Administrative architecture in more detail.

2.4 Dynamic Content

Using Web Server 7.0, in addition to hosting and serving static content, you can serve dynamic content written in various scripting languages.

2.4.1 Common Gateway Interface

Content deployed as Common Gateway Interface (CGI) programs are handled by the CGI subsystem. CGI is a standard for external programs to interface with a web server. CGI programs are typically written in scripting languages such as Perl and Bourne shell. On Windows platforms, CGI programs written in a Windows-specific language such as Visual Basic are handled by the Shell CGI subsystem in Web Server.

CGI specifies an interface for a web server to accept data from an HTTP client, pass the data to an external program for processing, and then forward the result back to the HTTP client.

Figure 2.4 shows the typical relationship between Web Server and the CGI program. Upon receiving a request for a CGI program, the server creates the CGI process and then exchanges data with the CGI program using the standard file descriptors for input, output, and error. After executing a request, the CGI program terminates.

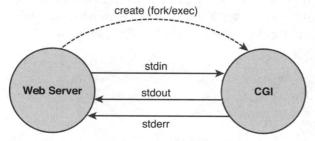

Figure 2.4   Web Server—CGI Process Interaction

On UNIX platforms, the CGI subsystem in Web Server enforces a number of security restrictions on what it will execute as whom. The CGI subsystem in Web Server can also be configured to run CGI programs as different UNIX users, limit the amount of memory that a CGI can consume, and specify the run priority of the CGI program. Web Server includes a Perl interpreter to run CGI programs that are written in the Perl programming language.

2.4.2 Server-Parsed HTML (SHTML)

The SHTML subsystem processes requests for HTML files that contain tags/ directives that are executed on the server. Server-Parsed HTML or Server-Side Includes is a basic server-side scripting language that is HTML for the most part, but it also has a limited set of dynamic directives for including other files, printing HTTP environment variables, executing programs on the server, displaying when a file was last modified, and so on. In Web Server, you can also define your own server-parsed HTML directives and embed Java servlets in HTML files. The Web Server parses server-side tags only if server-side parsing has been enabled. The SHTML subsystem in Web Server also includes a cache that accelerates processing of SHTML content.

2.4.3 FastCGI

FastCGI is an extension to the Common Gateway Interface that mitigates many of CGI's limitations and provides high performance for applications that interoperate with Web Servers. For each request for a CGI application, a separate process is created. Depending on the nature of the CGI application, this can be a time- and resource-expensive operation. The life cycle of FastCGI applications is not tied to client requests, thereby eliminating the process creation overhead and enabling FastCGI applications to maintain state (such as content caches and connection pools) across requests. Applications that run in a FastCGI environment operate in a separate process from the Web Server. FastCGI may be used to run applications written in any language, such as Perl, Python, PHP, Ruby, and so on.

Figure 2.5 shows that the Web Server process and the FastCGI process communicate over a persistent full-duplex socket connection. The socket is either a TCP socket or UNIX socket. Unlike the CGI process model, the FastCGI process isn't created and destroyed for each request.

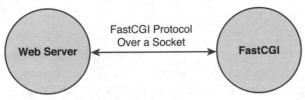

Figure 2.5   Web Server—FastCGI Process Interaction

The FastCGI protocol is client/server based, and this gives the administrator the flexibility to host FastCGI applications on a remote computer. This process separation is an ideal way to use applications that might not be thread-safe with a multi-threaded server such as Web Server. Web Server 7.0 includes a FastCGI plug-in that enables using dynamic scripting languages such as PHP, Perl, Python, and so on to work well with Web Server.

2.4.4 Java

Requests for Java Web Application content are processed by the Java Web Container shown previously in Figure 2.2. Java Web Application technologies include servlets, JavaServer Pages, JavaServer Faces, and Web Services. The Java Web Container in Web Server also supports the Java Naming and Directory Interface (JNDI) API and the Java Database Connectivity (JDBC) API.

Unlike Apache HTTP Server deployments, where requests for Java Web Application content are typically delegated to another process (e.g. Tomcat Web Server), the Java Web Container in Web Server 7.0 is embedded in the worker process itself. This eliminates the need to use interprocess communication protocols (e.g. Apache JServe Protocol) and channels (e.g. sockets and pipes). A tighter integration (via a programmatic API) between the Web Server and the Java Web Container enables the server to process requests for Java content more efficiently and enables the Java Web Container to leverage subsystems in the Web Server (such as the high-performance file cache).

2.5 Multi-Threaded Architecture

Multi-threading is an efficient programming model wherein multiple threads exist within a single process, sharing the process' resources but able to execute simultaneously. Threads in the same process share the same address space. Context switching between threads within a process is generally more efficient than context switching between processes. Multi-threaded programs can perform faster on computers that have multiple CPUs.

Web Server's multi-threaded design supports massive connection scalability without sacrificing performance or unnecessarily wasting system resources. Depending on the load on the server, Web Server 7.0 automatically switches from operating in low-latency mode to operating in high-concurrency mode and vice versa. Typically, a light workload is one in which the number of incoming requests is less than the number of worker threads. A heavy workload is one where there are far more incoming requests than there are worker threads. A lightly loaded server operates in low-latency mode, wherein for Keep-Alive connections, worker threads themselves poll for new requests. In high concurrency mode, worker threads pass the connection onto the keep-alive subsystem after finishing the request. In this mode, the keep-alive subsystem polls all Keep-Alive connections for new requests and passes these connections back to the worker threads via the connection queue.

Wise design choices in creating and configuring different pools of threads have resulted in a highly scalable, high-performance, world-class web server.

On UNIX platforms, you can use the pstack command to see the different threads running within a process. The following example demonstrates how you can use this command to look into the processes that Web Server creates.

Start your instance as follows (the Java plug-in was not installed on the server instance for the purposes of this example):

```
% bin/startserv
Sun Java System Web Server 7.0 B12/04/2006 10:15
info: HTTP3072: http-listener-1: http://test:9000 ready to accept
    requests
info: CORE3274: successful server startup
```

Using the ps -ef UNIX command, determine the process IDs of the watchdog, primordial, and worker processes, respectively:

```
% ps -ef | grep webservd
    root 29473 29472   1 15:20:20 ?          0:00 webservd -d
/opt/webserver7/https-test/config -r /opt/webserver7 -t /tmp/https-
    root 29472    1    0 15:20:20 ?          0:00 webservd-wdog -d
/opt/webserver7/https-test/config -r /opt/webserver7 -t /tmp/h
webservd 29474 29473   0 15:20:21 ?          0:00 webservd -d
/opt/webserver7/https-test/config -r /opt/webserver7 -t /tmp/https-
```

Looking at the entries, the following is evident:

- Process 29472 is the watchdog process.
- Process 29473 is the primordial process.
- Process 29474 is the worker process.

Using the pstack command to examine the current execution call stack of each thread within the watchdog process shows that there is only one thread. (The c++filt command is used to demangle C++ symbol names, thus making them easier to read.)

```
% /usr/bin/pstack 29472 | /opt/SUNWspro/bin/c++filt
29472: webservd-wdog -d /opt/webserver7/https-test/config -r
/opt/webserver7
 fee457c8 pollsys  (8d008, 3, ffbff460, 0)
 fede1d24 poll     (8d008, 3, 2710, 10624c00, 0, 0) + 7c
 0001923c int wdLSmanager::Wait_for_Message() (2c45c, 0, 12c, 0, 14c, 0)
   + 20
 00017268 main     (8, 1, 2c45c, 0, 2bc20, 2cff0) + 12a8
 000130a0 _start   (0, 0, 0, 0, 0, 0) + 108
```

Examination of the primordial process shows that it too has only one thread:

```
% /usr/bin/pstack 29473 | /opt/SUNWspro/bin/c++filt
29473: webservd -d /opt/webserver7/https-test/config -r /opt/
   webserver7 -t /t
 fd5c57c8 pollsys  (ffbff808, 4, ffbff798, 0)
 fd561d24 poll     (ffbff808, 4, 64, 10624c00, 17d784, 5f5e100) + 7c
 fe85c700 _pr_poll_with_poll (64, ffbff808, 2710, 7eac8, 4, 3) + 42c
 ff197654 void ParentAdmin::poll(unsigned) (25eae8, 2710, ff2a3c00,
   ff2a3c00, ff2a3c00, ff2f4400) + c
 ff19e8ac PRStatus WebServer::Run() (25eae8, ff2a3f24, ffffffff,
   ff2a4000, 6, 1) + 494
 00010fd4 main     (9, ffbffbc4, ffbffbec, 21400, 0, fd134fc0) + 1c
 00010b98 _start   (0, 0, 0, 0, 0, 0) + 108
```

The following command shows the various threads in the worker process:

```
% /usr/bin/pstack 29473 | /opt/SUNWspro/bin/c++filt
```

The worker process, however, has multiple threads. When examining the pstack output of a program that has multiple threads, note that each thread is demarcated with a line of the form

```
---------------- lwp# 6 / thread# 6 --------------------
```

where the lwp (lightweight process) number identifies the operating system–level thread and the thread number identifies the user-level thread.

Although the output of the pstack command for a worker process is too verbose to be included in its entirety, the rest of this section identifies thread stacks corresponding to threads in some of the subsystems in the worker process.

The following stack trace of lwp# 1 shows the call stack of the main thread in the worker process that detects when the server is shut down:

```
---------------- lwp# 1 / thread# 1 --------------------
fd5c4a9c lwp_park (0, ffbff8d0, 0)
fd5beae8 cond_wait_queue (154c90, 25eae8, ffbff8d0, 0, 0, 0) + 28
fd5bef60 cond_wait_common (154c90, 25eae8, ffbff8d0, 0, 0, 0) + 298
fd5bf0f8 _cond_timedwait (154c90, 25eae8, ffbffa60, 0, 0, 0) + 34
fd5bf1ec cond_timedwait (154c90, 25eae8, ffbffa60, b1a13000, 989680,
    4e736350) + 14
fd5bf22c pthread_cond_timedwait (154c90, 25eae8, ffbffa60, 48ce32a4, 0,
    1dce6ab8) + c
fe857b1c PR_WaitCondVar (154c88, 0, 87f20, 0, 1dce6ab8, 0) + 170
ff19f7ac PRStatus WebServer::Run() (ff2a4000, ff2a4000, 6, 2a5cf8, 3d,
    ff26a4b6) + 1394
00010fd4 main     (9, ffbffbc4, ffbffbec, 21400, 0, fd134fc0) + 1c
00010b98 _start   (0, 0, 0, 0, 0, 0) + 108
```

The following shows the thread stack of a thread that is used to dynamically reconfigure the server:

```
---------------- lwp# 6 / thread# 6 --------------------
fd5c4a9c lwp_park (0, 0, 0)
fd5beae8 cond_wait_queue (2af190, 32e368, 0, 0, 0, 0) + 28
fd5bf068 cond_wait (2af190, 32e368, 0, 1c, 0, fcf21300) + 10
fd5bf0a4 pthread_cond_wait (2af190, 32e368, 1, fe878510, 64c, 400) + 8
fe857a10 PR_WaitCondVar (2af188, ffffffff, 293cb0, 0, 0, 0) + 64
ff1758dc PRStatus PSQueue
<ConfigurationManagerListener*>::get(ConfigurationManagerListener*&)
(c6848, fcd8fec4, 2a4878, ffffffff, c684c, 1) + 50
ff17535c void ConfigurationManager::run() (ff2a3000, 3, 2, 2, fcd8fec4, 0)
    + 10
fefa6de4 ThreadMain (2af138, 293cb0, 0, fefb9c00, ff17534c, ff2a33a8) + 1c
fe85e04c _pt_root (293cb0, fefa6dc8, 400, fe876bb8, 1, fe878914) + d4
fd5c49fc _lwp_start (0, 0, 0, 0, 0, 0)
```

The following illustrates the stack trace of a thread in the Keep-Alive subsystem:

```
---------------- lwp# 8 / thread# 8 --------------------
fd5c4a9c lwp_park (0, 0, 0)
fd5beae8 cond_wait_queue (2aef38, 759aa8, 0, 0, 0, 0) + 28
fd5bf068 cond_wait (2aef38, 759aa8, 0, 1c, 0, fcf22300) + 10
fd5bf0a4 pthread_cond_wait (2aef38, 759aa8, 1, fe878510, 64c, 400) + 8
fe857a10 PR_WaitCondVar (2aef30, ffffffff, 27a7a8, 0, 0, 0) + 64
ff16f910 void PollArray::GetPollArray(int*,void**) (8ef48, fcd2fec0,
    fcd2fec4, 0, 2, ff2a2c00) + 5c
```

```
ff1701c0 void KAPollThread::run() (21a5f8, 0, 4, ff2a2c00, ff2f4584,
  fcd2fec4) + 6c
fefa6de4 ThreadMain (21a5f8, 27a7a8, 0, fefb9c00, ff170154, ff2a2f9c) + 1c
fe85e04c _pt_root (27a7a8, fefa6dc8, 400, fe876bb8, 1, fe878914) + d4
fd5c49fc _lwp_start (0, 0, 0, 0, 0, 0)
```

The following call stack of lwp#12 is that of an acceptor thread:

```
---------------- lwp# 12 / thread# 12 --------------------
fd5c57c8 pollsys  (fcabfc88, 1, fcabfc08, 0)
fd561d24 poll     (fcabfc88, 1, 1388, 10624c00, 0, 0) + 7c
fe858654 pt_poll_now (fcabfcf4, 1, fcabfd24, fcabfc88, 20, ffffffff) + 4c
fe859ef8 pt_Accept (230408, fcabfe58, ffffffff, 13, 0, ffffffff) + cc
ff177690 PRFileDesc*ListenSocket::accept(PRNetAddr&,const unsigned)
  (1b9ac8, fcabfe58, ffffffff, ff000000, 0, fd5f4784) + c
ff171c30 void Acceptor::run() (128398, 7, 0, 6, 2, ffffffff) + 4c
fefa6de4 ThreadMain (128398, 2531a8, 0, fefb9c00, ff171be4, ff2a30a0) + 1c
fe85e04c _pt_root (2531a8, fefa6dc8, 400, fe876bb8, 0, fe878914) + d4
fd5c49fc _lwp_start (0, 0, 0, 0, 0, 0)
```

The following is an example of the call stack of a worker thread:

```
---------------- lwp# 15 / thread# 15 --------------------
fd5c4a9c lwp_park (0, 0, 0)
fd5beae8 cond_wait_queue (4e9e8, 2b1f88, 0, 0, 0, 0) + 28
fd5bf068 cond_wait (4e9e8, 2b1f88, 0, 1c, 0, fcf25b00) + 10
fd5bf0a4 pthread_cond_wait (4e9e8, 2b1f88, 1, fe878510, 64c, 400) + 8
fe857a10 PR_WaitCondVar (4e9e0, ffffffff, 117828, 0, 2a5a18, 0) + 64
ff171440 Connection*ConnectionQueue::GetReady(unsigned) (89cc8, ffffffff,
  ffffffff, 89cc8, 64c, 2a5a28) + c4
ff168014 int DaemonSession::GetConnection(unsigned) (14b948, ffffffff,
  ff2f4400, 0, ff266400, ff2a2400) + 18
ff168794 void DaemonSession::run() (798008, 14b948, 14b968, 14b9f0, 2000,
  ffffffff) + 150 fefa6de4 ThreadMain (14b948, 117828, 0, fefb9c00,
  ff168644, ff2a2850) + 1c
fe85e04c _pt_root (117828, fefa6dc8, 400, fe876bb8, 1, fe878914) + d4
fd5c49fc _lwp_start (0, 0, 0, 0, 0, 0)
```

The following shows some of the extra threads (started by the Java Virtual Machine) that are present in the pstack trace of a worker process with the Java plug-in enabled:

```
---------------- lwp# 12 / thread# 12 --------------------
fd5c5cd0 lwp_cond_wait (70c3a8, 70c390, f977fb60, 0)
fd5b05f0 _lwp_cond_timedwait (70c3a8, 70c390, f977fc38, 3e8, 0, 6dde6) +
  1c
```

```
fc5c16e0 int Monitor::wait(int,long) (25d238, 7ea08, fff0bc00, fcbce000,
    6400, 70c368) + 328
fc7681b4 void VMThread::run() (fcc228a8, fcc31064, 0, fcc31050, fcc31060,
    1) + 1b4
fca70738 void*_start(void*) (7ea08, 735b, fcbce000, 0, 4fe8, 4c00) + 208
fd5c49fc _lwp_start (0, 0, 0, 0, 0, 0)
----------------- lwp# 13 / thread# 13 --------------------
fd5c5cd0 lwp_cond_wait (70f128, 70f110, 0, 0)
fc6b178c void ObjectMonitor::wait(long long,int,Thread*) (802058,
fcc34140, 13ee30, 0, 13ed88, 9400) + 5a0 fc6b2788 void ObjectSynchronizer::
    wait(Handle,long long,Thread*)
(80205a, 8808, 0, 13ed88, 8800, fcbce000) + e8
fc6b2438 JVM_MonitorWait (0, 222964, 13ed88, fcc23154, 0, 1) + 31c
f680c280 * java/lang/Object.wait(J)V+1
f680c224 * java/lang/Object.wait(J)V+0
f6805764 * java/lang/Object.wait()V+2 (line 474)
f6805764 * java/lang/ref/Reference$ReferenceHandler.run()V+46 (line 116)
f6800218 * StubRoutines (1)
fc599d8c void
JavaCalls::call_helper(JavaValue*,methodHandle*,JavaCallArguments*,
    Thread*) (1, 13ed88, f967fc80, f967fb80, 4, f967fd70) + 5a0 fc6bffac void
JavaCalls::call_virtual(JavaValue*,Handle,KlassHandle,symbolHandle,
symbolHandle,Thread*) (7bc0, 13ed88, 222950, 22295c, 222958, e24005f0) +
    188
fc6df584 void thread_entry(JavaThread*,Thread*) (f242f700, 13ed88,
    222d3c, fcc34a24, fcc34af8, fcc34510) + 134
fc6db120 void JavaThread::run() (13ed88, fcc267ac, 6f68, 0, 6c00,
    f9600000) + 2b0
fca70738 void*_start(void*) (13ed88, 735b, fcbce000, 0, 4fe8, 4c00) + 208
fd5c49fc _lwp_start (0, 0, 0, 0, 0, 0)
```

You can also use the `pstack` command to analyze the call stacks of threads while the server is processing requests. Commands such as `pstack`, `ptree`, and `truss` can give you useful insights into what is under the hood of Web Server.

2.6 64-bit Support

With the increasing amount of data that is being exchanged over the Internet and the ready availability of high-capacity storage devices, there is a need for applications such as Web Server to access large amounts of data on disk and in memory. Although the Internet is currently dominated by 32-bit computers, many of today's computer manufacturers offer 64-bit platforms as well. The main difference between a 32-bit application and a 64-bit one is the amount of virtual address space (memory) that each can access. A 32-bit application's virtual address space is limited to 4GB, whereas 64-bit applications can theoretically access terabytes (1 terabyte = 1,000 gigabytes) of memory.

What does it mean when you read a statement that says "Web Server 7.0 includes 64-bit support"? When installing on supported 64-bit UNIX platforms, Web Server 7.0 gives you the option of installing its 64-bit binaries. After installing the binaries, you can use the Administration interface to configure the server to run as a 32-bit application or as a 64-bit one. The 64-bit Web Server can then leverage its 64-bit address space and manage more connections (hundreds of thousands) and store more data in its cache. So if you are running a large benchmark such as SPECweb2005 or have a busy web site you might benefit from running the 64-bit version of Web Server 7.0.

2.7 Summary

Web Server's multi-threaded, multi-process architecture provides a secure, scalable platform for hosting both static and dynamic content on a variety of operating systems. All aspects of the server can be configured and managed using the Administration Server, either via the Graphical User Interface or using the Command Line Interface.

2.8 Self-Paced Labs

Use the information contained in this chapter to perform the following exercises. These will help validate your understanding of the concepts described in this chapter.

1. Start both your server instance and your Administration Server. Correctly identify the process IDs of the watchdog, primordial, and worker processes corresponding to each instance.

2. Start your server instance. Examine the logs/errors file of your instance and for each message in the file and identify which of the three processes wrote the line to the log file. Hint: Use the process IDs of the watchdog, primordial, and worker processes to help you find the answer.

3. If you have access to both a Solaris and a Linux computer, install Web Server 7 on both those operating systems. Start your instance on each of the computers and compare the outputs of the `ps -ef` command on Solaris and Linux. Why are there so many `webservd` processes on Linux?

Note: Go to www.sunwebserver.com for detailed instructions on how to perform each of these exercises.

3

Web Server 7.0 Installation and Migration

THIS chapter provides the information necessary to perform a successful installation of Web Server 7.0 or migration to Web Server 7.0 from a previous version.

Before you can begin using Web Server 7.0, you must first install the software on a supported operating system using one of three different installation methods. After that has been completed, you can then customize the configuration and begin delivering both static and dynamic content to various user agents.

The installation process creates the environment necessary to run Web Server 7.0 on your local system. This includes the extraction of the Web Server binaries, shared objects (or dynamically linked libraries), configuration files, and various scripts for managing Web Server. The migration process enables you to take a previous Web Server installation and update it to the latest version.

3.1 Supported Platforms

Web Server 7.0 can be installed on multiple flavors of UNIX and provides unparalleled security on Windows platforms as well. Before attempting to install Web Server 7.0 you should determine that your system has enough memory and available storage and that you are installing the software on a supported platform.

Table 3.1 summarizes the operating system platforms supported by Web Server 7.0.

Table 3.1   Operating System Platforms

Architecture	Operating System
PowerPC	IBM AIX 5.2, 5.3
PA-RISC	HP-UX 11i
Intel x86/AMD	Windows 2003 Server Enterprise Edition Windows XP Professional
UltraSPARC	Solaris 8, 9, and 10 OS
Intel x86 (32-bit)	Solaris 9 and 10 OS
AMD (64-bit)	Solaris 10 OS
Intel x86/AMD	Red Hat Linux Enterprise 3.0, 4.0 Advanced Server SuSE Linux 9 Enterprise Server

The minimum amount of random access memory (RAM) that Sun recommends for each of these platforms is 128MB (but 512MB is preferred). In each case, you will need about 550MBs of hard disk space for the initial Web Server installation. This will increase depending on how you use your web server and the type of content being served.

Note: You should install the latest patch cluster on Solaris Operating System for proper installation and execution of Web Server 7.0. Incompatible patches can affect Web Server startup and result in the server not responding to some requests. In such cases, Sun provides information about compatible patches that support efficient operation of Web Server 7.0.

On Solaris OS platforms, the Web Server 7.0 installer checks for required patches and does not install if the required patches are not found.

Refer to the Sun Java System Web Server 7.0 Release Notes for the latest information about platforms and patches.

3.2 Obtaining the Software

The Sun Java System Web Server (Web Server) is a component of the Sun Java Enterprise System (Java ES). Web Server 7.0 is available in version 5 of the Java ES and can be installed with the Java ES installer.

You can access and download the Java ES software from Sun's web site at http://www.sun.com/software/swportfolio/get.jsp. This book does not provide instructions for using the Java ES installer. For information about installing Web Server 7.0 as a component of Java ES v5 or about upgrading the Web Server from a previous Java ES release, refer to the Java ES documentation found at http://docs.sun.com/app/docs/prod/entsys#hic.

Web Server 7.0 is also available as a separate download. You can obtain the standalone version of the software by performing the following steps:

1. Access Sun's software download page at www.sun.com/download/.
2. Click the View by Category tab.
3. Select the Web Servers link in the bottom-right corner. This takes you to the main download page for Web Server content. This page contains links to several releases of the Web Server as well as links to various Web Server add-ons.
4. Select the Download link for the latest release of Web Server 7.0 (for example, Web Server 7.0 Update 5). This takes you to the product download page for Web Server 7.0. This page contains an overview of Web Server 7.0.
5. Select the platform on which you want to install the software, and the appropriate language.
6. Select the Sun Software Portfolio License Agreement link to understand Sun's terms and conditions for downloading and installing the software.
7. If you agree to these terms and conditions, select the checkbox next to the text, I agree to the Sun Software Portfolio License Agreement.
8. Click the Continue button.
9. Select the link for the appropriate distribution (for example, sjsws-7_0u5-windows-i586.zip). This starts the download process.
10. Save the file into a temporary directory on your local file system. The file is approximately 150MB for most platforms. The format of the file name is as follows:

    - `sjsws-release-platform.tar.gz` (for Unix-based systems)
    - `sjsws-release-platform.tar.zip` (for Windows systems)

11. You have now downloaded a copy of the software and are ready to proceed to the installation.

3.3 Preparing for Installation

Web Server 7.0 software is distributed as a compressed archive—a GNU zip archive (*.gz) for UNIX-based systems and a zip archive (*.zip) for Windows systems. Before installing the software, you must first decompress the archive to a temporary location on your disk. The extracted files require approximately 250MB of free disk space.

On UNIX-based systems you can use the following command sequence to decompress and extract the files (this will leave the original distribution file in its original location, intact):

```
gzip -dc sjsws-release-platform.tar.gz | tar xvf -
```

The latest releases of the Windows operating system (such as Windows XP and Windows Vista) support the zip file format natively and you can use the Windows Explorer utility to decompress the file. For older versions of the operating system, you need a utility such as WinZip to extract the files.

Table 3.2 provides an example of the contents of your installation directory after the files have been extracted.

Table 3.2   Installation Directory Contents

File/Directory	Description
Legal	This directory contains licensing information for this software release, as well as any third-party products included in this release.
README.txt	This file contains additional information that might be considered useful. This can include the location of Web Server 7.0 documentation or mailing lists for product support.
setup or setup.exe	This is the main installation file. You execute this command to start the installation process.
WebServer	This directory contains the Web Server 7.0 installation components.

3.4 Installing the Software

You can use any one of three methods to install the Web Server 7.0 software: graphical, command-line, and silent. These methods are available on any distribution and enable you to install the software in either an interactive or non-interactive fashion.

3.4.1 The setup Command

You begin the installation process by executing the setup command. The syntax for this command is as follows:

```
setup [--help] [--console] [--silent state_file]
      [--savestate] [--javahome java_dir] [--id]
```

You may select the desired mode of installation by providing the appropriate options to the setup command. Table 3.3 provides a list of these options.

Table 3.3   Options for the setup Command

Option	Description
./setup --help	Displays the options for the setup command.
./setup	Runs the installer in graphical mode.
./setup --console	Runs the installer in command-line mode.
./setup --savestate	Runs the installer in graphical mode and also creates an installation configuration file (state file) based on this installation. The state file can then be used to perform a silent (non-interactive) installation. The state file is created and saved in the installation directory. The default name of the file is statefile, but it can be changed.
./setup --console --savestate	Runs the installer in command-line mode and also creates an installation configuration file (state file) based on this installation.
./setup --silent state_file	Runs the installer in silent (noninteractive) mode. Installation parameters are read from the specified state file (state_file), which was first created using the --savestate option.
./setup --javahome java_dir	Defines the location of the JDK installation that should be used for the installer Java Virtual Machine (JVM). This installation is performed in graphical mode.

Table 3.3   Options for the `setup` Command   *continued*

Option	Description
`./setup --console --javahome java_dir`	Defines the location of the JDK installation that should be used for the installer JVM. This installation is performed in command-line mode.
`./setup --id`	Shows the unique identifier for the installer build. This option is provided to simplify reuse of installer state files between software builds, if necessary. Each installer build has a unique identifier. To reuse installer state files created by different installer builds, the unique identifier referenced in the installer state file must match the one in the current installer build. The `--id` option enables you to determine this value so you can edit the value in the state file. See Section 3.4.4.2, "Build Identifier," for more information.

3.4.2 Graphical Installation

Web Server 7.0 includes a graphical installation wizard (simply named the Install Wizard) that walks you through the installation process. The Install Wizard guides you through a series of screens where you are prompted for the information and preferences necessary to install the software.

As indicated in the previous section, graphical installation is the default mode when the installation program is started without any options. You can install Web Server 7.0 in graphical mode by performing the following steps:

1. Log in to your system as the `root` user (on UNIX-based systems) or `Administrator` (on Windows systems).

2. Launch the Install Wizard without any options as follows:

   - `./setup` (for UNIX-based systems)
   - `setup.exe` (for Windows systems)

   The Install Wizard Welcome screen opens as shown in Figure 3.1.

 Note: On UNIX systems, the installation interface defaults to command-line mode if either the DISPLAY environment variable has not been exported to your local machine or X Windows is not supported. To install in command-line mode, follow the instructions covered in the following "Command-Line Installation" section.

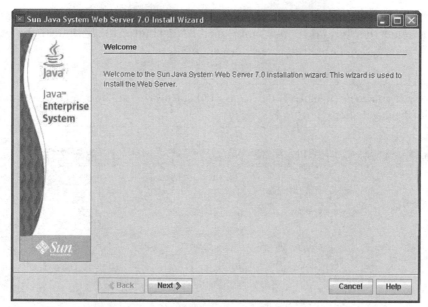

Figure 3.1 Install Wizard—Welcome Screen

3. Click the Next button to continue to the Software License Agreement screen as shown in Figure 3.2.

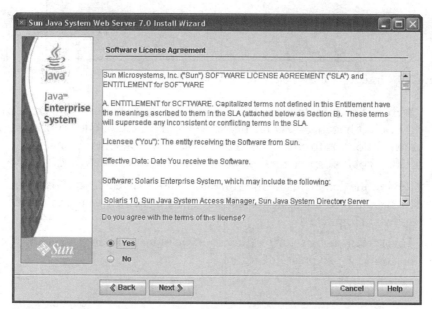

Figure 3.2 Install Wizard—Software License Agreement Screen

4. Review the software license agreement. If you agree to the license terms, select the Yes radio button and click the Next button to continue to the Select Installation Directory screen shown in Figure 3.3.

Note: If you do not to agree to the license agreement, you will be unable to continue with the installation.

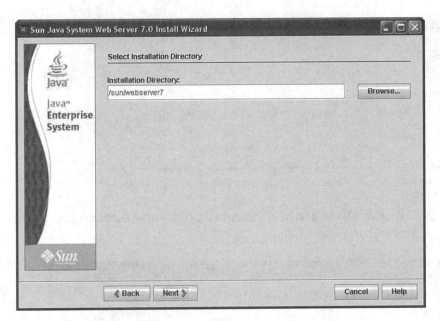

Figure 3.3   Install Wizard—Select Installation Directory Screen

Web Server 7.0 components will be installed in the directory specified by the Select Installation Directory screen. If the directory does not exist, you have the option to create it. Keep in mind that you will need at least 550MB of disk space for the initial installation.

5. Review the default installation directory and change it if you wish. Click the Next button to continue to the Select the Type of Installation screen, as shown in Figure 3.4.

This screen enables you to select the type of installation you will be performing—Express or Custom.

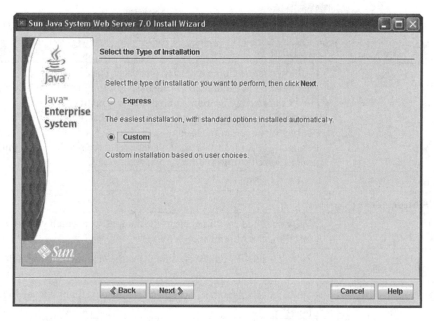

Figure 3.4   Install Wizard—Select the Type of Installation Screen

An Express installation enables you to quickly install Web Server using the most common options and predefined defaults. Express installation is the default installation type and makes various assumptions, such as hostname, port numbers, and Java Development Kit (JDK) installation. If you select Express, you do not specify these settings during installation. Settings are configured automatically, using the defaults listed in Table 3.4.

Table 3.4   Express Installation Defaults

Setting	Default
General Settings	
Administration instance	Configured as Administration Server.
JDK	Installs the JDK bundled with the Web Server.
Components	Installs the following: Server Core: Installs the core binaries needed to set up the Web Server environment. Server Core 64-bit Binaries (Solaris SPARC and AMD64 only): The 64-bit binaries required for setting up the 64-bit runtime for Web Server instances. This option is available only if the system on which you are installing has 64-bit support. Both the 64- and 32-bit binaries are installed.

Table 3.4   Express Installation Defaults   *continued*

Setting	Default
	Administration Command Line Interface: The command-line administration client used to manage and configure the Web Server and its hosted applications from the command line. Sample Applications: Sample applications that demonstrate Web Server features and functionality. Language Packs: Installs the language resource bundles containing the localized strings for the Web Server.
Start on boot	No
Administration Server Settings	
Server host	Fully qualified domain name of the computer on which you are installing the Administration Server.
SSL port	8989 if available; otherwise defaults to the next highest available port.
Non-SSL Port	8800 if available; otherwise defaults to the next highest available port.
Runtime User ID (Unix)	For root installation, default is root. For non-root installation, default is the user performing the installation.
Web Server Instance (Administration Node) Settings	
Server name	The name of the computer on which you are installing the default Web Server instance.
HTTP port	Default value depends upon the run-time user ID of Administration Server instance. If the Administration Server instance's runtime user ID is non-root, the default is 8080. If the Administration Server instance's runtime user ID is `root`, the default is 80.
Runtime User ID (Unix)	If the Administration Server instance's runtime user ID is non-root, the default is the same as Administration Server instance's runtime user ID. If the Administration Server instance's runtime user ID is `root`, the default is `webservd`.
Document root directory	*install_dir*/`https-`*server_name*/`docs`
64–bit configuration (Solaris SPARC and AMD64 only)	No

Selecting the Express installation type is recommended if you are new to Web Server 7.0 or if you are performing an evaluation of the product. Choose a Custom installation if you want to customize your installation. The remaining steps provide details for performing a Custom installation.

6. Select the Custom radio button and click the Next button to continue to the Component Selection screen, as shown in Figure 3.5.

This screen gives you the opportunity to select various components to be installed. In general, these choices are based on the role the server will play as either a standalone server or within a server farm environment. Additionally, you may select other options based on various administration considerations.

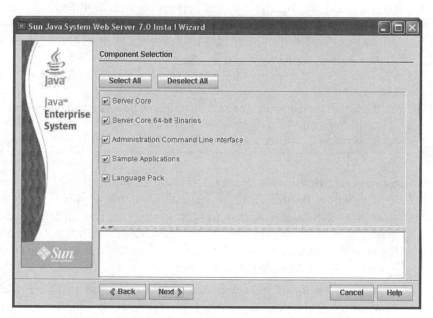

Figure 3.5   Install Wizard—Component Selection Screen

The following items provide additional information for each of these components:

- **Server Core**—Refers to the core binaries required for the Web Server environment. If Server Core is selected, an Administration instance is created and it can be configured as either the Administration Server or an Administration Node, both of which are described later in this chapter. If the Administration instance is configured as Administration Server, a default Web Server instance is installed. These installation options are used in server farm environments in which a centralized Administration Server resides on one of the nodes and Administration Nodes reside on the rest.

- **Server Core 64-bit Binaries (Solaris SPARC and AMD64 Only)**—If this option is selected, the 64-bit binaries required for setting up the 64-bit runtime for the default Web Server instance are installed. This option is selected by default and displays only if 32-bit binaries are installed.
- **Administration Command Line Interface**—The Administration Command Line Interface is used to administer and configure all Administration Server and Web Server instances in a server farm. This tool can be used to manage locally installed servers as well as those installed on remote servers. You can specify only this option to install the tools necessary to remotely administer other servers without installing any Web Server instances on your local machine.

Note: You can install the Administration Command Line Interface component without installing the Server Core, but you cannot install the Server Core without installing the Administration Command Line Interface.

- **Sample Applications**—If you select Sample Applications in the component selection portion of the installation, sample applications demonstrating Web Server features and functionality are installed. The default installation location is *install_dir*/samples. For more information about the sample applications, see the *Sun Java System Web Server 7.0 Developer's Guide to Java Web Applications*.
- **Language Pack**—If you select Language Pack in the component selection portion of the installation, the language resource bundles containing the localized strings for the Web Server are installed. Web Server 7.0 supports languages such as Japanese, Korean, Spanish, French, German, Traditional Chinese, and simplified Chinese. Core messages that are part of Server Core are available in the supported locale language. For example, to see the Administrative Console in Japanese, change the browser locale to Japanese.

7. Select each of the components shown in this panel and click the Next button to continue to the Java Configuration screen, as shown in Figure 3.6.

   You can decide to install the JDK bundled with Web Server 7.0 (the default) or specify the absolute path to an existing JDK.

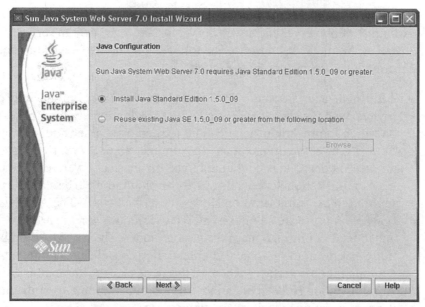

Figure 3.6   Install Wizard—Java Configuration Screen

8. Select the Install Java Standard Edition 1.5.0_09 radio button (if necessary), and click the Next button to continue to the Administration Options screen, as shown in Figure 3.7.

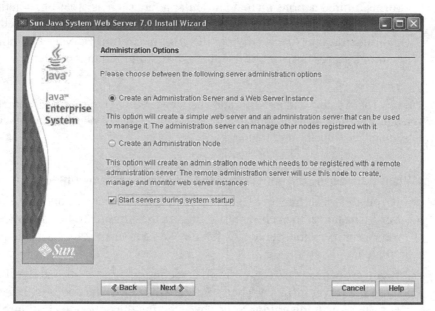

Figure 3.7   Install Wizard—Administration Options screen

This screen enables you to specify whether to install both the Administration Server and a Web Server instance (the default) or just to install an Administration Node. The following items provide additional information as to each of these options:

- **Administration Server**—The Administration Server is a specially configured Web Server instance used only for administration purposes and on which administration applications are deployed. Each node in a server farm or cluster environment has an Administration Server running on it. Of these nodes, one is configured to be the master server, referred to as the Administration Server, and the rest are configured to be slave servers, referred to as Administration Nodes (described next). The Administration Server is used to administer all Web Server instances in a server farm and to push configurations to the various nodes. The master Administration Server runs the graphical administration console and command-line administration interface, whereas the nodes in the farm run just the Administration Node application. The Administration Server maintains the configuration repository for all instances.

- **Administration Node**—The Administration Node is a Web Server instance without the features and functionality of the Administration Server (no graphical console, for example). The Administration Node receives commands from the designated Administration Server and performs limited actions on that particular node, such as creating, deleting, starting, and stopping Web Server instances. Instances can be created on Administration Nodes only by the Administration Server. The nodes within a server farm or cluster cannot be configured independently.

Warning: The Administration Node must be registered with the Administration Server, either during the installation or after installation. The Administration Server must be running during the registration.

When considering the options, use the following general guidelines:

- If you are not setting up a server farm and simply want a standalone Web Server instance, then choose to configure the Administration instance as the Administration Server. A default Web Server instance will also be created.

- If you are setting up a server farm, first configure the centralized Administration Server instance. Then configure the rest of the nodes in the server farm as Administration Nodes by selecting the option to configure the

Administration instance as an Administration Node. If you configure the Administration instance as the Administration Server, a default Web Server instance is also created.

9. Select the Create an Administration Server and a Web Server Instance radio button to create an Administration Server instance and Administration Node instance.

10. You can also select the Start Servers During System Startup check box if you want both of these instances to start when your system reboots. Selecting this option creates the appropriate startup scripts for UNIX-based systems and registers the instances as services for automatic startup for Windows systems.

Note: If you select Start servers during system startup, various scripts are created on the following UNIX-based systems:

- **Solaris:** /etc/init.d/webserver7-*
- **Linux:** /etc/init.d/webserver7-*
- **AIX:** /etc/rc.d/webserver7-*
- **HPUX:** /sbin/init.d/webserver7-*

An asterisk * in the script name refers to the unique hash code generated during each installation. An example of a startup script would be webserver7-99bbdd.

The script contains the variable WS_START_ONBOOT, which is set to 1 if you selected the Start Servers During System Startup check box. To disable this, change the WS_START_ONBOOT value to 0.

Be careful to choose the correct script for your system. Each installation includes its own script with a different hash code.

---

11. Click the Next button to continue to the Administration Server Setting screen, as shown in Figure 3.8.

This screen enables you to configure various Administration Server settings, as shown in Table 3.5. You see this screen only if you are configuring the administration instance as an Administration Server.

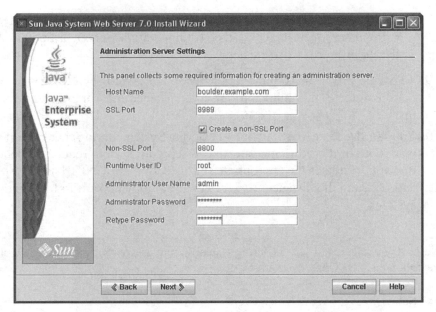

Figure 3.8 Install Wizard—Administration Server Settings Screen

Table 3.5 Administration Server Settings

Setting	Value
Host Name	Specify the fully qualified domain name of the computer on which you are installing the Administration Node instance.
SSL Port	Specify the SSL port for the Administration Node instance or accept the default. The default is 8989 unless that port is unavailable, in which case this defaults to the next highest available port.
Create a non-SSL Port	Select this check box if you would like to enable non-SSL access to the Administration Server. After it is selected, the server enables you to enter a non-SSL port number.
Non-SSL Port	Specify the non-SSL port for the Administration Node instance or accept the default. The default is 8800 unless that port is unavailable, in which case this defaults to the next highest available port.
Runtime User ID	(UNIX only) Specify the UNIX username to use when running the Administration Server. For root installations, the default is root. For non-root installations, the default is the username you used at login.
Administrator User Name	Specify the name of the administrator user. This is the user you will use to log in to the graphical user interface. The default is admin.
Administrator Password	Specify the password for the administrator user.
Retype Password	Confirm the administrator password.

Table 3.6 provides sample values for completing the data found on this screen.

Table 3.6   Sample Administration Server Settings

Setting	Value
Host Name	Accept (or enter) the fully qualified host.domain name for your computer.
SSL Port	Accept the default port of **8989**.
Create a non-SSL Port	Do not select this box.
Non-SSL Port	Not Applicable (the Create non-SSL Port was not selected).
Runtime User ID	Accept the default user of **root**.
Administrator User Name	Accept the default user of **admin**.
Administrator Password	Enter a password of **password**.
Retype Password	Confirm the password of **password**.

12. Complete the Administration Server settings as shown in Table 3.6, and click the Next button to continue to the Web Server Settings screen. This is shown in Figure 3.9.

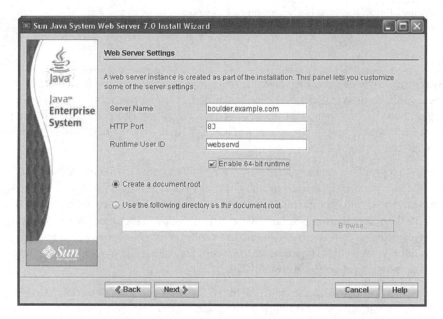

Figure 3.9   Install Wizard—Web Server Settings Screen

This screen enables you to configure various settings for the default Web Server instance. See Table 3.7.

Table 3.7   Web Server Settings

Setting	Value
Server Name	Specify the fully qualified domain name of the computer on which you are installing the default Web Server instance. The information you enter here will be used to create the name of the initial configuration, instance, and virtual server.
HTTP Port	Default value depends upon the runtime user ID of the Administration Server instance. If the Administration Server instance's runtime user ID is non-root, the default is 8080. If the Administration Server instance's runtime user ID is root, the default is 80.
Runtime User ID	(UNIX only) If the Administration Server instance's runtime user ID is root, then the default runtime user ID is webservd. If the Administration Server instance's runtime user ID is non-root, then the default is the same as Administration Server instance's runtime user ID.
Enable 64-bit runtime	Specify whether the 64-bit runtime should be enabled for the default Web Server instance. The default is No (the option is not selected). This option is not displayed if the 64-bit mode is not supported on this platform.
Create a default document root directory	Specify whether the default document root should be created during installation. The default is *install_dir*/https-*server_name*/docs. The server's content files reside in this directory.
Use the following directory as DocumentRoot	Specify a document root other than the default.

Warning: The root user on UNIX-based systems can start and stop processes bound to any port. Non-root users, however, can only start and stop processes that are listening on ports greater than 1024 (these are considered non-privileged ports). For non-root users to start and stop processes less than or equal to port 1024, the user must be granted the appropriate privileges.

Solaris 10 provides an alternative way for non-root users to bind to ports less than 1024. On Solaris 10, you must provide net_privaddr privileges to a non-root user and start the server. For example, to start the Web Server instance as webservd (the default Web Server user on Solaris 10) you would need to log in as root and execute the following command: /usr/sbin/usermod -K defaultpriv=basic, net_privaddr webservd. The webservd user would now have the appropriate privileges to stop and start processes less than 1024.

For more information on usermod, see http://docs.sun.com/app/docs/doc/816-5166. For more information on privileges, see http://docs.sun.com/app/docs/doc/816-5175.

Table 3.8 provides sample values for completing the data found on this screen.

Table 3.8 Sample Web Server Settings

Setting	Value
Server Name	Accept (or enter) the **fully qualified** *host.domain* name for your computer.
HTTP Port	Accept the default port of **80**.
Runtime User ID	Accept the default of **webservd**.
Enable 64-bit runtime	Do not select this box.
Create a default document root directory	Select this radio button.
Use the following directory as DocumentRoot	Do not select this radio button.

13. Complete the Web Server settings as shown in Table 3.8, and click the Next button to continue to the Ready to Install screen. This is shown in Figure 3.10.

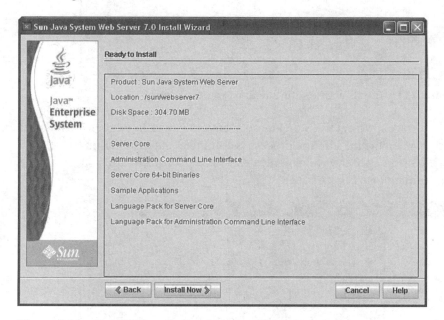

Figure 3.10 Install Wizard—Ready to Install Screen

14. Verify your settings and click the Install Now button to begin the installation process. A new window opens that displays where you are in the installation process. This can be seen in Figure 3.11.

    You can select the Stop button at any time to terminate the installation. When the installation process is complete, the Installation Complete screen appears, which indicates whether the installation succeeded or failed (see Figure 3.12). This screen also provides useful information about using the Administration Server and reviewing the installation log file. Take note of the information provided in this screen for future reference.

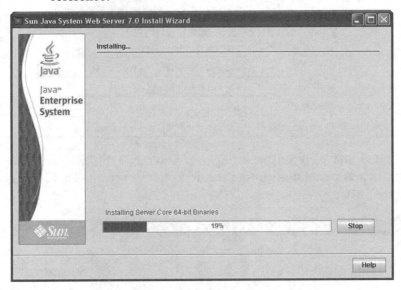

Figure 3.11   Install Wizard—Installation Progress Screen

You can select the Stop button at any time to terminate the installation. When the installation process is complete, the Installation Complete screen appears, which indicates whether the installation succeeded or failed (see Figure 3.12).

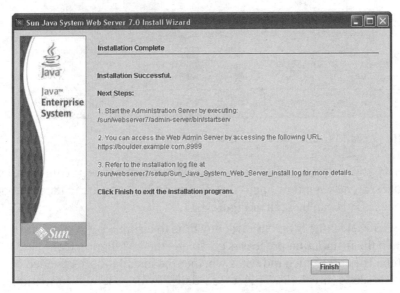

Figure 3.12   Install Wizard—Installation Complete Screen

This screen also provides useful information about using the Administration Server and reviewing the installation log file. Note the information provided in this screen for future reference.

15. Your installation is now complete. Click the Finish button to exit the Install Wizard.

16. Refer to the "Verifying the Installation" section, later in this chapter, to verify that you have successfully installed Web Server 7.0 on the target system.

3.4.3 Command-Line Installation

Web Server 7.0 includes a command-line installer that provides a method for performing an interactive, text-based installation from a terminal window. This is particularly useful if you are remotely accessing the target system with TELNET or SSH. Just like the graphical Install Wizard, the command-line installer walks you through the installation process and prompts you for the information and preferences necessary to install the software. You can install Web Server 7.0 in command-line mode by performing the following steps:

1. Log in to your system as the root user (on UNIX-based systems) or Administrator (on Windows systems).

2. Launch the Install Wizard with the `--console` option as follows:

   `./setup --console` (UNIX-based systems)

   `setup.exe --console` (Windows systems)

   (See Section 3.4.1, "The `setup` Command," for a complete list of options for the `setup` command.)

   The command-line installation program panel opens. You will see text similar to the following:

   ```
   You are running the installation program for Sun Java System Web
   Server 7.0. You will be asked to specify preferences that determine
   how Sun Java System Web Server 7.0 is installed and configured.
   ```

   The installation program pauses as questions are presented so you can read the information and make your choice. When you are ready to continue, press Enter (Return on some keyboards).

   ```
   <Press ENTER to Continue>
   ```

3. Press the Enter key to continue displaying text as follows:

```
Some questions require that you provide more detailed
information. Some questions also display default values in brackets
[]. For example, yes is the default answer to the following ques-
tion:


Are you sure? [yes]

To accept the default, press Enter.


To provide a different answer, type the information at the command
prompt and then press Enter.

<Press ENTER to Continue>
```

4. Press the Enter key to continue. You will be prompted for the same information (in the same order) as requested by the graphical Install Wizard. Refer
to Section 3.4.2, "Graphical Installation," for an overview of the installation
process and an explanation of each prompt.

5. See Section 3.5, "Verifying the Installation," to verify that you have successfully installed Web Server 7.0 on the target system.

3.4.4 Silent Installation

Silent installation enables you to install the Web Server in a non-interactive mode.
This is accomplished by providing an input file to the installation process that
contains the options that would normally be provided by an administrator during
an interactive installation. Silent installations enable you to conform to corporate
standards by providing a predictable installation based on parameters specified in
the input file (*state file*). A non-interactive installation also eliminates user error
and enables you to quickly install the software on multiple systems.

To install in silent mode, you must first generate the state file (described in the following section). After that has been completed, you can then start the installation
program using the `--silent` option (`./setup --silent state_file`). After the silent
mode is activated, installation takes place without additional user input.

3.4.4.1 Generating a State File

The installer configuration file (state file) is created when the `--savestate` option
is used with the `setup` command to start an interactive installation (either graphi-

cal or command-line). Examples of how to create a state file on a UNIX-based system are as follows:

```
./setup --savestate          (graphical installation)
./setup --console --savestate (command-line installation)
```

Settings are captured during the interactive installation and saved in a state file. This file forms the template for a silent installation, which can be used to install the product on one or more systems in a non-interactive mode.

The state file is created and saved into the installation directory that you specify during installation (/sun/webserver7 by default on Unix, C:\Program Files\sun\ webserver7 on Windows). The default name of the file is statefile, but it can be changed to another name after it has been created.

An example state file for a UNIX-based system might look as follows:

```
#
# Wizard Statefile created: Mon Jan 22 08:52:30 EST 2007
#         Wizard path: /ws7-extract/WebServer/WebServer.class
#

#
# Install Wizard Statefile section for Sun Java System Web Server
#
#
[STATE_BEGIN Sun Java System Web Server cb2498a60eaeb-
    712daf267df27293b963730573b]
defaultInstallDirectory = /sun/webserver7
currentInstallDirectory = /sun/webserver7
UPGRADE = false
SELECTED_COMPONENTS =
    svrcore,admincli,svrcore64,devsupport,svrcore_l10n,admincli_l10n
USE_BUNDLED_JDK = true
JDK_LOCATION =
IS_ADMIN_NODE = false
STARTUP_ONBOOT = true
ADMIN_HOST = boulder.example.com
ADMIN_SSL_PORT = 8989
ADMIN_PORT = 8800
ADMIN_UID = root
ADMIN_NAME = admin
ADMIN_PASSWD = password
NODE_HOST =
NODE_SSL_PORT =
REGISTER_NODE =
```

```
WEB_SERVERNAME = boulder.example.com
WEB_PORT = 80
WEB_UID = webservd
WEB_DOCROOT =
SIXTYFOURBIT_INSTALL = true
CONFIG_NAME = boulder.example.com
SKIP_INSTANCE_CREATION =
[STATE_DONE Sun Java System Web Server cb2498a60eaeb-
    712daf267df27293b963730573b]
```

Note: This particular state file was generated from the graphical installation steps demonstrated in Section 3.4.2, "Graphical Installation."

Table 3.9 provides an explanation of each of these parameters. Note that the parameters are in alphabetical order, not the order in which they appear in the state file.

Table 3.9   Common State File Parameters

Parameter	Possible Values	Description
ADMIN_PORT	0–65535	Administration Server port number for non-SSL communication.
ADMIN_SSL_PORT	0–65535	Administration Server port number for SSL communication.
ADMIN_UID	Valid UNIX user ID	(UNIX only) Valid UNIX user ID to run the Administration Server.
CONFIG_NAME	https-host.domain	Default configuration name used by the Web Server to create a configuration, associate it with a node, and create an instance.
currentInstall-Directory		Location for storing installation binaries and other components.
defaultInstall-Directory	/sun/webserver7 (Unix) C:\Program Files\Sun\WebServer7 (Windows)	Default location for storing installation binaries and other components.
IS_ADMIN_NODE	true or false	Valid only for Administration Server and Administration Node installations; null for Administration Command Line installations.

Parameter	Possible Values	Description
JDK_LOCATION		Path to the JDK used for this Web Server. It either contains the path to an existing JDK on your system, or is empty if you set the USE_BUNDLED_JDK parameter to `true`.
NODE_HOST		Fully qualified name of the computer on which you are installing the Administration Node.
NODE_SSL_PORT	0–65535	Administration Node port number for SSL communication.
REGISTER_NODE	`true` or `false`	Specifies whether the Administration Node instance should be registered with the Administration Server instance at the time of installation or later.
SELECTED_COMPONENTS		Comma-separated list of product components selected for installation.
SIXTYFOURBIT_INSTALL	`true` or `false`	Identifies a 64-bit installation.
SKIP_INSTANCE_CREATION	`true` or `false`	True will not create default instances.
STARTUP_ONBOOT	`true` or `false`	Start on system boot option.
USE_BUNDLED_JDK	`true` or `false`	Install the JDK bundled with the installer; if false, JDK_LOCATION cannot be empty.
WEB_DOCROOT		The primary document directory for the Web Server instance; if this is empty, a default document directory is created.
WEB_PORT	0–65535	Valid default port to run the Web Server instance under HTTP mode.
WEB_SERVERNAME		Fully qualified name of the computer on which you are installing the Web Server instance.
WEB_UID	Valid UNIX user ID	(UNIX only) Valid UNIX user ID to run the Web Server Instance.

Variables such as ADMIN_HOST, ADMIN_PORT, ADMIN_NAME, and ADMIN_PASSWD act differently based on the configuration. Table 3.10 provides additional information for these parameters.

Table 3.10   Configuration Parameters for an Administration Server Instance

Parameter	Possible Values	Description
ADMIN_HOST		Fully qualified name of the computer on which you are installing the Administration Node.
ADMIN_PORT	0–65535	Administration Server port number for non-SSL communication.
ADMIN_NAME		Administrator username for the initial server instance. This is the username of the administrator used to gain access to the Administration Server through the command-line interface (CLI) or graphical user interface (GUI).
ADMIN_PASSWD		Administrator password for the initial server instance. This is the password that the administrator uses to gain access to the Administration Server through the command-line interface (CLI) or graphical user interface (GUI). This password is stored in plain text in the state file.

Warning: Passwords are stored in the state file in plain text. Because of this, you should either use a generic password (such as `password`) and change it immediately after installation, or you should make the state file readable only to the user who is performing the silent installation (for instance, `root`).

Table 3.11 contains fields that might be found if you decided to install the server as an Administration Node as well as an Administration Server.

Table 3.11   Configuration Parameters for an Administration Node Instance

Parameter	Possible Values	Description
ADMIN_HOST		Fully qualified name of the computer on which you are installing the Administration Node.
ADMIN_SSL_PORT	0–65535	Administration Server port number for SSL communication.
ADMIN_NAME		Administrator username for the initial server instance. The Administration Server instance uses this username to remotely manage the Administration Node.
ADMIN_PASSWD		Administrator user password for the initial server instance. The Administration Server instance uses this password to remotely manage the Administration Node.

3.4.4.2 Build Identifier

A state file contains an identifier that is associated with the product build from which the state file was created. State files created from different builds of the Web Server will have different identifiers and cannot be used across the different builds. The following is an example of the build identifier contained in the state file:

```
[STATE_BEGIN Sun Java System Web Server cb2498a60eaeb-
    712daf267df27293b963730573b]
state file parameters
[STATE_DONE Sun Java System Web Server cb2498a60eaeb-
    712daf267df27293b963730573b]
```

If you would like to use an older state file with a later version of the software, you first need to update the state file with the build identifier for the build you would like to use. To accomplish this, you would use the `setup --id` command on the build you would like to use to determine the build identifier.

```
./setup --id
05ff73ff18c2c641920463c5ce6000160e281ee5
```

You would then update the state file with the new build identifier and initiate a silent installation.

> **Note:** State file parameters may change between product releases. As such, you might find that a later release either adds or deletes certain parameters. If you attempt to use a state file that has changed between releases (even with the new build identifier), you will see an error message specific to the missing or added parameter.

3.4.4.3 Performing a Silent Installation

You can perform a silent installation of Web Server 7.0 by performing the following steps:

1. Log in to your system as the root user (on UNIX-based systems) or Administrator (on Windows systems).
2. Launch the Install Wizard with the `--silent` option and specify the name of the state file as follows:

`./setup --silent` *state_file* (UNIX-based systems)

`setup.exe --silent` *state_file* (Windows systems)

(See Section 3.4.1, "The `setup` Command," for a complete list of options to the `setup` command.)

You will not see any indication that the installation has started.

3. After the installation has successfully completed, you will see a message that is similar to the following:

```
Installation Successful.

Next Steps:

1. Start the Administration Server by executing:

/sun/webserver7/admin-server/bin/startserv

2. You can access the Web Admin Server by accessing the following
URL:

https://boulder.example.com:8989

3. Refer to the installation log file at /sun/webserver7/setup/Sun_
Java_System_Web_Server_install.log for more details.
```

4. Refer to Section 3.5, "Verifying the Installation," to verify that you have successfully installed Web Server 7.0 on the target system.

3.5 Verifying the Installation

The installation process enables you to configure the installation as an Administration Server (with a Web Server instance) or an Administration Node. Depending on your selection, the installation process creates the appropriate structure on the file system for each instance. It then places various files such as libraries, binaries, and configuration files into that directory structure to support each instance.

There are several ways to verify that the installation completed as expected. The next section describes these methods in more detail.

3.5.1 Installation Log Files

The installation process creates various output (or log) files that contain messages pertaining to the installation process. These log files can be used to verify a proper Web Server installation or troubleshoot a failed installation and fall into two categories:

- Web Server Install Log (located in the Web Server installation directory)
- Low-Level (Java Enterprise System) log files (Solaris and Linux only, located in product registry for the particular operating system)

Reviewing the data found in these files provides an insight into the steps performed during the installation process. If your installation has succeeded, then it is not necessary to look in these log files. If your installation has failed, however, you should review each log file to determine the nature of the error.

3.5.1.1 Web Server Install Log

The Web Server Install Log is located in the `setup` directory, which is directly beneath the installation directory that you specified during the installation process. An example of this would be

```
/sun/webserver7/setup/Sun_Java_System_Web_Server_install.log
```

This file contains entries that specify the actions performed during the installation, the package used to perform the action, the outcome (or result) of the action, and the cause of the failure (if applicable). Each entry in this file spans two lines and has the following syntax:

```
[timestamp] [package] [action]
[result]: [cause]
```

Results fall into various categories. Table 3.12 describes each of these categories in more detail.

Table 3.12   Install Log Entry Categories

Category	Description
INFO	Indicates normal completion of a particular installation task.
FINE	Indicates normal completion of a particular installation task. This message contains more detail than INFO, but not as much as FINEST.
FINEST	Indicates normal completion of a particular installation task. This message contains the greatest amount of detail. It is the most verbose of all.
WARNING	Indicates non-critical failures. Warning-level messages contain information about the cause and nature of the failure, and point to possible remedies.
ERROR	Indicates critical failures and reports the installation status as failed. Error-level messages provide detailed information about the nature and cause of the problem.

The following is a snippet from a successful installation. Spacing has been added between each entry for readability.

```
Jan 22, 2007 9:17:28 AM com.sun.web.installer.web.actions.PostIn-
   stall_core install
INFO: Start core server configuration

Jan 22, 2007 9:17:28 AM com.sun.web.installer.web.actions.PostIn-
   stall_core install
FINE: Initialized the variable in PostInstall_core install

Jan 22, 2007 9:17:28 AM com.sun.web.installer.web.actions.PostIn-
   stall_core
   installJDK
FINE: Starting the copy of JDK

Jan 22, 2007 9:18:35 AM com.sun.web.installer.web.actions.PostIn-
   stall_core
   installJDK
FINE: Successfully copied JDK

Jan 22, 2007 9:18:35 AM com.sun.web.installer.web.actions.PostIn-
   stall_core
   createScript
FINE: Replacing
/sun/webserver7/lib/install/templates/scripts/configureServer.tem-
   plate to
/sun/webserver7/setup/configureServer...

Jan 22, 2007 9:18:36 AM com.sun.web.installer.web.actions.PostIn-
   stall_core
   createScript
```

```
FINE: ...done

Jan 22, 2007 9:18:36 AM com.sun.web.installer.web.actions.PostIn-
   stall_core
   configureServer
FINE: Successfully created the configurator script

Jan 22, 2007 9:18:36 AM com.sun.web.installer.web.actions.PostIn-
   stall_core
   configureServer
INFO: Successfully created the install.properties file to be used by
   the backend
   configurator

Jan 22, 2007 9:18:40 AM com.sun.web.admin.configurator.ConfigureServer
   main
FINEST: Starting configuration of webserver...

[entries deleted]

Jan 22, 2007 9:19:54 AM com.sun.web.installer.web.actions.PostIn-
   stall_core
   configureServer
INFO: Returned successfully from the backend configurator

Jan 22, 2007 9:19:54 AM com.sun.web.installer.web.actions.PostIn-
   stall_core install
INFO: End core server configuration

Jan 22, 2007 9:19:54 AM com.sun.web.installer.web.actions.PostIn-
   stall_core
   createInfFile
INFO: Successfully created the install.inf file

Jan 22, 2007 9:19:54 AM com.sun.web.installer.web.actions.PostIn-
   stall_core
   copyMsgJar
INFO: Successfully copied the messages.jar file

Jan 22, 2007 9:19:54 AM com.sun.web.installer.web.actions.PostIn-
   stall_core
   moveUninstaller
INFO: Successfully moved the Uninstall class file to setup directory
```

The Web Server Log file is useful in resolving errors that might have been experienced during the installation process. If your installation has failed, you should review the log file to determine the nature of the error. Start at the end of the log file and work your way backward until you see an error message that indicates why the installation has failed. Not enough storage space or attempting the installation as a user that does not have appropriate permissions are common reasons why installations fail. After you determine the reason why your installation failed, you can then take the appropriate action(s) and restart the installation process.

3.5.1.2 Low-Level Log Files

Web Server 7.0 is a component of the Java Enterprise System (Java ES). As such, the installation process creates log files specific to the Java ES environment. Low-level log file names have the following syntax (where *mm* is the two-digit month, *dd* is the two-digit day, *HH* is the two-digit hour, and *MM* is the two-digit minute that the installation was performed):

```
Sun_Java_System_Web_Server_install.AmmddHHMM
Sun_Java_System_Web_Server_install.BmmddHHMM
```

These files can be found in different directories (depending on the operating system), as shown in Table 3.13.

Table 3.13   Low-Level Log File Locations

Operating System	Location of the Low-Level Log File
Solaris (installation as the root user)	`/var/sadm/install/logs`
Solaris (installation as a non-root user)	`/var/tmp/`
Linux, HP-UX, AIX	`/var/tmp/`
Windows	`%tmp%`

The following is a snippet from the first of the two low-level log files (Sun_Java_System_Web_Server_install.A*mmddHHMM*):

```
Installing Sun Java System Web Server
   Log file: /var/sadm/install/logs/Sun_Java_System_Web_Server_in-
   stall.BmmddHHMM
Install complete.
```

It should be noted that the contents of this file simply point to the location of the second low-level log file for the Web Server installation. The second of these two files (Sun_Java_System_Web_Server_install.B*mmddHHMM*) contains the specific installation information as follows:

```
Installing Sun Java System Web Server
    Log file: /var/sadm/install/logs/Sun_Java_System_Web_Server_in-
    stall.BmmddHHMM
Installed: /sun/webserver7/uninstall.class
Uninstaller is at: /sun/webserver7/uninstall.class

Installing Sample Applications
Installed:/sun/webserver7/include
Installed:/sun/webserver7/include/base
Installed:/sun/webserver7/include/base/buffer.h
Installed:/sun/webserver7/include/base/cinfo.h
Installed:/sun/webserver7/include/base/crit.h
Installed:/sun/webserver7/include/base/daemon.h
Installed:/sun/webserver7/include/base/ereport.h
Installed:/sun/webserver7/include/base/file.h
Installed:/sun/webserver7/include/base/net.h
Installed:/sun/webserver7/include/base/pblock.h
Installed:/sun/webserver7/include/base/pool.h
Installed:/sun/webserver7/include/base/regexp.h
...
Installed:/sun/webserver7/lib/webapps/search/images/search_ko.jpg
Installed:/sun/webserver7/lib/webapps/search/images/search_zh_CN.jpg
Installed:/sun/webserver7/lib/webapps/search/images/search_zh_TW.jpg
Installed:/sun/webserver7/lib/webserv-rt-l10n.jar
Install complete.
```

The second file contains the specific details for each component installed during the Web Server 7.0 installation. On UNIX systems, you can use the grep command to obtain an overview of the components installed.

```
# grep Installing Sun_Java_System_Web_Server_install.BmmddHHMM

Installing Sun Java System Web Server
Installing Sample Applications
Installing Server Core 64-bit Binaries
Installing Administration Command Line Interface
Installing Language Pack for Administration Command Line Interface
Installing Server Core
Installing Language Pack for Server Core
```

The return values should correlate with the components selected during the installation process (refer to Figure 3.5).

3.5.2 Server Processes

Instances created during the Web Server 7.0 installation have their own specific purpose and have different configuration settings that reflect that purpose. Each instance responds to client requests and has server processes that listen on a particular listen socket to process those requests.

The Administration Server contains a specially configured administrative instance of the Web Server. This instance is used to manage configuration information and can be accessed through a graphical or command-line interface. As such, the administration instance has an HTTP process that listens on a particular listen socket for administrative commands.

The Administration Node provides the interface for HTTP user agents to access content being served by the Web Server. This instance has its own process that listens on a separate port and may even exist on a separate server altogether.

In addition to processes listening for client requests, both instances also have internal processes that are used to provide a level of high availability at the process level. In general, three processes are created for each instance. These are the *watchdog* process, the *primordial* process, and the *worker* process, and their relationship to each other is demonstrated in Figure 3.13.

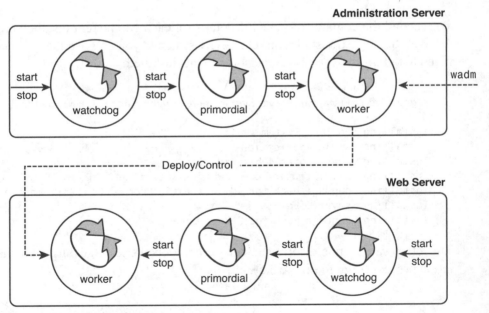

Figure 3.13   Web Server Processes

The worker process listens on a particular port for client requests. HTTP clients interact directly with the worker process. The watchdog and primordial processes are not accessible through the listen socket, so HTTP clients cannot communicate directly with these processes. Scripts used to start and stop each of the instances communicate directly with the watchdog process. The watchdog process interacts directly with the primordial process, which in turn interacts with the worker process. There is no direct interface to the primordial process.

The worker process is responsible for processing HTTP requests from clients. If the worker process terminates for any reason, then it is the duty of the primordial process to restart it (so that it can continue processing client requests). If the primordial process terminates, then the watchdog process restarts it.

The watchdog process is started when you execute the `startserv` script. The purpose of the watchdog and primordial processes is to provide a limited level of high availability within the server processes.

You can have multiple Web Server processes running within a single instance. The primordial process is responsible for launching each of these processes. When you start a single instance, the primordial process does not play much of a role; its true benefit comes into play, however, when you start multiple Web Server instances and the primordial process can monitor and restart all of them. This is the main purpose of the primordial process.

The primordial and worker processes are both named `webservd`. The name of the watchdog process is `webservd-wdog`. On UNIX servers, these processes can be seen with the `ps -ef` command. The following example demonstrates each of the processes for an Administration Node:

```
# ps -ef | grep http

webservd 14857 14856  0  Jan 22 ?        33:12 webservd -d
/sun/webserver7/https-boulder.example.com/config -r /sun/webserver7

    root 14856 14855  0  Jan 22 ?         7:19 webservd -d
/sun/webserver7/https-boulder.example.com/config -r /sun/webserver7

    root 14855    1  0  Jan 22 ?         0:04 webservd-wdog -d
/sun/webserver7/https-boulder.example.com/config -r /sun/webse
```

Note: The ps command provides important information regarding the process owner, the process ID, the parent process ID, the date the process was started, the daemon process that is running, and the parameters that were passed to the process.

The first column specifies the process owner, which, in this case, is root for the watchdog and primordial processes. This is required if your Web Server is listening to a port less than 1024 (a privileged port on UNIX). If the port is greater than 1024, then the watchdog and primordial process can be a non-root user. The user for the worker process owner is specified during the installation process. In this case the process owner is webservd, which is the default user.

The second column is the process ID of the running process, and the third column is the process ID of the parent process (or the process that started this process).

Looking at the entries from bottom to top, the following can be observed:

- Process 14855 is the watchdog process. It was started by the init process (which is indicated by a process ID of 1).
- Process 14856 is the primordial process. It was started by the watchdog process.
- Process 14857 is the worker process. It was started by the primordial process.

There is a parent/child relationship between the various processes. You can use the UNIX ptree command on the watchdog process to determine this relationship as follows:

```
# ptree 14855

14855 webservd-wdog -d /sun/webserver7/https-boulder.example.com/
   config -r /sun/webse

14856 webservd -d /sun/webserver7/https-boulder.example.com/config -r
/sun/webserver7

   14857 webservd -d /sun/webserver7/https-boulder.example.com/config
   -r /sun/webserver7
```

3.5.3 Directory Structure

During the installation process, you selected the directory where you wanted the Web Server files to be placed. This is referred to as the installation directory or *server root*.

The installation program places various folders, configuration files, executables, library files, and binaries beneath the server root, as shown in Figure 3.14.

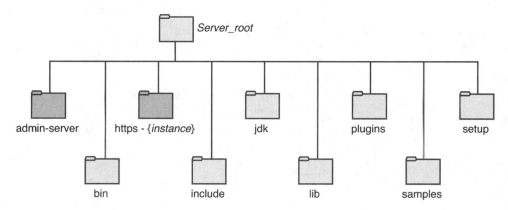

Figure 3.14   Server Root Contents

The `admin-server` and `https-{instance}` folders are the individual instance folders that were created during the installation process. Each one contains information that is specific to its particular instance. All other folders contain information that is considered to be global to all server instances. A brief description of the information contained in each of the folders shown in Figure 3.14 can be found in Table 3.14.

Table 3.14   Server Root Contents

Folder	Description
`admin-server`	The administrative instance for this server. The information beneath this folder varies depending on whether the server is configured as an Administration Server or Administration Node.
`bin`	Binaries and scripts for global use. (Global to the `admin-server` and any other server instances.)
`https-{instance}`	The default Web Server instance. This is created on an Administration Server by default during installation. This is not created on an Administration Node until that instance has been created.

Table 3.14   Server Root Contents   *continued*

Folder	Description
`include`	Include files for compiling plug-ins for Web Server 7.0. These files are global to all server instances.
`jdk`	This folder contains the Java Development Kit (JDK) that ships with the Web Server.
`plugins`	This folder contains plug-ins that are supported by the Web Server. Default plug-ins are installed in this folder by default. It is a good practice to add your own plug-ins to this folder as well.
`samples`	Sample applications that ship with the Web Server. This folder is created if you selected the Sample Applications component during installation.
`setup`	This folder contains the files associated with the installation of the Web Server (such as the installation log). It also contains information that allows you to uninstall the Web Server.
`lib`	This folder contains internal server files necessary to run the Web Server. This includes Java archive (`.jar`) files, shared objects (`*.so`), scripts, and properties files. This folder is considered a PRIVATE INTERFACE and should not be modified directly.

Warning: You should never create dependencies on files that are considered a *private interface*. The files and/or file structure contained within the private interface are not documented and are subject to change between product releases.

Information specific to the Administration Server instance can be found beneath the `admin-server` folder. Figure 3.15 demonstrates the file system layout for the Administration Server.

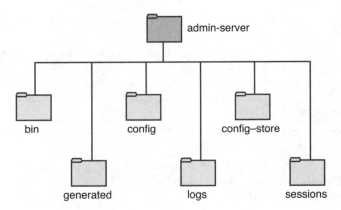

Figure 3.15   Administration Server Folder Contents

A brief description of the information contained in each of the folders shown in Figure 3.15 can be found in Table 3.15.

Table 3.15 Administration Server Folder Contents

Folder	Description
`bin`	Binaries and scripts specific to the Administration Server instance.
`config`	Administration Server configuration files. This folder is considered a PRIVATE INTERFACE and should not be modified directly.
`config-store`	The configuration repository for managed instances. This folder is considered a PRIVATE INTERFACE and should not be modified directly.
`generated`	Internal data that has been generated for the Administration Server. This includes compiled JSPs for the Administration Server. This folder is considered a PRIVATE INTERFACE and should not be modified directly.
`logs`	Administration Server log files.
`sessions`	Session data specific to the Administration Server web application. This folder is considered a PRIVATE INTERFACE and should not be modified directly.

Warning: You should never create dependencies on files that are considered a private interface. The files and/or file structure contained within the private interface are not documented and are subject to change between product releases.

To maintain compatibility with future releases, you should use the Administration Console or the `wadm` command to read or write to configuration files.

Information specific to the Administration Node instance can be found beneath the `https-{instance}` folder (where `{instance}` is the name you have given your Web Server instance). Figure 3.16 demonstrates the file system layout for Administration Nodes.

A brief description of the information contained in each of the folders shown in Figure 3.16 can be found in Table 3.16.

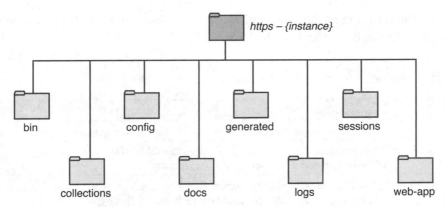

Figure 3.16   Administration Node Folder Contents

Table 3.16   Administration Node Folder Contents

Folder	Description
bin	Binaries and scripts related to the Administration Node instance. Earlier versions of the Sun Web Server stored these files in the instance's main folder. These are now located in the instance's bin folder.
config	Administration Node configuration files. Some files in the config directory are considered private and should not be modified directly. Refer to the Sun Java System Web Server 7.0 Administrator's Configuration File Reference for more information.
docs	Default directory for documents (such as .html files) served by this instance. This is also known as the *docroot* directory.
collections	Search collections used for the site search web application. This folder is considered a PRIVATE INTERFACE and should not be modified directly.
generated	Internal data that has been generated for the Administration Node. This directory contains compiled Java Server Pages that were located in the ClassCache directory in previous versions of the Sun Web Server. This folder is considered a PRIVATE INTERFACE and should not be modified directly.
logs	Administration Node log files.
sessions	Session data specific to the Administration Node web application. This folder is considered a PRIVATE INTERFACE and should not be modified directly.
web-app	Default web application data for this server instance. This folder is considered a PRIVATE INTERFACE and should not be modified directly.

Warning: You should never create dependencies on files that are considered a private interface. The files and/or file structure contained within the private interface are not documented and are subject to change between product releases.

To maintain compatibility with future releases, you should use the Administration Console or the wadm command to read or write to configuration files.

3.5.4 Non-Windows Product Registry Entries

The product registry is a repository on non-Windows systems where all packages are registered when they are installed. The registry contains information such as installation location, product version, and component dependencies. All Web Server 7.0 installed packages generate entries in the product registry.

The product registry can be found in different locations as follows:

- **Solaris OS:** /var/sadm/install/productregistry
- **Linux:** /var/opt/sun/install/productregistry
- **HP-UX:** /var/adm/sw/productregistry

During the installation process, you select various components that you would like to install as part of the Web Server 7.0 installation. This includes components such as Server Core, Server Core 64-bit Binaries, and the Administration Command Line Interface. Components have a set of packages that are installed to provide the functionality of that component. When you install a component, you create entries in the product registry that reference each package that was installed for a particular component. For example, the following code demonstrates the product registry entries for one of the packages that provides the Administration Command Line Interface functionality:

```
<compid>admincli_zip
      <compversion>1.0
            <uniquename>admincli_zip
            </uniquename>
            <compinstance>1
                  <parent>admincli
                        <instance>1
                              <version>7.0
                              </version>
                        </instance>
                  </parent>
                  <comptype>COMPONENT
                  </comptype>
                  <location>/opt/webserver7
                  </location>
                  <dependent>
                        <compref>admincli
```

```
                                  <instance>1
                                          <version>7.0
                                          </version>
                                  </instance>
                          </compref>
                      </dependent>
                  </compinstance>
          </compversion>
      </compid>
```

If Web Server 7.0 installation files are removed incorrectly (for example, if the files are manually deleted instead of being removed by the uninstaller), the files might be gone from the file system but the Web Server entries remain in the product registry. If you then try to re-install to that same location, a message displays indicating that an existing installation has been detected, even though it appears that the installation does not exist. To remedy the situation, go to the product registry and delete the entries manually. This includes the opening and closing compid tags.

The following entries are considered Web Server 7.0 product registry entries:

- svrcore64_zip
- svrcomponents64_zip
- svrcore64
- admincli_zip
- clicomponents_zip
- uninstall
- admincli
- svrcore_zip
- svrcomponents_zip
- svrcore
- Sun Java System Web Server

Note: Consider making a backup copy of the product registry before installing the Web Server. This enables you to easily identify those entries that are specific to your installation.

If for some reason you need to manually remove entries from the product registry, you should always make a backup copy of the product registry before deleting any entries.

3.5.5 Windows Specific Entries

Installation on Windows-based operating systems produces additional entries that are not found on UNIX-based systems. This section contains details about Windows-specific entries.

3.5.5.1 Windows Program Group

The installation process creates a program group called Web Server 7.0 that can be found in the following location:

```
Programs -> Sun Microsystems -> Web Server 7.0
```

This program group contains various icons used to start and stop the Administration Server instance, access the Administration Console through a web browser, and initiate an uninstallation of the product. The specific items contained in this group are as follows:

- Administration Console
- Start Administration Server
- Stop Administration Server
- Uninstall

3.5.5.2 Windows Service Entries

Web Server 7.0 instances (such as the Administration Server and Administration Nodes) run as Windows services. As such, you will see entries in the Services application (`services.msc`) similar to the following:

- Sun Java System Web Server 7.0 (https-*configname*)
- Sun Java System Web Server 7.0 Administration Server

A service entry will be created for each configuration that has been deployed on the Windows server—there will be one entry per instance. You can manually start and stop instances from the Services application or configure instances to start or stop automatically when the server starts or shuts down.

3.5.5.3 Windows Registry Entries

The installation process creates or modifies several entries in the Microsoft registry. The following entries are created or modified during the installation process:

- KEY_LOCAL_MACHINE\SOFTWARE\Microsoft\Windows\Current-Version\ Uninstall\Sun Java System Web Server

  This adds Sun Java System Web Server to the list of applications that can be uninstalled using the Add or Remove Programs functionality accessed from the Control Panel. This key is removed when the product is uninstalled by the uninstaller.

- HKEY_LOCAL_MACHINE\SOFTWARE\Microsoft\Windows\Current-Version\App Management\ARPCache\Sun Java System Web Server

  ARP stands for Add/Remove Program. Similar to the previous entry, this registry entry is used to recognize currently installed programs that can be removed with the Add/Remove Programs tool under the Control Panel.

- Control Set Entries such as :HKEY_LOCAL_MACHINE\SYSTEM\Control Set001\Enum\Root\LEGACY_HTTPS-ADMSERV70, HKEY_LOCAL_MACHINE\SYSTEM\ControlSet002\Enum\Root\LEGACY_HTTPS-*CONFIGNAME*, and HKEY_LOCAL_MACHINE\SYSTEM\CurrentControlSet\Services\https-admserv70

  These entries contain configuration data for the last known successful launch of each Web Server instance.

Note: See the Microsoft Knowledgebase article, "What Are Control Sets? What Is CurrentControlSet?" found at http://support.microsoft.com/kb/100010, for more information about Control Set entries.

3.6 Post-Installation Tasks

After installation has completed, you might need to perform several tasks to begin using your Web Server instance(s). This section provides details for interacting with the Web Server after the installation has completed.

3.6.1 Starting and Stopping Web Server 7.0

The installation process creates various Web Server control scripts that can be used to start, stop, and restart Web Server 7.0 instances. There is a separate set of scripts for each server instance (including the Administration Server). The scripts that are created for each server instance are described in Table 3.17.

Table 3.17   Web Server Control Scripts

Script	Description
startserv or startserv.bat	Starts the watchdog process for the appropriate instance. This in turn starts the primordial and worker processes, respectively. (See Section 3.5.2, "Server Processes," for more information.) This allows the server instance to begin processing client requests.
stopserv or stopserv.bat	Terminates the watchdog process for the appropriate instance. This in turn terminates any subsequent processes (including the primordial and worker processes, respectively). (See Section 3.5.2, "Server Processes," for more information.) The termination of these processes prevents the server instance from processing client requests.
restart or restart.bat	Stops and then restarts the server processes.

As indicated previously, each instance has its own set of process control scripts. The control scripts used to stop, start, and restart the Web Server instance may be found in the following location:

    install_dir/instance/bin/script

where the following is true:

install_dir is the directory where Web Server 7.0 has been installed.

instance is the name of the Web Server instance (for example admin-server or https-www.example.com).

script is the name of the script.

3.6.1.1 Output from `startserv` Commands

Executing the `startserv` script for the Administration Server instance produces the following output:

```
Sun Java System Web Server 7.0U1 B06/12/2007 22:48
info: CORE3016: daemon is running as super-user
info: CORE5076: Using [Java HotSpot(TM) Server VM, Version 1.5.0_09]
   from [Sun Microsystems Inc.]
info: WEB0100: Loading web module in virtual server [admin-server] at
   [/admingui]
info: WEB0100: Loading web module in virtual server [admin-server] at
   [/jmxconnector]
info: HTTP3072: admin-ssl-port: https://www.example.com:8989 ready to
   accept requests
info: CORE3274: successful server startup
```

The following items provide a description of the data found in this output.

- The first three lines of the output provide release information, the name of the process owner, and the version of Java that the Administration Server is using.
- The fourth and fifth lines specify two web applications that are loaded into the Administration Server.

  The first web application provides the graphical user interface for managing configurations and Web Server instances (this web application is not found on Administration Nodes).

  The second web application provides the JMX-based administrative interface for performing remote administration.

- The sixth line specifies the connection information for accessing the Administration Server from a browser.
- The seventh line specifies that the startup was successful.

Executing the `startserv` script for the Administration Node instance produces the following output:

```
Sun Java System Web Server 7.0U1 B06/12/2007 22:48
info: CORE5076: Using [Java HotSpot(TM) Server VM, Version 1.5.0_09]
   from [Sun Microsystems Inc.]
info: HTTP3072: http-listener-1: http://www.example.com:80 ready to
   accept requests
info: CORE3274: successful server startup
```

The following items provide a description of the data found in this output.

- The first two lines specify the release information and version of Java that the Administration Node is using.
- The third line specifies the connection information for accessing the Administration Node with a browser.
- The fourth line specifies that the startup was successful.

3.6.1.2 Automatic Starting of Web Server Instances

During the installation process, you had the opportunity to select an option that allowed you to start the server processes during system startup. If you selected this option on UNIX-based systems, then start and stop scripts were also created in the appropriate directory (see 3.4.2, "Graphical Installation," for more details). The start and stop scripts call the `startserv` and `stopserv` scripts, respectively, and do so for all instances contained in the *install_dir* directory.

> **Warning:** The Administration Server instance is started in the default start script. You should consider disabling the automatic startup of the Administration Server because leaving this instance running might be considered a security risk.
>
> On UNIX-based systems, you can disable the automatic startup of a particular server instance by creating a `.noStartOnBoot` file in the instance's main directory. One way of creating this file is to use the UNIX `touch` command as follows:
>
> ```
> touch install_dir/instance/.noStartOnBoot
> ```
>
> This creates an empty file in the instance's main directory with a name of `.noStart-OnBoot`. The start script is configured to bypass the startup of any instance that has this file in its instance directory.
>
> On Windows-based systems, you can disable the automatic starting of a particular process through the Services application (`C:\WINDOWS\system32\services.msc`). Launch this application and change the Startup Type to Manual for the instance you would like to disable.

3.6.2 Accessing Web Server 7.0 Instances

Administration Servers and Administration Nodes are Web Server instances. As such, you can use a standard Internet browser to communicate with each instance once it has been started.

Table 3.18 provides an overview of the default Web Server 7.0 URLs for accessing each server instance.

Table 3.18   Default Web Server URLs

Instance	Description
Administration Server	`http://host.domain:8989` (default URL—SSL) `http://host.domain:8800` (default URL—non-SSL)
Administration Node	`http://host.domain:80` (default URL—installed as root user) `http://host.domain:8080` (default URL—installed as non-root user)

3.6.2.1 Accessing the Administration Server

The default port for the Administration Server is 8989. This instance is configured to communicate over SSL and is protected by a self-signed digital certificate that was generated during the installation process. If you selected the default values for the Administration Server during installation, the URL for accessing the Administration Server would be `https://host.domain:8989`.

> **Note:** If you inadvertently use the HTTP protocol while attempting to access the secure port on the Administration Server, your browser is redirected to the same host and port number, but the protocol is changed from HTTP to HTTP(S).
>
> For example, a request for **http**:`//host.domain:8989` is redirected to **https**:`//host.domain:8989`.

You see a certificate warning when you access the Administration Server on its secure port because the SSL certificate is self-signed and not issued by a trusted Certificate Authority (CA). Figure 3.17 provides an example of a certificate warning.

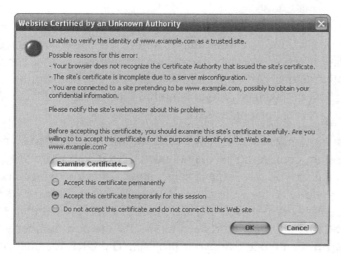

Figure 3.17 Administration Server Unknown Certificate

To access the Administration Server you can choose to trust the certificate for this session only (the default) or you can choose to trust the certificate permanently. Trusting the certificate permanently adds the Administration Server's Certificate Authority to your browser's list of trusted entities and you will not see this certificate warning in the future. If you decide not to trust the certificate, you are unable to access the Administration Server.

The Administration Server can be configured to listen on a non-secure port as well. This is not the default behavior, so you must specify this by selecting the appropriate option during the installation process. If you do select this option, then the default port for a non-SSL based server is 8800 and the URL for accessing the Administration Server on its non-SSL port is `http://host.domain:8800`.

Warning: It is not advisable to configure the Administration Server to listen on a non-secure port if you are accessing the server over the Internet. The potential exists for sensitive data to be exposed as it is sent between the browser and the Administration Server in an unencrypted mode.

You are required to enter a username and password to gain access to the Administration Server. Enter the values that you used in step 11 of the "Graphical Installation" section when prompted for these values. You are now able to perform such operations as starting and stopping Web Server instances and creating and modifying Web Server configurations. Refer to Chapter 4, "Web Server 7.0 Administration," for more information on administering Web Server 7.0.

3.6.2.2 Accessing the Administration Node

During the installation process you were able to select whether you wanted to install an Administration Server (combined with an Administration Node) or simply perform an installation of an Administration Node by itself. Both options create an Administration Node instance, which is nothing more than a default Web Server instance for delivering content to users.

On UNIX-based systems, only root users can configure software to listen on ports less than 1024 (these are considered privileged ports). So if you performed the installation as the root user, you were able to select port 80 and you would access the Administration Node with the following URL: `http://host.domain`. If you installed the software as a non-root user, you had to select a port greater than 1024 (the default is port 8080) and you would need to specify the port number when accessing the Administration Node from your browser. The URL for this would be `http://host.domain:port`.

You will see a default web page displayed containing information about the features of Web Server 7.0. This information is contained in the default a configuration that was created as part of the installation process.

3.6.3 Creating an Initial Configuration

The Administration Node that was created during the installation process contains a default configuration that has limited use other than showing you that you have successfully accessed the node correctly. One of the first things that you want to do after you have installed the software is to create and deploy a new configuration that contains information specific to your own needs.

Refer to Chapter 4 for more information on creating and modifying a configuration.

3.7 Uninstalling Web Server 7.0

The uninstallation process removes an existing Web Server 7.0 installation from your local system. This includes binaries, log files, and configuration data that was used or modified after an initial installation was performed. Similar to the installation process, three methods can be used to uninstall the Web Server 7.0 software: graphical, command-line, and silent. These methods are available on any distribution and enable you to uninstall the software in either an interactive or non-interactive fashion.

3.7.1 The uninstall Command

The uninstall command is used to remove Web Server 7.0 software from your server. The command can be found under the *install_dir*/bin directory and has the following syntax:

```
uninstall [--help] [--console] [--silent]
          [--javahome java_dir] [--saveinstances]
```

You may select the desired mode (graphical, command-line, or silent) by providing the appropriate options to the uninstall command. Table 3.19 provides a list of these options as well as an explanation of each.

Table 3.19   Options for the uninstall Command

Option	Description
./uninstall --help	Displays the options for the uninstall command.
./uninstall	Runs the uninstaller in graphical mode.
./uninstall --console	Runs the uninstaller in command-line mode.
./uninstall --silent	Runs the uninstaller in silent mode.
./uninstall --javahome *java_dir*	Defines the location of the JDK that should be used for the uninstaller JVM. This uninstallation is performed in graphical mode.
./uninstall --console --javahome *java_dir*	Defines the location of the JDK that should be used for the uninstaller JVM. This uninstallation is performed in command-line mode.
./uninstall --saveinstances	Runs the uninstaller in graphical mode with the Save Instances check box preselected. This enables you to save all instance information during the uninstallation process.
./uninstall --silent --saveinstances	Runs the uninstaller in silent mode and automatically saves any instances during the uninstallation process.

3.7.2 Graphical Uninstallation

Web Server 7.0 includes a graphical uninstallation wizard (simply named the Uninstall Wizard) that walks you through the uninstallation process. The Uninstall Wizard guides you through a series of screens where you are prompted for the information and preferences necessary to uninstall the software.

As indicated in the previous section, graphical uninstallation is the default mode when the uninstallation program is started without any options. You can uninstall Web Server 7.0 in graphical mode by performing the following steps:

1. Log in to your system as the root user (on UNIX-based systems) or Administrator (on Windows systems).

2a. (UNIX only) If you are performing an uninstallation from a UNIX-based system, launch the Uninstallation Wizard as follows: /install_dir/bin/uninstall.

2b. (Windows only) If you are performing an uninstallation from a Windows-based system, navigate Windows Explorer to the directory where you installed the software and double-click the uninstall.exe command.

Note: On Windows-based systems, you can also launch the Uninstall Wizard by using any of the following three methods:

1. Run uninstall.exe from the command line.

2. Click Start, Control Panel, Add or Remove Programs, Sun Java System Web Server 7.0.

3. Click Start, Programs, Sun Microsystems, Web Server 7.0, Uninstall.

The Uninstall Wizard Welcome screen opens as shown in Figure 3.18.

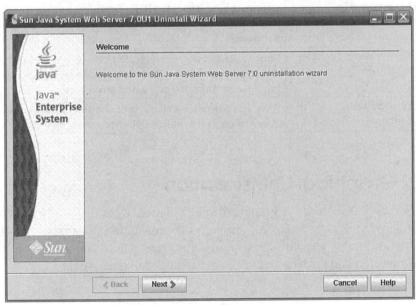

Figure 3.18   Uninstall Wizard—Welcome Screen

Note: On UNIX systems, the uninstallation interface defaults to command-line mode if either the DISPLAY environment variable has not been exported to your local machine or X Windows is not supported. To uninstall in command-line mode, follow the instructions covered in Section 3.7.3, "Command-Line Uninstallation."

3. Click the Next button to continue to the Uninstall Options Selection Panel screen, as shown in Figure 3.19.

   Selecting the Save Instances check box (not selected by default) retains all the server instance directories in the Web Server's installation directory. Saving instances enables you to reuse the configurations by copying them to the Configuration Store of a new Administration Server instance.

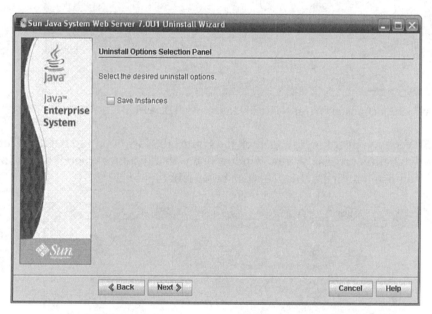

Figure 3.19 Uninstall Wizard—Uninstall Options Selection Panel Screen

4. Click the Next button to continue to the Ready to Uninstall screen, as shown in Figure 3.20.

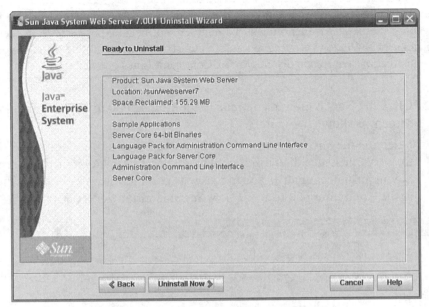

Figure 3.20   Uninstall Wizard—Ready to Uninstall Screen

5. Verify your settings, and click the Uninstall Now button to begin the uninstallation process. A new window opens that displays where you are in the uninstallation process. This can be seen in Figure 3.21.

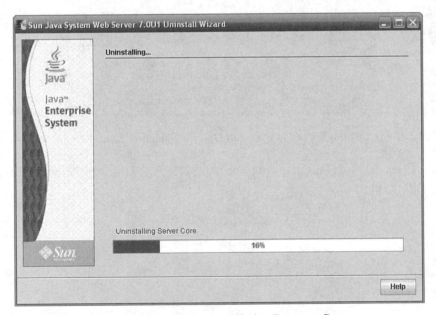

Figure 3.21   Uninstall Wizard—Uninstallation Progress Screen

When the uninstallation process is complete, the Uninstallation Summary screen appears, which indicates the results of the uninstallation process (see Figure 3.22).

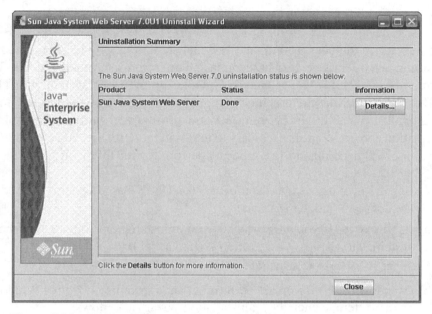

Figure 3.22 Uninstall Wizard—Uninstallation Summary Screen

6. Your uninstallation is now complete. Click the Close button to exit the Uninstall Wizard.

Similar to the installation process, the uninstallation process provides log files that provide insight into the steps performed by the Uninstallation Wizard. These log files may be found in the following locations:

High-Level Log File:

```
install_dir/setup/Sun_Java_System_Web_Server_uninstall.log (High
Level)
```

Low-Level Log Files:

```
Sun_Java_System_Web_Server_install.AmmddHHMM
Sun_Java_System_Web_Server_install.BmmddHHMM
```

(where *mm* is the two-digit month, *dd* is the two-digit day, *HH* is the two-digit hour, and *MM* is the two-digit minute that the uninstallation was performed).

Consider reviewing the data found in these files if errors occur during the uninstallation process.

3.7.3 Command-Line Uninstallation

Web Server 7.0 includes a command-line uninstaller that provides a method for performing an interactive, text-based uninstallation from a terminal window. This is particularly useful if you are remotely accessing the target system with TELNET or SSH. Just like the graphical Uninstall Wizard, the command-line uninstaller walks you through the uninstallation process and prompts you for the information and preferences necessary to uninstall the software. You can uninstall Web Server 7.0 in command-line mode by performing the following steps:

1. Log in to your system as the root user (on UNIX-based systems) or Administrator (on Windows systems).

2a. (UNIX only) If you are performing an uninstallation from a UNIX-based system, launch the Uninstallation Wizard as follows:

    `/install_dir/bin/uninstall --console`

2b. (Windows only) If you are performing an uninstallation from a Windows-based system, launch the Uninstallation Wizard as follows:

    `\install_dir\bin\uninstall.exe --console`

    The command-line uninstallation program opens. You will see text similar to the following:

    ```
    Welcome to the Sun Java System Web Server 7.0 uninstallation wizard.

    This wizard is used to uninstall the Web Server. It is strongly
    recommended that you exit all programs before starting the uninstal-
    lation. If other programs are running, type Control-C to stop the
    uninstallation, then close the programs and start the uninstalla-
    tion program again.

    Press Enter to move through the program (Return on some keyboards).
    Default options are shown in brackets [].

    <Press ENTER to Continue>
    ```

3. Press the Enter key to continue displaying text as follows:

    ```
    Select the desired uninstall options.

        Save Instances [Yes/No] [no] {"<" goes back, "!" exits}:
    ```

4. Press the Enter key to accept the default to not save the instances. You will see text similar to the following:

```
Product: Sun Java System Web Server

Location: /sun/webserver7

Space Reclaimed: 155.29 MB

-----------------------------------

Sample Applications

Server Core 64-bit Binaries

Language Pack for Administration Command Line Interface

Language Pack for Server Core

Administration Command Line Interface

Server Core



Ready to Uninstall


1. Uninstall Now

2. Start Over

3. Exit Uninstallation


What would you like to do [1] {"<" goes back, "!" exits}?
```

5. Press the Enter key to accept the default to begin the uninstallation process. You will see text indicating that the Web Server is being uninstalled. Additionally, you will see a text-based progress bar indicating the status of the uninstallation. Wait until you see that the uninstallation has been completed with text similar to the following:

```
Uninstalling Sun Java System Web Server

|-1%-------------25%----------------50%----------------75%-----
---------100%|



Uninstallation Details:
```

```
    Product                      Result  More Information
1.  Sun Java System Web Server  Done    Available


2.  Done


Review uninstallation details, or enter 2 to exit the uninstallation
program
   [2] {"!" exits}:
```

6. Press the Enter key to exit the uninstallation wizard.

Consider reviewing the data found in the uninstallation log files if errors occur during the uninstallation process. For more information on the location of these log files, see Section 3.7.2, "Graphical Uninstallation."

3.7.4 Silent Uninstallation

A review of the questions asked during a graphical uninstallation or command-line uninstallation process demonstrates that the interactive nature of the uninstallation process is very minimal. As such, you can perform an uninstallation of the product without having to answer questions at all. This is called a silent uninstallation and is the quickest way to remove a Web Server 7.0 installation from your system. To perform an uninstallation in silent mode, you simply have to specify the `--silent` parameter with the `uninstall` command as follows:

```
./uninstall --silent [--saveinstances]
```

The uninstallation process would then proceed without any prompts. Optionally, you can provide the `--saveinstances` option if you want to save instance configuration information before the Web Server is uninstalled. This is useful if you are planning on moving your instances to another server and simply want to capture existing instance information. Otherwise, all instance-specific information is removed during the uninstall process.

3.8 Migrating to Web Server 7.0

Migration is the process of updating product software from an earlier version to a later one. If you are currently running Web Server 6.0 or 6.1, you can migrate your server instances directly to Web Server 7.0.

Note: If you are running a previous version of the Web Server, such as iPlanetWeb Server 4.0 or Sun ONE Web Server 4.1, you must first migrate your instance to Web Server 6.1 and then you can migrate to Web Server 7.0.

3.8.1 The Migration Process

Web Server 7.0 enables you to perform your migration using either a graphical user interface or an administrative command-line interface. The process is the same no matter which method you select. You must first migrate a Web Server 6.0 or 6.1 *instance* to a Web Server 7.0 *configuration* (see Chapter 4 regarding this terminology). The configuration is then stored in the Web Server 7.0 Configuration Store, but it is not yet deployed so clients cannot interact with it. The next step is to deploy the configuration to an Administration Node and test the newly created instance.

Specific steps for performing a migration are as follows:

1. Commit all pending configuration changes on Web Server 6.0 or Web Server 6.1.
2. Confirm that the existing Web Server version is working as expected.
3. Stop the Web Server instance that you are migrating (to avoid port conflicts).
4. Execute the migration tool from either CLI or GUI.
5. Review the migration log file.
6. Perform manual configurations (as necessary).
7. Verify migration.

Note: The server being migrated and the Web Server 7.0 Administration Server must reside on the same physical host. This is necessary to extract data from configuration files and repurpose it for Web Server 7.0. After the new configuration has been created, it can be deployed to any Administration Node anywhere within your server environment.

Some settings might not migrate and must be reconfigured manually. Detailed migration information is provided during and after the migration process. This information includes a list of the settings and configurations that were and were not migrated, a warning about changes that need to be made manually, and an indication whether the migration succeeded or failed. This information is recorded in the following migration log file:

install_dir/admin-server/logs/MIGRATION_*yyyymmddhhmmss*.log

You can specify an alternate pathname for this file if you use the `--logdir` option when performing the migration from the command line.

Note: You should check the log file after the migration has completed to determine which settings (if any) must be configured manually.

3.8.2 What Is and Is Not Migrated

Web Server 7.0 is a major new release of the Sun Web Server product. It has adopted a different paradigm for administration and as such there have been numerous changes in configuration files and directories. The intent of these changes was designed to perform the following:

- Reduce the number of files
- Simplify and improve configuration file syntax
- Enhance flexibility and functionality in existing files

As part of the redesign, no new configuration files have been introduced, but a number of changes have been made to consolidate instance-specific configuration files into the instance's `config` directory.

The migration process takes these changes into account and rewrites, relocates, and removes those files as appropriate. In some cases, it is not possible to migrate certain information. In such cases, the migration process flags these events in the migration log and you must manually migrate that information. The remainder of this section defines those items that are migrated as well as those that are not.

3.8.2.1 What Is Migrated

The following items are migrated during the migration process. In some cases files are moved into configuration-specific directories (as in the case of ACL files), and in other cases the data from one file has been migrated to another. An example of this can be seen with the movement of entries from the `dbswitch.conf` file to elements now found in the `server.xml` file.

- ACL files
- Configuration files
- Scheduler settings

- Configuration settings for file cache tuning
- Key and certificate databases and certificate mappings
- Listen socket settings
- MIME type settings
- NSAPI information
- SHTML settings
- SNMP settings
- SSL information
- User databases
- Virtual server settings
- Web applications
- WebDAV settings (but not the physical collections and locks)
- Web Server 6.1 search collections information (but not the indexes and document root for search collections)

3.8.2.2 What Is Not Migrated

Support for some features has been antiquated in Web Server 7.0 and therefore this functionality is not migrated. Examples of this include legacy servlets and certain session managers. In other cases manual changes to scripts must be reapplied to maintain functionality post-migration. Finally, the migration process does not move data such as CGI scripts, Web applications, or data in the document root directory. Instead, the new instance simply points back to the data contained in the Web Server 6.x location.

> **Warning:** Do not remove files from old instances until you are completely sure that everything has been migrated over. A common mistake is to perform a removal of old instance directories that still contain data such as CGI scripts or Web applications.

The following items are NOT migrated during the migration process:

- CGI directories (the new instance will point to these directories; the data will not be moved)
- Virtual Server Classes (these are no longer supported in Web Server 7.0)
- Command-line scripts (such as `startsvr`, `stopsvr`, `restart`, and `reconfig`)

- The document root directory (the new instance points to this directory; the data itself is not moved)
- Web applications (the new instance points to the old location for Web applications; the data itself is not moved)
- Legacy servlets (legacy servlets are not supported in Web Server 7.0)
- Log files (log files are not be moved; nor does the new instance point to the old log file location)
- Simple Session Manager and JDBC Session Manager (these session managers are no longer supported)
- User libraries and some plug-ins
- WebDAV physical collections and locks (settings are migrated, but not the collections and locks)
- Search configuration and collections (settings are migrated, but not the indexes and document root)

3.8.3 Migrating Using the Graphical User Interface

Web Server 7.0 includes an easy-to-use Migration Wizard to perform a migration from the graphical user interface. The following procedure describes how to perform the migration of one or more server instances using this tool.

1. Log in to the Administration Console and click the Configurations tab. The Configuration screen opens.
2. In the Configuration screen, click the Migrate button. The Migration Wizard opens.
3. In the Migration Wizard, enter the absolute path of the installation directory for the Web Server 6.0 or 6.1 instance that you want to migrate. Click Next. The Select Instances screen opens.
4. Select one or more check boxes next to the instance(s) you would like to migrate.
5. Enter a configuration name next to each instance you are migrating. Use descriptive names such as `migrated-WS61`, and click Next. The Choose Migration Options screen opens.
6. (Optional) Select the Migrate Search Collections check box if you want to migrate search collections from Web Server 6.1 only.
7. (Optional) Provide the absolute path to the directory where Web Server 6.1 search collections may be found.

8. (Optional) Provide the absolute path to the directory where the log files will be generated.

9. Click Next. The Review screen appears.

10. Review the data found in this screen and click Finish to begin the migration process.

11. When the migration process has completed, you will see a message similar to the following:

```
Instance Migration Successful

Migration of instance(s) was successful Migration log file can be
viewed at: /sun/webserver7/admin-server/logs/MIGRA-
TION_20071107032642.log
```

12. Review the migration log file and address any issues.

 Note: The Migration Wizard creates a Web Server 7.0 configuration based on the Web Server 6.1 configuration. At least one instance of this configuration must be successfully deployed to a node for the site to be live.

3.8.4 Migrating Using the Command-Line Interface

Web Server 7.0 includes a command-line tool that enables you to perform various management tasks without the need for a web browser. This tool is particularly useful when you must connect through two or more servers to gain access to the Web Server. The wadm utility is located in the *install_dir*/bin directory and takes various subcommands to perform its management tasks.

One such subcommand is migrate-server. This subcommand is used to migrate server instances and create Web Server 7.0 configurations. The syntax for this command is as follows:

```
wadm> migrate-server <connect_options> [--echo|-e] [--no-prompt|-Q]
[--verbose|-v] [--search-collection-copy-path|-s directory] [--log-
   dir|-d directory] ([--all|-l]|[--config|-c newconfigname]|
      [--instance|-n instancename]) --server-root|-r path
```

Optional arguments (or options) are displayed within square brackets []. See Table 3.20 for a complete list of the parameters for the migrate-server subcommand.

Table 3.20   Options for the migrate-server Subcommand

Option	Description
<connect_options>	Use connect_options to connect to the Administration Server. Connect_options includes the administration username, password file, host, port (SSL/non-SSL), and an optional preferences file. These options are common for all commands. In shell mode, the connect_options options that you provide while invoking wadm are used automatically for every command that you execute. A list of connect_options is as follows: [--user|-u admin-user] [--password-file|-w admin-pswd-file] [--host|-h admin-host] [--port|-p admin-port] [--no-ssl|-N] [--rcfile|-R rcfile]
[--echo|-e]	Specify this option to print this command on the standard output before executing. This option also prints the default value for all the non-mandatory options that you do not provide in the command.
[--no-prompt|-Q]	If you specify this option, wadm will not prompt you for passwords while executing this command. Use this option if you have defined all passwords in a password file and specified the file using the --password-file connect option.
[--verbose|-v]	Specify this option to display a verbose output.
[--search-collection-copy-path|-s *directory*]	Specify the directory where the search collections can be found in the old instance.
[--log-dir|-d *directory*]	Specify the directory for creating the migration log files, for example, install_dir/admin-serv/logs.
[--config|-c *newconfigname*]	Specify the name of the new configuration that will be created after migration.
[--instance|-n *instancename*]	Specify the name of the instance to be migrated.
[--all|-1]	Specify this option to migrate all server instances.
--server-root|-r *path*	Specify the installation location (directory) where a previous version of Web Server—that is, 6.0 or 6.1—is installed.

An example of the use of the `migrate-server` subcommand and the resulting text is as follows:

```
wadm> migrate-server --config=migrated-config --server-root=/opt/
    SUNWwbsvr --instance=https-www.example.com
CLI186 Migration log file stored on the administration server machine
    at: /sun/webserver7/admin-server/logs/MIGRATION_20071107043025.log
```

3.9 Summary

Web Server 7.0 is an extremely dynamic product that makes it as easy to install and manage an entire server farm as it is to manage a single server instance. The tools and wizards provided with Web Server 7.0 make it a powerful yet flexible product that makes installing, migrating, or uninstalling Web Server instances a simple and straightforward process.

3.10 Self-Paced Labs

Use the information contained in this chapter to perform the following exercises. These will help validate your understanding of the concepts described in this chapter.

1. Verify that your computer supports Web Server 7.0.
2. Download the latest copy of Web Server 7.0 to your workstation.
3. Install Web Server 7.0 and configure it as a standalone server (Administration Server with a Web Server instance). Use available ports for each instance and select your own passwords when prompted to do so. (Consider using the `--savestate` option to enable yourself to reference the values you used for installation.)
4. Verify the installation was successful by accessing the default Web Page and Administration Server GUI.

Note: Go to http://www.sunwebserver.com for detailed instructions on how to perform each of these exercises.

5. Additional Exercises:

   If you have an existing Web Server 6.x installation, perform a migration using the Migration Wizard.

   If you do not have an existing Web Server 6.x installation, consider downloading and installing Web Server 6.1 from Sun's web site.

   Customize the product and perform a migration using the graphical user interface. Repeat the process using the command-line interface. (Consider using a different configuration name for the command-line migration and compare the two configurations.)

4

Web Server 7.0 Administration

WEB Server 7.0 includes a completely redesigned administration infrastructure that makes managing Web Server instances much easier than it was in previous versions. It includes a robust command-line tool that provides access to all features available in the graphical (web) interface. The new command-line tool provides extensive configuration management, configuration distribution, server monitoring, and remote diagnostics, and can be installed on the Administration Server or remote workstations. This allows flexibility in a safe and secure environment when administering your Web Server instances.

The graphical interface has been redesigned to support internationalization and 508 accessibility requirements. It provides better manageability and a more intuitive set of tasks. The interface is based on the everyday tasks that an administrator will perform rather than on functional areas (as with previous versions of the Web Server). The graphical interface reduces complexity by providing wizards and reasonable defaults to reduce user input while still allowing administrators to change the defaults as they see fit.

This chapter describes the newly redesigned administration framework and how it makes management of several instances (as in the case of a server farm) as easy as management of a single Web Server instance.

4.1 Web Server 7.0 Administration Framework

Web Server 7.0 provides a framework for administering server farms as easily as a single server instance. It accomplishes this by allowing you to manage both local and remote servers from a central administration hub called the *Administration Server*. The Administration Server allows you to control, configure, and monitor Web Server instances from a single interface. You can access the Administration Server across the network through either a command-line or graphical user interface.

Figure 4.1 provides a high-level overview of the Web Server 7.0 administration framework.

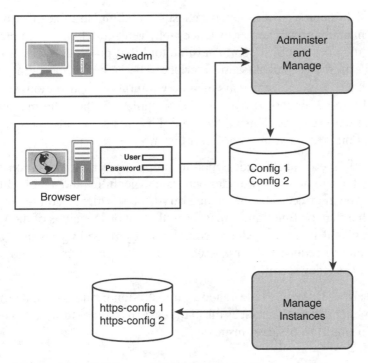

Figure 4.1   Web Server 7.0 Administration Framework

Administrators access the *Administration Server*, where they manage Web Server *configurations*. They can then deploy these configurations to an *Administration Node*, where they become Web Server *instances*. Web Server instances are accessible to HTTP clients and can be grouped (or *clustered*) together to share configuration data. This enables you to manage configuration data across multiple servers as easily as if it were being configured on a single server. Section 4.2 provides a detailed explanation of the terms introduced here.

4.2 Terminology

You might already be familiar with some of the terminology in the previous section. If not, a general review of server farms, clusters, configurations, and other related terms is helpful to understanding Web Server 7.0's administrative framework.

Figure 4.2 provides a model of the various components and how they interact together. The remainder of this section provides further detail on each of these components and how they are used within the Web Server 7.0 administration framework.

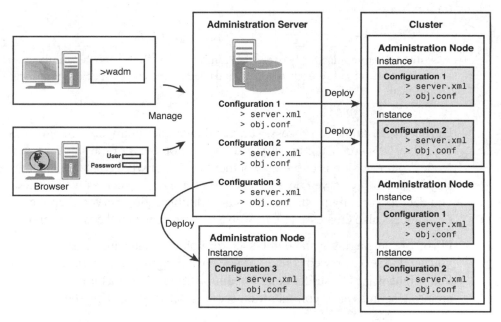

Figure 4.2   Centralized Administration

4.2.1 Administration Server

The *Administration Server* is a specialized Web Server 7.0 instance that is used to manage configuration data on one or more Administration Nodes. There is a master/slave relationship between the Administration Server and any Administration Node(s) that it has been configured to manage. Administrators access the Administration Server through either a graphical user interface or a command-line interface and perform various operations that update configuration data. This functionality is provided through the following web applications that have been deployed within the Administration Server:

- `admingui`—Provides functionality for the graphical user interface
- `jmxconnector`—Provides functionality for the command-line interface

Configuration data for each Web Server instance is stored in a centralized repository on the Administration Server and distributed (or *deployed*) to each Administration Node.

Note: All communication between the Administration Server and the Administration Node is transmitted securely over SSL and takes place across a special administrative interface.

During the installation process, you decide whether you would like to configure the server you are installing as an Administration Server or as an Administration Node. Your decision is based on whether this server will be used to manage other servers or simply serve content to HTTP user agents (such as web browsers). If you decide to configure the server as an Administration Server, then the installation process also creates a default Web Server instance on that same server.

If you are managing a standalone server, you now have all the components that you need to serve up web content. If you are managing a server farm environment, you might want to use the default Administration Node as a temporary staging area to test and verify configuration settings before deploying them to your production servers.

4.2.2 Administration Node

A *node* is a network resource, such as a server or a host. In a typical data center, a network of nodes is called a *server farm*. An *Administration Node* is a node where

Web Server 7.0 has been installed and where it provides content to HTTP/S user agents (such as web browsers). Content is provided by a Web Server instance that has been created on the Administration Node. Instances are created when a configuration is deployed to the Administration Node by the Administration Server.

An Administration Node can contain zero or more Web Server instances that are used to provide content to user agents. When you first install the Administration Node, it has zero instances configured. It is not until you deploy a configuration to the node that you get your first Web Server instance.

Each Administration Node contains a special Web Server instance that is used by the Administration Server to control the Administration Node. This includes tasks such as deploying configurations to the Administration Node and creating server instances. It also includes starting and stopping the instances and gathering instance data for monitoring purposes.

Administration Nodes must be registered with a single Administration Server. This can be performed during the installation process or after the fact through the administration Command Line Interface (CLI) contained on the Administration Node. Registration with a particular Administration Server creates a trusted relationship between the Administration Server and the Administration Node. After it is established, only the registered Administration Server is allowed to communicate to the Administration Node on the default administrative instance.

Warning: You cannot directly access the administrative instance on an Administration Node because this instance is reserved for the Administration Server. As such, administrators are required to perform all tasks through the appropriate Administration Server.

4.2.3 Configuration

A *configuration* is a set of meta-data that is used to configure the runtime services of a Web Server 7.0 instance. A configuration consists of configuration files (such as `magnus.conf`, `server.xml`, and `obj.conf`), web applications that have been deployed to the server instance, search engine collections, and shared objects for implementing built-in services and third-party NSAPI plug-ins that have been installed in the Web Server instance.

The configuration meta-data is used by the server runtime to load built-in services (service application functions or SAFs) and third-party plug-ins and set up other server extensions, such as database drivers.

The primary function of the administration infrastructure is to manage configurations from a central location (the Administration Server). These configurations can then be distributed to one or more Administration Nodes, where they become server instances.

> **Note:** Data centers typically dedicate a subset of Administration Nodes for a specific service or content. An example of this is finance.yahoo.com, which hosts a stock quote web application along with other content, such as research material and graphs.
>
> To ease administration and supportability, the nodes within this subset are typically of the same operating system and hardware platform. In addition, they might share other data center resources such as a network file system (NFS) for the document root. In Web Server 7.0, the subset of nodes running a given configuration is called a *cluster*.

Web Server instances can be clustered (or grouped) together so that configuration information (and, therefore, runtime services) can be identical across multiple nodes.

4.2.4 Configuration Store

Configurations are stored on the Administration Server's file system in an area called the *Configuration Store*. The Configuration Store can be found in the following location:

```
install_dir/admin-server/config-store
```

During installation of the Administration Server, an initial configuration is created and stored beneath this directory with a name reflective of the server's hostname and domain name. This configuration is used to create the default Web Server instance that is included with the Administration Server (see Section 4.2.1, "Administration Server"). You can use the Administration Server to create additional configurations as well. Each new configuration is stored in a separate subdirectory beneath the Configuration Store as follows:

```
install_dir/admin-server/config-store/configname
```

Files that are part of an instance's configuration (for example, `magnus.conf`, `server.xml`, and `mime.types`) are included in this directory, as well as applications that have been deployed to virtual servers within the instance, third party plug-ins used by this instance, and search collections defined within this instance.

Any changes made to the server configuration using the command line interface or graphical administrative interface are first made to files within the Configuration Store and then deployed to the appropriate node(s) when you are satisfied with the changes. During the deployment process, a copy of the previous configuration (prior to the deployment) is captured and saved in the Configuration Store beneath the following directory:

> *install_dir*/admin-server/config-store/*configname*/backup

This enables you to restore (or *roll back*) a previous configuration based on a given timestamp.

In cases where web applications are part of a configuration, the entire web application and all configuration directories beneath the `config-store` directory are zipped up and copied to the appropriate server instance. The zipped information is contained in a file called `current.zip` and can be found beneath the appropriate configuration directory.

Warning: Do not manually edit any file under the Administration Server's `config-store` directory or base any user-written scripts on these files. The files under this directory are created by the Web Server for internal use only and are subject to change without notice.

Configuration files may be edited and altered directly on a particular Administration Node (see Section 4.5.3, "Manually Editing Configuration Files"). Configuration files that are no longer synchronized with those in the Configuration Store are detected by the Administration Server and noted in the graphical administrative interface. System Administrators can elect to pull the changes from the Administration Node and update the copies in the Configuration Store, or they can choose to overwrite the files on the Administration Node with those contained in the Configuration Store. If the changes are pulled from the Administration Node, the corresponding files in the Configuration Store are updated and redeployed to any other servers that may be part of the cluster.

4.2.5 Instance

An *instance* refers to the environment necessary to run a Web Server 7.0 daemon or service on a given Administration Node. This includes its configuration, log files, and other runtime artifacts, such as lock databases, caches, and temporary files. For management purposes, an instance can be started, stopped, restarted, or dynamically re-configured.

When the Administration Server deploys a configuration to one or more Administration Nodes, an instance of that configuration is created on that node. Each instance is located directly beneath the installation root directory and has a name of `https-configname`. The following example demonstrates the directory structure associated with an instance of the `default-config` configuration:

```
# cd /sun/webserver7/https-default-config/
# ls
bin          config    generated    logs      web-app
collections       docs       lock-db   sessions
```

4.2.6 Cluster

A *cluster* is a set of instances that span one or more Administration Nodes. These Administration Nodes can be overlapped by more than one cluster, so for simplicity, all nodes in a cluster must be homogeneous. That is, Administration Nodes must run on the same operating system version (including the patch level) and be identically configured to offer the same runtime services.

Warning: Sun supports clusters across nodes that are homogeneous. This means that all nodes within the cluster must be running the same operating system and patch level.

4.2.7 Virtual Server

A *virtual server* is a fully functioning "virtual" web server that resides within a particular Web Server instance and utilizes the resources and configuration settings that make up the instance. You can inherit settings (or *elements*) from the configuration or you can override certain elements for each virtual server. This enables you to customize and differentiate the virtual server. Examples of elements that you can specify for a particular virtual server include

- Document root directory
- MIME types file
- Log files
- Access control list file(s)
- Authentication database(s)

Note: Refer to the virtual-server element in the Sun Java System Web Server 7.0 Administrator's Configuration File Reference for a complete list of subelements that you can use to customize your virtual server.

Virtual servers enable you to offer companies or individuals their own domain names, IP addresses, and some server monitoring capabilities with a single installed server. For the users, it is almost as if they have their own web servers, though you provide the hardware and basic web server maintenance.

4.3 Administrative Architecture

Java Management Extensions (JMX) provides the foundation for the Web Server 7.0 administrative framework. JMX was an extension available in previous versions of the JDK and is now a feature in version 5.0 of the Java Platform, Standard Edition (J2SE). It provides the tools for building distributed, modular, and dynamic solutions for managing and monitoring devices, applications, and service-driven networks.

Web Server 7.0 implements the JMX framework with the jmxconnector that is deployed to both the Administration Server and each Administration Node. Through its implementation of the JMX API, Web Server 7.0's administrative infrastructure is designed to manage and monitor Web Server instances across clustered Web Server deployments. Functionality for managing and monitoring applications within this environment is contained within managed beans (or MBeans).

MBeans are located in an MBean server, which is a type of container that provides management applications access to MBeans. Applications do not access MBeans directly, but instead access them through the MBean server with their unique

ObjectNames. Three types of MBeans are implemented in Web Server 7.0: Monitoring MBeans, Task MBeans, and Agent MBeans. The relationship between the various MBeans and the Web Server administrative components is shown in Figure 4.3.

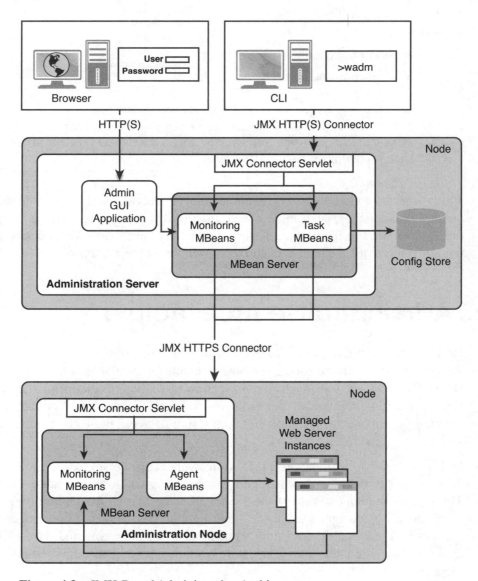

Figure 4.3   JMX-Based Administration Architecture

4.3.1 Monitoring MBeans

Monitoring MBeans are created on both the Administration Server and the Administration Node during startup of the respective administrative instance. They fetch the monitoring data for the instance, using the Java Native Interface (JNI) layer, which connects to running instances, using the UNIX socket (for the Solaris and Linux OSs) and pipe (for Microsoft Windows).

Monitoring MBeans provided in the Administration Node level can expose data specific to a particular instance or can aggregate data from multiple instances. This information can then be displayed through the graphical administrative interface or command line interface. In some cases, the information may even be displayed through a specific URL configured for the Administration Server instance. (See Chapter 7, "Monitoring Web Server 7.0," for more information.)

4.3.2 Task MBeans

Task MBeans are registered within an MBean Server that is running on the Administration Server. These MBeans expose only composite administration tasks and do not model configuration files. Therefore, these MBeans do not expose getting and setting specific attributes on configuration files.

The command line interface and graphical user interface invoke operations on Task MBeans that are located on the Administration Server, using JMX remote connectors based on JSR-160. These connectors are also used by the Task MBeans to invoke operations on Agent MBeans running on Administration Nodes on other nodes. The JMX connector used by the administration infrastructure is layered on top of the HTTP protocol and can thus be run on SSL as well to provide a secure transport layer. The connection is handled on the server side by a special JMX connector servlet.

Note: Web Server 7.0 utilizes the Sun reference JMX implementation, which ships with HTTP and RMI protocol handlers.

4.3.3 Agent MBeans

Agent MBeans are a subset of the Task MBeans that expose the tasks related to managing Web Server instances. Agent MBeans expose operations such as creating and deleting instances, deploying a configuration to an instance, performing life cycle operations on the instance, and monitoring the instance. Only the Administration Node has Agent MBeans registered on its MBean Server.

The JMX API infrastructure provides a common interface for both the command line interface and graphical user interface to initiate administrative tasks within Web Server 7.0.

Note: Refer to the Sun Developer forum at http://java.sun.com/products/JavaManagement/ for more information about the JMX application programming interface (API).

4.4 Starting and Stopping Administrative Instances

To manage configurations on the Administration Server, an administrative instance must be running on that node. To deploy, monitor, or stop/start instances on Administration Nodes, administrative instances must be running on those nodes as well.

4.4.1 Starting on UNIX-based Systems

On UNIX-based systems, you can easily determine whether an administrative instance is running on the respective node by using a combination of the ps and grep commands as follows:

```
ps -ef | grep admin-server
```

If the Administration Server instance is running, you will see a response similar to the following:

```
root  1419  1418  5 10:22:11 ?        0:46 webservd -d /sun/webserver7/
    admin-server/
config -r /sun/webserver7 -t /tmp/admi
root  1417     1  0 10:22:09 ?        0:00 webservd-wdog -d /sun/
    webserver7/
admin-server/config -r /sun/webserver7 -t /tmp
root  1418  1417  0 10:22:09 ?        0:02 webservd -d /sun/webserver7/
    admin-server/
config -r /sun/webserver7 -t /tmp/admi
```

Note: An explanation of Web Server processes can be found in Chapter 3, "Web Server 7.0 Installation and Migration."

If you do not see the administration instance running, you can start it with the `startserv` command, as follows:

install_dir/admin-server/bin/startserv

Running this command on an Administration Server provides a response similar to the following:

```
Sun Java System Web Server 7.0 B12/04/2006 10:15
info: CORE3016: daemon is running as super-user
info: CORE5076: Using [Java HotSpot(TM) Server VM, Version 1.5.0_09]
   from [Sun Microsystems Inc.]
info: WEB0100: Loading web module in virtual server [admin-server] at
   [/admingui]
info: WEB0100: Loading web module in virtual server [admin-server] at
   [/jmxconnector]
info: HTTP3072: admin-ssl-port: https://boulder.example.com:8989
   ready to accept requests
info: CORE3274: successful server startup
```

The response on an Administration Node is slightly different. In this case you will see a response similar to the following:

```
Sun Java System Web Server 7.0 B12/04/2006 10:15
info: CORE3016: daemon is running as super-user
info: CORE5076: Using [Java HotSpot(TM) Server VM, Version 1.5.0_09]
   from [Sun
   Microsystems Inc.]
info: WEB0100: Loading web module in virtual server [admin-server] at
   [/jmxconnector]
info: HTTP3072: admin-ssl-port: https://www.example.com:8989 ready to
   accept
   requests
info: CORE3274: successful server startup
```

Note: The Administration Server includes the admingui web application; the Administration Node does not. This application provides the graphical interface to the Administration Server. You cannot directly access an Administration Node through the graphical administrative interface, so this web application is not applicable. Additionally, all administrative communication between the Administration Server and the Administration Node is performed over SSL. As such, you cannot configure a non-SSL port for the Administration Node.

4.4.2 Stopping on UNIX-based Systems

On UNIX-based systems, you can stop an administration instance with the stopserv command, as follows:

> *install_dir*/admin-server/bin/stopserv

When the server has stopped, you will see a response similar to the following:

> server has been shutdown

There is no way to centrally start/stop administration instances across multiple nodes. You will, therefore, need to connect to each node over SSH or TELNET and manually run the stopserv command on each node.

4.4.3 Starting and Stopping on Windows Systems

There are various ways to stop and start the administration instance on a Windows platform.

4.4.3.1 Command Line Method

Similar to UNIX-based systems, on a Windows-based system you can run the start and stop scripts directly from the command line as follows:

- *install_dir*/admin-server/bin/startserv.bat
- *install_dir*/admin-server/bin/stopserv.bat

4.4.3.2 Program Group Method

In addition, the installation process creates a program group called Web Server 7.0 where it groups several icons for interfacing to the Administration Server. This group can be found at the following location:

```
Programs -> Sun Microsystems -> Web Server 7.0
```

The program group includes various icons for starting, stopping, or accessing the administrative interface on the Administration Server:

- Administration Console
- Start Administration Server
- Stop Administration Server

Simply click on the Start Administration Server icon to start that server process.

4.4.3.3 Services Method

The Administration Server runs as a services applet. As such, you can also use the Services application (`services.msc`) to start and stop this service directly.

4.5 Methods for Administering Web Server 7.0

Methods for administering Web Server 7.0 are the same for UNIX-based or Windows systems. You can manage your Sun Java System Web Server by using any of the following:

- Administration Console (graphical user interface - GUI)
- Command Line Interface (CLI)
- Direct editing of configuration files

The following sections describe these methods further.

4.5.1 Administration Console

The Administration Console is a specially designed web application that has been deployed to the Administration Server only. It consists of HTML Pages, JavaServer Pages (JSP), JavaScript technology, core Java technology-based classes and XML-based deployment descriptors, data files for various components, and so on. The files that make up the Administration Console are private; there is no need for an administrator to edit them.

4.5.1.1 Accessing the Administration Console

Administrators access the Administration Console with a browser. Communication with the Administration Console is typically performed over SSL (by default), but you can specify a non-SSL administrative port during installation. The following URL provides an example of how you would access the Administration Console if you were to use the default settings:

```
https://adminhost.admindomain:8989
```

> **Note:** Clients attempting to connect to the secure port using standard HTTP protocol are redirected automatically to the secure port through the use of HTTP over SSL (HTTPS).

If the Administration Server instance is running, the login screen shown in Figure 4.4 appears in your browser window.

Enter the credentials that you supplied during the installation process to log in to the Administration Console. Administrators authenticate through forms-based authentication, which authenticates the user to the Web Container. Forms-based authentication allows administrators to log off without having to close the browser window.

4.5.1.2 Administration Console Layout

You perform various administrative tasks by navigating through a combination of tabs and subtabs (also known as parent and child tabs) and providing input through a variety of web form elements. The information provided on each page of the Administration Console has been designed to make navigation easy and to provide access to valuable information. Figure 4.5 demonstrates the Administration Console window that provides access to virtual server properties.

Figure 4.4 Administration Console Login Screen

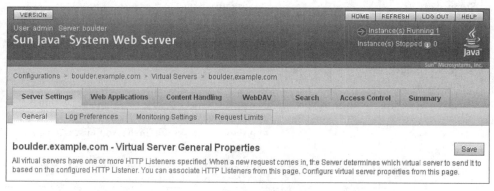

Figure 4.5 Administration Console—Console Layout

Table 4.1 summarizes the various components contained on this page.

Table 4.1   Administration Console Components

Name	Type	Location	Description
VERSION	Button	Upper left	This button allows immediate access to the version of the Web Server installed on your system. An example of the data displayed when you click on this button is as follows: Sun Java System Web Server 7.0U1 B06/12/2007 22:48.
User: admin	Label	Upper left	Indicates the username of the administrator currently logged in to the Administration Server.
Server: boulder	Label	Upper left	Indicates the name of the server to which the administrator is currently logged in.
HOME	Button	Upper right	Clicking this button takes you to the Common Tasks page.
REFRESH	Button	Upper right	Clicking this button refreshes the current page.
LOG OUT	Button	Upper right	Clicking this button logs you out of the Administration Console.
HELP	Button	Upper right	This button launches a context-sensitive help window. The data displayed in the window is based on the current page.
Instance(s) Running: 1	Label	Upper right	This label tells you how many server instances are currently running.
Instance(s) Stopped: 0	Label	Upper right	This label tells you how many server instances are currently stopped.
Configurations > boulder.example. com > Virtual Servers > boulder. example.com	Bread-crumb	Upper left	This breadcrumb shows you where you are in the Administration Console. You can click on links within the breadcrumb to take you back to previous pages.
Parent tabs (tabs)	Button	Upper middle	Parent tabs are top-level tabs for pages within the Administration Console. These tabs provide a high-level grouping of tasks within the Administration Console. The parent tabs displayed on this page are Server Settings, Web Applications, Content Handling, WebDAV, Search, Access Control, and Summary.
Child tabs (subtabs)	Button	Upper middle	Child tabs exist beneath parent tabs and provide granular access to tasks within a particular grouping. In Figure 4.5, the Server Settings tab has been selected. The child tabs displayed for this tab are as follows: General, Log Preferences, Monitoring Settings and Request Limits.
Content	N/A	N/A	The remainder of the page consists of forms, labels, and general information for data applicable to a particular tab and/or subtab.

Clicking any of the parent tabs may result in child tabs appearing on the page directly beneath the parent. The actions provided by the child tabs are specific to the parent tab functionality.

Clicking on a particular tab or subtab opens the associated page in the same window. Some tasks, however, require the gathering of data over a series of steps and hence require multiple pages. The Administration Console has a wizard interface for such tasks; wizards always open in a new window.

4.5.1.3 Common Tasks

The Administration Console has been designed according to customer usage patterns based on previous versions of the Web Server. The interface is task-based (rather than functionality-based) and provides access to the most common tasks immediately after you log in. The Administration Console includes wizards for the most common tasks; this includes wizards for creation of configurations, virtual servers, and requesting server certificates.

Figure 4.6 provides an overview of the common tasks available immediately after you log in to the Administration Console.

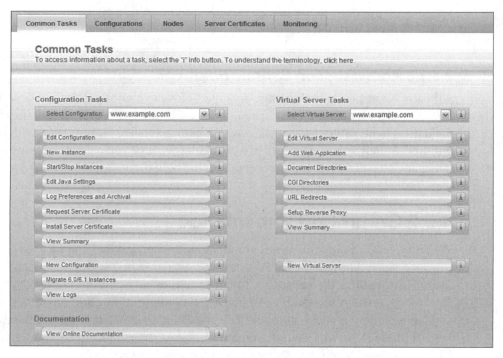

Figure 4.6 Administration Console—Common Tasks

You can select one of the many common tasks from this screen or you can drill down on any particular area by selecting the appropriate tab (such as Configurations or Nodes).

4.5.1.4 Up-to-Date News

The Common Tasks page also includes links to various sources (such as blogs, wikis, and developer articles) to keep you informed of the latest information on Web Server 7. Figure 4.7 demonstrates examples of information that may be found beneath News.

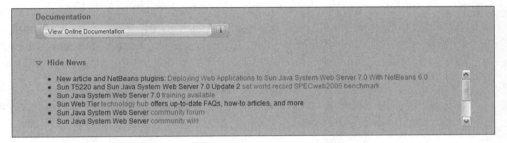

Figure 4.7   Administration Console—News

4.5.1.5 Administration Console Help

All form elements and other page-specific fields have information that describes how data is to be entered for a particular form. The help information specifies how the data is to be validated as well as which parameters are required and which are optional. When accessing pages in a particular wizard, you can click on the Help tab at any step in the wizard to receive specific help for a particular task.

4.5.2 Command Line Interface

Web Server 7.0 includes a robust command line interface that can be used to perform the same administrative tasks as those available in the graphical user interface. This includes the capability to create and deploy configurations, start and stop server instances, monitor instances and configurations, and any other tasks available in the graphical interface. The command line interface takes full advantage of the JMX administrative framework and as such, a local installation of the CLI can be used to manage remote Administration Servers.

The command line interface is a scripting framework based on Java Command Language (JACL); which is essentially a Java implementation of the TCL language. CLI functionality is implemented with the `com.sun.web.admin.cli.shelladapter.WSadminShell` Java class and is launched with the `wadm` script.

Web Server 7.0 ships with several pre-configured administrative scripts (see Table 4.3) that use TCL syntax to access administrative subcommands. With some basic knowledge of TCL, you can create your own administrative scripts and therefore extend the Web Server administration environment to meet your own specific needs.

Administrators can use the command line interface in one of three modes:

- **Single mode**—The entire command (including options) is included in one line.
- **File mode**—A series of commands are stored in a file and input in to `wadm`.
- **Shell mode**—Commands are entered in an interactive JACL shell

Previous versions of Web Server provided commands such as `HttpServerAdmin`, `wdeploy`, and `flexanlg`, which provided only a subset of the functionality provided in the graphical Administration Server interface. The CLI has been redesigned, however, to provide access to 100% of the functionality provided in the Administration Server.

Note: The `wdeploy` command is still supported in Web Server 7.0, but only for backward compatibility with Web Server 6.x versions. It works only on the web instance included with the Administration Server.

The command line interface is included with both Administration Server and Administration Node installations, but you can also install the CLI by itself. The latter option is useful if you simply want to use the CLI to manage remote servers from your own desktop.

4.5.2.1 Running the Command Line Interface

The `wadm` script can be found in the *install_dir*/`bin` directory. When you launch the script, it attempts to bind itself to a particular Administration Server instance to perform its tasks. As such, the Administration Server you are communicating with needs to be running before you launch the CLI. You can specify the hostname and port number for a particular Administration Server to access the administration instance on that node. If you do not provide this information, the CLI attempts to connect to the local host on port 8989 (the default value).

To ensure that only authorized users are allowed to access the Administration Server, you need to specify the Administrator User Name and the Administrator Password credentials that were entered during installation (see Figure 3.8 in Chapter 3). If you do not provide the Administrator User Name, the CLI assumes that you are trying to perform this operation as the admin user. No assumption is made for the password value.

The following example demonstrates how you can specify the host, port, and user parameters when launching the wadm script:

```
install_dir/bin/wadm --host adminhost --port adminport --user
   adminuser
```

Refer to Section 4.5.2.3, "Syntax," for an overview of the usage and syntax for the wadm script.

If secure socket layer (SSL) is enabled on the Administration Server, then all traffic is encrypted between the wadm script and the Administration Server. The certificate passed by the Administration Server is verified against the truststore file (located at ~/.wadmtruststore). If the certificate exists and is valid, then the command proceeds normally. Otherwise, the wadm script displays the certificate and gives the user the choice of accepting it. If the user accepts it, the certificate is added to the truststore file and the command proceeds normally.

Note: A truststore is a database file that contains the public keys for various servers. The public key is stored in the truststore as a signer certificate.

4.5.2.2 Shell Variables

Any parameter provided on the command line can also be supplied as an environment variable from the shell invoking the wadm script or by setting the variable within the wadm shell, itself. Use of these *shell variables* enables you to avoid having to type common parameters such as the hostname and port number each time you launch the wadm script.

The shell variable name for a particular parameter is derived by prefixing the string "wadm_" to the parameter name. For instance, the hostname, port number, and administration users parameters may be referenced by the following shell variables:

- `wadm_host`
- `wadm_port`
- `wadm_user`

If a particular parameter contains a dash (such as `document-root`), the dash is replaced by the underscore character in the corresponding shell variable (`wadm_document_root`).

In UNIX operating systems, `rc` files are used to provide configuration settings for various applications. For example, `~/.bashrc` provides the configuration settings for the bash shell. The `rc` files found under `/etc` define system-wide settings, whereas the ones found in a user's home directory are specific to a particular user.

Note: rc file /R-C fi:l//n./ [Unix: from 'runcom files' on the CTSS system ca.1955, via the startup script '/etc/rc'] Script file containing startup instructions for an application program (or an entire operating system), usually a text file containing commands of the sort that might have been invoked manually once the system was running but are to be executed automatically each time the system starts up.

Source: Cool Jargon of the Day http://www.jargon.net/jargonfile/r/rcfile.html.

The `.wadmrc` file is the default `rc` file for the `wadm` command. This is a TCL file that is typically located in the user's home directory on UNIX-based systems. The contents of this file are processed before any `wadm` command is executed. You can use the `--rcfile` or `-R` command-line options to specify the location and name of a particular `rc` file. This is particularly useful on Windows-based systems where you may or may not have a home directory. The following example demonstrates how you would reference an `rc` file on a Windows-based system:

```
C:\Sun\WebServer7\bin>wadm -R c:\wadmrc
```

Note: The `wadm` script uses the value of the `USERPROFILE` environment variable when searching for the `.wadmrc` file on Windows-based systems. This environment variable is not set by default.

Variables may be defined within the .wadmrc through the use of the set command. The following is an example of a .wadmrc file that sets default values for the user, host, and port parameters:

```
set wadm_host host01.example.com
set wadm_port 8989
set wadm_user admin
set wadm_password password
```

Note: You can also specify the administrative password in the .wadmrc file with the wadm_password variable. This is highly discouraged, however, because of the security implications associated with saving the password on the file system.

If you need the CLI to be more verbose, you can set the wadm_verbose to true. Or if you are interested in looking at the complete command that goes to the administration server, set wadm_echo to true. To enable JACL, set wadm_script to true. The following is an updated .wadmrc file with these values set:

```
set wadm_host host01.example.com
set wadm_port 8989
set wadm_user admin
set wadm_password password
set wadm_verbose true
set wadm_echo true
set wadm_script true
```

Web Server 7.0 enables you to set shell variables in various locations (on the command line, in the .wadmrc file, and so on). As such, it can be confusing when trying to determine which definition takes precedence when a variable has been defined multiple times. The CLI follows certain rules that define the order of precedence that is followed when it detects that a variable has been defined in multiple places. The CLI user can set shell variables in the following ways, in their increasing order of precedence:

1. Options supplied directly on the command line take precedence over any shell variables.

2. Options defined as environment variables in the shell from which the user invokes the wadm command are next.

3. Options defined within a .wadmrc file are processed next.

4. Options defined using `set/unset` commands within the `wadm` shell are processed last.

If you are unsure about which variables are currently set, you can use the `info` subcommand to list the current values as follows:

```
wadm> info vars

wadm_echo argv wadm_histfile auto_execs auto_index errorInfo wadm_user
    wadm_ssl auto_oldpath wadm_script tcl_library errorCode wadm_
    verbose wadm_password argc wadm_port wadm_savehist wadm_mode tcl_
    patchLevel wadm_host tcljava tcl_platform env tcl_version
    tcl_interactive wadm_prompt argv0 auto_path

wadm>
```

4.5.2.3 Syntax

Understanding the syntax for a new command can be a daunting task, to say the least. You can read through the 500 or so pages of the Sun Java System Web Server 7.0 CLI Reference Manual, or you can try to learn the command through trial and error. Fortunately, Web Server 7.0 provides an intuitive way to learn the syntax through use of the command itself.

The usage of the `wadm` script is as follows:

```
Usage: wadm --version|-V
   or  wadm --help|-?
   or  wadm [--user=admin-user] [--password-file=admin-pswd-file]
[--host=admin-host] [--port=admin-port] [--no-ssl] [--rcfile=rcfile]
[--no-prompt] [--commands-file=filename]
```

This information is displayed any time you specify a parameter on the command line that does not agree with the usage. The easiest way to obtain this information is to simply type the `wadm` command without providing any parameters (this assumes that a `.wadmrc` file has not been defined).

Options have both long and short versions for a particular parameter. For instance, the following two commands provide the same output:

- `wadm --version` (long version)
- `wadm -V` (short version)

Note: You can use the `--help` option to see a complete list of options for the `wadm` script. Information is similar to a UNIX man page entry. To obtain help for a particular command, use the following format: `install_dir/bin/wadm command --help` (where *command* is the command for which you are seeking additional help).

The `wadm` script takes a series of subcommands and options to perform various administrative tasks. It should be noted that options can be different between subcommands, even though they might have the same short version. For example, a parameter of `-f` is used to specify the *search filter* for the `create-ldap-authdb` subcommand, but it *forces* the creation of an instance (and overwrites existing instances) when used with the `create-instance` subcommand.

Figure 4.8 provides an illustrative example of the structure for the `wadm` script with a `restart-instance` subcommand.

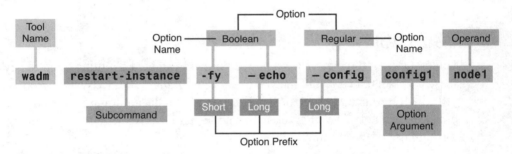

Figure 4.8   Use of the Command Line Interface

The following items describe the details found in Figure 4.8:

- The *Tool name* is the executable program or script that processes a set of arguments and then performs the operation in the manner the arguments specify. The tool name for the Web Server 7.0 is `wadm`.

- All arguments provided on the command line (including the *subcommand*) are optional. If there is no subcommand provided, then the script launches into an interactive shell.

- All options are dependent upon a specific subcommand. Every option has an *Option prefix*, *Option name*, and *Option argument*.

- All options have a long name and most of them have a synonymous short name. An option prefix is a single dash (`-`) for short options and two consecutive dashes (`--`) for long options.

- Boolean options can be grouped (for example, in UNIX, `ls -la` is equivalent to `ls -l -a`), but only with their short option names. In this example, the `-f` and `-y` options are grouped together.

- Options can be specified in any order.
- The command line is scanned from the left, and after all the options and their values are exhausted, the remaining portion is treated as operands.
- If an option is repeated with a different option argument on the command line, the last option value is used and a warning message is displayed.
- The argument -- acts as a delimiter indicating the end of options. Any following arguments are treated as operands, even if they begin with the - character. The -- option should not be used as an argument.
- The CLI exits with a code of 0 if the command succeeded or a non-zero value if there was a failure in command execution. Table 4.2 details the exit codes and their meaning.

Table 4.2   Exit Codes for the Command Line Interface

Exit Code	Type
0	Command exited successfully
1–4	Connection failure errors
10–22	Parsing error
33–43	Input/Output errors
44–56	General errors (for instance, invalid configuration value)
76–96	Generic back-end errors
110–123	Errors that are specific to MBeans
125	Unknown errors

4.5.2.4 Tab Completion (Shell Mode Only)

The wadm command provides an interactive shell that is both powerful and easy to use. (See Section 4.5.2.5 for more information on running wadm in shell mode.)

One extremely powerful feature is the ability to use the Tab key to auto-complete subcommands or see available command-line options for a particular subcommand. The following information provides a demonstration of the use of the Tab key to provide auto-completion. The <TAB> notation is used to designate the user pressing the Tab key on the keyboard.

```
wadm><TAB>

Display all 342 possibilities? (y or n)
```

You can press the Tab key without specifying any subcommands. Doing so allows you the opportunity to list all available subcommands within the CLI. This might prove useful when first learning the CLI, but can quickly become cumbersome. If you have an idea of what type of command you are looking for (for instance you want to list something), then type the string list, and press the Tab key as follows:

```
wadm> list-<TAB>

list-acls                            list-auth-realm-userprops
list-auth-realms                     list-authdb-userprops
list-authdbs                         list-backups
list-certs                           list-cgi-dirs
list-cgi-envvars                     list-ciphers
list-config-files                    list-configs
list-crls                            list-custom-resource-userprops
list-custom-resources                list-dav-collections
list-document-dirs                   list-error-pages
list-events                          list-external-jndi-resource-user
                                     props
list-external-jndi-resources         list-fastcgi-handlers
list-group-members                   list-groups
list-http-listeners                  list-instances
list-jdbc-resource-userprops         list-jdbc-resources
list-jvm-options                     list-jvm-profilers
list-lifecycle-module-userprops      list-lifecycle-modules
list-locks                           list-mail-resource-userprops
list-mail-resources                  list-mime-types
list-nodes                           list-org-units
list-reverse-proxy-headers           list-reverse-proxy-uris
list-search-collections              list-search-events
list-soap-auth-provider-userprops    list-soap-auth-providers
list-tokens                          list-uri-patterns
list-url-redirects                   list-users
list-variables                       list-virtual-servers
list-webapps
```

This displays all subcommands that begin with the string list. You can scan this list to locate the subcommand you are looking for or continue with the process to narrow your search down even further.

```
wadm> list-a<TAB>

list-acls                   list-auth-realm-userprops
list-auth-realms            list-authdb-userprops
list-authdbs
```

After you have identified the subcommand you are looking for, the Tab key also enables you to see the options that are applicable to the subcommand.

```
wadm> list-authdbs<TAB>

wadm> list-authdbs --
```

In this case, pressing the Tab key once produces two dashes following the sub-command. This indicates that you are now looking at the long options for this command. If you press the Tab key again, you will see the options themselves as follows:

```
wadm> list-authdbs --<TAB>

--config*     --vs        --echo      --no-prompt   --all
--verbose

wadm> list-authdbs --
```

You can continue using the Tab key to select your options. After an option has been selected, however, it is no longer listed as being available. This is demonstrated in the following:

```
wadm> list-authdbs --echo --<TAB>

--config*     --vs        --no-prompt   --all        --verbose

wadm> list-authdbs --echo --
```

Note how the echo option is no longer available after it has been used.

The auto-completion feature reduces the time necessary to understand and remember the various subcommands (and command-line options) that are available in the CLI. This enables you to concentrate on the administrative task at hand and not have to worry about the command specifics.

4.5.2.5 Modes

There are three ways that you can invoke the `wadm` script. The method that you select depends on your level of experience and how much interaction you plan on using. The three modes of invocation are as follows:

- Standalone Mode
- Shell Mode
- File Mode

Standalone Mode

In *standalone mode*, you invoke the `wadm` script from a command shell (such as a terminal window on UNIX or a command window on Windows). You specify the desired subcommand along with any options or operands required for execution on the command line. When the subcommand completes, all control is returned back to the command shell from whence it was spawned. An example of the `wadm` script operating in a standalone mode is as follows:

```
$ wadm list-configs --user=admin --host=www.example.com --password-
   file=./admin.pwd
www.example.com
$
```

Users are prompted for a password if it has not been provided through a password file or defined in the `.wadmrc` rc file. If the password is provided through either of these methods, then the user is not prompted and the script operates in non-interactive execution.

> **Note:** Passwords cannot be passed to the `wadm` script on the command line. You can, however, specify a password file that contains a clear text version of the password and use the `--password-file` option to reference the file when executing the `wadm` script. Be sure to make the file readable only to yourself if you elect to use this method.

Standalone mode is useful if you know the various subcommands and subcommand syntax. It enables you to quickly specify and execute a subcommand with little overhead. You cannot, however, use the Tab completion capability described in Section 4.5.2.4.

Shell Mode

In *shell mode*, you invoke the wadm script from a command shell without providing a subcommand. After the initial parameters have been verified (for instance, host, port, user, and password-file), then the wadm script enters into its own shell (called the wadm shell) where it waits for the user to enter a subcommand.

```
$ wadm --user=admin --host=www.example.com -password-file=./admin.pwd
Connected to localhost:8989
Sun Java System Web Server 7.0U2 B12/12/2007 08:48
wadm>
```

After a subcommand has been executed, control is returned back to the wadm shell, where it waits for another subcommand.

```
$ wadm --user=admin --host=www.example.com -password-file=./admin.pwd
Connected to localhost:8989
Sun Java System Web Server 7.0U2 B12/12/2007 08:48
wadm> list-configs
www.example.com
wadm>
```

You can exit the wadm shell by typing either the exit or quit subcommand.

Note: To provide additional features on UNIX boxes, you can access UNIX commands and external scripts within the CLI while running in shell mode. For instance, you can access the UNIX ls command from within the shell as follows:

```
wadm> ls
certutil
htpasswd
jspc
modutil
pk12util
schemagen
uninstall
wadm
wdeploy
wsgen
wsimport
xjc
wadm>
```

Shell mode is useful if you are planning on performing multiple commands and are not quite sure of the syntax. There is overhead associated with launching into shell mode but it is minimal, however, after you have established the wadm shell. Shell mode is quite helpful when you are first learning how to use the CLI.

File Mode

In *file mode*, you can specify a list of subcommands in an external file and pass the file as an argument to the wadm script. The CLI reads the subcommands from that file and executes them in the order in which they appear. The wadm script uses the --commands-file or -f options to specify the name of the file that contains the subcommands. Suppose, for instance, that you have a file called restart-instance. cmds with the following subcommands defined:

```
stop-instance --config=www.example.com
start-instance --config=www.example.com
```

You can pass this file into the wadm script as an argument as follows:

```
$ wadm --user=admin --host=www.example.com --password-file=./admin.pwd
    --commands-file=restart-instance.cmds
```

The script then executes each of the subcommands found in the file and returns control back to the original shell when each of the subcommands has been completed.

The *install_dir*/samples/admin/scripts directory contains several predefined scripts that come with the Web Server 7.0 distribution (see Table 4.3). These scripts can be used to perform various common administrative tasks and provide a demonstration of how new utilities can be built on top of existing commands.

Note: The wadm script is built on a Java-based Tcl engine and as such, you can include Tcl scripting in the command file. See Section 4.5.2.6 for more information pertaining to Tcl support.

Table 4.3   Administrative Scripts

Script	Description	Usage
`enable-ssl.tcl`	Enables SSL on a given Virtual Server and port.	`wadm -f enable-ssl.tcl <config> <vs> <server> <port>`
`filter-mime.tcl`	Fetches the matching mime types from the given Configuration and Virtual Server	`wadm -f filter-mime.tcl "<regex>" <config> <vs>`
`remove-mime.tcl`	Removes the matching mime types from the given Configuration and Virtual Server	`wadm -f remove-mime.tcl "<regex>" <config> <vs>`
`add-mime-ext.tcl`	Adds the specified extension to the matching mime types in given Configuration and Virtual Server	`wadm -f add-mime-ext.tcl "<regex>" "ext" <config> <vs>`
`summary.tcl`	Provides a summary of the installation. It contains list of listeners, port, SSL status, bound virtual servers.	`wadm -f summary.tcl`
`list-webapps.tcl`	Provides a summary of all the deployed webapps.	`wadm -f list-webapps.tcl`
`collate-logs.tcl`	Provides collated logs across multiple nodes.	`wadm -f collate-logs.tcl <config> <node1> <node2> ..`
`renew-selfsigned-cert.tcl`	Allows renewal of self-signed certificates with a given nickname.	`wadm -f renew-selfsigned-cert.tcl <config> <cert-nickname> [<valid-ity>]`

The *install_dir*/samples/admin/scripts directory also contains several utilities and wizards that can be used to interact with your Web Server 7.0 installation. Review the README file in that directory for a complete list of files found there and a description of each.

File mode is useful if you have a sequence of subcommands that you execute on a regular basis. This enables you to make a single call that performs multiple events. This is particularly useful if you want to schedule the execution of multiple subcommands to run on a periodic basis without user intervention (as is the case with the UNIX cron job). File mode is also quite powerful in that it enables you to extend administrative processes through scripting.

4.5.2.6 Tool Command Language (Tcl) Support

JACL (or the Java Command Language) is a Java implementation of the Tcl scripting language created by Dr. John Ousterhout. The command line interface implements full Tcl support through JACL and therefore has adopted all the features of the language. As such you can use Tcl commands at the wadm prompt while in shell mode or within scripts created in file mode. Examples of Tcl commands and their syntax can be seen in the sample administration scripts found in the `install_dir/ samples/admin/scripts` directory.

> **Note:** The Tcl Reference Manual can be found at http://tmml.sourceforge.net/doc/ tcl/. This page includes details describing Tcl commands, variable handling, control constructs, and other information that will be useful in developing your own Tcl-based scripts.

4.5.3 Manually Editing Configuration Files

You can make changes to any configuration file on an Administration Node by manually editing and saving the file. Depending on the file(s) changed, you may have to restart or reload the configuration file(s) for the node to detect the changes. Keep in mind that manually editing configuration files on a node makes that instance's configuration different from the one stored on the Administration Server's Configuration Store as well as other nodes that might be clustered together.

Configuration files that are no longer synchronized with those in the Configuration Store are detected by the Administration Server and noted in the graphical administrative interface. You can elect to pull the changes from the Administration Node and update the copies in the Configuration Store, or you can choose to overwrite the files on the Administration Node with those contained in the Configuration Store. If the changes are pulled from the Administration Node, the corresponding files in the Configuration Store are updated and redeployed to any other servers that may be part of the cluster.

The Administration Server uses the following steps to detect and process manual edits:

1. Before deploying any configuration through the Administration Console, the Administration Server verifies whether any instance of the configuration has manual edits.

2. If any instance has been found to have manual edits, then the deployment of the configuration is paused and the user is presented with the option to update the configuration in the Configuration Store or overwrite the changes on the Administration Node with the existing configuration.

3. If the user elects to use the edited configuration, then the Administration Server pulls the entire configuration from that instance into the Configuration Store and the existing configuration is overwritten.

4. After the configuration has been updated, it is deployed to all instances that share the configuration within a particular cluster.

Warning: Do not manually edit any files in the Configuration Repository. The files under this directory are created by the Web Server for internal use only.

4.6 Localization and Accessibility

Products that are *localized* have been translated into other languages or cultures. Products that are said to be *accessible* can be read and used by people with disabilities and meet governmental standards such as 508 compliance. The Administration Console (graphical user interface) and the command line interface both support localization and meet accessibility standards that make them *508 compliant*.

Note: The terms *localization* and *internationalization* have been abbreviated as L10n and i18n, respectively. The numbers 10 and 18 in these abbreviations refer to the number of letters between the starting letter and the ending letter of each word. The capital letter, "L", on L10n helps to distinguish it from the lowercase letter "i" in i18n.

Section 508 of the United States Rehabilitation Act defines the electronic and information technology accessibility guidelines that should be followed to make information accessible to people with disabilities. Products that adhere to these guidelines are said to be *508 compliant*. For more information on 508 compliance, see http://www.section508.gov/.

4.6.1 Localization of the Administration Console

Web browsers can be configured to specify the languages that a user can read. Web servers can detect this information and elect to return data back to the browser in the specified language. This information is passed from the web browser to Web Server in the Accept-Language request header as follows:

```
GET / HTTP/1.1
Host: localhost:8989
User-Agent: Mozilla/5.0 (Windows; U; Windows NT 5.1; en-US;
    rv:1.8.1.12) Gecko/20080201 Firefox/2.0.0.12
Accept: text/xml,application/xml,application/xhtml+xml,text/
    html;q=0.9,text/plain;q=0.8,image/png,*/*;q=0.5
Accept-Language: es,en-us;q=0.7,en;q=0.3
Accept-Encoding: gzip,deflate
Accept-Charset: ISO-8859-1,utf-8;q=0.7,*;q=0.7
Keep-Alive: 300
Connection: keep-alive
```

The Administration Console is an application that automatically detects the Accept-Language header and returns content in a localized fashion. As such, there is no need to configure anything within the Administration Server for localization. Figure 4.9 demonstrates a localized login screen for the Spanish language.

4.6.2 Localization of the Command Line Interface

You achieve localization of the command line interface by adding localization-specific elements to the Administration Server's server.xml file. The second-level localization element contains a subelement named default-language, which specifies the IANA language tag as specified in RFC 4646 (Tags for Identifying Languages).

Note: The Internet Assigned Numbers Authority (IANA) is one of the Internet's oldest institutions, with its activities dating back to the 1970s. IANA allocates and maintains unique codes and numbering systems that are used in the technical standards ("protocols") that make up the Internet.

Figure 4.9 Administration Console Localized for the Spanish (es) Language

An example of the use of the localization tag to set the default language to Spanish (Latin America) is as follows:

```
<localization>
<default-language>es-419</default-language>
</localization>
```

After this element is set, any interaction with the CLI would produce messages in Spanish. For instance, the following error is returned when requesting configuration statistics for an invalid configuration name:

```
wadm> get-config-stats --config=foobar
ADMIN3725: No hay datos de supervisión disponibles para la configura-
    ción:    foobar
wadm>
```

This is roughly translated as, "There is no data available for the configuration, foobar."

All messages are returned in the language specified by the `default-language` element. Subcommands, options, and operands, however, do not change.

> **Note:** Refer to the Web Server 7.0 Release Notes for a list of languages supported by the Administration Console and the command line interface.

4.6.3 Accessibility

Applications that are 508 compliant return content that can be read by persons with disabilities. An example of this would be a sight-impaired person who can interact with the application through a screen reader. Applications and web sites that are compliant with section 508 must provide data in a format that can be read easily by such devices. A web site is said to be in compliance with the 508 standards if it meets the standards set in the following areas:

- Text Tags
- Multimedia Presentations
- Color
- Readability
- Server-Side Image Maps
- Client-Side Image Maps
- Data Table (i) Frames
- Flicker Rate
- Text-Only Alternative
- Scripts
- Applets and Plug-Ins
- Electronic Forms
- Navigation Links
- Time Delays

Sun Microsystems spent a great deal of time ensuring that the Administration Console and the command line interface are both 508 compliant. These interfaces went through a major redesign from the previous versions to ensure that data was organized in such a way to meet these standards.

4.7 Managing Web Server Configurations

In reviewing the information contained in this chapter, it should be clear that the *configuration* is at the very center of the administration infrastructure. In fact, the primary purpose of the administration infrastructure in Web Server 7 is to manage configurations from a central location (the Administration Server) and distribute them to Administration Nodes, where they become instances.

Management of Web Server 7 is focused on creating new configurations, editing existing configurations, and deploying configurations in order for them to become instances. Thinking in terms of configurations (rather than instances) will help you to better understand how to effectively manage your Web Server.

4.7.1 Creating a New Configuration

A default Web Server instance was created when you installed the Administration Server. During the installation process, an initial configuration was created beneath the Configuration Store and subsequently deployed to the same node as the Administration Server. This is how that default instance was created.

If you are managing a standalone server, you now have all the components you need to serve up web content. You can elect to customize the existing (default) configuration or create a new configuration with your customizations. It is a best practice to leave the initial configuration untouched and create a new configuration that contains your customizations. This enables you to create a baseline that you can use for comparison purposes later if need be.

There are two basic ways to create a new configuration:

- Create a new (empty) configuration
- Copy an existing configuration

4.7.1.1 Creating a New (Empty) Configuration

You can use either the Administration Console or command line interface to create a new configuration.

To use the Administration Console to create a new configuration, complete the following steps:

1. Open the Administration Console and click the Configurations tab to access the main configuration page.

2. Click the New button found on that page. The New Configuration Wizard Page appears.

3. Complete the Configuration Information form as follows:

   • Enter a Name for your configuration. This is a human-readable name that helps you identify the configuration from other configurations found in the interface.

   • Enter a Server Name for your configuration. This is the host and domain name by which others will access your server.

   • Enter or update the Document Root directory. This is the location where content will be served.

4. Click the Next button.

5. Complete the Listener Properties form as follows:

   • Enter a Port for your configuration. This is the listen socket where a deployed instance will listen for HTTP traffic.

   • Enter an IP Address for your configuration. This is the Internet protocol address of the server where your configuration will be deployed. If you do not know your server's address or if you want your server to listen on all available IP addresses, then enter an asterisk (*) character.

6. Click the Next button.

7. You can elect to enable/configure Java, CGI, and SHTML on the Configuration properties page, or you can do this later. Click the Next button.

8. You can elect to create the instance now by selecting an available node or you can do this later. Click the Next button.

9. Review the information found in the Review page and click Finish if you are satisfied.

10. A new configuration is created. Click the Close button to close the New Configuration Wizard.

11. You will see the new configuration appear in the Configurations table, along with information that indicates whether the configuration has been deployed or not.

The New Configuration Wizard guides a user through the process of creating a new configuration. The `create-config` subcommand in the CLI can be used as an alternative to the Administration Console and may in fact be faster and more flexible. The following information provides an overview of this subcommand:

```
wadm> create-config --<TAB>
--http-port*      --server-name*     --echo        --no-prompt
--verbose         --document-root    --jdk-home    --server-user
--ip              --platform
```

The `create-config` subcommand actually enables you to specify additional parameters that are not available in the New Configuration Wizard. To specify these values in the Administration Console, you would need to edit the configuration after it has been created; this is a two step process. The command line interface enables you to complete both steps in one. The following demonstrates how the `create-config` subcommand can be used to create a new configuration:

```
wadm> create-config --server-name=www.example.com --document-root=../
   docs --http-port=80 --ip=* "My Test Config"
CLI201 Command 'create-config' ran successfully
wadm>
```

To make comparisons easier, the subcommand options have been listed in the order in which they appear in the New Configuration Wizard. Note that the name of the configuration is listed last. If you would like to include spaces in your configuration name, you need to use double quotes (as shown).

4.7.1.2 Copying an Existing Configuration

Using an existing configuration as a template can often be easier than creating a new configuration. You can use this functionality when you want to try something before updating an existing (tested) configuration. Web Server 7 enables you to copy an existing configuration in the Administration Console as follows:

1. Open the Administration Console and click the Configurations tab to access the main configuration page.

2. Select the check box next to the configuration you would like to use as a template and click the Duplicate button found on that page. The New Configuration Wizard Page appears.

3. Enter a Name for your configuration. This is a human-readable name that helps you identify the configuration from other configurations found in the interface. Click the OK button.

4. You will see the new configuration appear in the Configurations table. You can now edit the configuration and apply your customizations.

The `copy-config` subcommand in the CLI can be used as an alternative to the Administration Console. The following information provides an overview of this subcommand:

```
wadm> copy-config --<TAB>
--config*    --echo     --no-prompt   --verbose
```

The following demonstrates how the `copy-config` subcommand can be used to copy one configuration to another:

```
wadm> copy-config --config="My Test Config" "My Second Test Config"
CLI201 Command 'copy-config' ran successfully
wadm>
```

Note: You cannot create a server instance during the process of copying a configuration.

4.7.2 Deploying an Existing Configuration

A configuration is nothing more than a set of files that can be used to instantiate a Web Server instance. You need to *deploy* the configuration to one or more nodes before you can see the customizations contained in your configuration. The process of deployment simply copies all the configuration files from the Configuration Store to one or more nodes and creates an instance of the server on the node(s). After you have created the instance, you can then start it to see the customizations you have made.

You can deploy a configuration by using either the Administration Console or the command line interface.

To use the Administration Console to deploy a configuration, complete the following steps:

1. Open the Administration Console and click the Configurations tab to access the main configuration page.

2. Select the check box next to the configuration you would like to deploy and click the Deploy button. You will see a window appear indicating that a deployment is pending.

3. Click the Deploy button.

4. After the configuration has been deployed, click the Close button. You are returned to the main configuration page.

5. Select the check box next to the configuration you would like to deploy and click the Deploy button. A window appears indicating that a deployment is pending.

The preceding steps assume that you are not currently editing a configuration when you want to deploy it. This is not always the case. You often want to test your configuration changes immediately after making them. After you make changes to a configuration through the Administration Console, a message appears in the upper-right corner indicating that a deployment is pending. This message can be seen in Figure 4.10.

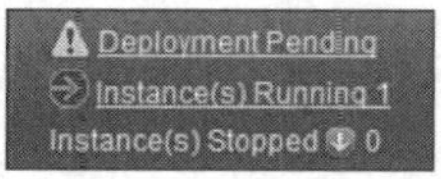

Figure 4.10   Deployment Pending Notification

You can continue making changes to your configuration or click the Deployment Pending link to initiate the deployment process. Clicking the Deployment Pending link while editing a configuration eliminates the first two steps detailed in the preceding list.

The `deploy-config` subcommand in the CLI can be used as an alternative to the Administration Console. The following information provides an overview of this subcommand:

```
wadm> deploy-config --<TAB>
--echo         --no-prompt    --verbose      --force        --restart
--no-reconfig
```

The following demonstrates how the `deploy-config` subcommand can be used to deploy a configuration to applicable node(s):

```
wadm> deploy-config "My Test Config"
CLI201 Command 'deploy-config' ran successfully
wadm>
```

4.7.3 Rolling Back to a Previous Configuration

There may be times when the changes that you make to a configuration cause problems and you need to remove the changes to restore functionality. In such cases you can simply edit the configuration and restore the configuration settings back to their previous values. But what if you do not know which changes caused the problem? In this case, you may want to restore (or *roll back*) to a previous version of the configuration.

The Administration Server makes a backup copy of the existing (deployed) configuration before it deploys a configuration that has been updated. This occurs whether you perform the operation from the Administration Console or command line interface, but only occurs if there have been actual changes made to the configuration. Backups are stored in the Configuration Store beneath each configuration-specific directory in a subdirectory named backup. The full path to the backup directory is as follows:

```
install_dir/admin-server/config-store/config_name/backup
```

Files contained in this directory are recognized by the timestamp of the time when the configuration was created.

Each of these files is a complete archive of the previously deployed configurations.

```
20080116_203853.zip
20080116_204142.zip
20080116_204409.zip
```

The format of each filename found in this directory is yyyymmdd_HHMMSS.zip (where yyyy is the four-digit year, mm is the two-digit month, dd is the two-digit day, HH is the two-digit hour [in 24-hour format], MM is the two-digit month, and SS is the two-digit second).

You can access the backup configurations through the Administration Console by performing the following steps:

1. Open the Administration Console and click the Configurations tab to access the main configuration page.
2. Click the link for the configuration whose backups you would like to see.
3. Click the General tab. This opens a window that enables you to perform general functionality for this configuration. One such item is the ability to view and restore previously deployed configurations.

4. Click the Restore subtab. You see a list of the previously deployed versions of this configuration. An example of this is shown in Figure 4.11.

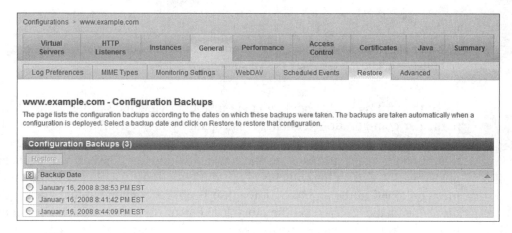

Figure 4.11   Configuration Backup Screen

You can select the radio button for any of these configurations and click the Restore button to restore any and all nodes with a previous version of a configuration. You will be prompted to determine whether you really want to perform this action before continuing.

In addition to the Administration Console, you can also use the `list-backups` subcommand in the CLI to show a list of backups for a particular configuration, as follows:

```
wadm> list-backups --config=www.example.com
20080116_203853
20080116_204142
20080116_204409
wadm>
```

You can then restore any of these configurations with the `restore-config` subcommand. The following information provides an overview of this subcommand:

```
wadm> restore-config --<TAB>
--from-backup*    --echo          --no-prompt      --all
--verbose
```

The following demonstrates how the `restore-config` subcommand can be used to restore a previous configuration:

```
restore-config --from-backup=20080116_204142 "www.example.com"
CLI201 Command 'restore-config' ran successfully
wadm>
```

Note: The roll-back functionality was introduced in Web Server 7.0 PU2. This capability cannot be found in previous versions of the software.

As of the writing of this book, you are unable to view the settings defined for a particular configuration version. (This capability is not available through either the Administration Console or the CLI.) So how do you know whether the configuration you are restoring is the one you are looking for? The best way to accomplish this is to extract the contents of the configuration zip archive and look at the files contained in the archive. Although it is not recommended that you modify files beneath the `config-store` directory, looking into the configuration zip archives is the only way you can be sure to restore the appropriate configuration.

4.7.4 Deleting an Existing Configuration

Old configurations that are no longer in use can be deleted from the file system through either the Administration Console or the CLI. To delete configurations through the Administration Console, perform the following steps:

1. Open the Administration Console and click the Configurations tab to access the main configuration page.

2. Select the check box next to the configuration you would like to delete and click the Delete button found on that page. The Delete Configuration page appears. This page provides information on any deployed instances of this configuration.

3. Click the OK button to perform the following tasks:

    • Stop any running instances of this configuration on any nodes where it has been deployed

    • Remove the instance from the node(s) where it has been deployed

    • Remove the configuration from the Configuration Store on the Administration Server

4. You will see the configuration disappear from the Configurations table.

The `delete-config` subcommand in the CLI can be used as an alternative to the Administration Console. The following information provides an overview of this subcommand:

```
wadm> delete-config --<TAB>
--echo        --no-prompt   --verbose    config-name
```

The following demonstrates how the `delete-config` subcommand can be used to delete a configuration:

```
wadm> delete-config "My Test Config"
CLI201 Command 'delete-config' ran successfully
wadm>
```

Unlike the Administration Console, the `delete-config` subcommand does not enable you to delete deployed configurations. If you attempt to delete a deployed configuration, you receive the following error message:

```
wadm> delete-config "My Test Config"
ADMIN3653: Cannot delete the configuration 'My Test Config'. It has been
    deployed to '1' node(s).
wadm>
```

To perform this task, you must first delete any instance(s) from the node(s) on which it has been deployed. Then you can safely remove the configuration. The following command sequence demonstrates how to accomplish this from the command line:

```
wadm> delete-instance --config="My Test Config" www.example.com
CLI201 Command 'delete-instance' ran successfully
wadm> delete-config "My Test Config"
CLI201 Command 'delete-config' ran successfully
wadm>
```

4.8 Summary

Web Server 7.0 provides several methods for administering the Web Server configurations. Although many administrators use the graphical Administration Console to learn the product, many soon migrate to the command-line tools or even direct editing of the configuration files. Whether your preference is graphical, tool-based, or direct edit, Web Server 7 allows you the ultimate flexibility to manage your Web Server the way you want to.

4.9 Self-Paced Labs

Use the information contained in this chapter to perform the following exercises. These will help validate your understanding of the concepts described in this chapter.

Use the Graphical Administration Console to perform the following steps:

1. Review the settings in the default configuration. Correlate the settings to the parameters you entered during the installation process.
2. Stop and Start the default configuration and verify that you can access it with a web browser.
3. Make a copy of your default configuration; call it "My New Config".
4. Edit the "My New Config" configuration and change the port number to an available port on your server.
5. Deploy the "My New Config" configuration.
6. Start the instance for the "My New Config" configuration.
7. Verify that you now have two new configurations deployed on your server, both listening on different ports.
8. Add a URL redirect to the "My New Config" configuration, using the following parameters:

   Source: URL Prefix: /foo

   Target URL: The URL of your default server instance (for instance, http://localhost:80)

9. Deploy the updated configuration and access the /foo URI on your "My New Config" instance. Verify that you are redirected to the default server instance.
10. Restore the "My New Config" configuration to the previous version.
11. Deploy the restored "My New Config" configuration and verify that you are no longer redirected, using the /foo URI.
12. Delete the "My New Config" configuration.
13. Repeat Steps 1–12 using the command line interface.

Note: Go to http://www.sunwebserver.com for detailed instructions on how to perform each of these exercises.

5

Web Server 7.0 Configuration Files

CHAPTER 4, "Web Server 7.0 Administration," introduced the concept of a Web Server *configuration*. That chapter described that a configuration consists of various components that are used to configure the runtime services of a Web Server 7.0 instance. Included in these components are various configuration files (such as `magnus.conf`, `server.xml`, and `obj.conf`) that are used to specify global variables and define how the server responds to specific events and client requests.

Each Web Server configuration has its own set of files that are located beneath the config directory for the server instance. Table 5.1 provides an overview of the configuration files associated with Web Server 7.0, as well as a brief description of their purpose.

Table 5.1 Web Server 7.0 Configuration Files

Filename	Overview
`cert8.db`	Network Security Services (NSS) certificate database. This database stores publicly accessible objects (such as certificates, certificate revocation lists, and S/MIME records) and works with the `key3.db` database for certificate management. This file is part of the instance's trust database.
`certmap.conf`	Certificate to LDAP DN mapping configuration.
`default-web.xml`	Default values for all web applications.
`default.acl`	Default access control list (ACL) file for the server instance. This file contains the default rules governing access within the server instance.
`key3.db`	NSS private key database. This database stores the private keys generated by the server and works with the `cert8.db` database for certificate management. This file is part of the instance's trust database.

Table 5.1   Web Server 7.0 Configuration Files   *continued*

Filename	Overview
`keyfile`	File containing usernames and hashed passwords for flat file authentication.
`login.conf`	Information for file authentication used by the Java Authentication and Authorization Service (JAAS).
`magnus.conf`	Contains the Netscape server application programming interface (NSAPI) plug-in initialization directives and settings that control the way NSAPI plug-ins are run.
`mime.types`	Multipurpose Internet mail extension (MIME) type mapping file. This file contains a mapping of file extensions to MIME types and enables the server to determine the content type of a requested resource.
`obj.conf`	NSAPI request processing configuration file. This file contains the instructions that tell the Web Server how to handle various HTTP requests from clients.
`secmod.db`	NSS PKCS #11 module database. This database stores PKCS #11 module configuration information that is used for various cryptographic modules (for example, hardware accelerator cards).
`server.policy`	Policy controlling the access that applications have to resources.
`server.xml`	The main instance configuration file, which contains the majority of settings necessary to run the server.

Configuration files are updated when you perform administrative tasks through the Administration Console or command line interface. Additionally, you can directly edit each configuration file and modify it as appropriate.

Warning: You are permitted to edit configuration files for an instance on an Administration Node, but do not edit any files beneath the Administration Server's `config-store` directory. The files in this directory are modified by the Administration Server and command line interface and are for internal use only.

This chapter takes a closer look at each configuration file as well as the syntax, usage, and considerations for each file. Although the configuration files in Table 5.1 appear in alphabetical order, the following sections discuss Web Server 7.0's configuration files in order of importance.

5.1 The `magnus.conf` File

The `magnus.conf` file contains the directives necessary to initialize Netscape Server Application Programming Interface (NSAPI) plug-ins. Directives may also contain additional settings that control the way the NSAPI plug-ins are run.

> **Note:** A *directive* is a statement that defines a setting within the Web Server.

The Web Server consists of functionality that enables you to perform basic request processing immediately after installation. This functionality is provided by server application functions (SAFs) that are part of the Web Server platform.

You can change the way the server responds to client requests by adding or modifying directives in the magnus.conf and obj.conf files. Each directive references a SAF that is used to perform the work during a particular stage of request processing. You can elect to add directives that call SAFs provided by Web Server 7.0, or extend the functionally of the Web Server by creating your own shared libraries (or plug-ins) through the NSAPI. Additionally, you might find it necessary to include functionality that is provided by third-party vendors or by other Sun Microsystems products.

Plug-ins must be registered with the Web Server in the magnus.conf file; this is accomplished with the Init directive. Once registered, you can use the SAFs contained within the plug-ins to customize request processing within the obj.conf.

Example 5.1 demonstrates the use of the Init directive in a customized magnus.conf file.

Example 5.1 Sample magnus.conf File

```
#
# Copyright 2006 Sun Microsystems, Inc.  All rights reserved.
# Use is subject to license terms.
#
Init fn="load-modules"now)"
Init fn="load-modules" shlib="libfastcgi.so"
Init fn="load-modules"
  shlib="/sun/webserver7/plugins/myplugin/myplugin.so"
  funcs="myfunc1,myfunc2"
```

The load-modules SAF is used to load and register a plug-in with the Web Server. This function is most often used to load third-party plug-ins into the Web Server to provide functionality that is not included in the base platform. An example of this might include a plug-in that is used to provide an interface to an application server.

This example specifies three plug-ins that are registered during the initialization process. The libj2eeplugin.so and libfastcgi.so plug-ins are included with Web Server 7.0. The myplugin.so plug-in is a user-created shared library that can be found beneath the `/sun/webserver7/plugins/myplugin` directory. The `shlib` parameter specifies the local file system path to the shared library.

> **Note:** If you do not specify the fully qualified filename in the `shlib` parameter, the Web Server searches for the plug-in in the path specified by the `SERVER_LIB_DIR` variable defined in the startup script (`startserv`). If you installed your Web Server in the `/sun/webserver7` directory, the default value for `SERVER_LIB_DIR` would be `/sun/webserver7/lib`.

The `shlib_flags` parameter (as seen in the first directive) specifies how a shared library will be loaded into the Web Server process. After it is started, the Web Server process uses the `dlopen` function to load additional library files into memory. The options of `global` and `now` shown in the first directive refer to the `dlopen` options of `RTLD_GLOBAL` and `RTLD_NOW`, respectively. You can read more about these and other options by using the UNIX `man` command as follows:

```
# man dlopen
```

The third `Init` directive also demonstrates the capability to register specific functions within a particular plug-in (i.e., `myfunc1` and `myfunc2`). The `funcs` parameter is not specified in the first two directives, so all functions defined within those plug-ins are available for use.

> **Note:** Refer to the Sun Java System Web Server 7.0 NSAPI Developer's Guide (document number 819-2632) for additional information on Web Server directives.

5.1.1 Syntax

Table 5.2 provides the general syntax for the `magnus.conf` file.

Table 5.2   `magnus.conf` Syntax

Syntax	Rules
Case Sensitivity	Items in the `magnus.conf` file are case-sensitive, including function names, parameter names, parameter values, and pathnames.
Comments	Hash symbols (#) are used to designate comments in the `magnus.conf` file. Any text that appears to the right of a hash symbol is ignored by the Web Server. The first four lines of Example 5.1 include comments.

Syntax	Rules
Directives	Directives in the `magnus.conf` file either set a value or invoke a SAF. You can add directives or edit existing directives in the `magnus.conf` file, but be very careful when doing so. Simple mistakes can make the server fail to operate correctly. There are three `Init` directives in Example 5.1. Each of these invoke the `load-modules` SAF to load the appropriate plug-in. The `Init` directives load and initialize server modules and NSAPI plug-ins. Refer to the Sun Java System Web Server 7.0 NSAPI Developer's Guide for a complete list of directives available in the `magnus.conf` file.
Directive Parameters	For predefined SAFs, the number and names of parameters depend on the function. The order of parameters on the line is not important.
Path Names	Always use forward slashes (/) rather than backslashes (\) in path names, even on the Windows platform. A backslash character is used to escape the character that follows it.
Quotation Marks	Quotation marks (") are required around the value strings only when there is a space in the string; otherwise, they are optional. Each open quotation mark must be matched by a closed quotation mark.
Spacing	Directives in the `magnus.conf` file appear on their own line. You may continue long directives on the next line by beginning the next line with a space or tab. Spaces are not allowed before or after the equal (=) sign that separates a name and value. Spaces are not allowed at the end of a line or on a blank line. Line continuation is demonstrated for the first and third directives in Example 5.1. The second line for both of these directives begins with a space.

5.1.2 Context

An Administration Node may contain multiple configurations that have been deployed to the node by the Administration Server. These deployed configurations are called instances. Each instance can contain only one `magnus.conf` file; therefore, there is a one-to-one correspondence between an instance and the `magnus.conf` file. The directives defined within the `magnus.conf` file apply to the entire server instance and therefore any virtual servers defined within that instance.

5.1.3 Modifications

Some changes made through the Administration Console or the command line interface update the `magnus.conf` file. If this file is updated as a result of changes made through either of these two interfaces, you must deploy the updated configuration before the changes are reflected on the appropriate Administration Node(s).

The `magnus.conf` file is read when the instance is started; therefore, any changes made to the `magnus.conf` file require a server restart for the changes to take effect. The Administration Console and command line interface detect changes to the `magnus.conf` file during the deployment process. If you use these tools to deploy the new configuration, you are prompted to restart the instance. If you directly edit the `magnus.conf` file, you need to restart the sever on your own.

The `magnus.conf` file is validated at start-up time. Errors found within the file might prevent the server from starting or processing requests properly.

5.2 The `server.xml` File

The `server.xml` file is the main configuration file for a Web Server instance. It contains initial values for listen sockets, virtual servers, and other components that were configured during the installation process. It also contains several default settings that allow the Web Server to work immediately after installation. You can modify the values for these settings through the Administration Console or the command line interface, or by editing the `server.xml` file on a particular Administration Node.

> **Note:** The `server.xml` file is one of the most important configuration files. It is important that you understand the syntax of this file and how it is structured if you decide to manually edit it.

5.2.1 Syntax

As the name indicates, the `server.xml` file contains information in an extensible markup language (XML) format. As such, an understanding of basic XML structure and terminology is essential to understanding the `server.xml` file.

An XML document contains a hierarchy of *elements* and *values*. An element is a unit of XML data and is the basic building block of an XML document. Elements can have associated with them either values or other subelements; thus forming a parent/child relationship.

Elements are delimited by opening and closing tags that have a structure similar to what you might see if you viewed the source of an HTML document (they use the < and > brackets). Elements begin with an opening tag, for example `<virtual-server>`, and end with the closing tag, for example `</virtual-server>`. The tags are case-sensitive.

An example of the `platform` element for a Web Server running in 64-bit mode is as follows:

```
<platform>64</platform>
```

An XML document must contain a single *root* element, which is the topmost element of the hierarchy. Like any other XML element, the root element can contain subelements. The `<server>` element is the root element of the `server.xml` file. The `<server>` element has many subelements, many of which have subelements of their own.

Example 5.2 demonstrates the `server.xml` file for the default Administration Node.

Example 5.2 Sample `server.xml` File

```
<?xml version="1.0" encoding="UTF-8"?>

<!--
  Copyright 2006 Sun Microsystems, Inc.  All rights reserved.
  Use is subject to license terms.
-->

<server>
  <cluster>
    <local-host>boulder.example.com</local-host>
    <instance>
      <host>boulder.example.com</host>
    </instance>
  </cluster>

  <log>
    <log-file>../logs/errors</log-file>
    <log-level>info</log-level>
  </log>

  <platform>64</platform>

  <temp-path>/tmp/https-boulder.example.com-6accbd0a</temp-path>
```

```
  <user>webservd</user>

  <jvm>
    <java-home>/sun/webserver7/jdk</java-home>
    <server-class-path>
/sun/webserver7/lib/webserv-rt.jar:/sun/webserver7/lib/pwc.jar:
/sun/webserver7/lib/ant.jar:${java.home}/lib/tools.jar:
/sun/webserver7/lib/ktsearch.jar:/sun/webserver7/lib/webserv-jstl.jar:
/sun/webserver7/lib/jsf-impl.jar:/sun/webserver7/lib/jsf-api.jar:
/sun/webserver7/lib/webserv-jwsdp.jar:/sun/webserver7/lib/
    container-auth.jar:
/sun/webserver7/lib/mail.jar:/sun/webserver7/lib/activation.jar
</server-class-path>
    <debug>false</debug>
    <debug-jvm-options>
-Xdebug -Xrunjdwp:transport=dt_socket,server=y,suspend=n,address=7896
</debug-jvm-options>
    <jvm-options>-Djava.security.auth.login.config=login.conf
      </jvm-options>
    <jvm-options>-Xms128m -Xmx256m</jvm-options>
  </jvm>

  <thread-pool>
    <max-threads>128</max-threads>
    <stack-size>131072</stack-size>
  </thread-pool>

  <default-auth-db-name>keyfile</default-auth-db-name>

  <auth-db>
    <name>keyfile</name>
    <url>file</url>
    <property>
      <name>syntax</name>
      <value>keyfile</value>
    </property>
    <property>
      <name>keyfile</name>
      <value>keyfile</value>
    </property>
  </auth-db>

  <acl-file>default.acl</acl-file>

  <mime-file>mime.types</mime-file>

  <access-log>
    <file>../logs/access</file>
  </access-log>
```

```
<http-listener>
  <name>http-listener-1</name>
  <port>80</port>
  <server-name>boulder.example.com</server-name>
  <default-virtual-server-name>boulder.example.com</default-
    virtual-server-name>
</http-listener>

<virtual-server>
  <name>boulder.example.com</name>
  <host>boulder.example.com</host>
  <http-listener-name>http-listener-1</http-listener-name>
  <document-root>/sun/webserver7/https-boulder.example.com/docs
    </document-root>
</virtual-server>
</server>
```

If a given variable name is defined at both the `<virtual-server>` and `<server>` levels, the `<virtual-server>` value takes precedence.

Note: A detailed explanation for each of the data elements found in this example can be found in Appendix A, "A Detailed Look at the `server.xml` File."

5.2.2 XML Schema

An XML schema provides a means for defining the structure, content, and semantics of XML documents. It can specify the constraints (that is, valid element names, data types, and values) on XML documents, using an XML-based language. An XML schema is hierarchical, so it is easier to create an unambiguous specification, and it's possible to determine the scope over which a comment is meant to apply.

Web Server 7.0 validates the format and content of the `server.xml` against the `sun-web-server_7_0.xsd` schema. This file can be found in the `lib/dtds` subdirectory; directly beneath the Web Server 7.0 installation directory. An understanding of this file will help you understand valid element names and the structure of those elements as they are found in the `server.xml` file.

For example, the following definition provides the structure for the <user> element:

```
<xs:element name="user" type="userType" minOccurs="0"
    maxOccurs="1"/>
```

The userType attribute describes the format of the data (such as the minimum length) and can also be found in the schema file. The <user> element is optional in the file because the minOccurs value is set to 0. If this element appears in the server.xml file, however, the maximum number of times it can occur is once (as specified by the maxOccurs value).

Note: Refer to the XML Schema Primer at http://www.w3.org/TR/xmlschema-0/ for more information.

5.2.3 Context

Each instance can contain only one server.xml file; therefore, there is a one-to-one correspondence between an instance and the server.xml file. The server.xml file contains definitions for each virtual server contained within the instance, so there is a one-to-many relationship between the server.xml file and virtual servers.

5.2.4 Modifications

Some changes made through the Administration Console or the command line interface update the server.xml file. If this file is updated as a result of changes made through either of these two interfaces, you must deploy the updated configuration before the changes are reflected on the appropriate Administration Node(s).

The server.xml file is validated against the sun-web-server_7_0.xsd schema when you start or dynamically reconfigure the instance. Errors found at that time prevent the server from starting properly. You can use the -configtest option to the startserv script to validate the server.xml file before you stop the server. This enables you to detect errors to the file without impacting a running server instance.

5.3 The `obj.conf` File

The `obj.conf` (or object configuration) file contains instructions on how to process HTTP client requests. This file consists of various directives that map directly to request processing stages and enable your Web Server to process client requests immediately after installation.

An initial object configuration file is created for each Web Server configuration; the name of the file is simply `obj.conf`. Additional object configuration files may also exist for any virtual servers created using the Administration Console or command line interface. The default name for each virtual server object configuration file is *vsname*-`obj.conf` (where *vsname* is the name of the virtual server). The `<object-file>` element in the `server.xml` file specifies the name of the object configuration file to use to process requests for that virtual server. Example 5.3 demonstrates the use of the `<object-file>` element in the `server.xml` file.

Example 5.3   Virtual Server Definition for the Object Configuration File

```
<virtual-server>
  <name>www.example.com</name>
  <http-listener-name>http-listener-1</http-listener-name>
  <host>www.example.com</host>
  <object-file>www.example.com-obj.conf</object-file>
  <document-root>/export/home/example.com/public_html</document-root>
  <access-log>
  <file>/export/home/example.com/logs/access</file>
  </access-log>
</virtual-server>
```

When the Web Server receives a request, it uses information contained within the `server.xml` file to select an appropriate virtual server. It then uses the file specified by the `<object-file>` element to determine how to process the request. Multiple object configuration files allow the flexibility to process requests differently for each virtual server.

5.3.1 File Structure

The `obj.conf` file contains a series of instructions (or directives) that tell the server what to do at each stage of the request-handling process. These directives are grouped together by `<Object>` tags. Each directive invokes a SAF with one or more arguments.

Example 5.4 demonstrates the obj.conf file for the default Administration Node.

Example 5.4   Default obj.conf File

```
#
# Copyright 2006 Sun Microsystems, Inc.  All rights reserved.
# Use is subject to license terms.
#

# You can edit this file, but comments and formatting changes
# might be lost when you use the administration GUI or CLI.

<Object name="default">
AuthTrans fn="match-browser" browser="*MSIE*"
  ssl-unclean-shutdown="true"
NameTrans fn="ntrans-j2ee" name="j2ee"
NameTrans fn="pfx2dir" from="/mc-icons" dir="/opt/webserver7/lib/icons"
  name="es-internal"
PathCheck fn="unix-uri-clean"
PathCheck fn="find-pathinfo"
PathCheck fn="find-index-j2ee"
PathCheck fn="find-index" index-names="index.html,home.html,index.jsp"
ObjectType fn="type-j2ee"
ObjectType fn="type-by-extension"
ObjectType fn="force-type" type="text/plain"
Service method="(GET|HEAD)" type="magnus-internal/directory"
  fn="index-common"
Service method="(GET|HEAD|POST)" type="*~magnus-internal/*"
  fn="send-file"
Service method="TRACE" fn="service-trace"
Error fn="error-j2ee"
AddLog fn="flex-log"
</Object>

<Object name="j2ee">
Service fn="service-j2ee" method="*"
</Object>

<Object name="es-internal">
</Object>

<Object name="es-internal">
</Object>

<Object name="cgi">
ObjectType fn="force-type" type="magnus-internal/cgi"
Service fn="send-cgi"
</Object>
```

```
<Object name="send-precompressed">
PathCheck fn="find-compressed"
</Object>

<Object name="compress-on-demand">
Output fn="insert-filter" filter="http-compression"
</Object>
```

5.3.2 Syntax

Directives in the object configuration file follow a syntax similar to those contained in the `magnus.conf` (refer to Table 5.2 for details). The exception is that the object configuration file also contains objects (called *templates*) for grouping directives together. Templates enable you to process directives on a conditional basis.

Note: For information on how requests are processed on a conditional basis, see Chapter 6, "Web Server 7.0 Request Processing."

The overall structure of the object configuration file is as follows:

```
<Object name="default">
directives
</Object>

<Object name="objectname">
directives
</Object>
...
<Object name="objectname">
directives
</Object>
```

The order of these templates is not important, but there must exist one template with the name `default`. The directives contained in the `default` template are used to process every request. The object configuration file for Web Server 7 contains a standard `default` template with directives for standard request processing. This enables you to process requests immediately after installation.

Warning: Do not change the name of the default template or you cannot process requests. The instance will start without a default template, but it will flag an error similar to the following during request processing:

```
[05/Aug/2007:07:28:02] config ( 3208): for host 127.0.0.1 trying to GET
/, process-uri-objects reports: HTTP2020: cannot find template default
```

Some syntax errors in the object configuration file might cause situations where the server instance cannot start, whereas others might not be noticed until a request is processed.

Examples of errors that prevent an instance from starting include an incorrect spelling of the directive name or the name of a directive parameter and can be found in the following example:

```
NameTrans func="pfx2dir" from="/mc-icons" dir="/opt/webserver7/lib/
    icons" name="es-internal"
```

In this example, the directive parameter, fn, has been incorrectly specified as func. If this were to occur, you would see an error similar to the following when you attempted to start the instance:

```
config: CONF2265: Error parsing file obj.conf, line 12, column 1:
    Missing parameter (need fn)
config: CORE3235: File server.xml line 71: Error processing
  <object-file> element: Error processing file obj.conf
failure: server initialization failed
```

Other syntax errors are not so easily noticed and might not be recognized until a request is processed. For example, if you specify an incorrect SAF in the function (fn) specification as follows:

```
NameTrans fn="badfunc" from="/mc-icons" dir="/opt/webserver7/lib/
    icons" name="es-internal"
```

you would see a warning message at start-up as follows:

```
config: trying to GET /, func_exec reports: HTTP2122: cannot find
    function named badfunc
```

and the following message in the errors log:

```
[22/Jul/2007:08:23:55] config ( 3546): for host 24.26.101.117 trying to
    GET /mc-icons/image.gif, func_exec reports: HTTP2122: cannot find
    function named badfunc
info: HTTP3072: http-listener-1: http://www.example.com:80 ready to
accept requests
info: CORE3274: successful server startup
```

These types of errors might not be noticed if the instance is configured to start when the server reboots. Instead, the server might start properly and flag an error message, but it isn't until a request comes in for that resource that the server error is noticed.

The following subsections contain an overview of directives and objects found in the object configuration file. Refer to Chapter 6 for a detailed explanation of request processing.

5.3.2.1 Directives

Directives in the object configuration file invoke SAFs at various request processing stages. The stage is specified as the first parameter of the directive.

> **Note:** The `magnus.conf` file contains directives that are processed only at instance startup time. The `obj.conf` file contains directives that are processed for every request.

Each directive calls a function and specifies zero or more parameters that are necessary for the SAF to process the request at that stage. The function name and/or parameters are specified with reserved words, so the order in which they appear in the directive is not important. In general, however, the syntax for each directive in the object configuration file is as follows:

```
Directive fn="function" name1="value1" ... nameN="valueN"
```

Where *Directive* is the stage at which the directive is processed. The value of the function (`fn`) parameter is the name of the SAF to execute. All directives must supply a value for the `fn` parameter; if there is no function, the instruction will do nothing. Function names can be composed of letters, digits, underscores (_), or hyphens (-). The remaining parameters are the arguments needed by the function, and they vary from function to function.

An example of a directive that applies to the NameTrans (Name Translation) stage of request processing would be

```
NameTrans fn="document-root" root="/opt/Sun/webserver7/https-www.
    example.com/docs"
```

In this example, the directive is executed during the NameTrans stage of request processing and invokes the document-root SAF to specify the document root directory for the server. The document-root SAF uses one parameter, root, to specify the path to the document root directory.

Parameters can contain references to variables and expressions. The variables can be predefined variables, variables defined at request time using the set-variable SAF, or variables defined in server.xml.

It is not required, but it is a best practice to group directives according to the stage in which they are processed (for example, all NameTrans directives should be grouped together). This enables you to easily recognize and debug problems within the object configuration file.

The order in which directives appear within a particular group becomes important if the directives are conditionally executed. A common error is to place directives that are processed unconditionally before those that are conditional in nature. In such a case, the conditional directives might never be processed.

Another best practice is to place directive groups in the order of request processing stages (for example, AuthTrans, NameTrans, PathCheck, ObjectType, Service, Error, and AddLog) because this also aids in debugging.

Note: This is the order in which the default directives in the object configuration file appear. You can reorder these if you want, but if you use the Administration Console or command line interface to manage your configuration, directives are reordered to follow this format.

5.3.2.2 Objects

Directives in the object configuration file are grouped together by *objects* (which are also referred to as *containers* or *templates*). Objects are specified by the <Object> tag and enable you to define directives that are executed only on certain conditions. Example 5.4 demonstrates various objects that are defined as part of the default object configuration file.

One of the most common attributes for the `<Object>` tag is the `name` attribute, which uniquely identifies the object within the configuration file. The syntax for objects that use the `name` attribute is as follows:

```
<Object name="objectname">
directives
</Object>
```

The object configuration file contains a `default` object that tells the instance how to process requests by default.

```
<Object name="default">
directives
</Object>
```

The object configuration file can contain objects that are executed only when certain conditions are true for a particular `NameTrans` directive. Two such conditions involve the use of additional named objects or `ppath` objects.

Named Object Processing

One such example of conditional processing is the use of the optional `name` attribute in the `NameTrans` directive. Assume that a client is requesting the following URL:

```
http://www.example.com/mc-icons/back.gif
```

During request processing, the server evaluates each `NameTrans` directive in the `default` object in an attempt to locate a match. In this case, the second directive is matched because the URI begins with `/mc-icons`.

```
NameTrans fn="ntrans-j2ee" name="j2ee"
NameTrans fn="pfx2dir" from="/mc-icons" dir="/opt/webserver7/lib/
  icons" name="es-internal"
```

The server then determines whether a `name` attribute has been specified for the directive.

```
NameTrans fn="pfx2dir" from="/mc-icons" dir="/opt/webserver7/lib/
  icons" name="es-internal"
```

If the directive specifies a name attribute, the value of the attribute *points to* another object that contains additional directives that should be used for processing the request.

```
<Object name="es-internal">
directives
</Object>
```

Any directives found in the additional object are processed prior to those found in the default object for the particular stage being processed.

Note: Request processing is discussed in more detail in Chapter 6.

ppath **Object Processing**

Another example of conditional processing is the use of the ppath (partial path) object.

```
<Object ppath="path">
directives
</Object>
```

The ppath object enables you to specify a path to a document or resource where directives contained in the object are executed only if the path to the resource can be found beneath the location specified in the ppath value. For example, suppose you specify a ppath object as follows:

```
<Object ppath="/opt/webserver7/https-www.example.com/docs/
    private/*">
directives
</Object>
```

During the processing of the NameTrans directive, if it is determined that the resource can be found beneath the /opt/webserver7/https-www.example.com/ docs/private/ directory, then any directives found within this ppath object are processed prior to those found in the default object.

In general, the server always starts processing requests with the default object and may process directives in other objects based on conditions within the

NameTrans directive. Each new object added to the object configuration file has the potential to modify the default object's behavior.

5.3.2.3 Variables

SAF parameters can contain references to variables and expressions. The variables can be predefined variables, variables defined at request time using the set-variable SAF, or variables defined in the server.xml file.

> **Note:** The set-variable SAF allows the dynamic creation of variables during request processing. This can be a very powerful feature, but it also can be somewhat confusing because undefined variables are not reported until they are used (during request time).

Within the server.xml file itself, a variable can be defined at various levels (for example, <server> and <virtual-server>). As such, the server must have a method for resolving duplicate variable definitions. The server consults the following namespaces (in the following order) when attempting to resolve a variable:

1. Predefined variables
2. Variables defined at request time through the use of the set-variable SAF
3. Virtual Server–specific variables defined at the <virtual-server> level
4. Server variables defined at the <server> level

Web Server variables begin with a dollar sign character ($), followed by either upper- or lowercase letters as the next character. Subsequent characters can include any combination of upper- or lowercase alphanumeric characters or underscores (_).

A regular expression notation for variable syntax would be as follows:

```
\$[A-Za-z][A-Za-z0-9_]*
```

Examples of valid variable names include $variable, $Variable, $var_iable, or $var9. Examples of invalid variable names include $_variable and $9variable.

5.3.3 Context

The `server.xml` file contains definitions for each virtual server contained within the instance, so there is a one-to-many relationship between the `server.xml` file and virtual servers.

Each virtual server can use a different object configuration file for processing requests. Therefore, there is a one-to-many relationship between an instance and the object configuration file(s), but there is a one-to-one relationship between the virtual server and its object configuration file.

5.3.4 Modifications

Some changes made through the Administration Console or the command line interface update the appropriate object configuration file. If this file is updated as a result of changes made through either of these two interfaces, you must deploy the updated configuration before the changes are reflected on the appropriate Administration Node(s).

The object configuration file is read when the instance is started or when a dynamic reconfiguration is performed. The syntax for the directives and parameters contained in the object configuration file is validated within the start-up or reconfiguration code base. They are not validated against a schema such as the `server.xml` file.

Errors found within the file may prevent the instance from starting or processing requests properly.

5.4 The `mime.types` File

The Multipurpose Internet Mail Extensions (MIME) types file contains mappings between file extensions and MIME types. This file is utilized during request processing to tell the server what type of resource is being requested. It bases this information on the extension of the resource (such as `.txt`, `.html`, or `.cgi`) and associates a type, language, or encoding method based on the extension.

An initial MIME types file is created for each Web Server configuration; the name of the file is simply `mime.types`. You may create additional MIME types files and associate them to different virtual servers by using the `<mime-file>` element in the server.xml. Example 5.5 demonstrates the use of the `<mime-file>` element in the server.xml file.

Example 5.5   Virtual Server Definition for the MIME File

```
<virtual-server>
  <name>www.example.com</name>
  <http-listener-name>http-listener-1</http-listener-name>
  <host>www.example.com</host>
  <object-file>www.example.com-obj.conf</object-file>
  <mime-file>mymime.types</mime-file>
  <document-root>/export/home/example.com/public_html</document-root>
  <access-log>
    <file>/export/home/example.com/logs/access</file>
  </access-log>
</virtual-server>
```

Associating different MIME files to each virtual server gives you the flexibility to support different resources at the virtual server level.

5.4.1 File Structure

The mime.types file contains a series of associations that helps the instance identity the request type and subsequently understand how to process the request. Example 5.6 demonstrates the MIME types file for the default Administration Node.

Example 5.6   Sample mime.types File

```
#--Sun Microsystems Inc. MIME Information
# Do not delete the above line. It is used to identify the file type.
#
# Copyright 2006 Sun Microsystems, Inc.  All rights reserved.
# Use is subject to license terms.
#

type=application/octet-stream           exts=bin
type=application/astound                exts=asd,asn
type=application/fastman                exts=lcc
type=application/java-archive           exts=jar
type=application/java-serialized-object exts=ser
type=application/java-vm                exts=class
type=application/mac-binhex40           exts=hqx
type=application/x-stuffit              exts=sit
type=application/mbedlet                exts=mbd
```

```
type=application/msword                      exts=doc,dot,wiz,rtf
type=application/oda                         exts=oda
type=application/pdf                         exts=pdf
type=application/postscript                  exts=ai,eps,ps
type=application/studiom                     exts=smp
type=application/timbuktu                    exts=tbt
type=application/vnd.ms-excel                exts=xls,xlw,xla,
                                             xlc,xlm,xlt

type=application/vnd.ms-powerpoint           exts=ppt,pps,pot

[entries deleted]

enc=x-gzip                                   exts=gz
enc=x-compress                               exts=z
enc=x-uuencode                               exts=uu,uue

type=magnus-internal/parsed-html             exts=shtml
type=magnus-internal/cgi                     exts=cgi,exe,bat

type=application/x-x509-ca-cert              exts=cacert
type=application/x-x509-server-cert          exts=scert
type=application/x-x509-user-cert            exts=ucert
type=application/x-x509-email-cert           exts=ecert

type=application/vnd.sun.xml.writer          exts=sxw
type=application/vnd.sun.xml.writer.template exts=stw
type=application/vnd.sun.xml.calc            exts=sxc
type=application/vnd.sun.xml.calc.template   exts=stc
type=application/vnd.sun.xml.draw            exts=sxd
type=application/vnd.sun.xml.draw.template   exts=std
type=application/vnd.sun.xml.impress         exts=sxi
type=application/vnd.sun.xml.impress.template exts=sti
type=application/vnd.sun.xml.writer.global   exts=sxg
type=application/vnd.sun.xml.math            exts=sxm

type=application/vnd.stardivision.writer         exts=sdw
type=application/vnd.stardivision.writer-global  exts=sgl
type=application/vnd.stardivision.calc           exts=sdc
type=application/vnd.stardivision.draw           exts=sda
type=application/vnd.stardivision.impress        exts=sdd
type=application/vnd.stardivision.impress-packed exts=sdp
type=application/vnd.stardivision.math           exts=smf,sdf
type=application/vnd.stardivision.chart          exts=sds
type=application/vnd.stardivision.mail           exts=sdm
```

5.4.2 File Structure

The format is similar to the format of request/response information that is exchanged between a web browser and the Web Server to which it connects. This related format is specified as part of the Hypertext Transfer Protocol (HTTP) and has the following rules:

The first line in the MIME types file identifies the file format:

```
#--Sun Microsystems MIME Information
```

Other uncommented lines have the following format:

```
type=type/subtype exts=[file extensions]
```

where `type/subtype` refers to the MIME type and `subtype` and `exts` refers to the file extensions associated with this type. For example, the MIME types file uses the following mapping to associate the extensions `.html` and `.htm` to the type `text/html`:

```
type=text/html exts=htm,html
```

Note: For the definitive information on HTTP, you should consult RFC 2616, "Hypertext Transfer Protocol—HTTP/1.1."

5.4.3 Processing

The MIME types configuration file determines how your Web Server's virtual server maps filename extensions to MIME types that are returned to the browser. Your browser then maps these MIME types to "helper" applications or in-line plug-ins.

The following subsections describe how MIME mappings are used on both the Web Server and the user agent during request/response processing.

5.4.3.1 Server Processing

When the Web Server receives a request for a resource from a client, it uses the MIME type mappings to determine what kind of resource is being requested.

During the `ObjectType` stage in the request handling process, the server determines the MIME type attribute of the resource requested by the client. Several different SAFs can be used to determine the MIME type, but the most commonly used one is `type-by-extension`. This function tells the server to look up the MIME type according to the requested resource's file extension in the MIME types table (stored in the MIME types file).

MIME types are defined by three attributes: language (`lang`), encoding (`enc`), and content-type (`type`). At least one of these attributes must be present for each type. The most commonly used attribute is `type`. When the server sends the response to the client, the type, language, and encoding values are transmitted in the `Content-Type` headers of the response.

Note: The server frequently considers the `type` attribute when deciding how to generate the response to the client in the Service directive stage. (The `enc` and `lang` attributes are rarely used.)

If there is more than one `ObjectType` directive, the server applies all the directives in the order in which they appear. However, after a directive sets an attribute of the MIME type, encoding, or language, further attempts to set the same attribute are ignored.

Figure 5.1 demonstrates a client making a request for a particular file and how the server uses the `mime.types` file to determine how to process that request.

The following steps indicate a high-level overview of how the server processes this request:

1. A client makes a URL request of http://www.example.com/index.html.
2. The server accepts the request and selects the appropriate virtual server (not shown).
3. The server determines the name of the object configuration file, based on the virtual server's `object-file` settings (not shown). This instructs the server on how to process the request (not shown).
4. The server executes the request-response process, as dictated by the object configuration file.

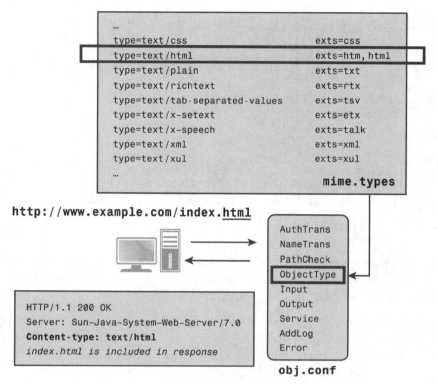

Figure 5.1 MIME File Usage During Request Processing

5. At the point when the server reaches the `ObjectType` stage, it reads the MIME types file and searches for an extension that matches the file requested (in this case it is an HTML file).

6. The server finds a match and sets the type to `text/html`.

7. The server selects the appropriate service to process the request (not shown).

8. The server sends the response to the client with the appropriate `Content-type` set in the response header.

5.4.3.2 Client Processing

The SAF defined for the appropriate service stage generates the data and sends it back to the client that made the request. When the server sends the data to the client, it also sends headers. These headers include the MIME type attributes that are known (which are usually defined by type attributes).

The client maintains its own MIME types table, as shown in Figure 5.2.

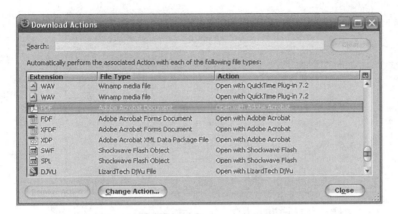

Figure 5.2   Client MIME Definitions

When the client receives the header, it uses the information contained in its own MIME types table to determine what to do with the data. For browser clients, the usual action is to display the data in the browser window.

Sometimes the requested resource cannot be displayed in the browser window and needs to be handled by another application. In such cases, the Content-type sent back by the server typically starts with application/; for example, application/x-pdf (for .pdf file extensions) or application/x-maker (for .fm file extensions).

The client has its own set of user-editable mappings that tells the browser which application to use for certain data types. For example, if the type is application/x-pdf, the client usually handles it by opening the Adobe Acrobat Reader application to display the file.

5.4.4 Context

The server.xml file contains definitions for each virtual server contained within the instance, so there is a one-to-many relationship between the server.xml file and virtual servers.

Each virtual server can use a different MIME types file for mapping associations. Therefore, there is a one-to-many relationship between an instance and the MIME types file(s), but there is a one-to-one relationship between the virtual server and its MIME types file.

5.4.5 Modifications

Although the default MIME types file includes a definition of the most commonly known MIME types, you are free to modify the file to add support for any additional MIME types. To add a new MIME type definition, simply append the definition to the existing MIME types in the file in the following format (where type/subtype is the MIME type of the document whose filename ends with one of the extensions listed):

```
type=type/subtype exts=extension1,extension2,...,extensionN
```

The extension list includes any number of comma-separated filename extensions. Examples of MIME type entries can be found in the default MIME types file included with your virtual server.

You can also use the Administration Console or the command line interface to update the MIME types file for the virtual server. After the file is updated, you must deploy the updated configuration before the changes are reflected on the appropriate Administration Node(s).

The MIME types file is read when the instance is started or when a dynamic reconfiguration is performed. The syntax contained in the MIME types file is validated within the start-up or reconfiguration code base. Errors found within the MIME types file or within the server.xml file (as it pertains to the <mime-file> attribute) may prevent the instance from starting.

5.5 Trust Database Files (*. db Files)

The Web Server stores security-based information in three Network Security Services (NSS) libdbm database files as follows:

- cert8.db—Stores publicly accessible objects (such as certificates, certificate revocation lists, and S/MIME records)
- key3.db—Stores the private keys generated by the server
- secmod.db—Stores PKCS #11 module configuration information

The combination of these files is commonly called the *trust database*, and each file plays a different role in securing your Web Server.

For example, the cert8.db and key3.db files are used to store public and private keys and certificates used for enabling secure socket layer (SSL). The secmod.db file stores information for enabling and configuring additional security modules that can be used with the Web Server (such as hardware accelerator cards). See Chapter 8, "Securing Web Server 7.0," for more information about how these files are used to provide security for your Web Server.

Note: NSS is a set of libraries designed to support cross-platform development of security-enabled client and server applications. Applications built with NSS can support SSL v2 and v3, TLS, PKCS #5, PKCS #7, PKCS #11, PKCS #12, S/MIME, X.509 v3 certificates, and other security standards. For more information on NSS, go to https://www.mozilla.org/projects/security/pki/nss/.

5.5.1 File Structure

Trust database files are formatted in a Berkeley DB 1.85 hash format so they are not viewable or editable with a standard text editor. You can, however, use a hex editor or the UNIX `strings` command to obtain an insight into the contents of these files. Example 5.7 provides a sample of the `cert8.db` file.

Example 5.7   Snippet of Hex Output from the `cert8.db` File

```
. . . . .
0000bc10   00 00 08 03 00 00 01 00 15 00 00 63 65 72 74 2d   . . . . . . . . . . cert-
0000bc20   66 6f 6f 2e 65 78 61 6d 70 6c 65 2e 63 6f 6d 00   foo.example.com.
0000bc30   00 6f 00 00 00 87 1b db 31 30 68 31 0b 30 09 06   .o...‡.Û10h1.0..
0000bc40   03 55 04 06 13 02 55 53 31 0b 30 09 06 03 55 04   .U....US1.0...U.
0000bc50   08 13 02 46 4c 31 0e 30 0c 06 03 55 04 07 13 05   ...FL1.0...U....
0000bc60   54 61 6d 70 61 31 0d 30 0b 06 03 55 04 0a 13 04   Tampa1.0...U....
0000bc70   54 65 73 74 31 13 30 11 06 03 55 04 0b 13 0a 57   Test1.0...U....W
0000bc80   65 62 20 53 65 72 76 65 72 31 18 30 16 06 03 55   eb Server1.0...U
0000bc90   04 03 13 0f 66 6f 6f 2e 65 78 61 6d 70 6c 65 2e   ....foo.example.
0000bca0   63 6f 6d 03 30 68 31 0b 30 09 06 03 55 04 06 13   com.0h1.0...U...
0000bcb0   02 55 53 31 0b 30 09 06 03 55 04 08 13 02 46 4c   .US1.0...U....FL
0000bcc0   31 0e 30 0c 06 03 55 04 07 13 05 54 61 6d 70 61   1.0...U....Tampa
0000bcd0   31 0d 30 0b 06 03 55 04 0a 13 04 54 65 73 74 31   1.0...U....Test1
0000bce0   13 30 11 06 03 55 04 0b 13 0a 57 65 62 20 53 65   .0...U....Web Se
0000bcf0   72 76 65 72 31 18 30 16 06 03 55 04 03 13 0f 66   rver1.0...U....f
0000bd00   6f 6f 2e 65 78 61 6d 70 6c 65 2e 63 6f 6d 08 01   
oo.example.com..
. . . . .
```

If you look closely at the text portion of the file (the far right column), you can see certain data elements that can be found within the details of the certificate shown in Table 5.3.

Table 5.3   Sample Certificate

Attribute	Value
Nickname	`cert-foo.example.com`
Subject	`CN=foo.example.com,OU=Web Server,O=Test,L=Tampa,` `ST=FL,C=US`
Issuer	`Self Signed`
Key Type	`RSA`
Key Size (bits)	`1024`
Valid From	`August 29, 2007 7:21:30 PM EDT`
Valid Till	`August 29, 2008 7:21:30 PM EDT`
Finger Print	`0B:DE:C8:80:17:38:EC:C6:6F:98:5A:5C:8F:3A:54:76`
Serial Number	`00:87:1B:DB:31`

5.5.2 Context

Each server instance has its own trust database; therefore, there is a one-to-one correspondence between the server instance and the trust database.

5.5.3 Modifications

You cannot edit files within the trust database directly. These files must be managed with the Administration Console or the command line interface. If any of these files are updated through either of these two interfaces, you must deploy the updated configuration before the changes are reflected on the appropriate Administration Node(s).

5.6 The `server.policy` File

Web Server 7 is a Java EE 1.4–compliant web server. As such, it follows the recommendations and requirements of the Java EE specification, including the optional presence of the Security Manager, which is the Java component that enforces policy, and a limited permission set for Java EE application code.

Each Web Server instance has its own standard Java Platform, Standard Edition (Java SE platform) server policy file named `server.policy`. The server policy file controls the access that applications have to the resources such as files on the file system.

5.6.1 Syntax

Directives in the server policy file grant explicit permission to access a particular resource. Without this permission, they are implicitly denied access. Server policy directives adhere to the following syntax:

```
grant [codeBase "path"] {
permission permission_class "package", "permission_type";
...
};
```

For example, the following directive grants web applications explicit permission to access shared system library files:

```
grant codeBase "file:/usr/share/lib/-" {
    permission java.security.AllPermission;
};
```

 Note: Refer to the *Sun Java System Web Server 7.0 Developer's Guide to Java Web Applications* for more information on how to modify the server policy file for your web application.

5.6.2 Context

Each server instance has its own server policy file; therefore, there is a one-to-one correspondence between the server instance and the server policy file.

5.6.3 Modifications

In Web Server 7, the Java SE SecurityManager (the Java component that enforces the policy) is not active by default. The policies granted in the server policy file do not have any effect unless the SecurityManager is enabled in the server.xml. You can enable the Java SE SecurityManager by adding the following Java Virtual Machine (JVM) options to the server.xml file:

```
<jvm>
    <jvm-options>-Djava.security.manager</jvm-options>
    <jvm-options>-Djava.security.policy=instance_dir/config/
      server.policy
    </jvm-options>
</jvm>
```

You can also add JVM options by using the Administration Console or the command line interface. After this has been performed, you must deploy the updated configuration before the changes are reflected on the appropriate Administration Node(s).

The Administration Console and command line interface do not provide a method for managing the server policy file. As such, directives must be added to the server.policy file directly on a particular Administration Node. After this has been performed, the modifications must be pulled back into the configuration and then pushed out to additional Administration Nodes as appropriate.

5.7 The `certmap.conf` File

Web Server 7 can be configured to allow client authentication through the use of an X.509 digital certificate. This can be performed under the SSL settings for a particular HTTP listener.

When a server receives a request from a client, it can ask for the client's certificate before proceeding. A client is programmed to respond by sending a client certificate to the server.

After checking that a client certificate chain ends with a trusted Certificate Authority (CA), the Web Server can optionally determine which user is identified by the client certificate and then look up that user's entry in a directory server. The Web Server authenticates the user by comparing the information in the certificate with the data in the user's directory entry.

To locate user entries in the directory, a server must know how to interpret certificates from different CAs. You provide the server with interpretation information by means of the certificate mapping configuration file (`certmap.conf`). This file provides three kinds of information for each listed CA:

- It maps the distinguished name (DN) in the certificate to a branch point in the LDAP directory.
- It specifies which DN values from the certificate (username, e-mail address, and so on) the server should use for the purpose of searching the directory.
- It specifies whether the server should go through an additional verification process. This process involves comparing the certificate presented by the client for authentication with the certificate stored in the user's directory entry. By comparing the certificate, the server determines whether to allow access or whether to revoke a certificate by removing it from the user's directory entry.

If more than one directory entry contains the information in the user's certificate, the server can examine all matching entries to determine which user is trying to authenticate. When examining a directory entry, the server compares the presented certificate with the certificate stored in the entry. If the presented certificate doesn't match any directory entries or if matching entries don't contain matching certificates, client authentication fails.

After the server finds a matching entry and certificate in the directory, it can determine the appropriate kind of authorization for the client. For example, some servers use information from a user's entry to determine group membership, which in turn can be used during evaluation of access control instruction ACIs to determine what resources the user is authorized to access.

Note: See Chapter 8 for more information about access control instructions.

5.7.1 File Structure

The `certmap.conf` file contains information on how a client certificate is mapped to a directory server entry. Example 5.8 demonstrates the certificate mapping configuration file for the default Administration Node.

Example 5.8   Default `certmap.conf` File

```
#
# Copyright 2006 Sun Microsystems, Inc.  All rights reserved.
# Use is subject to license terms.
#


#
# This file configures how a certificate is mapped to an LDAP entry.
# See the documentation for more information on this file.
#
# The format of this file is as follows:
#    certmap <name> <issuerDN>
#    <name>:<prop1> [<val1>]
#    <name>:<prop2> [<val2>]
#
# Notes:
#
# 1.  Mapping can be defined per issuer of a certificate.  If mapping
#     doesn't exists for a particular 'issuerDN' then the server uses
#     the default mapping.
#
# 2.  There must be an entry for <name>=default and issuerDN "default".
#     This mapping is the default mapping.
#
# 3.  '#' can be used to comment out a line.
#
# 4.  DNComps & FilterComps are used to form the base DN and filter
#     resp. for performing an LDAP search while mapping the cert to a
#     user entry.
#
# 5.  DNComps can be one of the following:
#    commented out - take the user's DN from the cert as is
#    empty        - search the entire LDAP tree (DN == suffix)
#    attr names   - a comma separated list of attributes to form DN
#
```

```
# 6.  FilterComps can be one of the following:
#    commented out - set the filter to "objectclass=*"
#    empty         - set the filter to "objectclass=*"
#    attr names    - a comma separated list of attributes to form the
#                     filter
#

certmap default        default
#default:DNComps
#default:FilterComps    e, uid
#default:verifycert     on
#default:CmapLdapAttr   certSubjectDN
#default:library        <path_to_shared_lib_or_dll>
#default:InitFn         <Init function's name>
```

5.7.2 Syntax

The file contains one or more named mappings, each applying to a different certificate authority (CA).

Hash symbols (#) at the beginning of a line indicate that the line is a comment. These are ignored by Web Server. Additional lines have the following syntax:

```
certmap <name> <issuerDN>
<name>:<property> [<value>]
```

The first line uses the name parameter to specify a name for the certificate mapping. It uses the issuerDN parameter to specify the attributes that form the distinguished name found in the CA certificate.

The name attribute is arbitrary; you can call it whatever you want it to be. The issuerDN attribute, however, must exactly match the distinguished name of the CA who issued the client certificate. For example, the following two issuerDN lines differ only in the spaces separating the attributes, but the server treats these two entries as different:

```
certmap name ou=Example CA,o=Example,c=US
certmap name ou=Example CA, o=Example, c=US
```

The second and subsequent lines of a mapping identify the rules that the server should use when searching the directory for information extracted from a certificate:

```
certmap name issuerDN
name:property1 [value1]
name:property2 [value2]
...
```

These rules are specified through the use of one or more of the following properties: DNComps, FilterComps, VerifyCert, CmapLdapAttr, Library, and InitFn. Additionally, you could use the certificate API to customize your own properties.

Table 5.4 describes each of the properties contained in the certificate mapping configuration file.

Table 5.4 certmap.conf Properties

Property	Description
DNComps	A list of comma-separated attributes used to determine where in the LDAP directory the server should start searching for entries that match the user's information (that is, the owner of the client certificate). The server gathers values for these attributes from the client certificate and uses the values to form an LDAP DN, which then determines where the server starts its search in the LDAP directory. For example, if you set DNComps to use the organization (o) and country attributes of the DN, the server starts the search from the o=*<organization>*, c=*<country>* entry in the LDAP directory, where *<organization>* and *<country>* are replaced with values from the DN in the certificate. Note the following situations: • If there isn't a DNComps entry in the mapping, the server uses either the CmapLdapAttr setting or the entire subject DN in the client certificate. • If the DNComps entry is present but has no value, the server searches the entire LDAP tree for entries matching the filter.

Table 5.4 `certmap.conf` Properties   *continued*

Property	Description
FilterComps	A list of comma-separated attributes used to create a filter by gathering information from the user's DN in the client certificate. The server uses the values for these attributes to form the search criteria used to match entries in the LDAP directory. If the server finds one or more entries in the LDAP directory that match the user's information gathered from the certificate, the search is successful and the server optionally performs a verification.
	For example, if `FilterComps` is set to use the e-mail and user ID attributes (`FilterComps=e,uid`), the server searches the directory for an entry whose values for e-mail and user ID match the end user's information gathered from the client certificate. E-mail addresses and user IDs are good filters because they are usually unique entries in the directory. The filter needs to be specific enough to match only one entry in the LDAP database.
	The following provides a list of valid X.509v3 certificate attributes:
	• `c`—Country
	• `o`—Organization
	• `cn`—Common name
	• `l`—Location
	• `st`—State
	• `ou`—Organizational unit
	• `uid`—User ID
	• `e` or `mail`—E-mail address
	Note that the attribute names for the filters must be attribute names from the certificate, not from the LDAP directory. For example, some certificates have an `e` attribute for the user's e-mail address; whereas LDAP calls that attribute `mail`.
verifycert	Tells the server whether it should compare the client's certificate with the certificate found in the LDAP directory. It takes two values, `on` and `off`. You should use this property only if your LDAP directory contains certificates. This feature is useful to ensure your end users have a valid, unrevoked certificate.
CmapLdapAttr	A name for the attribute in the LDAP directory that contains subject DNs from all certificates belonging to the user. The default for this property is `certSubjectDN`. This attribute isn't a standard LDAP attribute, so to use this property, you must extend the LDAP schema. Additionally, the search takes place more quickly if the attribute specified by `CmapLdapAttr` is indexed.
	If this property exists in the `certmap.conf` file, the server searches the entire LDAP directory for an entry whose attribute (named with this property) matches the subject's full DN (taken from the certificate). If the search doesn't find any entries, the server retries the search, using the `DNComps` and `FilterComps` mappings. This approach to matching a certificate to an LDAP entry is useful when it's difficult to match entries using `DNComps` and `FilterComps`.
Library	A property whose value is a pathname to a shared library or DLL. You need to use this property only if you create your own properties using the certificate API. For more information, see the *Sun Java System Web Server 7.0 Developer's Guide*.
InitFn	A property whose value is the name of an initialization (`init`) function from a custom library. You need to use this property only if you create your own properties by using the certificate API.

If you are using the `Library` and `InitFn` properties, a complete mapping might look like this:

```
certmap Example CA           ou=Example CA, o=Example, c=US
Example CA:CmapLdapAttr      certSubjectDN
Example CA:DNComps           o, c
Example CA:FilterComps       e, uid
Example CA:VerifyCert        on
```

In this example, the name of the certificate mapping is Example CA, and it is mapped to the issuer's distinguished name of `ou=Example CA, o=Example, c=US`.

> **Note:** Note how the remaining lines of the mapping's properties begin with the name of the certificate mapping (Example CA). This is how the Web Server knows that the properties apply to this mapping.

The `CmapLdapAttr` property tells the server to search the entire directory for an entry whose `certSubjectDN` matches the subject's full DN as listed in the client certificate. If the search doesn't yield any entries, the server retries the search, using the `DNComps` and `FilterComps` mappings.

The `DNComps` property indicates that the base distinguished name (`baseDN`) of the search should be created from the organization and country attributes that are extracted from the client certificate.

The `FilterComps` property indicates that the Web Server should search for entries that match the e-mail and user ID attributes extracted from the client certificate.

The `VerifyCert` property tells the server whether it should compare the client's certificate with the certificate found in the user's directory entry. A value of `on` ensures that the server does not authenticate the client unless the certificate presented exactly matches the certificate stored in the directory.

5.7.3 Context

Each server instance has its own certificate mapping configuration file; therefore, there is a one-to-one correspondence between the server instance and this file.

5.7.4 Modifications

The Administration Console and command line interface do not provide a method for managing the certificate mapping configuration file. As such, entries must be added to the `certmap.conf` file directly on a particular Administration Node. After this has been performed, the modifications must be pulled back into the configuration and then pushed out to additional Administration Nodes as appropriate.

5.8 The `default.acl` File

You can control access to the entire Web Server or to parts of the server (for example, directories, files, and file types). When the Web Server evaluates an incoming request, it determines access based on a hierarchy of rules called access control entries (ACEs). The Web Server uses the matching entries to determine whether the client request is allowed or denied.

The collection of ACEs is called an access control list (ACL). The Web Server processes the ACL list from top to bottom. If at any time an ACE evaluates to a value of `false`, then processing of the ACL stops and the user is denied access to the resource.

ACL files contain rules that define who can access resources stored on the Web Server. By default, the Web Server uses one ACL file (`default.acl`) that contains the default access list. You can change access control rules by editing this file or by creating additional ACL files for one or more instances. If you create additional ACL files, you can associate them to different virtual servers by using the `<acl-file>` element in the `server.xml`.

Example 5.9 demonstrates the use of the `<acl-file>` element to specify an additional ACL file for a particular virtual server:

Example 5.9   Virtual Server Definition for an ACL File

```
<virtual-server>
  <name>www.example.com</name>
  <http-listener-name>http-listener-1</http-listener-name>
  <host>www.example.com</host>
  <object-file>www.example.com-obj.conf</object-file>
  <mime-file>mime.types</mime-file>
  <acl-file>example.acl</acl-file>
```

```
<document-root>/export/home/example.com/public_html</document-root>
<access-log>
<file>/export/home/example.com/logs/access</file>
</access-log>
</virtual-server>
```

Associating different ACL files to each virtual server provides you with the flexibility to provide different access control at the virtual server level.

5.8.1 File Structure

The ACL file is a text file containing one or more ACLs. Example 5.10 demonstrates the access control list file for the default Administration Node.

Example 5.10   Default `default.acl` File

```
#--Sun Microsystems Inc. MIME Information
# Do not delete the above line. It is used to identify the file type.
#
# Copyright 2006 Sun Microsystems, Inc.  All rights reserved.
# Use is subject to license terms.
#
#
# Copyright 2006 Sun Microsystems, Inc.  All rights reserved.
# Use is subject to license terms.
#

version 3.0;
acl "default";
authenticate (user, group) {
  prompt = "Sun Java System Web Server";
};
allow (read, execute, info) user = "anyone";
allow (list, write, delete) user = "all";

acl "es-internal";
allow (read, execute, info) user = "anyone";
deny (list, write, delete) user = "anyone";
```

These access control rules allow anyone to read resources on the server but restrict listing, writing, and deleting resources to authenticated users.

5.8.2 Syntax

All ACL files must follow a specific format and syntax. All ACL files must begin with the version number they use. There can be only one version line and it can appear after any comment line. Web Server 7 uses version 3.0. For example:

```
version 3.0;
```

You can include comments in the file by beginning the comment line with the hash (#) character.

Each ACL in the file begins with a statement that defines its type. ACLs can follow one of the following three types:

- Path ACLs specify an absolute path to the resource they affect.
- URI ACLs specify a directory or file relative to the server's document root.
- Named ACLs specify a name that is referenced in the obj.conf file. Web Server 7 comes with a default named resource that allows read access to all users and write access to users in the LDAP directory. Even though you can create a named ACL from the Web Server user interface, you must manually reference the named ACLs with resources in the obj.conf file.

Path and URI ACLs can include a wildcard at the end of the entry, for example, /a/b/*. Wildcards placed anywhere except at the end of the entry do not work.

The type line begins with the letters acl and includes the type information in double quotation marks followed by a semicolon. Each type information for all ACLs must be a unique name, even among different ACL files. The following lines are examples of several different types of ACLs:

```
acl "default";
...
acl "path=C:/docs/mydocs/";
...
acl "uri=/mydocs/";
...
```

After you define the type of ACL, you can have one or more statements that define the method used with the ACL (authentication statements) and the users and computers who are allowed or denied access (authorization statements). The following sections describe the syntax for these statements.

5.8.2.1 General Syntax

Input strings can contain the following characters:

- Alphanumeric characters a through z or 0 through 9
- A period (.) or underscore (_) character

If you use any other characters, add double quotation marks around them. A single statement can be placed on its own line and terminated with a semicolon. Multiple statements are placed within braces. A list of items must be separated by commas and enclosed in double quotation marks.

5.8.2.2 Authentication Methods

ACLs can optionally specify the authentication method that the server must use when processing the ACL. There are three methods:

- `basic`
- `digest`
- `ssl`

The `basic` and `digest` methods both require users to enter a username and password before accessing a resource. The two differ, however, in the manner in which data is transmitted between the client and the Web Server and how the password is verified within the authentication database.

The `basic` authentication method enables users to enter a username and password and transmits the information to the Web Server in known Base 64-Encoded text. For security reasons, `basic` authentication is almost always used with SSL connections so that the username and password are encrypted before being sent from the client.

The `digest` authentication method prevents the client's username and password from being sent in known text. The browser uses the MD5 algorithm to create a message digest using the password and information sent by Web Server. The digest value is computed and compared on the server side using the Digest Authentication plug-in.

The `ssl` method requires the user to have a client certificate. The Web Server must have the encryption turned on, and the user's certificate issuer must be in the list of trusted certificate authorities (CAs) to be authenticated. See Section 5.7, "The `certmap.conf` File," for more information on using client certificates for authentication.

By default, the server uses the basic method for any ACL that does not explicitly specify a method. If you use the digest method, the server's authentication database must be able to handle digest authentication. Authentication databases are configured in server.xml with the <auth-db> element. See Chapter 8 for more information on configuring authentication databases.

Each authenticated line must specify the attribute (users, groups, or both users and groups) that the server authenticates. The following authentication statement, which appears after the ACL type line, specifies basic authentication with users matched to individual users in the database or directory:

```
authenticate (user) { method = "basic"; };
```

The following example uses ssl as the authentication method for users and groups:

```
authenticate (user, group) { method = "ssl"; };
```

The following example allows any user whose username begins with sales:

```
authenticate (user)
allow (all)
user = sales*
```

If the last line is changed to group = sales, the ACL will fail because the group attribute is not authenticated.

5.8.2.3 Authorization Statements

Each ACL entry can include one or more authorization statements. Authorization statements specify who is allowed or denied access to a server resource. Use the following syntax to write authorization statements:

```
allow|deny [absolute] (right[,right...]) attribute expression;
```

Start each line with either allow or deny. Because of the hierarchy rules, it is usually a good practice to deny access to everyone in the first rule and then specifically allow access for users, groups, or computers in subsequent rules. That is, if you allow anyone access to a directory called /my_stuff, and you have a subdirectory /my_stuff/personal that allows access to a few users, the access control on the subdirectory does not work because anyone allowed access to the /my_stuff directory is also allowed access to the /my_stuff/personal directory. To prevent this, create a rule for the subdirectory that first denies access to anyone and then allows it for the few users who need access.

In some cases, if you set the default ACL to deny access to everyone, your other ACL rules do not need a `deny all` rule.

The following line denies access to everyone:

```
deny (all) user = "anyone";
```

5.8.2.4 Hierarchy of Authorization Statements

ACLs have a hierarchy that depends on the resource. For example, if the server receives a request for the document (URI) `/my_stuff/web/presentation.html`, the server builds a list of ACLs that apply for this URI. The server first adds ACLs listed in the `check-acl` statement of its `obj.conf` file. Then the server appends matching URI and PATH ACLs.

The server processes this list in the same order. Unless absolute ACL statements are present, all statements are evaluated in order. If an `absolute allow` or `absolute deny` statement evaluates to `true`, the server stops processing and accepts this result.

If more than one ACL matches, the server uses the last statement that matches. However, if you use an absolute statement, the server stops looking for other matches and uses the ACL containing the absolute statement. If you have two absolute statements for the same resource, the server uses the first one in the file and stops looking for other resources that match.

Example 5.11 demonstrates how an ACL might be written to allow `user1` access to the content found at `/my_stuff/web/presentation.html`.

Example 5.11 Sample ACL Entries to Protect Web Server Content

```
version 3.0;
acl "default";
authenticate (user, group) {
prompt = "Sun Java System Web Server";
};
allow (read, execute, info) user = "anyone";
allow (list, write, delete) user = "all";
acl "uri=/my_stuff/web/presentation.html";
deny (all) user = "anyone";
allow (all) user = "user1";
```

5.8.2.5 Expression Attribute

Attribute expressions define *who* is allowed or denied access based on username, group name, hostname, or IP address. The following are examples of allowing access to different users or computers:

- user = "anyone"
- user = "smith*"
- group = "sales"
- dns = "*.sun.com"
- dns = "*.sun.com,*.mozilla.com"
- ip = "198.*"
- ciphers = "rc4"
- ssl = "on"

You can also restrict access to your server by time of day (based on the local time on the server) by using the timeofday attribute. For example, you can use the timeofday attribute to restrict access to certain users during specific hours.

Note: Use 24-hour time to specify times. For example, use 0400 to specify 4:00 a.m. or 2230 for 10:30 p.m.

The following example restricts access to a group of users called guests between 8:00 a.m. and 5:00 p.m.:

```
allow (read) (group="guests") and (timeofday<0800 or timeofday=1700);
```

You can also restrict access by day of the week. Use the following three-letter abbreviations to specify days: Sun, Mon, Tue, Wed, Thu, Fri, and Sat.

The following statement allows access for users in the premium group any day and any time. Users in the discount group get access all day on weekends and on weekdays, any time except 8:00 a.m. to 5:00 p.m.

```
allow (read) (group="discount" and dayofweek="Sat,Sun") or
    (group="discount" and (dayofweek="mon,tue,wed,thu,fri"
    and(timeofday<0800 or timeofday=1700)))or (group="premium");
```

5.8.2.6 Expression Operators

You can use various operators in an expression. Parentheses delineate the operator order of precedence. With `user`, `group`, `dns`, and `ip`, you can use the following operators:

- `and`
- `or`
- `not`
- `=` (equals)
- `!=` (not equal to)

With `timeofday` and `dayofweek`, you can use

- `>` (greater than)
- `<` (less than)
- `>=` (greater than or equal to)
- `<=` (less than or equal to)

5.8.3 Context

The `server.xml` file contains definitions for each virtual server contained within the instance, so there is a one-to-many relationship between the `server.xml` file and virtual servers.

Each virtual server can use one or more access control list files for protecting resources specific to that virtual server; therefore, there is a one-to-many relationship between an instance and the access control list file(s). Additionally, there is a one-to-many relationship between the virtual server and its access control list file(s).

5.8.4 Modifications

Administrators can update any of the access control list files through the Administration Console or the command line interface. If this file is updated as a result of changes made through either of these two interfaces, you must deploy the updated configuration before the changes are reflected on the appropriate Administration Node(s).

Access control list files are read when the instance is started or when a dynamic reconfiguration is performed. The syntax for the entries contained in these files is validated within the start-up or reconfiguration code base. They are not validated against a schema like the `server.xml` file is.

Errors found within the file may prevent the instance from starting or processing requests properly.

5.9 The `default-web.xml` File

The `default-web.xml` is a virtual server–specific web deployment descriptor file whose configuration settings are inherited by all web applications deployed on the virtual server. This file configures various servlets (such as the `DefaultServlet` and the `JspServlet`) and specifies the MIME types associated with specific extensions. (For more information about MIME mapping elements, see the Java Servlet specification.)

Individual web applications can override the configuration settings inherited from this file with settings contained in their own deployment descriptor file (`web.xml`).

Note: Deployment descriptor files for individual web applications are processed *after* the `default-web.xml` file is processed. This allows configuration settings in the web application's `WEB-INF/web.xml` file to override those contained in the `default-web.xml` file.

5.9.1 Syntax

The `default-web.xml` file is an XML-formatted file. All entries in this file are validated against the XML data type definition (DTD) for the Servlet 2.3 deployment descriptor as follows:

```
<!DOCTYPE web-app
    PUBLIC "-//Sun Microsystems, Inc.//DTD Web Application 2.3//EN"
    "http://java.sun.com/dtd/web-app_2_3.dtd">
<web-app>
```

5.9.2 Context

Each server instance has its own `default-web.xml` file; therefore, there is a one-to-one correspondence between the server instance and this file.

5.9.3 Modifications

The Administration Console and command line interface do not provide a method for managing the `default-web.xml`. As such, all modifications to this file must be made on a particular Administration Node. After this has been performed, the modifications must be pulled back into the configuration and then pushed out to additional Administration Nodes as appropriate.

5.10 The `login.conf` File

The Java Authentication and Authorization Service (JAAS) is a set of APIs that enable services to authenticate and enforce access controls upon users. It implements a Java technology version of the standard Pluggable Authentication Module (PAM) framework, and supports user-based authorization.

The JAAS can be used for two purposes:

- For authentication of users, to reliably and securely determine who is currently executing Java code, regardless of whether the code is running as an application, an applet, a bean, or a servlet.
- For authorization of users to ensure they have the access control rights (permissions) required to do the actions performed.

 Note: See the Java Authentication and Authorization Service page on Sun's web site at http://java.sun.com/products/jaas/ for more information.

The login configuration file (`login.conf`) contains the login module definitions used by the JAAS for client authentication. It is referenced in the JVM settings for a particular server instance, as shown in Example 5.12.

Example 5.12   Reference to Login Configuration File in the server.xml

```
<jvm>
  <java-home>/opt/webserver7/jdk</java-home>
  <server-class-path>...</server-class-path>
  <debug>false</debug>
  <debug-jvm-options>-Xdebug -Xrunjdwp:transport=dt_socket,
    server=y,suspend=n,address=7896</debug-jvm-options>
  <jvm-options>-Djava.security.auth.login.config=login.conf
  </jvm-options>
  <jvm-options>-Djava.util.logging.manager=com.sun.webserver.logging
    .ServerLogManager</jvm-options>
  <jvm-options>-Xms128m -Xmx256m</jvm-options>
</jvm>
```

5.10.1 File Structure

The login configuration file specifies the Java class used for each authentication realm. Example 5.13 demonstrates the `login.conf` file for the default Administration Node.

Example 5.13   Default `login.conf` File

```
/* Copyright 2006 Sun Microsystems, Inc.  All rights reserved.  */
/* Use is subject to license terms.                            */

fileRealm {
    com.iplanet.ias.security.auth.login.FileLoginModule required;
};

ldapRealm {
    com.iplanet.ias.security.auth.login.LDAPLoginModule required;
};

solarisRealm {
    com.iplanet.ias.security.auth.login.SolarisLoginModule required;
};

nativeRealm {
    com.iplanet.ias.security.auth.login.NativeLoginModule required;
};
```

5.10.2 Syntax

The basic format for the login module definitions contained in the login configuration file is as follows:

```
Application {
  ModuleClass  Flag    ModuleOptions;
  ModuleClass  Flag    ModuleOptions;
  ModuleClass  Flag    ModuleOptions;
};
```

Each entry in the login configuration file is indexed by an application name (*Application*). Each application contains a list of login modules configured for that application. Each login module is specified by its fully qualified class name (*ModuleClass*). Authentication proceeds down the module list in the exact order specified. The *Flag* value controls the overall behavior as authentication proceeds down the stack. Flags can be one of the following: Required, Requisite, Sufficient, or Optional.

ModuleOptions is a space-separated list of login module-specific values that are passed directly to the underlying login module. Options are defined by the login module itself and control the behavior within it.

Note: See the javax.security.auth.login class configuration page at http://java.sun.com/j2se/1.4.2/docs/api/javax/security/auth/login/Configuration.html for more information.

5.10.3 Context

Each server instance has its own login configuration file; therefore, there is a one-to-one correspondence between the server instance and this file.

5.10.4 Modifications

The Administration Console and command line interface do not provide a method for managing the login configuration file. As such, all modifications to this file must be made on a particular Administration Node. After this has been performed, the modifications must be pulled back into the configuration and then pushed out to additional Administration Nodes as appropriate.

5.11 The keyfile File

Authentication databases are repositories for maintaining user credentials. These credentials can be used to validate a user before granting access to resources on the Web Server. Common repositories include directory servers, databases, and flat files. Web Server 7 ships with a default file-based repository called keyfile that contains usernames and hashed passwords that can be used for flat file authentication.

The keyfile is empty by default, but entries can easily be added through the Administration Console. Before doing so, however, the server must be configured to use the keyfile as an authentication database.

Authentication databases are configured in server.xml at either the instance level, for a particular virtual server, or both. Example 5.14 demonstrates the settings for defining a keyfile as an authentication database.

Example 5.14   server.xml Authentication Database Definition for keyfile

```
<auth-db>
  <name>keyFile</name>
  <url>file</url>
  <property>
    <name>keyfile</name>
    <value>/opt/webserver7/https-www.example.com/config/keyFile</value>
  </property>
  <property>
    <name>syntax</name>
    <value>keyfile</value>
  </property>
</auth-db>
```

Table 5.5 provides an overview of the elements found in the authentication database definition.

Table 5.5   Authentication Database Properties

Element	Description
<auth-db>	Specifies the beginning and end of an authentication database definition.
<name>	The name of the authentication database. This is used to reference the database within the Web Server and must be unique. This value is arbitrary.
<url>	A value of file indicates that this is a file-based authentication database. Other values for this element might include an appropriate LDAP URL or pam.

Element	Description
`<property>`	Specifies a set of name/value property pairs for this authentication database. The first property listed is called `keyfile`. This indicates that the database is of type `keyfile`. The location of the `keyfile` database can be found at the following: /opt/webserver7/ https-www.example.com/config/keyFile. The next property specifies the file's syntax.

5.11.1 File Structure

The `keyfile` for an Administration Node is empty by default. Each new user creates an entry in the `keyfile`, as demonstrated in Example 5.15.

Example 5.15   Sample keyfile File

```
#
# Copyright 2006 Sun Microsystems, Inc.  All rights reserved.
# Use is subject to license terms.
#

# List of users for simple file realm. Empty by default.
rodale;{SSHA}OFata3ioPWgQhd8wXOUWNMKkL7J2FydGVyAA==;hr
relise;{SSHA}5QkLGJmZJ7Z2YaEobLcw5LEk1qdmVkZGVyAA==;it
wclay;{SSHA}h3y4+I6f75k7+5XH2EClfv6ZIixhZG1pbgAAAA==;qa
```

The Administration Server instance uses a `keyfile` to store its own authentication credentials. Example 5.16 demonstrates the default `keyfile` for the Administration Node:

Example 5.16   Default keyfile File for the Administration Server Instance

```
#
# Copyright 2006 Sun Microsystems, Inc.  All rights reserved.
# Use is subject to license terms.
#

# List of users for simple file realm. Empty by default.
admin;{SSHA}h3y4+I6f75k7+5XH2EClfv6ZIixhZG1pbgAAAA==;wsadmin
```

5.11.2 Syntax

The basic format for the keyfile is

     username; *hashedpassword*; *group*

The maximum length of a line in a file-based authentication database file is 255 characters. If any line exceeds this limit, the server fails to start and an error is logged in the errors log file.

5.11.3 Context

Each server instance has its own keyfile file; therefore, there is a one-to-one correspondence between the server instance and this file.

5.11.4 Modifications

You can configure authentication databases with either the Administration Console or the command line interface. This causes changes to the server.xml file. If this file is updated as a result of changes made through either of these two interfaces, you must deploy the updated configuration before the changes are reflected on the appropriate Administration Node(s).

The addition of users to the keyfile does not require a redeployment of the configuration.

Errors found within the file may prevent the instance from starting.

5.12 Summary

Knowing how to use the Administration Console or CLI tools is not enough to effectively manage your Web Server instances. You should have knowledge of the server's configuration files and how changes made with the Administration Console or CLI tools affect these files. You might never have to directly edit configuration files, but having the knowledge of how to do so will greatly increase your chances of successfully managing your server and debugging problems that arise from misconfigurations.

5.13 Self-Paced Labs

Use the information contained in this chapter to perform the following exercises. These will help validate your understanding of the concepts described in this chapter.

1. View the `server.xml` file for your default server installation. Do this for the files on the node, not beneath the `admin-server` instance.

2. Locate the `cluster` element. What is the name of the host of this instance? (Look for the `local-host` element.)

3. The `instance` element defines a member of the server cluster. What is the host name of the single instance that is part of this server cluster?

4. Locate the `log` element. What is the logging level for this server instance, and where is the log file located on your file system?

5. The `platform` element describes whether the server runs as a 32-bit or 64-bit process. As what platform does this server run?

6. Locate the `user` element (UNIX only). This is the system account the server runs as. As what account will the Web Server process run?

Tip: You can execute a `ps -ef | grep http` command string to verify that the process is running as this user.

7. Locate the `auth-db` element. This element replaces the functionality of `dbswitch.conf` from Web Server 6.1. What is the URL of the ACL authorization database?

8. The `auth-db` element contains `property` elements. All `property` elements must contain the `name` and `value` subelements (for a name/value pair). They can also contain a `description` subelement and for `auth-db` they might contain the encoded `subelement`, indicating that the value is Base 64–encoded. List the name/value pairs for the `property` elements defined in the `auth-db` element.

9. Locate the `acl-file` element. This element contains the name of the file that contains the access control list for this server instance. The value of this element can either be the absolute path to the file on the file system or the name of the file relative to the instance's `config` folder. What is the name of the file that controls access to this instance and where is it located?

10. Locate the `mime-file` element. This element contains the name of the file that contains the MIME types file used for request processing. What is the name of the file that contains the MIME type mappings, and where is it located?

11. Web Server 6.1 listen sockets are referred to as Web Server 7.0 HTTP listeners. You define HTTP listeners by using the `http-listener` element. What subelements are defined for the HTTP listener for this server?

12. Virtual servers are defined with the `virtual-server` element. Many of the elements that have been discussed thus far can be redefined within the body of a `virtual-server` element. This includes the `auth-db`, `acl-file`, and `mime-file` elements. Allowing the virtual server to redefine these elements provides the flexibility of having global settings for the server instance as well as localized settings for particular virtual servers. What subelements are defined for any virtual servers defined for this server?

13. Have these virtual servers redefined any of the global elements (`auth-db`, `acl-file`, or `mime-file`)? If so, which one(s)?

Note: Go to http://www.sunwebserver.com for detailed instructions on how to answer each of these questions.

14. Additional Exercises:

Make a backup of the `server.xml` file for your default server instance. Download a copy of a corrupted `server.xml` file from the http://www.sunwebserver.com web site and place this file in the `config` directory for your default server instance. Update the downloaded `server.xml` file with information specific to your host and domain. Change all occurrences of the string, `yourhost`, with your actual hostname and all occurrences of the string, `yourdomain`, with your actual domain name. Restart the default Web Server instance and resolve all errors found when attempting to start the server. This step is completed when you have addressed all errors and the server successfully starts and serves up data. After you have completed this exercise, restore the backup copy of your `server.xml` file or use the Administration Console to overwrite the configuration on the node (do not pull the configuration from the node or you will overwrite the data in the `config-store`).

6

Web Server 7.0
Request Processing

WHEN a Web Server instance is started, it performs certain initialization tasks as defined in the magnus.conf file and then waits for HTTP requests from clients. When it receives a request, the Web Server determines which virtual server in the server.xml is being accessed and then uses the appropriate object configuration file (obj.conf) to process the request.

Chapter 5, "Web Server 7.0 Configuration Files," discussed the format of the obj.conf file and how it contains default groupings (or *objects*) of directives that call server application functions (SAFs) to process requests. As such, a newly created Web Server 7.0 instance has the capability to process some requests right "out of the box." Other requests, however, require that you perform administrative tasks to enable or create the appropriate objects and directives before the server is able to process these requests.

This chapter explains the various request processing stages that the Web Server goes through on every request, the default behavior of request processing, and how (or why) you might want to change the default behavior. Specifically, this chapter discusses the following topics:

- Request processing stages
- Default request processing behavior
- Conditional processing
- Regular expressions
- Debugging request processing

6.1 Request Processing Stages

The request handling process involves a series of phases (or *stages*) in which a set of related functions have been grouped together to perform tasks within the request handling process. The Web Server has 11 predefined stages that define the entire request handling process from request initiation to server response.

While processing a particular stage, the server may call several functions to perform the work of request processing. There might be zero or more directives within each stage, and processing varies depending on the stage itself. Table 6.1 provides an overview of the request processing stages, along with a brief description as defined from Web Server's perspective. These stages are described in more detail throughout the remainder of this section.

Table 6.1   Web Server 7.0 Request Processing Stages

Stage	Description	From the Web Server's Point of View
AuthTrans	Authorization Translation	Do I know who you are? (Have you authenticated yourself to me?)
NameTrans	Name Translation	What resource are you asking me for?
PathCheck	Path Checking	Does the resource exist and are you allowed to see it?
ObjectType	Object Typing	What type of resource is this?
Input	Prepare to read input	Should I do something with your request before processing it?
Output	Prepare to send output	Should I do something with my response before returning it to you?
Route	Send the request to another server	Do I need to pass this request to a different server?
Service	Generate the response	What service do I need to use to process this request?
AddLog	Add log entries	I need to update my Access Log to keep track of this request.
Error	Service (only on error condition)	Do I need to update the Server Log? Has an error occurred during the processing of this request?

Note: The Init stage has purposely been left out of Table 6.1. The intent of this chapter is to discuss the stages that Web Server goes through for every request. The Init stage is processed only at instance startup. Refer to Chapter 5 for more information on the Init stage and its use in the magnus.conf file.

6.1.1 Authorization Translation (AuthTrans) Stage

The AuthTrans (or Authorization Translation) stage validates any authorization information provided in the HTTP request and translates it into a user and a group. The user and group information can then be used later in request processing to determine whether the user has the appropriate permissions to access the requested resource.

Web Server handles authorization of clients in two stages:

1. **The AuthTrans stage**—Validates authorization information sent by the client in the Authorization HTTP header. This is used to determine the user's identity.

2. **The PathCheck stage**—Determines whether the authorized user is allowed access to the requested resource. The user's permissions (if available) are reviewed before access is granted to a protected resource.

Generally, an AuthTrans function checks whether the username and password associated with the request are acceptable, but it does not allow or deny access to the request—it leaves that to a PathCheck function. When a request arrives, the AuthTrans stage checks whether the Authorization HTTP header exists; if it does, the AuthTrans stage validates the authenticity of the user's credentials.

After the server gets to the PathCheck stage, it then determines whether client access is granted to the resource. If the user is unknown at this point (and the resource is protected), then a PathCheck directive is responsible for sending a status code of 401 (Unauthorized) and request processing is passed to the Error stage, where the status is presented to the client, along with the realm being logged in to (if applicable).

When the client receives the status code, the client's usual response is to display a dialog box asking for the username and password to enter the appropriate realm. When the credentials are entered, the client resubmits the request, but this time it includes the username and password in the Authorization HTTP header.

The server once again processes any AuthTrans directives and attempts to validate the username and password against a defined database.

The following is an example of an AuthTrans directive that contains parameters for authenticating users against a database:

```
AuthTrans fn="basic-auth" userfn="chkauth" auth-type="basic"
    userdb="oracle"
```

This example demonstrates how you can create your own custom function to verify that the username and password provided by a remote client is accurate. This example calls the basic-auth function, which uses a user-defined authentication function (chkauth) to verify the authorization information sent by the client. The function uses a simple username and password (basic authentication) and relies on the database defined by the userdb definition. The Authorization header is sent as part of the basic server authorization scheme.

If there are more than one AuthTrans directives defined for the object, the Web Server processes each directive in sequential order until one succeeds in authorizing the user. As soon as a match occurs, processing within the stage is completed and subsequent AuthTrans directives are ignored. If the server is unable to find a match in any of the AuthTrans directives, then it simply continues to the next stage in request processing with a user's identity that has not been validated.

6.1.2 Name Translation (NameTrans) Stage

Clients use URLs to request resources on a Web Server. In addition to the protocol, host/domain and port, the client request includes a URI that provides the relative name of the resource being requested. Web Servers are services running on an operating system and think in terms of files and directory structures. When a client makes a request, the Web Server must evaluate the URI and then determine what resource the client is actually asking for.

The NameTrans (or Name Translation) stage is the step in the request handling process that translates the requested URI to a Web Server resource. Suppose, for instance, that a client makes a request for the following URL:

```
http://www.example.com/hr/hrdoc.html
```

The /hr/hrdoc.html URI might be associated with a path/file beneath the document root directory, it might be located elsewhere on the server, or it might be on a different server altogether. The client will most likely not care where the content is located, but to the Web Server, this is a very important consideration.

Consider the following NameTrans directive:

```
NameTrans fn="document-root" root="/sun/webserver7/docs"
```

The document-root function prepends the URI with a static, predefined path to create a fully qualified filename on the file system. A Web Server containing this NameTrans directive would automatically look for all content beneath the /sun/ webserver7/docs directory. Therefore a client request containing a URI of /hr/

`hrdoc1.html` would look for the file at the `/sun/webserver7/docs/hr/hrdoc1.html` location.

An example of a `NameTrans` directive that refers to resources outside the document root directory might be

```
NameTrans fn="pfx2dir" from="/hr" dir="/export/home/hruser/docs/"
```

This is a conditional `NameTrans` directive that uses the `pfx2dir` function to look for a particular string found at the beginning of the URI. The string is defined in the `from` parameter and in this case is "`/hr`". If the string is found, then the function prepends the URI with the value contained in the `dir` parameter (`/export/home/hruser/docs/`) and sets the resource's fully qualified pathname to `/export/home/hruser/docs/hr/hrdoc1.html`.

Finally, an example of a `NameTrans` directive that informs the client to look elsewhere for the content might be

```
NameTrans fn="redirect" from="/" url="http://hr.example.com/" sta-
    tus="301"
```

This example uses the `redirect` function to send a redirect status and location URL to the client to indicate that the content has been moved to another server. A status of `301` indicates that the data has been permanently moved to the location specified by the `url` parameter; it is the client's responsibility to follow the redirect and obtain the content from the new location.

Note: Web Server 7 introduces built-in reverse proxy functionality. After it has been determined in the `NameTrans` stage that a URI is requesting a resource on a different origin server, the `Route` directive can be used to instruct the Web Server to obtain that content on behalf of the client. This is an effective alternative to client redirects and is transparent to the client.

It is common to have more than one `NameTrans` directive in the `default` object container because this enables you to specify multiple resource locations based on different URIs. If more than one `NameTrans` directive is defined for the object, the Web Server processes each directive in sequential order until a match is found. After a match occurs, processing within the `NameTrans` stage is completed and subsequent directives are ignored.

Because `NameTrans` directives are processed in sequence, the order is very important. Consider a `default` object with the following `NameTrans` directives:

```
NameTrans fn="redirect" from="/" url="http://hr.example.com/"
   status="301"
NameTrans fn="pfx2dir" from="/hr" dir="/export/home/hruser/docs/"
NameTrans fn="document-root" root="/sun/webserver7/docs"
```

The first two directives are conditional; they match only if the URI defined in the from parameter matches the URI in the client request. The third directive is unconditional and matches only if any of the previous NameTrans directives do not succeed. If you rearrange the order of the directives as follows, the first directive always evaluates to logical TRUE and you will never process the second two directives:

```
NameTrans fn="document-root" root="/sun/webserver7/docs"
NameTrans fn="redirect" from="/" url="http://hr.example.com/"
   status="301"
NameTrans fn="pfx2dir" from="/hr" dir="/export/home/hruser/docs/"
```

Note: A directive that invokes document-root must be the final directive in the NameTrans stage so that it is executed if no other NameTrans directive is applicable. If any other NameTrans directive appears after the one that calls document-root, it is never executed, and the resulting physical directory always ends up under the /sun/webserver7/docs directory.

A NameTrans directive may also contain an optional name parameter. This parameter enables you to customize the request processing flow by defining additional directives that are to be processed should the NameTrans directive evaluate to logical TRUE. Additional information on conditional processing using the name parameter can be found in section 6.3, "Conditional Processing."

6.1.3 Path Check (PathCheck) Stage

After converting the logical URI to a pathname in the NameTrans stage, the server then executes PathCheck (or Path Check) directives to perform various tasks on the resulting path. In general, this includes the following tasks:

- Pathname preprocessing to clean up any malicious directories or save off any extra path information in the URI

- Determination of whether the path is a reference to a web application or a directory on the file system and verification that the resource actually exists

- Access control processing to determine whether the user is allowed access to the requested resource

Note: The Sun Java System Web Server 7.0 Administrator's Configuration File Reference contains a complete list of the tasks performed during the PathCheck stage.

Example 6.1 contains the default PathCheck directives immediately after installation. Line numbers have been added for reference purposes; they do not appear in the obj.conf file.

Example 6.1 Default PathCheck Directives in the obj.conf File

```
1. PathCheck fn="uri-clean"
2. PathCheck fn="check-acl" acl="default"
3. PathCheck fn="find-pathinfo"
4. PathCheck fn="find-index-j2ee"
5. PathCheck fn="find-index" index-names="index.html,home.html,index.jsp"
```

The next three sections describe the tasks performed during the PathCheck stage.

6.1.3.1 Pathname Preprocessing

One of the earliest vulnerabilities common to most web servers was the ability for a client to use periods (".") in the URI to gain access to documents outside the document root directory. Assuming that the document root directory was located at /sun/webserver7/https-myconfig/docs, then the following URI:

/../../../../etc/password

could pose a rather large security risk on UNIX-based systems. In Example 6.1, the uri-clean SAF in the first PathCheck directive looks for any path components containing /./ or /../ or // and sends an error 403 (Forbidden) status back to the client. This effectively blocks access to any client requesting access to any documents outside the document root directory.

> **Note:** Many browsers also attempt to eliminate this threat by stripping out path components that contain /./ or /../ or //. The uri-clean SAF is designed to respond to requests that were not cleaned up by browsers.

You can use the telnet command on UNIX or Windows systems to bypass the browser and force the execution of the uri-clean SAF. An example of how to use the telnet command in this manner is as follows:

```
telnet localhost 80
GET /../../../../etc/password HTTP/1.0
HTTP/1.1 403 Forbidden
Server: Sun-Java-System-Web-Server/7.0
Date: Mon, 28 Apr 2008 02:11:30 GMT
Content-length: 142
Content-type: text/html
```

Another task performed during path preprocessing involves the use of the find-pathinfo SAF. This function simply takes any extra path information contained in the URI (found after the filename) and stores it for use in the CGI environment variable, PATH_INFO. For instance, the find-pathinfo SAF would take a pathname of /sun/webserver7/https-myconfig/cgi-bin/runcgi.pl?attr1=foo&attr2=bar and store attr1=foo&attr2=bar in the PATH_INFO variable. This data could then be used for processing the request during the Service stage.

6.1.3.2 Pathname Verification

The find-index function determines whether a path generated in the NameTrans stage is actually a reference to a directory on the file system. If it is, then the find-index function searches for an index file in that directory (as specified in the index-names variable) and changes the path to reflect the index filename. For instance, if a path was determined to be /sun/webserver7/https-myconfig/docs/hr, then the find-index SAF defined in Example 6.1 would look for the following index files (in this order):

- /sun/webserver7/https-myconfig/docs/hr/index.html
- /sun/webserver7/https-myconfig/docs/hr/home.html
- /sun/webserver7/https-myconfig/docs/hr/index.jsp

If an index file is not found, then the server generates a directory listing (unless directory listing has been denied).

Note: A default home page may also be defined in the `NameTrans` stage with the home-page SAF as follows:

```
NameTrans fn="home-page"
  path="/sun/webserver7/https-myconfig/myHomePage.html"
```

If the Web Server cannot find any of the files specified by the find-index SAF in the document root directory, it returns the document specified by the home-page SAF instead.

The `find-index` function does not perform any actions if any of the following are found to be logical TRUE:

- The path contains a query string (see `find-pathinfo` in Section 6.1.3.1)
- The HTTP method is not GET
- The path is found to be a valid (existing) filename

Web applications can also specify a default entry point by using the `welcome-file-list` element defined in the `web.xml` deployment descriptor. If it is determined that the path is associated with a web application, then the `find-index-j2ee` function extracts a list of pages from the web application's deployment descriptor and performs an operation similar to the `find-index` function.

For instance, if it was determined that a path was referencing a web application (as defined in the `server.xml` file), and the web application existed in the /sun/webserver7/https-myconfig/webapps/webapp1 directory, and the web application's `web.xml` file contained the following `welcome-file-list` element definition,

```
<welcome-file-list>
    <welcome-file>index.html</welcome-file>
    <welcome-file>index.htm</welcome-file>
    <welcome-file>Home.jsp</welcome-file>
</welcome-file-list>
```

then the `find-index-j2ee` SAF defined in Example 6.1 would look for the following index files (in this order):

1. /sun/webserver7/https-myconfig/webapps/webapp1/index.html
2. /sun/webserver7/https-myconfig/webapps/webapp1/index.htm
3. /sun/webserver7/https-myconfig/webapps/webapp1/Home.jsp

If you plan on hosting both static web pages and web applications, then you should position the find-index-j2ee SAF above the find-index SAF as shown in Example 6.1. This position ensures that the ordering specified in the web.xml welcome-file-list takes precedence over the default index file order configured for the find-index SAF.

6.1.3.3 Access Control List Processing

An access control list contains information that specifies which users are allowed (or denied) access to Web Server resources. It can also specify under what conditions (i.e., client IP address, day of week, or authentication method) that the access is granted. The second PathCheck directive in Example 6.1 uses the check-acl SAF to build an access control list that determines whether the client (or user) is allowed access to the resource or not. The acl parameter in the check-acl directive specifies the name of the access control list that is to be used for access control processing.

It is possible that the Web Server may use more than one ACL during request processing. This can be accomplished by defining additional check-acl PathCheck directives in either the default object or in other named objects as well (i.e., <Object name="cgi">). If more than one ACL is defined for a particular request, the Web Server combines all the ACLs together (in the order in which they were specified) to make up one consolidated ACL.

In the case of Example 6.1, the ACL named, default, will be added to the overall ACL list. The default ACL is defined in the server.xml file with the following definition:

```
<acl-file>default.acl</acl-file>
```

The access control entries defined in this file are read and combined into the access control list along with other access control entries that might have been previously defined. The Web Server caches the ACLs returned by the check-acl function and as such, you should not include this SAF inside conditional logic such as Client, If, ElseIf, or Else containers.

Note: Debugging access control issues may become difficult as more and more access control lists are combined together. Web Server 7 introduces access control entry processing into the Server Log (errors) to help address this issue. Each access control entry is listed, along with the result of the evaluation of the entry and whether the user was permitted or denied access.

SAFs for other directives in a particular stage are processed in the order in which they are defined in the object. The check-acl SAF in the PathCheck directive, however, creates an exception to this rule. If a PathCheck directive specifies check-acl as the function, then that directive is moved to the front of the list. To ensure that the entire ACL list is cached before other PathCheck directives are processed, all check-acl functions are executed first regardless of the order in which PathCheck directives are defined in the object. In the case of Example 6.1, directives are defined as 1, 2, 3, 4, and 5, but they are processed as 2, 1, 3, 4, and 5.

> **Note:** If the NameTrans directive is assigned a name or generates a physical pathname that matches the name or ppath attribute of another object, the server first applies the PathCheck directives in the matching object before applying the directives in the default object. Additional information on conditional processing using the name parameter can be found in Section 6.3, "Conditional Processing."

After the order of all PathCheck directives is established, the server executes each directive until one of the following two conditions occurs:

- The user is unknown (the user needs to provide credentials).
- The user's access is denied (the user's identity is known but access to this resource is not allowed).

If an ACL specifies access based on a particular user or group and the user is not known (i.e., has not authenticated), Web Server responds to the client with a status of 401 (Unauthorized) and completes the processing of the request. This status informs the browser that it needs to open a dialog box to prompt the user for a username and password. The browser sends the credentials, along with the original URL, to the Web Server where they will then be validated in the AuthTrans stage. (Refer to Section 6.1.1, "Authorization Translation (AuthTrans) Stage," for more information.)

If access is denied, the server switches to executing directives in the Error stage, where a status code of 403 (Forbidden) is returned to the client.

6.1.4 Object Type (ObjectType) Stage

After the Web Server has determined what resource the client is requesting in the NameTrans stage and then determined whether the resource exists and the user is allowed access to it in the PathCheck stage, then the next step in request processing is to determine what *type* of object the client is requesting. This is performed in the ObjectType (or Object Type) stage.

During the ObjectType stage, the server determines the Multipurpose Internet Mail Extension (MIME) type attributes of the resource requested by the client. These attributes may be one or more of the following:

- type—The type of content being processed
- enc—How the content is encoded to the client
- lang—The language to use to read the content

When the server sends the response to the client, the type, enc, and lang values are transmitted in the headers of the response. This tells the client how to process the data and potentially which helper applications to use to display the data.

On the server side, the type attribute can be used to tell the Web Server which Service directive to execute to generate the response to the client. (See section 6.1.7, "Response Generation (Service) Stage," for more information on the Service directive.)

You can use different SAFs to determine the MIME type attributes. Example 6.2 contains the default ObjectType directives immediately after installation. Line numbers have been added for reference purposes; they do not appear in the obj.conf file.

Example 6.2   Default ObjectType Directives in the obj.conf File

```
1. ObjectType fn="type-j2ee"
2. ObjectType fn="type-by-extension"
3. ObjectType fn="force-type" type="text/plain"
```

The type-j2ee function in the first ObjectType directive sets the Content-Type response header for requests that map to resources in a Java web application. When configuring the server to host JSP-based web applications, type-j2ee must be the first ObjectType SAF in obj.conf. This ensures that any MIME type mappings specified in the web.xml file take precedence over the default MIME type mappings.

The most commonly used SAF is type-by-extension. This function can be seen in the second ObjectType directive and is used to search for the requested resource's file extension in the MIME types table. The MIME types table is stored in a MIME type file which is specified by the <mime-file> element defined in the server.xml file as follows:

```
<mime-file>mime.types</mime-file>
```

This file contains a mapping of file extensions to MIME types and enables the server to determine the content type of a requested resource. For example, the following two lines are part of a typical MIME types file:

```
type=text/html exts=htm,html
type=text/plain exts=txt
```

If the extension of the requested resource is `.htm` or `.html`, the `type-by-extension` function sets the `type` attribute to `text/html`. If the extension is `.txt`, the function sets the `type` attribute to `text/plain`.

> **Note:** See Section 5.4, "The `mime.types` File," in Chapter 5 for more information on the MIME types file.

If the `type-by-extension` function cannot find a matching file extension in the MIME types table, then the `type` attribute is `null`. In such cases, it is a good idea to specify a default `ObjectType` directive to force the `type` attribute to be `text/plain`. This enables the Web Server to respond to the client by sending the data in plain text. The function that forces the value of the `type` attribute is `force-type` and can be seen in the third `ObjectType` directive in Example 6.2.

Assume that the only values defined in the MIME file are those shown in Example 6.2. If the server receives a request for a file called `abc.texts`, it does not find a match for the `.texts` extension in the MIME types table and consequently the `type` attribute is not set. Because the `type` attribute has not already been set, the third (default) directive is successful and the `type` attribute is forced to `text/plain`.

> **Note:** It is important that the `force-type` SAF appear at the end of the list of `Object-Type` directives. After the `type` attribute has been set, it cannot be modified. Placing it before other `ObjectType` directives precludes the other directives from being able to set the `type` attribute.

Example 6.3 illustrates another use of the `force-type` SAF to force the `type` attribute based on the request. If a user makes a request for a URI that begins with `/cgi` (for example, `http://www.example.com/cgi/addrbook.cgi`), then the `type` attribute is forced to `magnus-internal/cgi` before the Web Server gets a chance to look in the MIME types table. This occurs because the `name` variable (set in the `NameTrans` directive) instructs the Web Server to process any `ObjectType` directives in the object named `cgi` before processing any defined in the `default` object. The object named `cgi` has one `ObjectType` directive that uses the `force-type` SAF to force the type to `magnus-internal/cgi`, therefore any attempt to reset the attribute in subsequent `ObjectType` directives is unsuccessful.

Example 6.3   `ObjectType` Directives in the `obj.conf` File

```
<Object Name="default">
...
NameTrans fn="pfx2dir" from="/cgi"
  dir="/sun/webserver7/https-myconfig/mycgi" name="cgi"
...
ObjectType fn="type-j2ee"
ObjectType fn="type-by-extension"
ObjectType fn="force-type" type="text/plain"
...
</Object>

<Object name="cgi">
ObjectType fn="force-type" type="magnus-internal/cgi"
Service fn="send-cgi"
</Object>
```

Note: Additional information on conditional processing using the `name` parameter can be found in Section 6.3, "Conditional Processing."

If there is more than one `ObjectType` directive, the server continues to process all directives in the order in which they appear even if a match has already occurred. After a directive sets a MIME attribute (`type`, `enc`, `lang`), further attempts to set the same attribute are ignored. This continuation of processing allows Web Server the flexibility to set one attribute in one directive (such as `type`) and a different attribute in a different directive (such as `lang`).

As with the `PathCheck` directives, if another object has been matched to the request as a result of the `name` attribute in the `NameTrans` stage, the server executes the `ObjectType` directives in the matching object before executing the `ObjectType` directives in the `default` object.

6.1.5 Input and Output Stages

All data sent to the server (such as the result of an HTML form) or sent from the server (such as the output of a Java Server Page) is passed through a set of filters known as a filter stack. The server creates a separate filter stack for each connection. While processing a request, individual filters can be inserted into and removed from the stack.

Different types of filters occupy different positions within a filter stack. Filters that deal with application-level content (such as filters that translate a page from XHTML to HTML) occupy a higher position than filters that deal with protocol-level issues (such as filters that format HTTP responses). When two or more filters are defined to occupy the same position in the filter stack, filters that were inserted later appear higher than filters that were inserted earlier.

Web Server 7.0 allows you to specify both Input and Output filters that enable you to modify client data either before or after it is processed by the Service stage.

6.1.5.1 Input Filters (Prepare to Read Input)

After the request's MIME type is determined by the ObjectType stage, the server prepares to generate the response to send to the client. This response is generated by the Service stage. However, before the Service stage generates the response, the server (or a plug-in) first attempts to read entity body data from the client and the Input directive is executed.

The Input directive selects filters that process incoming request data read by the Service stage. It enables you to invoke the insert-filter SAF to install filters that process incoming data. Suppose your Web Server serves up content to mobile devices such as personal digital assistants (PDAs). To increase performance over the wireless network, the PDA may compress the data before sending it to your Web Server. The Web Server needs to decompress the data received from the PDA before the Service stage can read the data and then process the response. This can be performed in the following Input directive:

```
Input fn="insert-filter" filter="http-decompression"
```

This directive instructs the insert-filter function to add a filter named http-decompression to the filter stack. This filter would effectively decompress incoming HTTP request data before passing it to the Service stage.

If another object has been matched to the request as a result of the `name` attribute in the `NameTrans` stage, the server executes the `Input` directives in the matching object before executing the `Input` directives in the `default` object.

6.1.5.2 Output Filters (Prepare to Send Output)

The `Output` directive selects filters that process outgoing response data generated by the `Service` step. The `Output` directive lets you invoke the `insert-filter` SAF to install filters that process outgoing data. All `Output` directives are executed when the server (or a plug-in) first attempts to write entity body data to the client.

Section 6.1.5.1, "`Input` Filters," introduced an example of a Web Server that provides content to mobile devices. In that example, all data sent from the wireless device to the Web Server is compressed and the Web Server must decompress it to allow the `Service` stage to process the data. After the `Service` stage has completed processing and a response has been generated, you may want to compress the response data before sending it back to the client. This can be performed in the following `Output` directive:

```
Output fn="insert-filter" filter="http-compression"
```

This directive instructs the `insert-filter` function to add a filter named `http-compression` to the filter stack, which would compress outgoing HTTP response data generated by the `Service` step.

If another object has been matched to the request as a result of the `name` attribute in the `NameTrans` stage, the server executes the `Output` directives in the matching object before executing the `Output` directives in the `default` object.

6.1.6 Request Routing (Route) Stage

Web Server 7.0 introduced the `Route` directive to allow other origin servers to service a client's request. If a `Service` directive requires that the HTTP request be sent to another server, the server executes `Route` directives to determine how the request should be routed. Routing a request can involve selecting the server that will ultimately service the request and selecting a proxy through which the request may be sent.

A common function used with the `Route` directive is `set-origin-server`. This SAF specifies the origin server that will service the request.

```
Route fn="set-origin-server" server="http://appserv.example.com:8000"
```

You can also specify multiple servers in this SAF to effectively distribute the load across a set of homogeneous HTTP origin servers. The following example demonstrates how this might occur:

```
Route fn="set-origin-server"
  server="http://appserv1.example.com:8000"
  server="http://appserv2.example.com:8000"
```

Note: Web Server uses a sticky round robin algorithm to load balance incoming HTTP and HTTPS requests.

6.1.7 Response Generation (Service) Stage

Web Server 7 has an extensive library of server application functions that are used to process client requests. Some SAFs may communicate with the web container to process web applications, whereas others may spawn a CGI process. Some SAFs may emulate a reverse proxy capability, whereas others simply process static content. After the server has determined what type of resource the client is requesting in the ObjectType stage, it then needs to call the appropriate SAF to generate a response to the client. This determination is made and the action is performed in the Service stage.

Example 6.4 contains the default Service directives immediately after installation. Line numbers have been added for reference purposes; they do not appear in the obj.conf file.

Example 6.4 Default Service Directives in the obj.conf File

```
1. Service method="(GET|HEAD)" type="magnus-internal/directory"
     fn="index-common"
2. Service method="(GET|HEAD|POST)" type="*~magnus-internal/*"
     fn="send-file"
3. Service method="TRACE" fn="service-trace"
```

Web Server evaluates each Service directive in an attempt to find the one that matches one or more of the following: type, method, and query string. It performs this evaluation sequentially in the order in which the directives appear in the obj.conf file. The manner in which Service directives are evaluated is similar to the way a programming language might evaluate a complex If statement. After the

Web Server finds a match, it uses the function defined in the method parameter to process the response, and subsequent Service directives are ignored.

> **Note:** If another object has been matched to the request as a result of the name attribute in the NameTrans stage, the server executes the Service directives in the matching object before executing the Service directives in the default object.

The first directive shown in Example 6.4 will be matched if the method presented by the client is either a GET or a HEAD and the type is set to magnus-internal/directory. If this is the case, Web Server will use the index-common SAF to generate a fancy (or common) list of files in the requested directory. Another way of reading the first Service directive is as follows:

```
If ( (method is either GET or HEAD) and (type is "magnus-
internal/directory") )
Then
use the index-common SAF to process the response
```

> **Note:** In the method parameter, parentheses are used for grouping methods together and the pipe symbol is used within an OR condition.

The second directive shown in Example 6.4 will be matched if the method presented by the client is a GET, HEAD, or a POST, and the type does NOT contain magnus-internal. If this is the case, then Web Server uses the send-file SAF to send the contents of the requested file to the client. This function provides the Content-Type, Content-Length, and Last-Modified headers. Another way of reading the first Service directive is as follows:

```
If ( (method is either GET, HEAD, or POST) and (type DOES NOT CONTAIN
"magnus-internal/*") )
Then
    use the send-file SAF to process the response
```

Note: The characters *~ mean anything that DOES NOT MATCH the following characters, so the expression *~magnus-internal/ means anything that does not match magnus-internal/. An asterisk by itself matches anything, so the whole expression *~magnus-internal/* matches anything that does not begin with magnus-internal/.

The third directive shown in Example 6.4 is matched if the method presented by the client is SERVICE. If this is the case, Web Server uses the service-trace SAF to trace the request. TRACE requests are typically used to diagnose problems with reverse proxy servers located between a web client and another Web Server. Another way of reading the first Service directive is as follows:

```
If (the method is TRACE)
Then
    use the service-trace SAF to process the response
```

It is a good practice to have a default Service directive that simply sends the file to the client should no other Service directives match the request sent by the browser. This default directive should appear last in the list of Service directives in the default object. This ensures that this directive is processed only if no other Service directives have succeeded. The second directive in Example 6.4 demonstrates a default directive for this purpose.

6.1.8 Adding Log Entries (AddLog) Stage

After the Web Server has generated a response and has sent it to the client in the Service stage, it then executes any AddLog directives it finds to add entries to the appropriate log file(s). You can have multiple AddLog directives, thus enabling you to add entries to multiple log files.

AddLog directives are processed after the response has been sent to the client. This minimizes the amount of time it takes to process a request from the client's perspective because it does not need to wait for Web Server to write information to log files.

An example of the default AddLog directive immediately after installation is as follows:

```
AddLog fn="flex-log"
```

This directive uses the flex-log SAF to log information about the current request. The data is sent to the file specified in the <access-log> element defined in the server.xml as follows:

```
<access-log>
  <file>../logs/access</file>
</access-log>
```

Note: File references can be specified as the fully qualified file name or you can specify a filename that is relative to the config directory for a particular server instance.

6.1.9 Error Handling (Error) Stage

If an error occurs during the request handling process then the currently executing SAF sets the HTTP response status code and then indicates that an error has occurred by returning the appropriate return code. When this occurs, the server stops processing the request and begins searching for an Error directive that has a reason attribute that matches either of the following two conditions:

- HTTP response status code (for instance, 403)
- Its associated reason phrase (for instance, Unauthorized)

If the Web Server finds a match, then it returns the document specified in the path variable. If the Web Server does not find a matching Error directive, it simply returns the response status code to the client. The following example demonstrates how to define an Error directive to return a customized error message rather than a generic error code response:

```
Error fn="send-error" reason="Unauthorized"
path="/sun/webserver7/errors/unauthorized.html"
```

In this example, Web Server sends the file in /sun/webserver7/errors/unauthorized.html whenever a client requests a resource that it is not authorized to access.

Note: It is a good practice for system administrators to create a custom HTML document to describe the problem to the user and provide possible solutions for resolving the problem (for instance, a web form that can be used to request access to the resource).

6.2 Default Request Processing Behavior

A newly created Web Server instance begins processing client requests as soon as the instance is started. The default request processing behavior is adequate if you are serving up basic content, but if you plan for your Web Server to reach its fullest potential, you may need to modify the way Web Server handles requests. This section builds upon the information covered in the previous section (6.1, "Request Processing Stages") and illustrates how requests are processed based on the default configuration files. The next section (6.3, "Conditional Processing") then discusses how you can alter the request processing flow to meet your needs.

Request processing involves multiple configuration files, but four of them are key to fully understanding how the Web Server processes client requests. These are

- `magnus.conf`—Performs the initialization of the SAFs involved in request processing
- `server.xml`—Determines the virtual server used to process the request and defines various files used in request processing (ACL file(s), `mime.types` file, access log, etc.)
- `obj.conf`—Defines the steps to follow during request processing
- `mime.types`—Provides an extension to MIME mapping to help determine the type of request being processed

Note: These configuration files are described in detail in Chapter 5.

This section takes a look at several different client requests and traces the path through the different request processing stages as defined in the `obj.conf` file. To accomplish this, the Web Server utilizes the information contained in two key files: `mime.types` and `obj.conf`.

Example 6.5 provides an excerpt from a default `mime.types` file. This information will be used as a reference to help describe request processing.

Example 6.5   Excerpt from the mime.types File

```
1. type=text/html exts=htm,html
2. type=text/plain exts=txt
3. type=magnus-internal/parsed-html exts=shtml
4. type=magnus-internal/cgi exts=cgi,bat
```

Example 6.6 provides a complete default obj.conf file. This information will be used as a reference to help describe request processing.

Example 6.6   Default obj.conf File

```
1  <Object name=default>
2
3  AuthTrans fn="match-browser" browser="*MSIE*"
     ssl-unclean-shutdown="true"
4  NameTrans fn="ntrans-j2ee" name="j2ee"
5  NameTrans fn="pfx2dir" from="/mc-icons" dir="/sun/webserver7/lib/
     icons" name="es-internal"
6  NameTrans fn="document-root" root="$docroot"
7
8  PathCheck fn="uri-clean"
9  PathCheck fn="check-acl" acl="default"
10 PathCheck fn="find-pathinfo"
11 PathCheck fn="find-index-j2ee"
12 PathCheck fn="find-index" index-names="index.html,home.html,index.jsp"
13
14 ObjectType fn="type-j2ee"
15 ObjectType fn="type-by-extension"
16 ObjectType fn="force-type" type="text/plain"
17
18 Service method="(GET|HEAD)" type="magnus-internal/directory"
     fn="index-common"
19 Service method="(GET|HEAD|POST)" type=*~magnus-internal/* fn="sendfile"
20 Service method="TRACE" fn="service-trace"
21
22 Error fn="error-j2ee"
23
24 AddLog fn="flex-log"
25
26 </Object>
27
28 <Object name="j2ee">
29 Service fn="service-j2ee" method="*"
30 </Object>
31
32 <Object name="es-internal">
```

```
33 PathCheck fn="check-acl" acl="es-internal"
34 </Object>
35
36 <Object name="cgi">
37 ObjectType fn="force-type" type="magnus-internal/cgi"
38 Service fn="send-cgi"
39 </Object>
40
41 <Object name="send-precompressed">
42 PathCheck fn="find-compressed"
43 </Object>
44
45 <Object name="compress-on-demand">
46 Output fn="insert-filter" filter="http-compression"
47 </Object>
```

6.2.1 Request for Static Content

Suppose a client makes a request for static content such as `http://www.example.com/index.html`. Which directives in the `obj.conf` file would the server execute to process this request? Referring to the `obj.conf` file specified in Example 6.6, the server would process the following directives (in this order):

```
 3  AuthTrans fn="match-browser" browser="*MSIE*"
    ssl-unclean-shutdown="true"
 6  NameTrans fn="document-root" root="$docroot"
 9  PathCheck fn="check-acl" acl="default"
 8  PathCheck fn="uri-clean"
10  PathCheck fn="find-pathinfo"
11  PathCheck fn="find-index-j2ee"
12  PathCheck fn="find-index" index-names="index.html,home.html,
    index.jsp"
14  ObjectType fn="type-j2ee"
15  ObjectType fn="type-by-extension"
16  ObjectType fn="force-type" type="text/plain"
19  Service method="(GET|HEAD|POST)" type=*~magnus-internal/*
    fn="sendfile"
24  AddLog fn="flex-log"
```

But how and why? Information contained in Table 6.2 provides insight into how this particular request is processed. Keep in mind the following rules when reviewing the content in Table 6.2:

- All AuthTrans directives are processed.
- Only one NameTrans directive is processed (either a match is found or the default is forced).
- All PathCheck directives are processed, but any containing the check-acl SAF are moved to the front of the list.
- All ObjectType directives are processed, but after a MIME attribute has been set, it cannot be changed.
- Only one Service directive is processed (either a match is found or the default is forced).
- All AddLog directives are processed.

Table 6.2   Directives Processed for Static Content

Line #	Directive	Explanation
3	AuthTrans	Older versions of Microsoft Internet Explorer contained a bug where the application did not properly close the TCP/IP session after SSL communications were completed. This impacted performance on multiple vendor web servers and each vendor had to provide their own workaround. Microsoft has since addressed the issue, but this directive remains in place should Web Server encounter an older version of Internet Explorer.
6	NameTrans	Directives 4 and 5 are evaluated, but only directive 6 is found to be true based on the URL. This is not a web application and the URI does not contain the /mc-icons prefix. Therefore processing falls into the default case where the path is simply the URI concatenated onto the contents of the document root directory (for instance /sun/webserver7/https-myconfig/docs/index.html). The $docroot variable is populated based on data found in the server.xml file. Note: The document-root NameTrans directive does not appear in the default obj.conf file for Web Server 7.0 instances; it does, however, in previous versions. This is now an *implied* directive in Web Server 7.0 and is processed when none of the previous NameTrans directives are found to be true. The directive was added to Example 6.6 for illustrative purposes only.
9	PathCheck	This directive updates the ACL for this instance. (Remember that PathCheck directives with the check-acl SAF are moved to the front of the list.)
8	PathCheck	The URI did not contain any potential security risks so processing continues.
10	PathCheck	The URI did not contain any extra path information (found after the filename) so the PATH_INFO variable was not populated.
11	PathCheck	The URI did not match a J2EE web application (as defined in the server.xml file) so the resource path information remains unaltered.
12	PathCheck	The requested resource was not a directory so the resource path information remains unaltered.

Line #	Directive	Explanation
14	ObjectType	The URI did not match a J2EE web application (as defined in the server.xml file) so the Content-Type header parameter is not updated.
15	ObjectType	The mime.types file defined in the server.xml is evaluated (see Example 6.5). The server locates an extension of .html and sets the Content-Type to be text/html.
16	ObjectType	The type has already been defined and force-type does not set enc or lang attributes. This directive is processed, but no changes occur.
19	Service	This is the only directive that matches based on the previous ObjectType directives. The send-file SAF is used to process and send the file to the client.
24	AddLog	The access log (as defined in the server.xml) is updated to reflect the client request and subsequent server response.

6.2.2 Request for a File that Does Not Exist

Suppose a client makes a request for a CGI script and CGI processing is not yet enabled. The client might request a URL, such as http://www.example.com/cgi/addrbook.cgi. Assuming that this is an initial installation and there is no /cgi/addrbook.cgi file beneath the document root directory, which directives in the obj.conf file would be executed to process this request? Referring to the obj.conf file specified in Example 6.6, the server would process the following directives (in this order):

```
 3  AuthTrans fn="match-browser" browser="*MSIE*"
    ssl-unclean-shutdown="true"
 6  NameTrans fn="document-root" root="$docroot"
 9  PathCheck fn="check-acl" acl="default"
 8  PathCheck fn="uri-clean"
10  PathCheck fn="find-pathinfo"
11  PathCheck fn="find-index-j2ee"
12  PathCheck fn="find-index" index-names="index.html,home.html,
    index.jsp"
14  ObjectType fn="type-j2ee"
15  ObjectType fn="type-by-extension"
16  ObjectType fn="force-type" type="text/plain"
19  Service method="(GET|HEAD|POST)" type=*~magnus-internal/*
    fn="sendfile"
22  Error fn="error-j2ee"
24  AddLog fn="flex-log"
```

The directives are similar to those found when processing static content (see Section 6.2.1) with the exception that an additional directive (line 22) has been processed to handle the fact that the file does not exist. Why is this an error in the first place? Keep in mind that even though the obj.conf file has the following object defined to process CGI scripts, the server has not been instructed to access these directives for request processing:

```
<Object name="cgi">
ObjectType fn="force-type" type="magnus-internal/cgi"
Service fn="send-cgi"
</Object>
```

The next section describes how you can incorporate additional functionality and alter the default processing flow to make request processing conditional.

6.3 Conditional Processing

The obj.conf file contains directives that instruct Web Server on how to handle client requests and provide the appropriate response. Directives in the obj.conf file are grouped into Object tags (also called *containers*). The default object contains directives that instruct Web Server on how to process requests by default. Each new object that you add or each existing object that you modify also modifies the behavior of the default object. You can modify and extend the request handling process by adding or changing directives in the obj.conf or simply alter the flow based on certain conditions.

Web Server 7.0 provides various ways that you can execute directives on a conditional basis. These are as follows:

- Directive parameters
- Name Translation (name) attributes
- Partial Path (ppath) parameters
- Client containers
- If/ElseIf/Else containers

Each method is different from each other and your decision to select one over another depends on the availability of information and the functionality you are trying to employ. This section describes each of these methods in more detail.

6.3.1 Directive Parameters

Certain directives can be executed based on conditions defined within the directive, itself. One such example has already been discussed in section 6.1.7, "Response Generation (Service) Stage." An example of a Service directive that specified whether the function should be executed is as follows:

```
Service method="(GET|HEAD)" type="magnus-internal/directory"
  fn="index-common"
```

In this case, the index-common SAF is executed only if the following conditions are true:

- The method from the client is either GET or HEAD
- The type selected in the mime.types file does not contain the string magnus-internal

If one or more of these conditions is false, then request processing proceeds to the next Service directive.

6.3.2 Name Translation (name) Attributes

During request processing, Web Server evaluates each NameTrans directive in the default object in an attempt to locate a match consistent with the URI being requested. If the matched NameTrans directive contains the name attribute, then the Web Server switches to processing any directives found in the object specified by the name attribute before processing the remaining directives in the default object.

An example of a NameTrans directive containing a name attribute is as follows:

```
NameTrans fn="pfx2dir" from="/cgi"
  dir="/sun/webserver7/https-myconfig/mycgi" name="cgi"
```

If a client requests a resource that begins with a URI of /cgi, then this NameTrans directive will be matched. The pfx2dir function will create the path to the resource by concatenating the value specified by the dir attribute with the remainder of the URI that follows the string, /cgi. This tells the Web Server where to look for the resource on the file system for processing, but even if it is found, the Service directives in the default object will not process the request properly. Instead, processing will fall to the default case and the request will be processed by the Service directive containing the send-file SAF.

NameTrans directives that include the name attribute provide a mechanism to inform the Web Server that another object contains additional directives that should be executed only when this NameTrans directive is found to be true. The following is an example of the cgi object that can be used in conjunction with the NameTrans directive:

```
<Object name="cgi">
ObjectType fn="force-type" type="magnus-internal/cgi"
Service fn="send-cgi"
</Object>
```

In essence, the name attribute *points to* another object that contains additional directives that should be used for processing the request. It should be noted that the value of the name attribute in the NameTrans directive must be the same as the name of the object for the two to match. In this case, both must share the name="cgi" value. If these are not consistent, then an error is returned during request processing.

6.3.3 Partial Path (ppath) Attributes

The ppath object enables you to specify a path to a document or resource where directives contained in the object are executed only if the path to the resource can be found beneath the location specified in the ppath value.

When the server completes processing the NameTrans directives in the default object, the URI of the request has been converted to a physical pathname. If this physical pathname matches the ppath attribute of another object, the server switches to processing the directives in that object before processing the remaining ones in the default object.

Example 6.7 provides a sample ppath object definition.

Example 6.7   Example of a ppath Definition

```
<Object ppath="/sun/webserver7/https-myconfig/docs/private/*">
directives
</Object>
```

After the NameTrans stage has been completed, the Web Server looks to see whether there are any objects that specify a ppath value that matches the path generated in the NameTrans stage. In the case of the ppath definition shown in Example 6.7, the server is looking to see whether the path generated in the NameTrans stage maps to any document found beneath the `/sun/webserver7/https-myconfig/docs/` `private` directory. If so, then any directives found within this `ppath` object are processed prior to those found in the `default` object.

6.3.4 `Client` Containers

The `Client` container is used to limit execution of a set of directives to requests received from specific clients and client-type requests. Directives listed between the `<Client>` and `</Client>` tags are executed only when information in the client request matches the parameter values specified.

> **Note:** `Client` containers can appear only inside other containers (for instance, the `default` object); they cannot stand on their own.

Examples of client parameters that you can query include the following:

- `browser`—The User-Agent string sent by a browser to the Web Server
- `dns`—The DNS name of the client
- `method`—The HTTP method used by the browser
- `type`—The type of document requested (such as `text/html` or `image/gif`)
- `urlhost`—TheDNS name of the virtual server requested by the client (the value is provided in the Host header of the client request)

Additionally, you can use wildcard patterns to provide more granular control over what is and is not matched.

The following example demonstrates the use of a `Client` container being placed within the `default` object:

```
<Object name="default">
AuthTrans ...
<Client urlhost="hr.example.com">
NameTrans fn="document-root"
    root="/sun/webserver7/https-myconfig/hrdocroot/"
</Client>
NameTrans ...
NameTrans ...
...
</Object>
```

The first NameTrans directive is evaluated if and only if the client is requesting content from the hr.example.com host.

In the following example, the Client tag and the AddLog directive are combined to direct the Web Server to log access requests from all clients except those from the specified subnet:

```
<Client ip="*~192.168.2.*">
AddLog fn="flex-log" name="access"
</Client>
```

The Client container also lets you create a negative match by setting the match parameter of the Client tag to a value of none. In the following example, access requests from the specified subnet are excluded as are all requests to the virtual server, foo.example.com:

```
<Client match="none" ip="192.168.2.*" urlhost="foo.example.com">
AddLog fn="flex-log" name="access"
</Client>
```

Note: Refer to the *Sun Java System Web Server Administrator's Configuration File Reference* document for additional parameters that you can query. Appendix B of the *Sun Java System Web Server Administrator's Configuration File Reference* provides details on the types of wildcard patterns supported by Web Server 7.0.

6.3.5 If/ElseIf/Else Containers

Web Server 7.0 introduced three additional containers that take full advantage of conditional logic, variables, and regular expressions to determine whether certain directives should be executed or not.

The If, ElseIf, and Else containers enable you to define the conditions under which a certain set of directives may be executed. These containers use standard if-then-else logic found in typical programming languages. Like the Client container, these new containers can appear only inside an existing object—they cannot exist on their own as a ppath or named object can. There are some key differences, however, between the two types of containers, as summarized here:

- If and ElseIf containers offer richer expression syntax, including support for regular expressions. This expression syntax is different from the Client syntax.

- If, ElseIf, and Else containers can contain other containers. Client containers cannot.

- If and ElseIf expressions are evaluated once per request, not once per contained directive.

- If, ElseIf, and Else containers can contain directives only of the same type; they cannot contain multiple types of directives within the same container. Client containers can.

- Directives within the If and ElseIf containers can use regular expression back references.

If, ElseIf, and Else containers are useful for executing directives under certain circumstances and can evaluate server variables to help determine whether the directives should be processed or not. Suppose, for instance, you were running a web site that was open only between the hours of 8:30 a.m. and 5:00 p.m. and wanted to display one set of pages when you were open and another set of pages when you were closed. You could play games with symbolic links and UNIX cron jobs (or come up with some other creative methods of changing the document root directory to reflect the hours of operation), or you could use a simple If container in the object configuration file to evaluate the current time of day as follows:

```
<If "$time_hour:$time_min" < "8:30" || "$time_hour:$time_min" >
"17:00">
AuthTrans fn="set-variable" $docroot="/var/www/docs/closed"
</If>
...
NameTrans fn="document-root" root="$docroot"
```

In this example, the Web Server evaluates the $time_hour and $time_min server variables to determine whether the server's time is earlier than 8:30 a.m. or later than 5:00 p.m. If either of these cases is found to be true, then the AuthTrans directive is processed and the set-variable SAF sets the document root directory variable ($docroot) to reflect a page indicating that you are currently closed. If, however, the request is processed during business hours, then the condition in the If container is found to be false and the NameTrans directive sets the document root directory to be the original value of $docroot as defined in the server.xml file.

Note: Variables set with the set-variable SAF have a higher order of precedence than those that are defined in the server.xml file, so other directives have no effect on the value of this variable. (See Chapter 5, Section 5.3.2.3, "Variables," for a description of the namespaces consulted when attempting to resolve a particular variable.)

In addition to the $docroot variable, this example also introduces the use of variables such as $time_hour and $time_min. Refer to Appendix A in the *Sun Java System Web Server Administrator's Configuration File Reference* document for a list of predefined variables and methods for defining your own variables in Web Server 7.0.

Although this example is simple, it demonstrates the power associated with being able to execute directives based on a simple if condition. A more complex example that demonstrates the use of multiple layers of If containers and introduces the ElseIf and Else containers is as follows:

```
<If $path = "/">
<If $browser =~ "MSIE">
NameTrans fn="rewrite" path="/msie.html"
</If>
<ElseIf $browser =~ "Mozilla">
NameTrans fn="rewrite" path="/mozilla.html"
</ElseIf>
<Else>
NameTrans fn="rewrite" path="/unknown.html"
</Else>
</If>
```

In this example, there is an outer If container that evaluates if the $path variable equals "/". (This condition occurs when the user does not specify any directories or files in the URI. There are three "child" containers within the outer If container: If, ElseIf, and Else. The If and ElseIf containers evaluate the $browser variable to determine what type of browser the user is using. This example demonstrates how the Web Server can be configured to present a different page based on whether the browser is Microsoft Internet Explorer, Mozilla, or another browser.

Note: When used, an ElseIf or Else container must immediately follow an If or ElseIf container. ElseIf and Else containers are skipped if the preceding If or ElseIf expression evaluates to logical TRUE.

This example also demonstrates the usage of regular expressions in the `If` and `ElseIf` conditional statements. The `$browser` variable is evaluated to determine whether the strings, MSIE, or Mozilla are part of the user-agent header data received from the client. The "`=~`" character sequence is a regular expression that means *contains*. Section 6.3 contains additional information on regular expression usage.

6.4 Pattern Matching and Regular Expressions

Pattern matching is the act of matching character strings using metacharacters or wildcard symbols. In the Web Server, effective use of pattern matching enables you to conditionally process directives and dramatically reduce the number of entries contained in your configuration files.

Note: A *metacharacter* is a special character that affects the way a pattern is matched. The letter *A* is an ordinary character. Searches that look specifically for the letter *A* return only matches that are (or contain) the letter A. The period (`.`), however, is a metacharacter that matches any single character other than a newline character. Searches that look for a period could match any letter of the alphabet, any single character number, any punctuation mark, or any other character other than a newline character. Metacharacters have special meaning to regular expressions and allow flexibility when performing pattern searches.

Two files that make use of pattern matching in Web Server 7.0 are the `server.xml` and `obj.conf` configuration files. The `server.xml` file limits its use of pattern matching to the `virtual-server/host` element, whereas the `obj.conf` file makes extensive use of pattern matching through regular expressions in evaluating variable content and performing URL rewrites.

The next two sections describe simple pattern matching and regular expressions and show how these are used in Web Server 7.0.

6.4.1 Simple Pattern Matching

In UNIX-based systems, pattern matching is typically used to perform OS-based operations like selecting multiple files with similar names. UNIX uses wildcard characters such as a question mark (?) or an asterisk (*) to match character strings as follows:

- Question mark—Matches any single character
- Asterisk—Matches one or more occurrences of any character

For instance, on a Solaris-based system you could use the asterisk wildcard to determine all the files in the /etc directory that begin with the letters rc as follows:

```
# ls -d /etc/rc*
/etc/rc0    /etc/rc1    /etc/rc2    /etc/rc3    /etc/rc5    /etc/rcS
/etc/rcm /etc/rc0.d /etc/rc1.d /etc/rc2.d /etc/rc3.d /etc/rc6
/etc/rcS.d
```

This shows all the files that begin with the letters rc. If you wanted to narrow down the files that are displayed to show only those that match rc0.d, rc1.d, rc2.d, rc3.d, and rcS.d, you would use the single character pattern matching operator as follows:

```
# ls -d /etc/rc?.d
/etc/rc0.d  /etc/rc1.d  /etc/rc2.d  /etc/rc3.d  /etc/rcS.d
```

In Web Server 7.0, pattern matching has been extended to support the host element in the server.xml file. Use of pattern matching in the virtual-server/host element enables you to minimize the number of elements defined. Example 6.8 contains an example of how you would configure a particular virtual server to respond to multiple hosts.

Example 6.8   Host Definitions Without Pattern Matching

```
<virtual-server>
    <name>https-foo.bar.example.com</name>
    <host>foo.bar.example.com</name>
    <host>foo.bar</name>
    <host>foo.eng.example.com</name>
    <host>foo.eng</name>
</virtual-server>
```

If DNS resolved each of these hosts to your server, then this virtual-server definition would allow you to process requests for any of these four hosts. But what if you wanted to continue adding additional DNS entries and did not want to have to edit your Web Server each time? You could use a wildcard pattern to accomplish this. A quick observation of the hosts listed in Example 6.8 reveals that each host element starts with the string pattern of foo. If you wanted to add foo.sales and foo.sales.example.com to DNS and have your server respond to one or both of those hosts without modifying your server.xml file, then you would need a virtual-server definition as shown in Example 6.9.

Example 6.9 Host Definitions with Wildcard Patterns

```
<virtual-server>
    <name>https-foo.bar.example.com</name>
    <host>foo.*</host>
</virtual-server>
```

Example 6.9 uses simple pattern matching to reduce the number of host elements from four to one. The definition accomplishes this because the asterisk matches any pattern of characters that follow the string foo. and therefore matches any host that begins with foo.

Note: Pattern matching applies to only the host element. Host comparisons are not case sensitive.

6.4.2 Regular Expressions

Regular expressions build upon simple pattern matching techniques to provide more complex matching conditions. They use metacharacters to match various types of data patterns and allow you to define expressions that match multiple, similar strings. For example, the regular expression statement, he[l]+o w[i|or]ld, would match either hello world or hello wild.

Note: See O'Reilly's man page on PERL regular expressions for an overview of the characters used in this statement. This can be found at http://www.perl.com/doc/manual/html/pod/perlre.html.

Web Server 7.0's support of regular expressions allows you to create very dynamic matching expressions and to configure fewer configuration settings. A generic example of a regular expression is as follows:

```
[a-z]*://.*\.example\.com/.*
```

This example contains various pattern matching expressions to dynamically match one or more URLs. This example presents some common pattern matching expressions.

First of all, character sets are defined by square brackets. In this example, the square brackets around the a-z defines a range of all lowercase letters from the letter *a* to the letter *z*. The asterisk character (*) matches zero or more occurrences of whatever preceeds it. Therefore, when you combine the asterisk with the character set in this example, you get a pattern match of zero or more letters from *a* to *z*. This would match the patterns http, ftp, gopher, or any other string.

You can also include actual string characters in the regular expression. In this example, the colon followed by two forward slashes (://) means that you are actually looking for that particular string.

A period (.) matches any single character except for a newline. Combining it with the asterisk (.*) means that you match one or more of almost any character. (This is affectionately called the *greedy* character.)

A backslash (\) is used as an escape character. This means that you take the actual value of the next character. In this example, the backslash before the period means that you are actually looking for a period character and not a pattern match of any single character except a newline.

In summary, this regular expression would match any protocol used to access any hosts from the .example.com domain serving up any types of documents from those hosts.

Regular expressions can be used within the obj.conf file to evaluate server variables and control the flow of request processing. Knowing how and when to use them, however, makes all the difference between streamlining request processing and configuring your server poorly.

6.4.2.1 Regular Expression Considerations

Regular expressions use the Perl-compatible syntax implemented by the Perl-compatible regular expressions (PCRE) library set. By default, regular expressions are case sensitive but you can use the (?i) option flag at the beginning of a regular expression to request case insensitivity.

Regular expressions are most effectively used in If/ElseIf/Else containers to determine when certain directives are to be executed. The =~ and !~ matching operators can be used to determine whether a variable contains or does not contain a particular pattern match, respectively. Use of containers, matching operators, and server variables allows you to create dynamic pattern matching scenarios to solve some very real situations.

Suppose for example that you have decided that you want to migrate content from one area of your site (beneath a particular folder) to an entirely new server. The following example demonstrates how you can use a regular expression to do this.

```
<If $uri =~ '^/folder'>
NameTrans fn="redirect" url="http://newsite.example.com"
</If>
```

The `If` container determines whether the `$uri` variable contains the string "`^/folder`" (where the caret character (`^`) is a metacharacter that represents the beginning of a string). This particular regular expression is matched for any request where the requested URI contains the string `folder` at the beginning. It would not match `/foo/folder` because the string `folder` does not appear at the beginning of the URI. All clients requesting URIs containing this string are redirected to the main page found at `http://newsite.example.com`.

Although this has the desired effect of redirecting the client to a new site, the fact that it directs all traffic to the main page of the new site can be quite restrictive. The next section shows how to address this problem by using backreferences.

6.4.2.2 Backreferencing

Regular expression metacharacters can match multiple strings within the data. As such, you may know that you have matched a string, but you are not quite sure what it was that you actually matched. Regular expressions use a concept called *backreferencing* to account for this. Various portions of the regular expression can be enclosed within parentheses to signify that you want to keep track of what it was the regular expression matched. You can refer to the predefined variables to see what each set of parenthesized metacharacters actually matched.

Regular expression backreference variables are of the form `$n` (where n is an integer that begins with any number between 1 and 9) and correspond to the capturing subpattern of the regular expression (that is, the order in which the parenthesized regular expression appears). To state it another way, backreference variables take the form of `$1`, `$2`, `$3`, ..., `$n`, where the first parenthesized regular expression is denoted by `$1`, the second parenthesized regular expression is denoted by `$2`, and so on.

Suppose the client request contained a URI as follows: `/folder1/folder2/folder3/file.html`.

If you applied a regular expression to the URI, you could match and capture each component of the URI and save them into backreferenced variables as follows:

```
$uri =~ '^/(.*)/(.*)/(.*)/(.*)'
```

This is a very simple example and would not match unless the client URI contained at least three directories. It does, however, demonstrate how to use backreferencing and how backreferenced variables are populated.

The caret (^) matches the beginning of the string in the `$uri` variable. The forward slashes (/) match each corresponding forward slash in the client request. The greedy character (.*) matches each component of the URI, and because they are parenthesized, the values that were matched would be stored into the backreferenced variables as follows:

- `$1 = folder1`
- `$2 = folder2`
- `$3 = folder3`
- `$4 = file.html`

Any expression can contain backreferences to earlier regular expressions within the same container. This enables you to use the data that was previously matched to perform additional operations or set other variables based on this data.

In Section 6.4.2.1 you saw an example of how to redirect a client to a new site based on the requested URI containing a particular folder name. In that example, you saw that all client requests—including those for files contained in subdirectories—were redirected to the new site's main page. Suppose you wanted to maintain the structure of the request from the old site to the new site so that if a user asked for a file several directories deep (for instance, http://www.example.com/folder/subfolder/file.html), that user would be redirected to the same directory structure on the new server (http://newsite.example.com/folder/subfolder/file.html). The following example demonstrates how you can use a backreferences to accomplish this.

```
<If $uri =~ '^/folder/(.*)'>
NameTrans fn="redirect" url="http://newsite.example.com/$1"
</If>
```

A client request could contain any combination of subdirectories or files beneath the directory, `folder`. Examples of potential client requests could be

- `/folder/foo.html`
- `/folder/subfolder/file.html`
- `/folder/subfolder1/subfolder2/file.html`

The backreferenced greedy character (`.*`) would match any such combination and store whatever was matched into the `$1` variable. The corresponding values of the `$1` variable for each of these potential client requests would be

- `foo.html`
- `subfolder/file.html`
- `subfolder1/subfolder2/file.html`

The `NameTrans` directive is able to reference the additional subdirectories (or files) with the `$1` variable and is then able to create a redirect location (`url`) based on the value of the URI as follows:

- http://newsite.example.com/foo.html
- http://newsite.example.com/subfolder/file.html
- http://newsite.example.com/subfolder1/subfolder2/file.html

An expression can contain references to saved backreferences within the same container expression as follows:

```
<If "foo" =~ '(.*)' and $1 eq "foo">
directives
</If>
```

But you cannot reference saved backreferences from one container in another container—even the child's parent container. The following example is invalid because the child container is attempting to perform a backreference to a value saved in the parent container's expression:

```
<If $path =~ "(.*)\\.css">
<If $browser =~ "MSIE">
AuthTrans fn="rewrite" path="$1-msie.css"
</If>
</If>
```

The rewrite will always contain a value of "-msie.css" because the $1 variable will always be empty in the child container.

6.4.2.3 Expression Functions

Expression functions are used to manipulate data for use in object configuration file expressions. The following provides an overview of various predefined expression functions:

- choose—Parses a pipe-separated string and randomly returns one of the values within the string.
- escape—Converts special octets to their percent-encoded equivalents.
- httpdate—Returns an RFC 1123 date/timestamp for use in HTTP header fields. Time must be specified in UTC (the number of seconds since January 1, 1970).
- lc—Converts all the US ASCII characters in the string to lowercase.
- length—Determines the length of the string argument.
- uc—Converts all the US ASCII characters in string to uppercase.
- unescape—Converts percent-encoded octets to their unencoded form.

As a rule, expression functions require at least one argument. Arguments are bound by a set of parentheses, and multiple arguments are separated by commas.

Expression functions are not the same as server application functions (SAFs). SAFs perform the actual work associated with an HTTP request, but expression functions are used within containers to aid in the processing of regular expressions or directly within directive parameters themselves. Specifically, expression functions are used within the following two places:

- In the body of a container expression to determine whether a particular set of directives are to be processed (and hence what SAFs will run).
- Within SAF parameters to perform some operation on the data before it becomes a SAF parameter.

An example of how to use an expression function within a SAF parameter is as follows:

```
<If $uri =~ '^/\~(.*)'>
NameTrans fn="document-root" root="/var/websites/people/$(lc($1))"
</If>
```

A common practice is to allow people their own home directories within the corporate intranet. The URL format for accessing the user's content is similar to the following: http://www.example.com/~rodale.

In this example, the If container is trying to determine whether the URI is referencing a person's home directory. It accomplishes this by looking for the tilde character (~) at the beginning of the URI string. If it is found, then the server uses a backreference to save the username. The NameTrans directive creates a dynamic document root directory based on the value of the username contained in the URI. The lc() expression function converts the username to lowercase—thus ensuring a single, consistent document root directory for the user.

Note: Refer to the *Sun Java System Web Server 7.0 Administrator's Configuration File Reference* for a complete list of available expression functions and examples of each.

6.5 Debugging Request Processing

With the addition of new containers and support for regular expressions, it is now easier than ever to misconfigure your server. As such, knowing how to gather information to debug request processing errors is essential. This section contains information on how to use the Server Log for debugging purposes.

6.5.1 The log SAF

Web Server 7.0 introduces a new SAF that can log arbitrary messages and/or parameter block (pblock) contents to the Server Log (errors log file). This SAF can be used in any stage of request processing and output can be tied to a specific log level. The new SAF is called log and it contains the following parameters:

- level—(Optional) Log level. This parameter defines the log level that must be defined in the server.xml file for the message to be sent to the Server Log. Valid values are finest, finer, fine, info, warning, failure, config, security, and catastrophe.

- `message`—The message to be recorded in the Server Log.
- `pblock`—(Optional) The name of a `pblock` whose contents should be logged. Valid values are `client`, `reqpb`, `headers`, `srvhdrs`, and `vars`.

Examples of the use of this SAF include the following:

```
AuthTrans fn="log" message="Received request from $ip" pblock="reqpb"
pblock="headers"

AddLog fn="log" level="info" message="$uri mapped to $path"
```

The log SAF provides simple output of data, but for more extensive debugging techniques, you should consider increasing the log level in the Server Log.

6.5.2 The Server Log

> **Note:** This section contains information specific to monitoring the client request processing stages. It does not provide specific information on the format, codes, or other detailed information on the Server Log file. To obtain a better understanding of the Server Log file in general, see Chapter 7, "Monitoring Web Server 7.0."

The Server Log contains errors, starts/stops, failures, and user-defined messages created with the `log` SAF. You can specify the verbosity of data sent to the Server Log by modifying the `log-level` element in the `server.xml` file.

```
<log>
    <log-file>../logs/errors</log-file>
    <log-level>info</log-level>
</log>
```

The default value for this element is `info`; this provides an adequate amount of information to determine how your server is processing requests, but it does not contain enough information to debug complex problems. To obtain information that is useful for debugging purposes, you should increase the log level to `finest`.

Note: Log level values include finest, finer, fine, info, warning, failure, config, security, and catastrophe.

For testing and debugging, it is recommended that you set the log-level to finest. For a production environment, the recommended log-level is failure or security. A log-level of catastrophe captures very few details.

Setting the log-level to finest enables you to see details of how requests are being processed. Example 6.10 provides the level of detail contained during request processing for a Web Server whose log level has been set to finest. Comments have been inserted (where appropriate) to explain what is being logged.

Example 6.10   Server Log with Log Level Set to finest

```
[04/May/2008:12:46:05] finest ( 1128): for host 127.0.0.1 trying to GET
  /index.html, process-uri-objects reports: processing objects for URI /
index.html
[04/May/2008:12:46:05] finest ( 1128): for host 127.0.0.1 trying to GET
/index.html, process-uri-objects reports: processing object
name="default"
```

The last entry indicates that the Web Server is starting to process the default object.

```
[04/May/2008:12:46:05] finest ( 1128): for host 127.0.0.1 trying to GET
/index.html, func_exec reports: executing fn="match-browser"
browser="*MSIE*" ssl-unclean-shutdown="true" Directive="AuthTrans"
  magnus-internal="1"
[04/May/2008:12:46:05] finest ( 1128): for host 127.0.0.1 trying to GET
/index.html, func_exec reports: fn="match-browser" browser="*MSIE*"
ssl-unclean-shutdown="true" Directive="AuthTrans" magnus-
  internal="1"
 returned -2 (REQ_NOACTION)
```

These two entries indicate that the server is currently processing in the AuthTrans stage and has just completed execution of the match-browser SAF. The return code from the call to the SAF is REQ_NOACTION. This indicates that the SAF took no action and that it should continue with the next SAF in the current server stage. (Refer to Table 6.3 for a complete list of SAF return codes.)

```
[04/May/2008:12:46:05] finest ( 1128): for host 127.0.0.1 trying to GET
 /index.html, func_exec reports: executing fn="ntrans-j2ee"
   name="j2ee"
Directive="NameTrans"
```

```
[04/May/2008:12:46:05] finest ( 1128): for host 127.0.0.1 trying to GET
/index.html, func_exec reports: fn="ntrans-j2ee" name="j2ee"
Directive="NameTrans" returned -2 (REQ_NOACTION)
```

These two entries indicate that the server is currently processing in the NameTrans stage and has just completed execution of the ntrans-j2ee SAF. The return code from the call to the SAF is REQ_NOACTION. This indicates that the SAF took no action and that it should continue with the next SAF in the current server stage. (Refer to Table 6.3 for a complete list of SAF return codes.)

```
[04/May/2008:12:46:05] finest ( 1128): for host 127.0.0.1 trying to GET
/index.html, func_exec reports: executing fn="pfx2dir" from="/
  mc-icons"
dir="C:/Sun/WebServer7/lib/icons" name="es-internal"
  Directive="NameTrans"
[04/May/2008:12:46:05] finest ( 1128): for host 127.0.0.1 trying to GET
/index.html, func_exec reports: fn="pfx2dir" from="/mc-icons"
dir="C:/Sun/WebServer7/lib/icons" name="es-internal"
  Directive="NameTrans"
returned -2 (REQ_NOACTION)
```

These two entries indicate that the server is currently processing in the NameTrans stage and has just completed execution of the pfx2dir SAF. The return code from the call to the SAF is REQ_NOACTION. This indicates that the SAF took no action and that it should continue with the next SAF in the current server stage. This is the last directive processed in the NameTrans stage and none of the previous directives matched. The default behavior when this occurs is to simply create a document path based on a concatenation of the $uri and $docroot variables.

```
[04/May/2008:12:46:05] finest ( 1128): for host 127.0.0.1 trying to GET
 /index.html, func_exec reports: executing fn="uri-clean"
Directive="PathCheck"
[04/May/2008:12:46:05] finest ( 1128): for host 127.0.0.1 trying to GET
/index.html, func_exec reports: fn="uri-clean" Directive="PathCheck"
returned 0 (REQ_PROCEED)
```

These two entries indicate that the server is currently processing in the PathCheck stage and has just completed execution of the uri-clean SAF. The return code from the call to the SAF is REQ_PROCEED. This indicates that the SAF successfully completed its objective (to clean the URI) and should continue with the next SAF in the current server stage. (Refer to Table 6.3 to see why a return code of REQ_PRO-CEED continues processing for PathCheck directives.)

At first glance, it would seem that the information contained in these two entries conflicts with the placement of the check_acl PathCheck directive. This is not the case. Similar to the processing of the internal SAF that created the default document root directory, the check_acl directive is hidden from the Server Log. You just need to be aware that the check_acl SAF is called for every request.

The remainder of the entries generated for this request as it processes the remaining stages (PathCheck, ObjectType, Service, AddLog) have been purposely left out. The data contained in those entries is similar to the entries already discussed.

Table 6.3 contains an explanation of the codes returned from each SAF call. Some of these return codes take on a different meaning based on the stage that is currently being processed. It is helpful to understand these codes to better understand request processing.

Table 6.3   SAF Return Codes

Return Code	Explanation
REQ_PROCEED	Indicates that the SAF achieved its objective. For some request-response steps (AuthTrans, NameTrans, Service, and Error), this code tells the server to proceed to the next request-response stage, skipping any other SAFs in the current stage. For the other request-response steps (Input, Output, Route, PathCheck, ObjectType, and AddLog), the server proceeds to the next SAF in the current stage.
REQ_NOACTION	Indicates that the SAF took no action. The server continues with the next SAF in the current server stage.
REQ_ABORTED	Indicates that an error occurred and an HTTP response should be sent to the client to indicate the cause of the error. A SAF returning REQ_ABORTED should also set the HTTP response status code. If the server finds an Error directive matching the status code or reason phrase, the server executes the SAF specified. If not, the server sends a default HTTP response with the status code and reason phrase, in addition to a short HTML page reflecting the status code and reason phrase for the user. The server then proceeds to the first AddLog directive.
REQ_EXIT	Indicates the connection to the client was lost. This code should be returned when the SAF fails in reading or writing to the client. The server then proceeds to the first AddLog directive.

In general, when you attempt to troubleshoot request processing issues, you should always check the log files. If they do not contain enough information to help determine the problem, then you should increase the log level to finest to increase the log verbosity. Then reproduce the problem and check the log files again.

6.6 Summary

Request processing in Web Server 7.0 is more robust than with previous product versions. To account for the additional complexity introduced into the object configuration file, the file parser was rewritten to catch more configuration errors and process others in a logical fashion. Even so, it is still easy to misconfigure your Web Server instance as you implement containers and complex regular expressions.

Make sure you follow best practices by saving your configuration before making drastic updates to the object configuration file and test your changes thoroughly on a non-production system before placing the configuration into production. If you do make mistakes, however, rest assured that you have several debugging techniques at hand to help determine and resolve the problem.

6.7 Self-Paced Labs

Use the information contained in this chapter to perform the following exercises. These will help validate your understanding of the concepts described in this chapter.

1. Create support for end-user home pages by performing the following steps: a) create a directory structure to contain user directories on your server, b) create a few user-specific directories beneath it, for example:

   - /var/websites/people/rodale
   - /var/websites/people/wclay
   - /var/websites/people/relise

   c) populate the user-specific directories with sample index.html files, and d) use an If container and an appropriate NameTrans directive to access content in each. Update the NameTrans directive to accept mixed-case letters for the end-user directories.

2. Create a single container and `NameTrans` directive to support server aliases and multiple web sites within one virtual server. Use regular expressions, expression functions, and backreferences to solve the problem. Use the following items for reference:

   - `www.example.com maps to /var/websites/sites/www.example.com`
   - `w3.example.com maps to /var/websites/sites/www.example.com`
   - `example.com maps to /var/websites/sites/www.example.com`

3. Send a user-defined message to the Server Log indicating what browser you are using.

4. Create a different web page for various browser types (i.e., `mozilla.html`, `msie.html`) and use an `If/ElseIf/Else` container structure to present a different web page for each browser.

5. Use the Administration Console to enable CGI as a directory. Review the changes made to the `NameTrans` directives in the object configuration file (you should see a new `pfx2dir` SAF for the CGI `NameTrans` directive). Verify that you have a new entry that calls the named `cgi` object when the `NameTrans` directive is matched. Place a script to echo "Hello World!" beneath the CGI directory and verify that you can access/process this script.

Note: Go to http://www.sunwebserver.com for detailed instructions on how to answer each of these questions.

---

6. Change the log level to `finest` and re-create the client requests that generate server responses for steps 1–6. Review the entries generated for each client request.

7

Monitoring Web Server 7.0

Effective monitoring of your Web Server is an essential task for maintaining an optimal production environment. By keeping a watchful eye you can identify performance bottlenecks, which in turn can enable you to tune the system for optimal performance. Monitoring the Web Server allows you to take a proactive approach to capacity planning by determining when you need additional nodes to serve a growing customer base. This is essential if you are planning on adding a new service or feature to your web site that is expected to draw more visitors. Monitoring enables you to determine whether your site has been configured incorrectly or simply has incorrect links within certain web pages. It enables you to detect and predict certain failures, perform root cause analysis in case of failures, and in some cases simply ensure that everything is functioning as expected.

This chapter explains the various methods you can use to monitor your Web Server. This may be as simple as keeping an eye on Web Server log files or as extensive as storing statistical data in a database and looking for trends. The amount and types of things that you monitor and what you do with the data is totally up to you.

This chapter looks at the monitoring subsystem within Web Server 7.0 and how you can extract data from the subsystem using various tools. It then explores how you can evaluate the data for patterns and use that knowledge to fine-tune your Web Server's performance. In general, we will discuss the following topics:

- Web Server statistics
- The Web Server monitoring subsystem
- Methods for monitoring the Web Server
- How to use monitoring data to tune the Web Server

7.1 Web Server Statistics

The Web Server maintains statistical data for each request received. This data enables you to monitor server activity and obtain information to help fine-tune the system. Statistics show you how many requests your server is handling and how well it is handling those requests. You can view statistical data for individual virtual servers, server instances, or configurations across multiple nodes.

Statistical data is communicated between each node and the Administration Server to which it has been registered. As such, you can review statistical data even if a server instance has been restarted. This can be particularly useful if you need to troubleshoot an instance that has either stopped responding or has been restarted.

Statistics can be configured on a per-instance basis. Unlike previous versions of the Web Server, statistics in Web Server 7.0 are enabled by default and configured in the server.xml file as follows:

```
<stats>
    <enabled>true</enabled>
    <interval>10</interval>
</stats>
```

This example demonstrates a server instance with statistics enabled and the information being updated every five seconds. The stats element is used to configure the statistics collection subsystem and may contain the following subelements:

- enabled—Whether the server collects statistics at runtime or not. Allowable values are either true or false; the default value is true.

- interval—Interval (in seconds) at which statistics are updated. Allowable values are between 0.001 and 3600; the default value is 5.

- profiling—Whether performance buckets are enabled or not. (Performance buckets are used to track NSAPI function execution times.) Allowable values are either true or false; the default value is true.

A review of the server.xml file for a particular instance may or may not contain the stats element. Absence of this element means that statistics are enabled and using the default configuration settings. There is no need to add the stats element unless you would like to override the default values.

7.2 The Web Server Monitoring Subsystem

The monitoring subsystem gathers statistical data from registered nodes and exposes the data for consumption by various clients. Default client interfaces include the following:

- Command Line Interface (CLI)
- Graphical User Interface (GUI)
- Java Enterprise System Monitoring Console (Java ES Monitoring Console)
- Simple Network Management Protocol (SNMP) client

Figure 7.1 provides a high-level overview of the Web Server 7.0 monitoring subsystem. It contains information on the various interfaces used to communicate and to gather the statistical data.

The Command Line Interface and graphical user interface both access statistical data through the Administration Server instance. The GUI accomplishes this through the Administration Console web application and the CLI communicates directly to the Java Management eXtensions (JMX) Connector Servlet.

Monitoring MBeans on the Administration Node fetch statistical data from each running server instance. These MBeans use the Java Native Interface (JNI) layer to connect to and retrieve the data. The information is then communicated back to the Administration Server, where it can be consumed by either the CLI or GUI interfaces.

Note: See Section 4.3 of Chapter 4, "Web Server 7.0 Administration," for more information on the administrative architecture for Web Server 7.0.

You can also use the Java ES Monitoring Console or a Network Management System to communicate with agent applications running on a particular Administration Node. This gives you the flexibility to obtain monitoring data from different standards-based client monitoring applications and display the data in a consistent manner. Figure 7.1 demonstrates how you might access the data in an environment that uses client applications such as these.

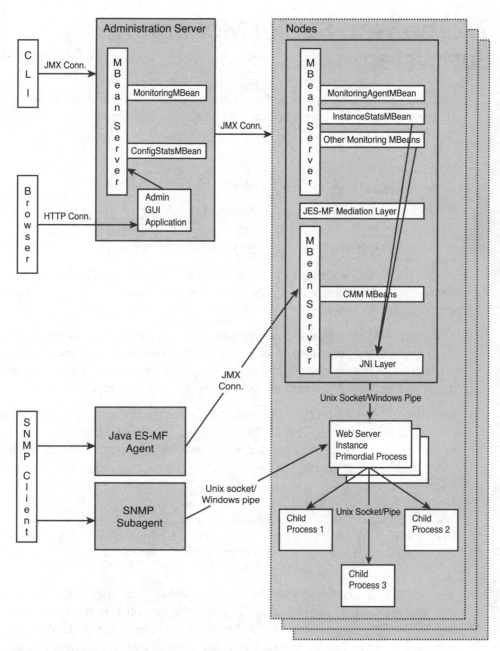

Figure 7.1   Web Server 7.0 Monitoring Subsystem Components

7.3 Methods for Monitoring the Web Server

Web Server 7.0 provides several methods for monitoring components within your Web Server. You can monitor data for all nodes that share a particular configuration, narrow down on a particular instance within the configuration, or even on a particular virtual server within a single instance. You can keep track of information at the process level or even look within the web container to monitor a web application or specific servlet.

The ability to monitor with such flexibility yet remain granular within the monitoring environment provides you with the information necessary to keep your Web Server running and serving a satisfied customer base.

This section describes various methods that you can use to monitor Web Server 7.0.

7.3.1 Web Server Log Files

Web Server log files are used to record your server's activity. You can use these logs to monitor your Web Server and get useful information for tuning or troubleshooting. Regular scanning of these log files is essential in monitoring or troubleshooting your Web Server. There are many ways for you to do this. You can view the raw data from the log files, use the log analysis tools that come with the Web Server, use third-party tools, or even develop your own scripts to parse the data in the log files.

Two log files are enabled by default on the Web Server; these are the Access Log and the Server Log. Each server instance has its own set of log files, which can be found beneath the instance's logs directory. You can change the location of these files by editing the server.xml file associated with your server instance.

Note: Server log files can be configured at the instance level or for a particular virtual server. Virtual server settings override those defined at the instance level.

7.3.1.1 Access Log File

The default name of the Access Log file is access and it records information about requests to the server and the responses that your server sends back to the client. You can configure the types of information recorded in the Web Server Access Log file and then use a log analyzer to determine valuable information regarding the interaction between the Web Server and its clients.

The access-log element is used to configure Access Log parameters in the server. xml file. The following provides an example of the default configuration for the access-log element.

```
<access-log>
   <file>../logs/access</file>
</access-log>
```

The file subelement is used to define the location of the Access Log file. If a fully qualified file name is not provided as a value to this element, then all file references are relative to the instance's config directory.

Note: See the Sun Java System Web Server 7.0 Administrator's Configuration File Reference for additional properties that may be configured for the Access Log.

Example 7.1 provides a sample Access Log file shortly after the server has started.

Example 7.1   Access Log File

```
format=%Ses->client.ip% - %Req->vars.auth-user% [%SYSDATE%]
"%Req->reqpb.clf-request%" %Req->srvhdrs.clf-status%
 %Req->srvhdrs.content-length%
10.100.2.101 - - [05/Oct/2006:15:00:50 -0500] "GET / HTTP/1.1" 200 9606
10.100.2.101 - - [05/Oct/2006:15:00:50 -0500] "GET /img/sun_logo.gif
   HTTP/1.1" 200 2349
10.100.2.101 - - [05/Oct/2006:15:00:51 -0500] "GET /img/a.gif HTTP/1.1"
   200 43
10.100.2.101 - - [05/Oct/2006:15:00:51 -0500] "GET /img/sjsws_
   title_text.gif HTTP/1.1" 200 1822
10.100.2.101 - - [05/Oct/2006:15:00:52 -0500] "GET /img/content_hline.gif
   HTTP/1.1" 200 473
10.100.2.101 - - [05/Oct/2006:15:00:52 -0500] "GET /img/foo.gif HTTP/1.1"
   404 292
```

The first line of Example 7.1 defines the format of each log entry and helps to interpret the remaining lines in the log file. Given this format, client IP addresses are logged first, followed by the authenticated username (if known). The system date is logged next, followed by the actual HTTP request from the client, the server's response to that request, and the length (in bytes) of the content transferred to the client.

Example 7.1 contains six GET requests and the associated responses that the Web Server sent the client for each request. There is one GET request for the main page and five additional GET requests for the images contained in the page. The first five requests contain a response code of 200 (which means the request was successful). The last request contains a response code of 404, which means that the item was not found on this server. This is most likely due to an incorrect image reference in the web page. You should scan your log files on a periodic basis and address issues such as these.

Server access logs can be in Common Logfile Format, or you can provide your own customized format. The Common Logfile Format is a commonly supported format across multiple vendor web servers and provides a fixed amount of information about the server. You can elect to customize your log file format through the use of parameter blocks (pblocks), which allow you to control what gets logged. For a list of customizable format parameters, see the Sun Java System Web Server 7.0 NSAPI Developer's Guide.

Note: You can alter the format of the Access Log through the Administrative Console, command line interface, or by directly editing the server.xml file for the appropriate server instance.

After an Access Log for a particular configuration has been created, you cannot change its properties until you either archive it or create a new Access Log file for the configuration.

7.3.1.2 Server Log File

The default name of the Server Log file is errors. This file lists all the errors the server has encountered as well as all server starts and stops. The Server Log contains messages generated when the Web Server runs events (such as loading a certificate revocation list) and you can even add your own entries to the Server Log, using the log SAF. You can configure the level of detail provided in the Server Log by modifying the log-level attribute in the server.xml file.

The basic format for the Server Log is as follows:

`[date] log-level (pid): error-message-number: error-message`

and can be described as follows:

- *date*—The date (or timestamp) for the entry. The date is bounded by a set of square braces.
- *log-level*—The severity of the entry. Different log levels contain different types or amounts of data. The following log levels are defined for the Web Server:
  - finest, finer, fine—Messages are verbose and may contain debug information. A log level of finest provides the most information.
  - info—Messages are informative in nature and usually contain information pertaining to the server configuration or server status. These messages do not indicate errors that need immediate action.
  - warning—Messages indicate a warning. The message would most likely be accompanied by an exception.
  - failure—Messages indicate a failure of considerable importance that can prevent normal application execution.
  - config—Messages relate to a variety of static configuration information, to assist in debugging problems that may be associated with particular configurations.
  - security—Messages indicate a security issue.
  - catastrophe—Messages indicate a fatal error.

  Items at the top of the list produce the most information, and the number of messages diminishes the farther down that you go. It is common to increase the log level to troubleshoot problems with the Web Server.
- *pid*—The process identifier for the Web Server process.
- *error-message-number*—The error message number associated with this entry.
- *error-message*—The error message associated with this entry. Error messages are free-form text.

Warning: The *error-message-number* and the *error-message* are created by the developer of the SAF and vary between functions. The Web Server shares code with other Sun Web–tier products (for instance, the Java Enterprise System Proxy Server), and although some of the information may be similar, you cannot count on the log entries to be the same.

The log element is used to configure Server Log parameters in the server.xml file. The following provides an example of the default configuration for the log element.

```
<log>
    <log-file>../logs/errors</log-file>
    <log-level>info</log-level>
</log>
```

The log-file subelement is used to define the location of the Server Log file. If a fully qualified filename is not provided as a value to this element, then all file references are relative to the instance's config directory. The log-level subelement is used to define the logging level and directly affects what types of entries are sent to the Server Log.

Note: See the Sun Java System Web Server 7.0 Administrator's Configuration File Reference for additional properties that may be configured for the Server Log.

Example 7.2 provides a sample Server Log file shortly after the server has started. The entries found in this file correspond to those found in Example 7.1.

Example 7.2   Server Log File

```
[05/Oct/2006:07:11:01] info ( 6940): CORE1116: Sun Java System Web Server
    7.00U1
B06/12/2007 22:13
[05/Oct/2006:07:11:05] info ( 6940): CORE5076: Using [Java HotSpot(TM)
Server VM, Version 1.5.0_09] from [Sun Microsystems Inc.]
[05/Oct/2006:07:11:19] info ( 6940): HTTP3072: http-listener-1:
http://www.example.com:80 ready to accept requests
[05/Oct/2006:07:11:19] info ( 6940): CORE3274: successful server startup
...
[05/Oct/2006:15:00:52] warning ( 6940): for host 10.100.1.62 trying to GET
/img/foo.gif, send-file reports: HTTP4142: can't find /sun/webserver7/
https-www.example.com/docs/img/foo.gif (File not found)
```

The first four entries in Example 7.2 are informational messages that provide standard start-up information. The entries can be described as follows:

- Entry 1—Contains the version of the Web Server.
- Entry 2—Contains the version of the standard Java Virtual Machine (JVM) and the Hotspot high-performance plug-in that the Web Server is using.
- Entry 3—Demonstrates that the listener is ready to accept requests on port 80.
- Entry 4—Indicates that the server has started up successfully.

The final entry in Example 7.2 provides the reason why the following entry in the Access Log returned an error response code of 404 to the client:

```
10.100.2.101 - - [05/Oct/2006:15:00:52 -0500] "GET /img/foo.gif
HTTP/1.1" 404 292
```

In most cases, the standard data found in the Server Log is enough to debug a problem involving content-related issues. If, however, you need to perform extensive troubleshooting of a particular problem, you should increase the log level to finest, reproduce the problem, and review the additional entries generated by the increased log level.

7.3.1.3 Accessing and Modifying Log Settings from the Administration Console

The Administration Console gives you an easy-to-use graphical web-based form that enables you to view and modify log settings for either the Access Log or Server Log. You can access the log file settings through the Administration Console by performing the following steps:

1. Open the Administration Console and click the Configurations tab to access the main configuration page.
2. Click the link for the configuration that contains the Server Log settings you want to modify.
3. Click the General tab. This opens a window that enables you to perform general functionality for this configuration, such as modifying log file preferences.
4. Click the Log Preferences subtab (if necessary). The main window appears for updating log file preferences for either the Access Log or Server Log.

Any changes made through the Administration Console update the access-log or log elements in the server.xml file (as appropriate).

7.3.1.4 Accessing and Modifying Access Log Properties from the Command Line Interface

The command line interface provides subcommands to quickly access and modify log file settings for the Access Log. These subcommands can be included in scripts to allow further functionality when performing administrative tasks.

The `get-access-log-prop` subcommand in the CLI can be used to obtain the current properties for the Access Log. The following information provides an overview of this subcommand:

```
wadm> get-access-log-prop --<TAB>
--config*     --vs     --uri-pattern  --echo     --no-prompt
--verbose
```

You can configure Access Log properties at either the server or virtual server level. As such, this subcommand enables you to obtain the properties for either level as well. The following demonstrates how the `get-access-log-prop` subcommand can be used to obtain the current Access Log properties for the My Test Config configuration:

```
wadm> get-access-log-prop --config="My Test Config"
enabled=true
file=../logs/access
format=%Ses->client.ip% - %Req->vars.auth-user% [%SYSDATE%] "%Req-
   >reqpb.clf-
request%" %Req->srvhdrs.clf-status% %Req->srvhdrs.content-length%
wadm>
```

The `enable-access-log` subcommand in the CLI is used to modify Access Log properties. The following information provides an overview of this subcommand:

```
wadm> enable-access-log --<TAB>
--config*        --file*      --format      --log-ip      --vs
--uri-pattern    --echo       --no-prompt   --verbose
```

You can configure Access Log properties at either the server or virtual server level. The following demonstrates how the `enable-access-log` subcommand can be used to set the Access Log's file location for the My Test Config configuration:

```
wadm>enable-access-log --config "My Test Config" --file="/foo.txt"
CLI201 Command 'enable-access-log' ran successfully
wadm>
```

Changes made with the `enable-access-log` subcommand update the appropriate `access-log` subelements in the `server.xml` file.

7.3.1.5 Accessing and Modifying Server Log Properties from the Command Line Interface

The command line interface provides subcommands to quickly access and modify log file settings for the Server Log. These subcommands can be included in scripts to allow further functionality to perform administrative tasks.

The `get-log-prop` subcommand in the CLI can be used to obtain the current properties for the Server Log. The following information provides an overview of this subcommand:

```
wadm> get-log-prop --<TAB>
--config*     --echo         --no-prompt  --verbose
```

You can configure Server Log settings at either the server or virtual server level. As such, this subcommand enables you to obtain the properties for either level as well. The following demonstrates how the `get-log-prop` subcommand can be used to obtain the current Server Log properties for the My Test Config configuration:

```
wadm> get-log-prop --config="My Test Config"
log-stdout=true
log-to-syslog=false
log-virtual-server-name=false
create-console=false
log-to-console=true
date-format=[%d/%b/%Y:%H:%M:%S]
log-level=info
archive-suffix=.%Y%m%d%H%M
log-file=../logs/errors
log-stderr=true
wadm>
```

The `set-log-prop` subcommand in the CLI can be used to set Server Log properties. The following information provides an overview of this subcommand:

```
wadm> set-log-prop --<TAB>
--config*     --echo         --no-prompt   --verbose
```

You can configure Server Log settings at either the server or virtual server level. The following demonstrates how the `set-log-prop` subcommand can be used to set the Server Log's log level for the My Test Config configuration:

```
wadm> set-log-prop --config "My Test Config" log-level=finest
CLI201 Command 'set-log-prop' ran successfully
wadm>
```

Changes made using the `set-log-prop` subcommand update the appropriate log subelements in the `server.xml` file.

7.3.1.6 Accessing Log Data from the Administration Console

The Log Viewer in the Administration Console provides you with a web-based interface for viewing log files. Within a single web page you can easily review Access Log or Server Log files for any configuration. This can be limited to a single node or used on all nodes within the configuration. You can sort the entries based on date, log level (Server Log only), or message identifier. You can even filter data based on a number of entries, the log level (Server Log only), or the server response code (Access Log only), or you can display entries that fall within a specific time frame.

To access the Log Viewer, perform the following steps:

1. Open the Administration Console and click the Configuration tab to access the main configuration page.
2. Click the View Logs button in the upper-right corner of the page. This opens a Log Viewer window.

Access to log data in the Administration Console is convenient if you already have the GUI open. Launching the graphical interface simply to look at log data may not be the right approach, however, if you need immediate access to your data. Fortunately, the Web Server also provides a method whereby you can view log files from the command line interface or view them directly on the file system. The next two sections describe how to access the log files using these two methods.

7.3.1.7 Accessing Log Data from the Command Line Interface

The command line interface provides the same functionality for accessing log data as the Administration Console does. Two specific subcommands are designated for this purpose—one for obtaining Access Log entries (`get-access-log`) and one for obtaining Server Log entries (`get-log`). These two subcommands are described in this section.

The `get-access-log` subcommand in the CLI can be used to retrieve Access Log entries for a particular configuration. The following information provides an overview of this subcommand:

```
wadm> get-access-log --<TAB>
--config*   --start-date   --end-date    --status-code --num-records
--vs        --echo         --no-prompt   --verbose
```

This command also enables you to filter data based on a number of entries, a particular server response code, or within a specific time frame. The following demonstrates how the `get-access-log` subcommand can be used to get the Access Log data for the www.example.com configuration:

```
wadm> get-access-log --config="www.example.com" www.example.com
10.100.2.101 - - [05/Oct/2006:15:00:50 -0500] "GET / HTTP/1.1" 200
    9606
10.100.2.101 - - [05/Oct/2006:15:00:50 -0500] "GET /img/sun_logo.gif
    HTTP/1.1"
200 2349
10.100.2.101 - - [05/Oct/2006:15:00:51 -0500] "GET /img/a.gif
    HTTP/1.1" 200 43
10.100.2.101 - - [05/Oct/2006:15:00:51 -0500] "GET /img/sjsws_title_
    text.gif
HTTP/1.1" 200 1822
10.100.2.101 - - [05/Oct/2006:15:00:52 -0500] "GET /img/content_
    hline.gif HTTP/1.1"
200 473
10.100.2.101 - - [05/Oct/2006:15:00:52 -0500] "GET /img/foo.gif
HTTP/1.1" 404 292
```

Note: The format entry is not returned when you retrieve the Access Log from the command line.

The `get-log` subcommand in the CLI can be used to retrieve Server Log entries for a particular configuration. The following information provides an overview of this subcommand:

```
wadm> get-log --<TAB>
--config*    --start-date   --end-date    --log-level    --num-records
--vs         --echo         --no-prompt   --verbose
```

This command also enables you to filter data based on a number of entries, a log level, or within a specific time frame. The following demonstrates how the `get-log` subcommand can be used to get the Server Log data for the www.example.com configuration:

```
wadm> get-log --config=www.example.com www.example.com
[05/Oct/2006:07:11:01] info ( 6940): CORE1116: Sun Java System Web
    Server 7.00U1
B06/12/2007 22:13
[05/Oct/2006:07:11:05] info ( 6940): CORE5076: Using [Java HotSpot(TM)
    Server VM,
Version 1.5.0_09] from [Sun Microsystems Inc.]
[05/Oct/2006:07:11:19] info ( 6940): HTTP3072: http-listener-1:
http://www.example.com:80 ready to accept requests
[05/Oct/2006:07:11:19] info ( 6940): CORE3274: successful server
    startup
...
[05/Oct/2006:15:00:52] warning ( 6940): for host 10.100.1.62 trying to
    GET
/img/foo.gif, send-file reports: HTTP4142: can't find /sun/webserver7/
    https-
www.example.com/docs/img/foo.gif (File not found)
```

7.3.1.8 Accessing Log Data from the File System

One of the most common ways to access log data is by viewing the content in the log files on the file system. You can then use operating system–specific commands to search for data, sort data, combine both log files, or simply keep a watchful eye on events within the file itself.

You can find the log files beneath the *server_root*/*configuration*/logs directory for a particular node.

7.3.2 XML Report

After a Web Server instance is started, it begins gathering statistical data that is useful for monitoring purposes and is accessible through an XML data report. The Administration Console and certain text reports extract information from the

XML data to provide you with a user-friendly interface. There are times, however, when you might need to review the raw XML data because it contains much more detailed information than a formatted web page or report.

Note: Web Server 7.0 continues to support the XML data stream found in previous Web Server versions and generated with the `stats-xml` SAF. Unlike previous versions, however, statistics gathering is enabled by default in Web Server 7.0 and the data now includes additional Java data values.

The XML Report is typically used by analysis tools and can be accessed through either the command line interface or through a user-defined URI.

7.3.2.1 Accessing the XML Report from the Command Line

The command line interface requires authentication to the Administration Server and all traffic between the CLI and the Administration Server is encrypted. As such, accessing the data from the CLI is both safe and easy.

The entirety of the Web Server's statistical data can be accessed by default using the `get-stats-xml` subcommand in the CLI, as follows:

```
wadm> get-stats-xml --<TAB>
--config*    --node*    --echo    --no-prompt  --verbose
```

You can obtain statistics for only a particular node within a configuration. The following example demonstrates how you can use the `get-stats-xml` command to retrieve the `stats-xml` data from the `node1` node in the `www.example.com` configuration.

```
wadm> get-stats-xml --config=www.example.com --node=node1
```

Note: See Appendix B, "Sample XML Report Data," for sample output for this command.

The CLI is useful for troubleshooting conditions where a server instance has stopped responding to HTTP requests. The last known statistical data for the hung instance is still available in the Administration Server and may be obtained through the command line. This information can be helpful in debugging the problem because it often includes the last request prior to the sever problem.

7.3.2.2 Accessing the XML Report from a User-Defined URI

Access from the command line interface is enabled by default, but you need to enable XML Reporting at the virtual server level if you would like to access the XML Report through a particular URI.

The Administration Console gives you an easy-to-use graphical web-based form that allows you to enable XML Reporting and configure the desired URI for accessing the data. You can access the form through the Administration Console by performing the following steps:

1. Open the Administration Console and click the Configurations tab to access the main configuration page.
2. Click the link for the configuration that contains the virtual server where you would like to enable XML Reporting. You will see a list of virtual servers.
3. Click the link for the virtual server where you would like to enable XML Reporting. You will see the virtual server general properties page.
4. Click the Server Settings tab (if necessary).
5. Click the Monitoring Settings subtab (if necessary). You will see the main window for enabling and configuring an XML Report for this virtual server.
6. Select the check box next to Enabled for XML Report and modify the URI (if necessary).

The command line interface can also be used to enable XML Reporting, disable XML Reporting, and query the status of XML Reporting for a particular virtual server. These tasks can be performed with the following subcommands:

- `get-stats-xml-prop`—Gets the properties for the XML Reporting configuration settings
- `enable-stats-xml`—Enable XML Reporting and provide an applicable URI
- `disable-stats-xml`—Disable XML Reporting

The `get-stats-xml-prop` subcommand can be used to determine if XML Reporting has been enabled for a particular virtual server or not. The following example demonstrates the usage for this subcommand:

```
wadm> get-stats-xml-prop --
--config*     --vs*          --echo        --no-prompt   --verbose
```

Access to XML Report data through a URI is disabled by default. You can verify this with the `get-stats-xml-prop` subcommand as follows:

```
wadm> get-stats-xml-prop --config=www.example.com --vs=www.example.com
enabled=false
uri=/stats-xml(|/*)
```

You can enable access to the XML Report through a URI with the `enable-stats-xml` subcommand from the CLI and use the `disable-stats-xml` subcommand to disable it once again. The `enable-stats-xml` subcommand takes the URI as an option. This enables you to specify your own URI when you enable XML Reporting. The following example demonstrates how you enable XML Reporting from the command line and specify a custom URI for accessing the data.

```
wadm> enable-stats-xml --config=www.example.com --vs=www.example.com
--uri-prefix=/wsstats(|/*)
CLI201 Command 'enable-stats-xml' ran successfully
```

After you enable URI access to XML Reporting data from either the Administration Console or the command line interface, the results of your performing these steps is a modified object configuration file that contains the following additions:

- A `NameTrans` directive to intercept the URI and associate a named object for further processing as follows:

```
NameTrans fn="assign-name" name="stats-xml"

    from="/wwstats(|/*)"
```

- The named object that specifies the appropriate service to dump the XML Report data as follows:

```
<Object name="stats-xml">

Service fn="stats-xml"

</Object>
```

You can now access the XML Report by providing the appropriate URI to your virtual server as follows:

```
http://www.example.com/wsstats/
```

The response to this request is a web page that contains XML data similar to that shown in Appendix B, "Sample XML Report Data."

Note: You can limit the amount of data provided in the XML Report by specifying a query string along with the URI. All XML elements are displayed by default, but you can "hide" certain elements by providing a value of 0 for the element that you want eliminated from the report. For instance, the following URI prevents the thread and process elements from being displayed in the XML Report:

`http://localhost:8080/wsstats/?thread=0&process=0`.

Some of the data contained in the XML Report may be considered sensitive in nature. As such, if you elect to enable access to the data from a URI, you should consider adding access control to the URI for this resource. Doing so limits the number of users who can view the XML Report from a browser.

The ACL file created to protect this URI must be referenced in the stats-xml named object definition in the object configuration file. For example, if you created a named ACL for the /wsstats URI and called this file stats.acl, then you would need to add a PathCheck directive in the object definition as follows:

```
<Object name="stats-xml">
PathCheck fn="check-acl" acl="stats.acl"
Service fn="stats-xml"
</Object>
```

Note: See Chapter 8, "Securing Web Server 7.0," for more information on creating ACL files.

7.3.3 Plain Text Report

service-dump is a Server Application Function (SAF) built into the Web Server that collects various pieces of performance data from the Web Server internal statistics (stats-xml) and displays them in an ASCII-formatted text report.

Note: You may see references to service-dump, perfdump, or a Plain Text Report in the Sun documentation. They all refer to the same functionality.

Plain Text Report data does not display all the statistics available through the CLI or the Administration Console, but it can still be a useful tool for monitoring your Web Server. A Plain Text Report can be obtained by using the `get-perfdump` subcommand in the CLI or by defining a URI to intercept and obtain the data.

A Plain Text Report provides statistics in the following categories:

- Connection queue information
- HTTP Listener (Listen Socket) information
- Keep-alive information
- Session creation (thread) information
- File cache information (static content)
- Thread pool information
- DNS cache information

7.3.3.1 Accessing Plain Text Report Data from the Command Line

Plain Text Report data can be accessed from the command line by default, using the `get-perfdump` subcommand as follows:

```
wadm> get-perfdump --<TAB>
--config*    --node*       --echo       --no-prompt   --verbose
```

Note: See Appendix C, "Sample Plain Text Report Data," for sample output and an explanation of the data provided from this subcommand.

Data contained in the Plain Text Report can provide valuable insight into how well your server is processing requests. `stats-xml` data provides a comprehensive view of all available statistical data and is quite useful for diving deeper into the data, but it may actually contain too much information. As an alternative, a Plain Text Report provides a formatted subset of the `stats-xml` data and gives you a dashboard view of your Web Server's overall performance.

7.3.3.2 Accessing Plain Text Report Data from a User-Defined URI

Access from the command line interface is enabled by default, but you need to enable the Plain Text Report at the virtual server level if you would like to access this information through a particular URI.

The Administration Console provides you an easy-to-use graphical web-based form that allows you to enable the Plain Text Report and configure the desired URI for accessing the data. You can access the form through the Administration Console by performing the following steps:

1. Open the Administration Console and click the Configurations tab to access the main configuration page.
2. Click the link for the configuration that contains the virtual server where you would like to enable the Plain Text Report. You will see a list of virtual servers.
3. Click the link for the virtual server where you would like to enable the Plain Text Report. You will see the virtual server general properties page.
4. Click the Server Settings tab (if necessary).
5. Click the Monitoring Settings subtab (if necessary). You will see the main window for enabling and configuring the Plain Text Report for this virtual server.
6. Select the check box next to Enabled for Plain Text Report and modify the URI (if necessary).

Note: These steps are similar to those found in section 7.3.2.2. The difference, however, is that you are now selecting Plain Text Report (rather than Enabled for XML) and specifying an appropriate URL to access the report.

The command line interface can also be used to enable the Plain Text Report reporting, disable the Plain Text Report, and obtain Plain Text Report data for a particular virtual server. These tasks can be performed with the following sub-commands:

- `get-perfdump-prop`—Get the properties for the Plain Text Report configuration settings
- `enable-perfdump`—Enable the Plain Text Report and provide an applicable URI
- `disable-perfdump`–Disable the Plain Text Report access through the URI

The `get-perfdump-prop` subcommand can be used to determine whether the Plain Text Report has been enabled for a particular virtual server or not. The following example demonstrates the usage for this subcommand:

```
wadm> get-perfdump-prop --
--config*    --vs*         --echo       --no-prompt  --verbose
```

Access to the Plain Text Report data through a URI is disabled by default. You can verify this with the `get-perfdump-prop` subcommand as follows:

```
wadm> get-perfdump-prop --config=www.example.com --vs=www.example.com
enabled=false
uri=/.perf
```

You can enable access to the Plain Text Report through a URI with the `enable-perfdump` subcommand from the CLI and use the `disable-perfdump` subcommand to disable it once again. The `enable-perfdump` subcommand takes the URI as an option. This enables you to specify your own URI when you enable Plain Text Reporting. The following example demonstrates how you enable Plain Text Reporting from the command line and specify a custom URI for accessing the data.

```
wadm> enable-perfdump --config=www.example.com --vs=www.
example.com
--uri=/.perf
CLI201 Command 'enable-perfdump' ran successfully
```

Note: The parameters for the `enable-stats-xml` and `enable-perfdump` subcommands are slightly different. For instance, the `enable-stats-xml` subcommand uses a `uri-prefix` parameter to specify the URI; the `enable-perfdump` subcommand uses the `uri` parameter.

After you enable URI access to the Plain Text Report by using either the Administration Console or the command line interface, the results of your performing these steps is a modified object configuration file that contains the following additions:

- A `NameTrans` directive to intercept the URI and associate a named object for further processing as follows:

```
NameTrans fn="assign-name" name="perf" from="/.perf"
```

- The named object that specifies the appropriate service to dump the Plain Text Report data as follows:

```
<Object name="perf">
Service fn="service-dump"
</Object>
```

You can now access the Plain Text Report by providing the appropriate URI to your virtual server as follows:

```
http://www.example.com/.perf
```

The response to this request is a web page that contains data similar to that shown in Appendix C, "Sample Plain Text Report Data."

Some of the data contained in the Plain Text Report may be considered sensitive in nature. As such, if you elect to enable access to the data from a URI, you should consider adding access control to the URI for this resource. Doing so limits the number of users who can view the data for your server from a browser.

The ACL file created to protect this URI must be referenced in the perf named object definition in the object configuration file. For example, if you created a named ACL for the /.perf URI and called this file, perfdump.acl, then you would need to add a PathCheck directive in the object definition as follows:

```
<Object name="perf">
PathCheck fn="check-acl" acl="perfdump.acl"
Service fn="service-dump"
</Object>
```

Note: See Chapter 8 for more information on creating ACL files.

7.3.4 Command Line Interface

The XML Report discussed in section 7.3.2 provides an XML data stream of all statistical data gathered by the Web Server since the instance was first started. The Plain Text Report in Section 7.3.3 provides a subset of the XML Report data that might be useful in monitoring the Web Server's performance. In addition to the get-stats-xml and get-perfdump subcommands already discussed, the CLI also provides the following subcommands for displaying subsets of the XML Report data:

- `get-config-stats`
- `get-virtual-server-stats`
- `get-webapp-stats`
- `get-servlet-stats`

The following sections provide additional information on each of these subcommands.

> **Note:** The examples provided in Sections 7.3.4.1–7.3.4.4 do not contain all possible command-line options. Use the `help` option for the particular subcommand to see the usage and complete syntax.

7.3.4.1 Obtaining Configuration Level Statistics

Statistical information can be obtained for all instances that are part of a configuration. The following is an example of the `get-config-stats` command and the output from the command:

```
wadm> get-config-stats --config=www.example.com
countRequests=690546
rpsLast1MinAvg=4491.7666
rpsLast5MinAvg=1844.6061
rpsLast15MinAvg=637.37305
countErrors=0
epsLast1MinAvg=0.0
epsLast5MinAvg=0.0
epsLast15MinAvg=0.0
maxResponseTime=0.30789953
rtLast1MinAvg=5.3970284
rtLast5MinAvg=5.208407
rtLast15MinAvg=35.56042
countBytesReceived=96800935
countBytesTransmitted=689929574
wadm>
```

The data returned from this subcommand includes the following:

- The total number of requests (`countRequests`)
- The average number of requests per second for the past 1, 5, and 15 minutes (`rpsLast1MinAvg`, `rpsLast5MinAvg`, and `rpsLast15MinAvg`)
- The total number of error responses (`countErrors`)
- The average number of errors per second for the past 1, 5, and 15 minutes (`epsLast1MinAvg`, `epsLast5MinAvg`, and `epsLast15MinAvg`)
- The maximum response time it took to process a request (`maxResponseTime`)
- The average response time for the past 1, 5, and 15 minutes (`rtLast1MinAvg`, `rtLast5MinAvg`, and `rtLast15MinAvg`)
- The number of bytes received from the client (`countBytesReceived`)
- The number of bytes sent to the client (`countBytesTransmitted`)

This subcommand aggregates data from all instances within a particular configuration. If the configuration consists of only a single node, then the information is not particularly interesting unless you specify the `--node` option. Doing so produces additional data that can be gathered for a particular node (but does not have meaning to an entire configuration). You can see the additional information in the bold-faced items in the following example:

```
wadm> get-config-stats --config=www.example.com --node=node1
timeStarted=1212978838
secondsRunning=84350
countRequests=690546
rpsLast1MinAvg=4491.7666
rpsLast5MinAvg=1844.6061
rpsLast15MinAvg=637.37305
countErrors=0
epsLast1MinAvg=0.0
epsLast5MinAvg=0.0
epsLast15MinAvg=0.0
maxResponseTime=0.30789953
rtLast1MinAvg=5.3970284
rtLast5MinAvg=5.208407
rtLast15MinAvg=35.56042
countBytesReceived=96800935
countBytesTransmitted=689929574
countChildDied=0
countVirtualServers=1
instanceName=https-www.example.com
process.1.countThreadPools=1
process.1.jdbcPoolCount=0
process.1.countThreads=2
```

```
process.1.fractionSystemMemoryUsage=0.0
process.1.countConnectionQueues=1
process.1.sizeResident=0
process.1.countIdleThreads=2
process.1.mode=1
process.1.sizeVirtual=0
process.1.countConfigurations=2
process.1.pid=5540
process.1.timeStarted=Jun 8, 2008 10:33:58 PM
...
process.1.threadPool.1.countQueued=0
process.1.threadPool.1.countThreadsIdle=1
process.1.threadPool.1.threadPoolId=NativePool
process.1.threadPool.1.maxThreads=128
process.1.threadPool.1.countThreads=1
process.1.threadPool.1.maxQueued=0
process.1.threadPool.1.peakQueued=0
process.1.threadPool.1.name=NativePool
wadm>
```

7.3.4.2 Obtaining Virtual Server Statistics

If you have configured multiple virtual servers within a configuration, you can obtain statistical information for all virtual servers across multiple nodes or for a particular node within the configuration. The following is an example of the get-virtual-server-stats command and the output from the command:

```
wadm> get-virtual-server-stats --config=www.example.com
   --vs=www.example.com
count200=1150
count2xx=1150
count302=0
count304=0
count3xx=0
count400=64
count401=0
count403=0
count404=2
count4xx=62
count5xx=0
countBytesReceived=497652
countBytesTransmitted=2219783
countErrors=0
countOpenConnections=0
countOther=0
```

```
countRequests=1212
rateBytesTransmitted=0
vsName=www.example.com
wadm>
```

The data returned from this subcommand includes the following:

- The total number of responses that returned a specific status code to the client. This includes the following values: `count200`, `count302`, `count304`, `count400`, `count401`, `count403` and `count404`.

- The total number of responses that returned a status code within a particular range. This number is inclusive of any specific status codes listed. For instance, `count4xx` includes all responses between 400 and 499 and includes `count400`, `count401`, `count403`, and `count404` (and any other responses in the 4xx range that are not explicitly shown).

- The number of bytes received from the client (`countBytesReceived`)

- The number of bytes sent to the client (`countBytesTransmitted`)

- The number of errors detected during request processing (`countErrors`)

- The total number of open connections (`countOpenConnections`)

- The total number of responses that are not included in any of the default response counters. This includes any 1xx responses (`countOther`).

- The total number of requests (`countRequests`)

- The average rate in which the bytes were transmitted to the client (`rateBytesTransmitted`)

- The name of the virtual server (`vsName`)

Note: Virtual server statistics may also contain Web Application statistics (such as the JSP count, session count, or servlet response cache statistics) and servlet statistics (such as the number of requests serviced by the servlet and the time spent in processing a request). This information is not shown when a web application has not been deployed to the virtual server.

This subcommand aggregates data from all virtual servers within a particular configuration. As with the `get-config-stats` subcommand, you can limit the information to a specific node by specifying the `--node` option.

7.3.4.3 Obtaining Web Container Statistics

Web Server 7.0 makes it possible to track statistics that pertain to the Web Container. This includes data that is specific to a particular web application or Java servlet. Previous versions of Web Server did not provide this level of granularity. Web Server 7.0 now enables you to keep track of how well components within the Web Container are operating.

The following example demonstrates how you can use the `get-webapp-stats` subcommand to obtain information for the URI, `/hello`:

```
wadm> get-webapp-stats --config=www.example.com --node=node1
    --vs=www.example.com --uri=/hello
countActiveSessions=1
countExpiredSessions=0
countJsps=1
countRejectedSessions=0
countReloadedJsps=1
countSessions=1
peakActiveSessions=1
secondsSessionAliveAverage=0
secondsSessionAliveMax=0
uri=/hello
vsName=www.example.com
wadm>
```

The syntax obtains statistics for a given web application deployed to a particular virtual server operating within an instance on a particular node. To obtain the aggregated web application statistics for a given configuration across all the nodes where the configuration has been deployed, use the command without the `--node` option.

The following example demonstrates how you can use the `get-servlet-stats` subcommand to obtain information for a particular servlet (`/myServlet`).

```
wadm> get-servlet-stats --config=www.example.com --node=node1
    --vs=www.example.com --uri=/myServlet
```

Notice how the `--uri` parameter is used in a similar fashion when specifying a servlet as it was when specifying a web application with the `get-webapp-stats` subcommand.

7.3.5 Administration Console

The Administration Console provides a convenient method for accessing and viewing statistical information from a graphical user interface. You can review information for a particular configuration, instance, virtual server, or obtain any performance-related information as with `perfdump`.

Table 7.1 provides an overview of the statistical categories that can be monitored in Web Server 7.0:

Table 7.1   Administration Console Monitoring Categories

Category	Description
General Statistics	Provides information on overall Request, Error, and Response statistics for a configuration.
Instance Statistics	Provides information on overall Request, Error, and Response statistics for the instances, along with information on server crashes and virtual server count.
Virtual Server Statistics	Provides information on overall Request, Error, and Response statistics for virtual servers, along with the number of open connections and total bytes received/transmitted.

To access server statistics from the Administration Console, go to the Common Tasks page, click the Monitoring tab, and click the Configuration tab (if necessary). You will see the Overall Configuration Statistics monitoring page, as shown in Figure 7.2.

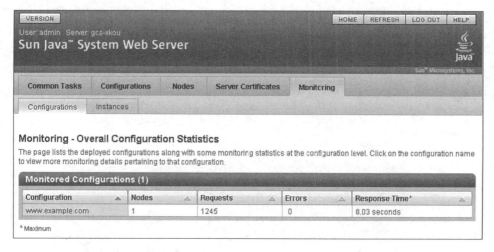

Figure 7.2   Overall Configuration Statistics

This page provides an overview of the various configurations that have been deployed to your Web Server environment. The table in Figure 7.2 provides a list of available configurations, along with the following:

- Nodes—The number of nodes to which the configuration has been deployed.
- Requests—The total number of requests received by all virtual servers within the configuration.
- Errors—The total number of errors logged across all virtual servers within the configuration.
- Response Time—The maximum response time for any virtual server contained within the configuration.

Click the configuration name to obtain statistics that are specific to the configuration. You will see the Configuration Monitoring Statistics page, as shown in Figure 7.3.

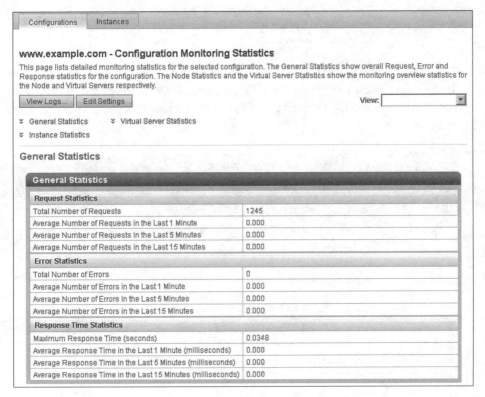

Figure 7.3   Configuration Monitoring Statistics

This page contains three categories of statistics: general statistics, instance statistics, and virtual server statistics.

Information found in the General Statistics section is the same as the information returned from the `get-config-stats` subcommand and is shown in Figure 7.3.

Information contained in the Instance Statistics section provides an overview of the various instances for which this configuration has been deployed. This can be seen in Figure 7.4.

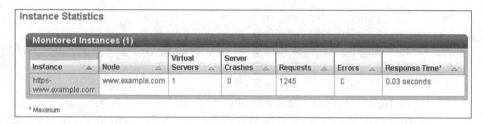

Figure 7.4   Configuration Instance Statistics Overview

The table in Figure 7.4 provides a list of available instances, along with the following:

- **Instance**—The name of the instance to which this configuration was deployed.
- **Node**—The name of the node where this instance is found.
- **Virtual Servers**—The number of virtual servers contained within this instance.
- **Server Crashes**—The number of times this particular instance has crashed and had to be restarted.
- **Requests**—The total number of requests received by all virtual servers within the instance.
- **Errors**—The total number of errors logged across all virtual servers within the instance.
- **Response Time**—The maximum response time for any virtual server contained within the instance.

Select the link for the instance name to see comprehensive information for the particular server instance. This includes general statistics, process-related statistics, thread pool statistics, and virtual server statistics. Information found on this page is the same as the information returned from the `get-config-stats` subcommand when you use the `--node` option. Information contained in the Virtual Server

Statistics section is the same as that found on the Configuration Monitoring Statistics page and provides an overview of the various virtual servers that are contained within the instance. This is shown in Figure 7.5.

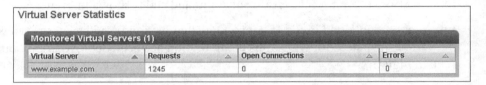

Figure 7.5   Virtual Server Statistics Overview

The table in Figure 7.5 provides a list of available virtual servers, along with the following:

- **Virtual Server**—The name of virtual servers within the configuration.
- **Requests**—The total number of requests received by the virtual server.
- **Open Connections**—The current number of open connections for this virtual server.
- **Errors**—The total number of errors logged within this virtual server.

Select the link for the virtual server name to see comprehensive information for the virtual server. Doing so takes you to the Virtual Server Monitoring Statistics page, where you can see the information contained in Figure 7.6.

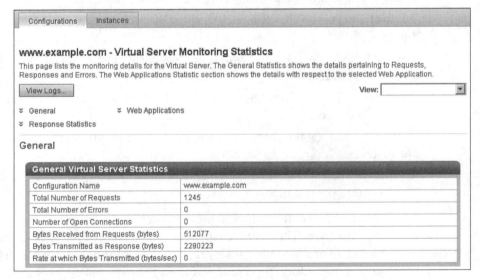

Figure 7.6   Virtual Server Monitoring Statistics (General Information)

On this page you can see general information about the virtual server (as shown in Figure 7.6), as well as detailed information about server responses from this virtual server (shown in Figure 7.7).

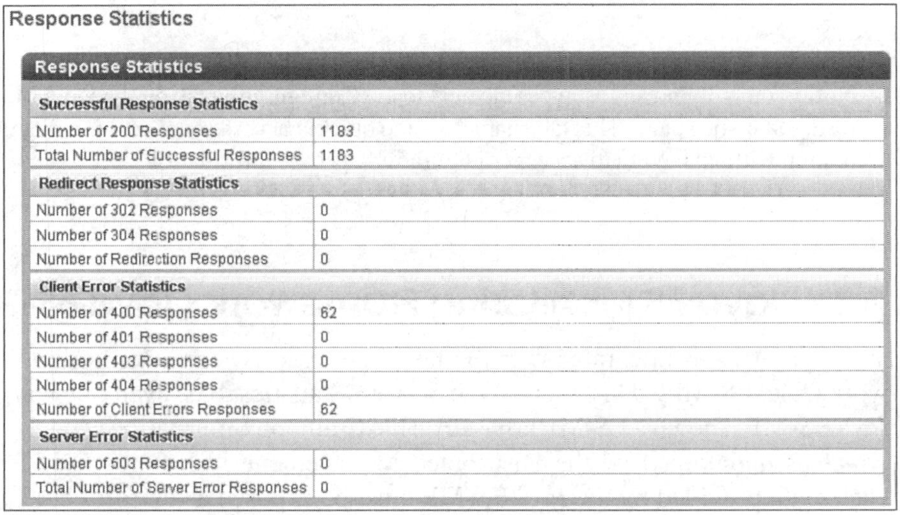

Response Statistics	
Response Statistics	
Successful Response Statistics	
Number of 200 Responses	1183
Total Number of Successful Responses	1183
Redirect Response Statistics	
Number of 302 Responses	0
Number of 304 Responses	0
Number of Redirection Responses	0
Client Error Statistics	
Number of 400 Responses	62
Number of 401 Responses	0
Number of 403 Responses	0
Number of 404 Responses	0
Number of Client Errors Responses	62
Server Error Statistics	
Number of 503 Responses	0
Total Number of Server Error Responses	0

Figure 7.7 Virtual Server Monitoring Statistics (Response Statistics)

You can obtain the statistics displayed in both Figure 7.6 and Figure 7.7 by using the get-virtual-server-stats subcommand and specifying a particular virtual server (--vs option) on a particular node (--node option).

In addition to the general and response statistics information described here, the Virtual Server Monitoring Statistics page provides statistical information on any Web Applications that may have been deployed to this virtual server. This information can be seen in Figure 7.8.

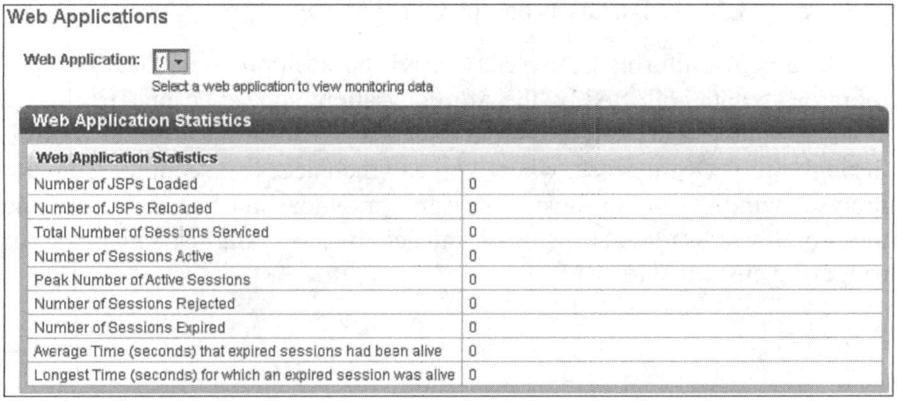

Web Applications	
Web Application: [/ ▾]	
Select a web application to view monitoring data	
Web Application Statistics	
Web Application Statistics	
Number of JSPs Loaded	0
Number of JSPs Reloaded	0
Total Number of Sessions Serviced	0
Number of Sessions Active	0
Peak Number of Active Sessions	0
Number of Sessions Rejected	0
Number of Sessions Expired	0
Average Time (seconds) that expired sessions had been alive	0
Longest Time (seconds) for which an expired session was alive	0

Figure 7.8 Virtual Server Monitoring Statistics (Web Application Statistics)

The information found in this table is the same as that returned by the get-webapp-stats command when you specify a particular web application (--uri option) in a particular virtual server (--vs option) on a particular node (--node option).

Note: You will find an Instances tab next to the Configuration tab on the main Monitoring Statistics page. This tab enables you to quickly access instance-specific information without having to access configuration-specific information.

7.3.6 Java ES Monitoring Framework (Java ES-MF)

Web Server 7.0 is integrated with the Java Enterprise System Monitoring Framework (Java ES-MF). This allows Web Server's statistics to be available within the Java ES-MF. The Java ES-MF is based on the Common Information Model (CIM), which is maintained by the Distributed Management Task Force (DMTF). As such, data provided by the Java ES-MF must be exposed as uniform objects and values consistent for comparable attributes.

Note: Go to http://www.dmtf.org/standards/cim for more information on CIM standards.

To support the Java ES-MF, the Web Server must provide data in the CIM format. To accomplish this, Administration Node instances in Web Server 7.0 contain a Java ES-MF mediation layer that takes the monitoring data and creates Common Monitoring Model (CMM) objects as per the CMM Mapping. These objects internally create CMM MBeans as per the CMM Model.

The Java ES Monitoring Console is the web-based application that displays all the monitoring data collected by the Administration Node. The Java ES Monitoring Console can be used to retrieve the data directly from the Administration Node through the JMX interface, where you can then access it securely from a simple browser window on any host. Using the graphical interface, you can then see monitored values in real time, view and acknowledge alarms, and create rules for triggering custom alarms.

Note: Java ES-MF monitoring is relevant only when installing the Web Server from the Java ES installer. There is no access to this functionality when installing the Web Server standalone.

7.3.7 Simple Network Management Protocol (SNMP)

You can also monitor Web Server instances with the simple network management protocol (SNMP). SNMP is a protocol used to issue commands or exchange data pertaining to an SNMP-managed device. Information such as server status and statistical data travels between the managed device and a network management station (NMS). In most cases, the NMS software provides a graphical display to show collected data or uses that data to make sure the server is operating within a particular tolerance.

Note: A *managed device* is anything that is able to process the SNMP protocol: hosts, routers, your Web Server, and other servers on your network. The network management station is a machine used to remotely monitor and manage SNMP-managed devices.

SNMP uses the default UDP port 161 for general SNMP messages and UDP port 162 for SNMP trap (or error) messages.

The NMS is usually a powerful workstation with one or more network management applications installed. A network management application such as HP Open-View or CA Unicenter graphically shows information about managed devices, such as your Web Servers. For example, it might show which servers in your enterprise are up or down, or the number and type of error messages received.

You can use the get-snmp-prop subcommand to determine whether SNMP has been enabled for a particular configuration as follows:

```
wadm> get-snmp-prop --config=www.example.com
wadm>
```

Nothing is returned if SNMP is not enabled.

You can then use the enable-snmp subcommand to enable SNMP and provide various parameters that help you identify and manage the agent for the configuration.

Each of these parameters corresponds to a child element that appears beneath the `snmp` element in the `server.xml`. The following example demonstrates how SNMP is enabled with this command and the various properties that are accepted as parameters to the `enable-snmp` subcommand:

```
wadm> enable-snmp
    --config=www.example.com
    --description=SunWebServer
    --organization=ExampleCorp
    --location=Tampa-2ndFloor-Grid3
    --contact=rodale@example.com
    --master-host=www.example.com
CLI201 Command 'enable-snmp' ran successfully
wadm>
```

Each of these parameters has a direct correlation to the elements configured in the `server.xml` when SNMP has been enabled as follows:

- `snmp`—Configures the server's SNMP subagent in the `server.xml`.
- `enabled`—Whether SNMP is enabled (default is `true`).
- `master-host`—Network address of the SNMP master agent (host name or IP address).
- `description`—Description of the server (text).
- `organization`—Organization responsible for the server (text).
- `location`—Location of the server (text).
- `contact`—Contact information of the person responsible for the server (text).

After it is enabled, you can use the `get-snmp-prop` subcommand to observe that data is now returned and the agent has been enabled for this configuration.

```
wadm> get-snmp-prop --config=www.example.com
contact=rodale@example.com
enabled=true
description=SunWebServer
master-host=www.example.com
location=Tampa-2ndFloor-Grid3
organization=ExampleCorp
wadm>
```

Finally, you can disable SNMP by using the `disable-snmp` subcommand as follows:

```
wadm> disable-snmp --config=www.example.com
CLI201 Command 'disable-snmp' ran successfully
```

7.4 How to Use Monitoring Data to Tune the Web Server

If you don't measure the system's behavior before and after making a change, you won't know whether the change was a good idea, a bad idea, or merely irrelevant. This chapter provides various ways that you can monitor your Web Server and provides specific examples of how you can determine how well the Web Server is performing.

Table 7.2 provides a recap of methods you can use to specifically monitor the performance of your Web Server.

Table 7.2   Methods of Monitoring Performance

Monitoring Method	How to Enable	How to Access	Advantages and Requirements
Statistics through the Administration Console	Enabled by default	In the Administration Console, for a configuration, click the Monitor tab	Accessible when session threads are hanging. The Administration Server must be running.

Statistics through individual wadm commands	Enabled by default	Through the wadm commands:
		`get-config-stats`
		`get-virtual-server-stats`
		`get-webapp-stats`
		`get-servlet-stats`
			Accessible when session threads are hanging. The Administration Server must be running.

XML-formatted statistics (`stats-xml`) through a browser	Enable through the Administration Console, by editing the object configuration file, or by running a wadm command.	Through a URI	The Administration Server does not need to be running.

Table 7.2   Methods of Monitoring Performance *continued*

Monitoring Method	How to Enable	How to Access	Advantages and Requirements
XML-formatted statistics (stats-xml) through the command line interface	Enabled by default	Through the wadm command, get-stats-xml	Accessible when session threads are hanging. The Administration Server must be running.
perfdump through a browser	Enable through the Administration Console, by editing the object configuration file, or by running a wadm command.	Through a URI	The Administration Server does not need to be running.
perfdump through the command-line interface	Enabled by default	Through the wadm command, get-perfdump	Accessible when session threads are hanging. The Administration Server must be running.
Java ES Monitoring	Enabled by default	Through the Java ES Monitoring Console	Only for Java ES installations. The Administration Server must be running.
SNMP Monitoring	Enable through the Administration Console, by editing the object configuration file, or by running a wadm command.		

In most cases, the default tuning parameters that ship with Web Server 7.0 are appropriate for all sites except those with very high volume, and even then the only settings that large sites might regularly need to change are the thread pool and keep-alive settings. You can tune these settings at the configuration level in either the Administration Console or by using wadm subcommands. It is also possible to tune the server by editing the elements directly in the server.xml file, but unless you know exactly what you are doing, you could cause more harm than good.

A good recommendation is to use the Plain Text Report (`perfdump`) to monitor statistics in various categories. (See Section 7.3.3, "Plain Text Report," and Appendix C, "Sample Plain Text Report Data," for more information on these settings.) In most cases these statistics are also displayed in the Administration Console, command line interface, and `stats-xml` output, but the Plain Text Report is a convenient way of obtaining all these statistics in one place.

Regardless of the method that you use to monitor the data, you should follow some general guidelines. As you tune your server, it is important to remember that your specific environment is unique. The impacts of the suggestions provided in this chapter will vary, depending on your specific environment. Ultimately you must rely on your own judgment and observations to select the adjustments that are best for you.

As you work to optimize performance, keep the following guidelines in mind:

- **Work methodically**—As much as possible, make one adjustment at a time. Measure your performance before and after each change, and rescind any change that doesn't produce a measurable improvement.
- **Adjust gradually**—When adjusting a quantitative parameter, make several stepwise changes in succession, rather than trying to make a drastic change all at once. Different systems face different circumstances, and you might leap right past your system's best setting if you change the value too rapidly.
- **Start fresh**—At each major system change, be it a hardware or software upgrade or deployment of a major new application, review all previous adjustments to see whether they still apply. After a Solaris upgrade, you should start over with an unmodified `/etc/system` file.
- **Stay informed**—Read the Sun Java System Web Server 7.0 Update 2 Release Notes and the release notes for your operating system whenever you upgrade your system. The release notes often provide updated information about specific adjustments.

 Warning: Be very careful when tuning your server. Always back up your configuration files before making any changes.

7.5 Summary

Continuous monitoring of the Web Server is one of the most overlooked tasks that system administrators perform. Often the Web Server is simply disregarded until you receive an e-mail or phone call that brings the problem to your attention. By then, however, it is too late and you are forced to react to a problem that could have been prevented.

Web Server 7.0 provides various mechanisms for monitoring your server and makes it quite easy to obtain statistics that can be used to determine both the health and well-being of your Web Server. By monitoring on a periodic basis (and actually evaluating the results), you can take a proactive approach and prevent most problems before they ever occur.

7.6 Self-Paced Labs

Use the information contained in this chapter to perform the following exercises. These will help validate your understanding of the concepts described in this chapter.

1. Generate several hundred requests for the default virtual server in the default configuration. For best results, ensure that your requests generate both successful responses (a server response of 200) as well as error responses (a server response of 404).

> **Note:** You can use a tool such as wget to generate these requests or you can use an Internet browser. If you use a browser, make sure that you use press the Shift key when you make your request to ensure that pages are not retrieved from the browser's cache.

2. Chapter 4 described how to use the command line interface in File Mode to perform various administrative tasks. Web Server 7.0 includes several predefined scripts to demonstrate this capability. One predefined script described in Table 4.3 (Administrative Scripts) is collate-logs.tcl. This script enables you to collate logs across multiple nodes. Use this script to review the access log files across any nodes where you may have deployed your configuration.

3. Enable logging at the virtual server level for the default configuration and specify log files that are unique to your virtual server and reflective of the type of log file (for instance, "`../logs/www.example.com-server.log`" and "`../logs/www.example.com-access.log`"). Review any changes made to the sub-elements for the default virtual server in the server.xml file. Verify that the new log files have been created and that they contain data specific to the default virtual server.

4. Use the Administration Console to enable the XML Report and Plain Text Report Monitoring Formats for the default configuration. Access both reports through the appropriate URI.

5. Use the command line interface to access the XML and Plain Text reports.

6. Use the command line interface to disable access to the XML and Plain Text reports.

7. Use the Administration Console to access configuration level statistics for the default configuration.

8. Use the Administration Console to access virtual server statistics for the default virtual server in the default configuration.

9. Repeat exercises 6 and 7 using the appropriate command-line subcommands.

Note: Go to http://www.sunwebserver.com for detailed instructions on how to perform each of these exercises.

---

10. Additional Exercise:

    Enable SNMP for a virtual server and use a tool such as `snmpwalk` to review the data provided by the server.

8

Securing Web Server 7.0

PUBLIC web servers are attractive targets for disgruntled employees, hackers, or business competitors seeking to embarrass organizations or simply prevent them from conducting business over the Internet. Although web servers may be considered a weak point in the security chain, Web Server 7.0, with its mature code base, security code reviews, and security-related features, has demonstrated a strong track record—all while powering the web sites of some of the world's most valuable companies.

Note: According to Netcraft (www.netcraft.com), the Sun Java System Web Server is #1 in Fortune 100 companies.

This chapter takes a look at some of the security-related features contained in Web Server 7.0 and how you can use them to secure your Web Server. In general, it covers the following topics:

- Controlling access to Web Server resources
- Using SSL certificates to secure data
- Automating maintenance of certificate revocation lists (CRLs)
- Detecting and responding to denial of service (DoS) attacks
- Using the Web Server as a reverse proxy to provide an additional layer of protection

8.1 Controlling Access to Web Server Resources

You can protect resources that reside on your Web Server through several security services and mechanisms, including authentication, authorization, and access control.

Authentication is the process of verifying that a person is who he or she claims to be. In the context of computer systems, authentication is commonly performed through the use of passwords. This, however, is one of the weaker forms of authentication as compared to digital certificates, tokens, or even biometric devices. Web Server 7.0 supports various methods of authentication by default and provides a way to extend processing to include user-defined methods as well.

After a person has been authenticated, the computer system must verify that the user is allowed to perform certain actions on the resources contained within the system. This process is called *authorization* and typically involves the querying of an authorization (or policy) data store to determine a user's rights as they pertain to resources provided by the Web Server. Policies are linked to users or groups and therefore authorization takes place after the user's identity has been determined.

Access control is the enforcement of the policies specified in the authorization data store and can be implemented by a number of security models, such as Web application security, htaccess, authentication realms, and more. Web Server 7.0 provides default access control that enables you to serve content immediately after installation. You can implement additional control on your Web Server by limiting access to one or more of the following resources:

- The entire server instance
- Parts of the server
- Files or directories
- File types
- Universal resource indicators (URIs)

8.1.1 User Authentication

Authentication is the process of determining that a user is who he or she claims to be. To verify a user's credentials, the Web Server must query a data store that contains the user's authentication information. This data store is called the *authentication database* and is specified by the auth-db element in the server.xml file.

Authentication databases are configured at the server level by default, but may be overridden by specifying the `auth-db` element within a particular virtual server.

Web Server 7.0 supports three types of authentication databases: file, directory service (ldap), and pluggable authentication module (pam). You can configure any number of authentication databases in any combination of these three types.

8.1.1.1 Using a File as an Authentication Database

Administrators can configure the Web Server to use a local file as an authentication database. This method of user data storage is particularly convenient during development or in small-scale deployments where no centralized user management is available (or desired). Web Server 7.0 supports three different file formats: keyfile, digestfile, and htaccess. The decision to select one file format over another depends on the type of authentication mechanism being implemented.

Table 8.1 provides an overview of each file format and how it can be used with the appropriate authentication mechanism.

Table 8.1   Comparison of File Formats to Authentication Mechanisms

File Format	Authentication Mechanism	Overview
keyfile	Basic authentication	A method designed to allow a User Agent to provide a username and password when making an HTTP request. The request has a format of the form: http://*username:password@host.domain*. Basic authentication does not provide any level of encryption. Instead, the username and password are passed to the Web Server in a Base64-encoded format.
digestfile	Digest authentication	A method similar to basic authentication, except the password is not sent in Base64-encoded text. In digest authentication, a valid response contains a checksum (by default, the MD5 checksum) of the username, the password, a nonce value (sent from the Web Server), the HTTP method, and the requested URI. An optional header allows the server to specify the algorithm used to create the checksum or digest, but by default the MD5 algorithm is used. Digest authentication is not as secure as Kerberos or X.509 certificates; it is intended only to be a replacement for basic authentication.
htaccess	Basic authentication	This method utilizes distributed access control files contained within the directories of the files they are seeking to protect. These access control files (typically named `.htaccess`) reference a centralized authentication file (typically `.htpasswd`) that is located outside the document root. Because the `.htaccess` files are distributed in the various directories requiring access control, their implementation and maintenance is more difficult than that of ACL files.

Note: RFC 2617 (HTTP Authentication: Basic and Digest Access Authentication) provides additional information on basic and digest authentication mechanisms.

The keyfile and digestfile authentication database types are supported immediately after installation. You can use either the GUI or CLI to create database files of these types or manage users within them.

The `create-file-authdb` subcommand in the CLI is used to create authentication databases of either type keyfile or disgestfile as follows:

```
create-file-authdb <connect_options> [--echo|-e] [--no-prompt|-Q]
[--verbose|-v] [--vs|-s name] [--syntax|-t keyfile|digestfile]
[--no-enabled|-n] --path|-P filepath --config|-c name authdb-name
```

Note: Although the contents of authentication database files may seem apparent, the format is considered private and subject to change between Web Server releases. As such, you should not create any programs, scripts, or assumptions based on these files.

Example 8.1 demonstrates a user-defined authentication database within the `server.xml` file.

Example 8.1   File-Based Authentication Database

```
<auth-db>
  <name>myKeyFile</name>
  <url>file</url>
  <property>
    <name>syntax</name>
    <value>keyfile</value>
  </property>
  <property>
    <name>keyfile</name>
    <value>keyfile</value>
  </property>
</auth-db>
```

This authentication database is referred to as `myKeyFile` as specified by the `name` element. This is the user-defined name that is used to reference the authentication database within the GUI or CLI. A `url` element with the value of `file` tells the Web Server that this authentication database uses file-based authentication. The type of file is specified by the `syntax` property, which indicates that this is a `keyfile` and therefore uses basic authentication. The location of the file on the file system is specified by the keyfile property. The value for this element can take either the fully qualified filename or a file that is relative to the instance's config directory. In this case, the filename is keyfile and it is located directly in the config directory.

A digestfile authentication database has the same format as shown in Example 8.1 with the only exception being that the syntax property is specified as digestfile. All other elements follow the same format as keyfile authentication databases.

The htaccess authentication database is maintained for compatibility with previous versions of Web Server, but it is recommended that administrators use either keyfile or digestfile instead. The htaccess authentication method is not enabled by default; you must enable it with either the GUI or CLI. Web Server 7.0 does not provide a mechanism through the GUI or CLI to manage users within the htaccess environment. Instead, you must use the htpasswd application located in the *install_dir*/bin directory to manage users in this authentication database.

8.1.1.2 Using a Directory Service as an Authentication Database

File authentication databases are convenient, but they suffer from performance and scalability limitations as the number of users increases. When this occurs, administrators turn to data storage applications (such as directory services or relational databases) that are more suited to large populations of users.

Many companies implement enterprise directory services in the form of the Sun Java System Directory Server (Sun Directory Server) or Microsoft Active Directory (Active Directory). These centralized servers typically contain the user population required for authentication and provide a convenient interface that supports the lightweight directory access protocol (LDAP) for accessing user records. These records contain a unique user identifier and password and can be used to verify a user's identity before allowing access to Web Server resources. Figure 8.1 demonstrates the relationship between the Web Server and a centralized directory server.

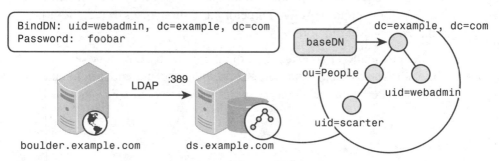

Figure 8.1   Web Server Interaction with a Directory Server

For a Web Server to use a directory service as an authentication database, it needs to know where on the network to find the service. For this it requires the hostname of the server hosting the directory service and the port number on which the service is listening. The Web Server uses this information to establish a connection to the directory server, using the LDAP protocol. In this relationship the Web Server acts as an LDAP client in a client-server interaction.

Directory services implement their own form of authentication and authorization; therefore, a Web Server needs to authenticate to the directory service as a user that is allowed access to specific information. For this to occur, it must provide the appropriate credentials in the form of a *bind* operation, using a specific *bindDN* and password.

Note: Each entry in the directory service database is identified by a unique *Distinguished Name* (DN). The DN is a string representation of the location of the entry in the directory tree. You can think of a DN as the full path from the object being modeled (for example, a user) to the root of the tree (or root suffix). This is analogous to the manner in which files are represented in a typical file system, only reversed! If you use a particular entry for authentication purposes, the DN of that entry is referred to as the *bindDN*.

After the Web Server has authenticated to the directory service, it needs to know where to start searching for users within the directory information tree (DIT) by providing a base distinguished name (or *baseDN*). This allows searches to be performed more quickly by eliminating portions of the tree that do not contain user information. Finally, the Web Server needs to know how to uniquely identify a user in the tree. It does this by presenting a filter that consists of the unique naming attribute used to identify a user. In Sun Directory Servers, the unique naming attribute is uid, and in Active Directory this is the sAMAccountName. Web Server 7.0 offers the flexibility to specify the unique naming attribute used to locate users and therefore supports Active Directory as a directory service. Previous versions of the Web Server did not.

All the information that is required to interact with a directory service is specified in the auth-db element. Example 8.2 provides the authentication database definition associated with the directory server shown in Figure 8.1.

Example 8.2   Directory Service Authentication Database

```
<auth-db>
  <name>ds.example.com</name>
  <url>ldap://ds.example.com:389/ou%3dPeople,dc%3dexample,dc%3dcom</url>
  <property>
    <name>binddn</name>
    <value>uid=webadmin,dc=example,dc=com</value>
  </property>
  <property>
    <name>bindpw</name>
    <value>cGFzc3dvcmQ=</value>
    <encoded>true</encoded>
  </property>
</auth-db>
```

In Example 8.2, the `name` element specifies the user-defined name that is used to reference the authentication database within the GUI or CLI. The `url` element specifies the information necessary to connect to the Directory Server. The value of this element includes the protocol used for connection (`ldap` or `ldaps`), the hostname and port number of the directory server to which you are connecting, and the location in the directory information tree where you would like to start searching for users (the *baseDN*). The format of the URL is `ldap(s)://host:port/baseDN` and uses hexadecimal characters to represent special symbols like the equality character (`=`).

Two optional properties are defined for this authentication database: The first is the `binddn` and contains a value of `uid=webadmin,dc=example,dc=com`. This is the distinguished name of the service account created to allow the Web Server to bind and perform lookup operations on user identifiers. The second property is the `bindpw` and this is the Base64-encoded password of the user specified in the `binddn` attribute.

If you do not specify a particular `binddn` and `bindpw`, the Web Server binds to the directory server as an anonymous user. Althugh this may seem convenient, you should verify that your directory service supports anonymous searches and that your security policy allows for this. Allowing searches from an anonymous user limits the amount of information contained in the directory service log files. As such, some companies require that the Web Server use a valid service account to bind to the directory service.

Figure 8.1 demonstrates the Web Server binding to the directory server using a bindDN of `uid=webadmin,dc=example,dc=com`. This is an entry that has been created for the sole purpose of allowing the Web Server to communicate with the directory server and is analogous to a service account on UNIX-type systems. Any operations performed by the Web Server (such as search operations) are easily traceable in the directory server log files.

> **Warning:** The Sun Directory Server contains a *superuser* account that is similar to the root user on a UNIX system. This account is referred to as the rootDN or Directory Manager account and by default is cn=Directory Manager. You should never use this account when binding to the Directory Server from the Web Server. The Directory Manager account is not affected by access control rules or search restrictions imposed on other accounts. Therefore, you can inadvertently affect both the performance and security on your Sun Directory Server. It is better to create an account in the Directory Server specifically for this Web Server, give that account permissions to manage users as appropriate, and bind to the Directory Server as that account.

Web Server 7.0 enables you to specify multiple directory servers for a given auth-db entry. This allows you to fail over to additional servers should the primary directory become unavailable. You configure this by specifying multiple directory servers in the url element as a space-delimited list. This can be seen in Example 8.3.

Example 8.3   Directory Service Failover

```
<auth-db>
  <name>ds.example.com</name>
<url>ldap://ds.example.com:389/ou%3dPeople,dc%3dexample,dc%3dcom
ldap://ds2.example.com:389/ou%3dPeople,dc%3dexample,dc%3dcom
ldap://ds3.example.com:389/ou%3dPeople,dc%3dexample,dc%3dcom</url>
  <property>
    <name>binddn</name>
    <value>uid=webadmin,dc=example,dc=com</value>
  </property>
  <property>
    <name>bindpw</name>
    <value>cGFzc3dvcmQ=</value>
    <encoded>true</encoded>
  </property>
</auth-db>
```

When multiple directory servers are provided, the Web Server attempts to contact the first server specified in the list. If that server is not available, an attempt is made to contact each subsequent server in the list. You can specify different baseDNs in the list and the servers, themselves, may even be different vendor types. The only requirement is that the `binddn` and `bindpw` properties must be consistent across all directory servers in the list.

Web Server 7.0 enables you to configure additional search parameters that were not available in previous versions of the product. This allows you to interact with other vendor-provided directory servers (such as Microsoft Active Directory) for user authentication and static group lookups. Additional parameters that you can specify in Web Server 7.0 include the following:

- `search-filter`—To search for users (default is `uid`)
- `group-search-filter`—To search for groups (default is `uniquemember`)
- `group-target-attr`—The LDAP attribute containing the name of the group (default is `cn`)

Example 8.4 demonstrates a configuration that uses Microsoft Active Directory as an authentication database. The `search-filter` property has been customized to use the `samAccountName` attribute and thus overrides the default attribute that is used to search for users.

Example 8.4   Flexible Search

```
<auth-db>
  <name>ldapMSAD</name>
  <url>ldap://msad.example.com:389/ou%3dPeople,dc%3dexample,dc%3dcom</url>
  <property>
    <name>binddn</name>
    <value>cn=webadmin,cn=special users,dc=example,dc=com</value>
  </property>
  <property>
    <name>bindpw</name>
    <value>cGFzc3dvcmQ=</value>
    <encoded>true</encoded>
  </property>
  <property>
    <name>search-filter</name>
    <value>samAccountName</value>
  </property>
</auth-db>
```

After the authentication database has been configured, the Web Server can then interact with the directory service to verify that a user is who he says he is. But how does this occur? When prompted, users do not present their credentials in the form of a directory server DN, so how is a Web Server able to make this determination? The process for authenticating users against an external directory service can be seen in Figure 8.2.

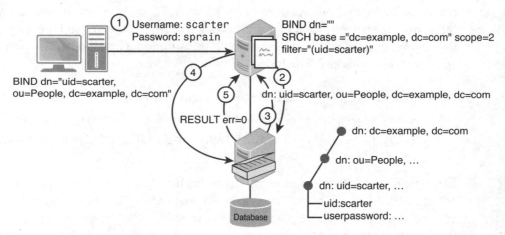

Figure 8.2   User Authentication Process

Three main components come into play during the authentication process: the browser, the Web Server, and the directory service. The general steps required to validate a user's identity can be summarized as follows:

1. A user attempts to access a page that has been restricted on the Web Server. The user is prompted for credentials and is required to respond so that the Web Server can determine identity. The user enters a username and password and submits the results to the Web Server.

2. The Web Server performs a bind operation using the distinguished name specified in the authentication database's `bindDN` property. In this case, the bind operation's distinguished name is empty so the operation is being performed as the anonymous user. After the bind operation has been completed, the Web Server takes the username provided by the browser and creates a search filter based on the appropriate naming attribute (`uid=scarter`). The Web Server then performs a search operation for entries that match this filter, starting at the `baseDN` (`dc=example,dc=com`) and continuing until operation has completed.

3. The search operation locates one entry that matches the filter. It returns the distinguished name of the entry to the Web Server. The Web Server terminates the connection with the directory service by unbinding.

Note: By default, the Web Server assumes that it will receive at most one entry from its search. If more than one entry is returned, then the Web Server logs an internal error and the authentication process terminates. If this occurs, then you may need to change the location where the search begins (baseDN), select a new search filter (search-filter), or ensure uniqueness within the directory service, itself. The Sun Directory Server has a plug-in called the UID Uniqueness plug-in that can be used for this purpose. If none of these options are feasible, then you may need to consider writing your own authentication function and incorporate this into the request processing process.

4. The Web Server performs a new bind operation, but this time it uses the distinguished name returned in step 3. It also uses the password provided by the browser in step 1.

5. If the password matches the value in the user's entry, then the bind operation succeeds and the directory service responds with an error code of zero. This indicates a successful bind operation and the Web Server has successfully verified the identity of the user. The Web Server terminates the connection with the directory service and allows the browser access to the requested resource.

The CLI includes a command for creating directory-specific authentication databases that differs from the one used to create file authentication databases. The create-ldap-authdb subcommand enables you to create an authentication database based on a directory service as follows:

```
create-ldap-authdb [--echo] [--no-prompt] [--verbose] [--vs=vs-name]
[--no-enabled] [--group-search-filter=filter] [--search-filter=filter]
[--dc-suffix=suffix] [--group-search-attr=attribute] [--bind-dn=bind-dn]
[--auth-expiring-url=url] [--timeout=timeout]
--ldap-url=ldap://server:port/dc=acme,dc=com --config=config-name
authdb-name
```

After the database has been created, you can use the create-user subcommand with the Web Server CLI or any of a number of LDAP-enabled tools to directly manage users in the directory database.

8.1.1.3 Using a Pluggable Authentication Module as an Authentication Database

Web Server 7.0 includes the ability to authenticate users against the Solaris operating system's pluggable authentication module (PAM) stack. This means that users can be authenticated against any supported Solaris operating system naming service that has been configured on the local host. This includes network information systems (NIS), directory servers, or even flat files such as /etc/passwd.

> **Note:** PAM is a new native authentication database supported by Web Server 7.0. Previous versions of the Web Server supported a Java Solaris Realm, which allowed Java Web applications to authenticate users with PAM. However, the native content (static files, CGIs, and so on) could not take advantage of this authentication mechanism.

Configuration of a PAM authentication database is supported on Solaris 9 Operating Systems and above. The Web Server can authenticate only against the PAM stack on the local system so there are no properties (other than the name of the authentication database) that are required for configuration of the auth-db element. Example 8.5 demonstrates the elements required to configure a PAM authentication database.

Example 8.5   Configuration of a PAM Authentication Database

```
<auth-db>
  <name>solarisAuth</name>
  <url>pam</url>
</auth-db>
```

Using PAM as the authentication database is another convenient method for authenticating users, but it has restrictions. First of all, you can configure this only on a Solaris 9 Operating System or above and you can use only username and password for authentication; smart cards and other authentication devices are not supported. Next, you cannot perform searches or modifications to users in the naming service. Finally, to use PAM as an authentication database, you need to be running your Web Server instance as the root user if you are accessing system files (such as /etc/passwd).

> **Note:** The Web Server does not need to be running as the root user if PAM is using NIS, NIS+, or LDAP for authentication.

8.1.1.4 Managing Users in an Authentication Database

After you have created an authentication database, you can use the GUI, the CLI, or one of various native tools to manage users within the database. The GUI provides a convenient method for managing users, but you must use a web browser to access this interface. To access the GUI interface for managing users, perform the following steps:

1. Open the Administration Console and click the Configurations tab to access the main configuration page.
2. Select the link for the configuration where you would like to manage users.
3. Click the Access Control tab.
4. Click the Users subtab.
5. Select the authentication database where you will be managing users.
6. Either click the New button to add a new user or search for users to manage.
7. A form appears, allowing you to add data for new users or modify existing user data.
8. After you have completed managing users, you need to deploy the updated configuration to all nodes.

The CLI provides a convenient method for managing users and does not require the use of a browser. You do, however, need to know the appropriate commands to use and the correct syntax for each of these commands. The `create-user` subcommand is used to create users within any of the authentication databases except for PAM or htaccess. The syntax to use this command is as follows:

```
create-user [--echo] [--no-prompt] [--verbose] [--first-name=name]
[--full-name=name] [--last-name=name] [--email=address]
[--phone=user-contact] [--title=title] [--realm=realm]
[--org-unit=org-unit] [--vs=vs-name] --config=config-name
--authdb=authdb-name userid
```

For instance, you can easily create a new user in the `mykeyfile` file authentication database, using the following command:

```
create-user --authdb=mykeyfile --user-password=foobar
--vs=https-www.example.com --config=https-www.example.com scarter
```

After a user has been created, the `set-user-prop` subcommand can be used to edit various properties for the user as appropriate for a particular authentication database. For file-based authentication databases, you can edit the user's password and realm. For LDAP-based authentication databases you can edit the user's last name (surname), full name (cn), e-mail address (mail), phone number (telephone-number), organizational unit (ou), password, and user title (title). The syntax of this command is as follows:

```
set-user-prop <connect_options> [--echo|-e] [--no-prompt|-Q]
[--verbose|-v][--vs|-s vs-name] [--org-unit|-o org-unit] [--realm|-L
   realm]
[--set-password|-r] [--user-password|-W] --config|-c config-name
--authdb|-a name --uid|-U userid (propertyname=value)
```

> **Warning:** As of the writing of this book, the Administration Console does not recognize changes made to file authentication databases without restarting the Web Server instance(s) that reference the file. Sun has acknowledged this issue and will be addressing it in a future release of the product.

Some authentication databases require that you use a different tool for managing users. These include those specified in the PAM and htaccess authentication databases because the Web Server has no direct method for managing those users. In such cases you would need to manage users with the native methods provided by those mechanisms. For instance, on a Solaris operating system that is using the `/etc/password` file as the authentication mechanism, you would need to use the `useradd` and `usermod` commands to manage those users.

8.1.2 Access Control

Access control is the enforcement of authorization policies (or rules) that have been defined for a particular resource. The Web Server provides default access control rules that allow users access to resources immediately after installation. These rules are stored in the `default.acl` configuration file by default and are referenced during the request processing stages defined in the object configuration file. You can modify these rules or implement additional access control within your Web Server by editing the `default.acl` file or by creating additional access control files. You can then control access at either the Web Server instance or the virtual server level. This enables you to provide general access control that applies to all virtual servers or fine-tuned access control that applies to only a specific virtual server.

You can specify whether you want to allow or deny access to server resources based on any of the following:

- Who is making the request (user and/or group)
- Where the request is coming from (Host-IP)
- When the request is happening (for example, time of day)
- What type of connection is being used (SSL)

Additionally, you can specify which rights you are permitting for those users you are allowing access.

> **Note:** Refer to Chapter 5, "Web Server 7.0 Configuration Files," for the structure and syntax of the `default.acl` file. An understanding of this file is helpful when trying to determine how the Web Server processes access control statements.

8.1.2.1 Access Control Rights

Access control rights restrict access to Web Server resources such as files and directories. In addition to allowing or denying all access rights (which is the default), you can achieve more granular control by specifying rules that explicitly allow or deny certain access rights. For example, you may want to allow users read-only access to files on your Web Server so they can view them, but you may not want to grant them permissions to modify the files.

Common rights that can be used for controlling access in an ACL file include `all`, `read`, `execute`, `info`, `write`, `list`, and `delete`. These rights correlate to the methods employed in the HTTP protocol, but one right may actually map to multiple methods and one method may require you to allow multiple rights. Table 8.2 provides a mapping between Web Server's access rights and the HTTP protocol methods.

Table 8.2   Mapping Between Access Control Rights and HTTP Methods

Rights	HTTP Methods
read	GET, HEAD, TRACE, OPTIONS, COPY, BCOPY
write	PUT, MKDIR, LOCK, UNLOCK, PROPPATCH, MKCOL, ACL, VERSION-CONTROL, CHECKOUT, UNCHECKOUT, CHECKIN, MKWORKSPACE, UPDATE, LABEL, MERGE, BASELINE-CONTROL, MKACTIVITY, BPROPPATCH
execute	POST, CONNECT, SUBSCRIBE, UNSUBSCRIBE, NOTIFY, POLL
delete	DELETE, RMDIR, MOVE, BDELETE, BMOVE
info	HEAD, TRACE, OPTIONS
list	INDEX, PROPFIND, REPORT, SEARCH, BPROPFIND

For example, if you wanted to allow a browser to obtain a directory listing of a particular folder on your Web Server, you would need to grant the `list` right. This in turn would allow the INDEX method, which would allow the Web Server to provide a directory listing.

Example 8.6 demonstrates how these rights can be used to provide granular access control for various types of users (line numbers have been added for demonstration purposes).

Example 8.6   Access Control Rights

```
1.  acl "uri=/";
2.  authenticate (user, group) {
3.    prompt = "Sun Java System Web Server";
4.  };
5.  deny (all) user="anyone";
6.  allow (read, execute, info) user="all";
7.  allow (list, write, delete) group = "superusers";
```

Lines 5–7 define the access control rights provided to three types of users. Line 5 denies all rights to users that fall under the `anyone` category. This includes both authenticated and anonymous users. Line 6 allows all authenticated users to `read`, `execute`, and obtain `info` for any resources on this Web Server (as specified by line 1). Line 7 allows users who are part of the group superusers to list, write, and delete pages on the Web Server. Users in the superusers group also have the rights specified by line 6 because they are part of all authenticated users.

Note: The entry on line 5 must appear first in the list. This entry denies all rights to any users (authenticated and unauthenticated users). This entry evaluates to TRUE, so the next entry in the list (line 6) is evaluated next. Subsequent ACEs are then defined to grant specific rights to certain users.

In addition to these rights, the Web Server allows you to configure access control based strictly on the HTTP method by using the http_*<method>* right. Suppose, for instance, that you want to block a particular host (or subnet) from issuing the GET method. In Web Server 7.0, you could create a deny rule similar to the following to achieve these results:

```
deny (http_GET) ip = "123.45.67.*";
```

Finally, you can control privileges associated with the distributed authoring and versioning (DAV) capabilities of the HTTP protocol in Web Server 7.0. For instance, you could create entries that either allow or deny DAV capabilities by specifying the appropriate privilege (such as dav:read-acl, or dav:read-current-user-privilege-set) within the ACE .

Note: For more information on the types of DAV privileges that can be controlled in Web Server 7.0, see RFC-3744 (Web Distributed Authoring and Versioning (Web-DAV) Access Control Protocol).

8.1.2.2 Access Control Processing

When the Web Server receives an incoming request, it selects the appropriate virtual server and determines whether the client is allowed or denied access, based on a hierarchy of rules called access control entries (or ACEs). The Web Server takes into account any general server ACEs and then determines whether any ACEs have been configured for the virtual server based on the client request. If so, the server evaluates each ACE to determine whether access should be granted or denied.

The collection of ACEs for a particular resource is called an access control list (or ACL). Access control lists are generated by scanning instance or virtual server–specific access control files for any ACEs that apply to the current request. Access control entries found in the default.acl are processed before those found in any virtual server–specific access control files. The order in which ACEs appear within those files is also important because previously defined ACEs appear before those defined later in the file.

After the ACL is generated, the Web Server processes it from top to bottom to determine whether the client is allowed or denied access. If at any time an ACE evaluates to FALSE, then processing of the ACL stops and the client is denied access to the resource. The server processes the list until it reaches the end or it reaches an *absolute* ACE. If processing reaches the end of the ACL without seeing a FALSE condition, then the user is granted access to the resource.

> **Note:** If an ACE resolves to TRUE, then the next ACE in the list is evaluated if and only if the ACE is not an *absolute* ACE. If an absolute ACE evaluates to TRUE, then the user is allowed or denied access based on the definition specified by the ACE, and no further processing of the list is performed. ACEs are made absolute when the keyword absolute is specified in the ACE definition as follows.
>
> ```
> allow absolute (read, execute, info) user = "anyone";.
> ```
>
> You can also specify this in the Administration Console (GUI) by deselecting the Continue check box when defining the ACE.

There are two ACLs defined (by default) in Web Server 7.0: default and es-internal. Figure 8.3 demonstrates how the default access control list appears in the Administration Console. Example 8.7 then provides the corresponding entries in the default.acl file (line numbers have been added for demonstration purposes).

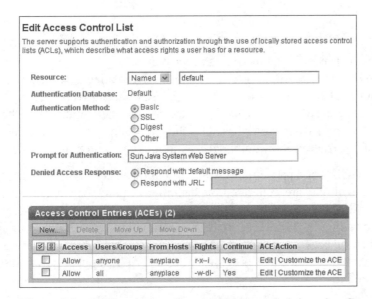

Figure 8.3   Editing Access Control with the Administration Console

Example 8.7   The default ACL

```
1.  acl "default";
2.  authenticate (user, group) {
3.    prompt = "Sun Java System Web Server";
4.  };
5.  allow (read, execute, info) user = "anyone";
6.  allow (list, write, delete) user = "all";
```

A description of the entries found in Example 8.7 is as follows:

- The first line specifies the name of the ACL. This correlates to the Resource text box shown in Figure 8.3.

- The second line specifies that authentication is required before the user is allowed to perform certain operations that are protected by subsequent ACEs. The Web Server uses the basic authentication method (the default) for verifying a user's identity.

- The third line specifies the prompt that is displayed in the username/password dialog box—opened by the User Agent. This correlates with the Prompt for Authentication text box shown in Figure 8.3.

- The fifth line specifies the first ACE in the list. This ACE allows all users (anyone; authenticated or not) the ability to read, execute, and obtain info on resources protected by this rule. This correlates to the first ACE shown in the table in Figure 8.3. This rule evaluates to TRUE because both authenticated and unauthenticated users are considered anyone.

- The sixth line specifies the second ACE in the list. This ACE allows all authenticated users (all) the ability to list, write, and delete resources protected by this rule. This correlates to the second ACE shown in Figure 8.3.

The first ACE does not require authentication and therefore does not request the user's identity. The second ACE requires authentication before allowing the user to perform the operations listed. If the user's identity is not known when this ACE is processed, then the user is prompted to enter credentials.

Let's take a final look at a simple ACL file and see how it is processed for various client requests. Example 8.8 contains a snippet of the default.acl file that has been modified to deny the info right to user bnelson. Line numbers have been added for demonstration purposes.

Example 8.8   Simple Access Control File

```
1.  acl "default";
2.  authenticate (user, group) {
3.    prompt = "Sun Java System Web Server";
4.  };
5.  allow (read, execute, info) user = "anyone";
6.  allow (list, write, delete) user = "all";
7.
8.  acl "/file.html";
9.  deny (info) user = "bnelson";
```

Table 8.3 provides various client requests and demonstrates how the access control entries in Example 8.8 are evaluated for each request. Refer to Table 8.2 to determine the rights to request mappings that are applicable to these requests.

Table 8.3   Applicability of ACEs to Client Requests

Request	Applicable ACEs	Request Results
HEAD /	ACEs that contain the following rights are applicable for this request: `all`, `read`, `http_head` and `info`. The ACL for HEAD / is as follows: `allow (read, execute, info) user = "anyone";`	The ACE defined on line 5 evaluates to TRUE. The HEAD request is allowed. *The ACE on line 9 is not evaluated because it is for a different URI.*
GET / or GET /file.html	ACEs that contain the following rights are applicable for this request: `all`, `read`, and `http_get`. The ACL for GET / or GET /file.html is as follows: `allow (read, execute, info) user = "anyone";`	The ACE defined on line 5 evaluates to TRUE. The GET request is allowed. *The ACE on line 9 is not evaluated because it is for a different right (info).*
HEAD /file. html (as user bnelson)	ACEs that contain the following rights are applicable for this request: `all`, `read`, `http_head` and `info`. The ACL for HEAD /file.html is as follows: `allow (read, execute, info) user = "anyone"; deny (info) user = "bnelson";`	The ACE defined on line 5 evaluates to TRUE and ACE processing continues. The ACE defined on line 9 evaluates to TRUE, but the request is denied for user bnelson.
HEAD /file. html (as user rodale)	ACEs that contain the following rights are applicable for this request: `all`, `read`, `http_head` and `info`. The ACL for HEAD /file.html is as follows: `allow (read, execute, info) user = "anyone"; deny (info) user = "bnelson";`	The ACE defined on line 5 evaluates to TRUE and ACE processing continues. The ACE defined on line 9 evaluates to FALSE, because the user is not bnelson. The HEAD request is allowed for user rodale.

Request	Applicable ACEs	Request Results
HEAD /file.html	ACEs that contain the following rights are applicable for this request: all, read, http_head and info. The ACL for HEAD /file.html is as follows: allow (read, execute, info) user = "anyone"; deny (info) user = "bnelson";	The ACE defined on line 5 evaluates to TRUE and ACE processing continues. The user has not authenticated, so the ACE defined on line 9 cannot be truly evaluated until this occurs. Until that time, access to the resource is denied.

Note: Although we do not have any deny ACEs for the anyone user, having an explicit deny or allow ACE for a particular user (as in line 9) implicitly denies access to unauthenticated users.

Processing of access control statements can be confusing at times. The next section demonstrates how you can observe which ACEs are executed during access control processing and which ones have either allowed or denied access to Web Server resources.

8.1.2.3 Observing Access Control Behavior

One of the most common causes of security-related calls to the Sun Support Desk is founded in the confusion surrounding how ACLs are evaluated. Previous versions of the Web Server did not offer much in the way of debugging tools to help understand why a particular set of rules accepted or denied a given request. In the past, trial and error was the only mechanism for diagnosing evaluation and interaction between each of the ACL rules, but this had the potential of adding risk in the process because ACL evaluation was fairly opaque.

To address this problem, Web Server 7.0 introduced a debug-level logging capability to make explicit the result of ACL processing. You can now view the results of ACL processing in the Server Log and even obtain more explicit information by setting the log-level attribute to finest.

Assume, for instance, that your default.acl file contains the entries as shown in Example 8.9 (line numbers have been added for demonstration purposes).

Example 8.9   Access Control File with URI Protection

```
1.  acl "default";
2.  authenticate (user, group) {
3.    prompt = "Sun Java System Web Server";
4.  };
5.  allow (read, execute, info) user = "anyone";
6.  allow (list, write, delete) user = "all";
7.
8.  acl "es-internal";
9.  allow (read, execute, info) user = "anyone";
10. deny (list, write, delete) user = "anyone";
11.
12. acl "uri=/topsecret/*";
13. authenticate (user,group) {
14.        database = "keyfile";
15.        method = "basic";
16. };
17. deny (all) user = "anyone";
18. allow absolute (all) user = "bnelson";
```

This particular file includes an ACL that allows the bnelson user contained in the keyfile authentication database all rights for all resources beneath the /topsecret URI. Any other users, whether they are contained in the database or not, should be denied access to this resource.

Example 8.10 demonstrates the Server Log entries that are generated when the rodale user attempts to access resources beneath the /topsecret URI. The rodale user exists in the keyfile authentication database, but is not allowed access to the resource as per line 18 in Example 8.9.

Example 8.10   Observing Access Control Behavior in the Server Log

```
[13/Oct/2008:21:59:05] fine ( 2056): for host 127.0.0.1 trying to GET /
   topsecret/, restarting request as /topsecret/index.html
[13/Oct/2008:21:59:05] fine ( 2056): GET requests for virtual server
   www.example.com cannot bypass ACL checks
[13/Oct/2008:21:59:05] fine ( 2056): acl: matched an acl for [uri=/
   topsecret/*]
```

[13/Oct/2008:21:59:05] fine (2056): acl user: match on user = (anyone)
[13/Oct/2008:21:59:05] fine (2056): acl user: match on user = (anyone)
[13/Oct/2008:21:59:05] fine (2056): acl: calling getter for (attr=user;
    method=basic, dbtype=file)
[13/Oct/2008:21:59:05] fine (2056): acl: calling getter for (attr=isvalid-
    password; method=basic, dbtype=file)
[13/Oct/2008:21:59:05] fine (2056): acl: calling getter for (attr=raw-
    user; method=basic, dbtype=file)
[13/Oct/2008:21:59:05] fine (2056): acl: calling getter for
    (attr=authorization; method=basic, dbtype=file)
[13/Oct/2008:21:59:05] fine (2056): acl: getter for (attr=authorization;
    method=basic, dbtype=file) returns -2
[13/Oct/2008:21:59:05] fine (2056): acl: getter for (attr=raw-user;
    method=basic, dbtype=file) returns -2
[13/Oct/2008:21:59:05] fine (2056): acl: getter for (attr=isvalid-pass-
    word; method=basic, dbtype=file) returns -2
[13/Oct/2008:21:59:05] fine (2056): acl: getter for (attr=user;
    method=basic, dbtype=file) returns -6
[13/Oct/2008:21:59:10] fine (2056): for host 127.0.0.1 trying to GET /
    topsecret/, restarting request as /topsecret/index.html
[13/Oct/2008:21:59:10] fine (2056): acl user: match on user = (anyone)
[13/Oct/2008:21:59:10] fine (2056): acl user: match on user = (anyone)
[13/Oct/2008:21:59:10] fine (2056): acl: calling getter for (attr=user;
    method=basic, dbtype=file)
[13/Oct/2008:21:59:10] fine (2056): acl: calling getter for (attr=isvalid-
    password; method=basic, dbtype=file)
[13/Oct/2008:21:59:10] fine (2056): acl: calling getter for (attr=raw-
    user; method=basic, dbtype=file)
[13/Oct/2008:21:59:10] fine (2056): acl: calling getter for
    (attr=authorization; method=basic, dbtype=file)
[13/Oct/2008:21:59:10] fine (2056): acl: getter for (attr=authorization;
    method=basic, dbtype=file) returns -1
[13/Oct/2008:21:59:10] fine (2056): acl: getter for (attr=raw-user;
    method=basic, dbtype=file) returns -1
**[13/Oct/2008:21:59:10] fine (2056): file authdb: Authenticating user
    [rodale]**

```
[13/Oct/2008:21:59:10] fine ( 2056): file authdb: Authentication succeeded
    for [rodale] (basic)
[13/Oct/2008:21:59:10] fine ( 2056): acl: getter for (attr=isvalid-pass-
    word; method=basic, dbtype=file) returns -1
[13/Oct/2008:21:59:10] fine ( 2056): acl: getter for (attr=user;
    method=basic, dbtype=file) returns -1
[13/Oct/2008:21:59:10] fine ( 2056): acl user: user [rodale] does not match
    user = (bnelson)
[13/Oct/2008:21:59:10] security ( 2056): for host 127.0.0.1 trying to GET
/topsecret/index.html while trying to GET /topsecret/, acl-state reports:
HTTP5191: access of /sun/webserver7/https-www.example.com/docs/topsecret/
index.html denied by ACL uri=/topsecret/* directive 1
```

The first 13 entries (with a timestamp of 13/Oct/2008:21:59:05) demonstrate the initial request made by the rodale user before they have authenticated to the database. The remaining 15 entries (with a timestamp of 13/Oct/2008:21:59:10) demonstrate the entries generated during the authentication process. Pay particular attention to the entries that indicate the user that is being authenticated and whether or not the authentication succeeded (these are the first two bold-faced entries listed in Example 8.10). Also pay attention to the last two bold-faced entries in Example 8.10; these provide details as to why the user's request to access this resource was denied.

The ACL for this particular resource consists of the two ACEs defined on lines 17 and 18. This example demonstrates that the user was prevented access to this resource by the first ACE that was evaluated (which is defined on line 17 of Example 8.9). This occurs because the second ACE resolved to FALSE because the user did not match bnelson.

8.1.2.4 Putting It All Together

Implementations of access control policies utilize both authentication and authorization to effectively protect Web Server resources. Before allowing users access to information, you must know who they are; this requires that you have an authentication database (of which the Web Server supports different types). As soon as you know who the user is, you can determine whether that user is allowed access (and in what manner) to the information based on the data defined within the policies. This requires you to have one or more access control files that define what rights you are defining for each Web Server resource. When both of these have been properly configured, you have established the foundation for protecting information contained within your Web Server.

Figure 8.4 demonstrates the communication between an HTTP user agent and the Web Server when implementing basic or digest authentication (simple username and password). It showcases the points in the request handling process where authentication and authorization come into play and the common manner in which both parties respond to the information they receive.

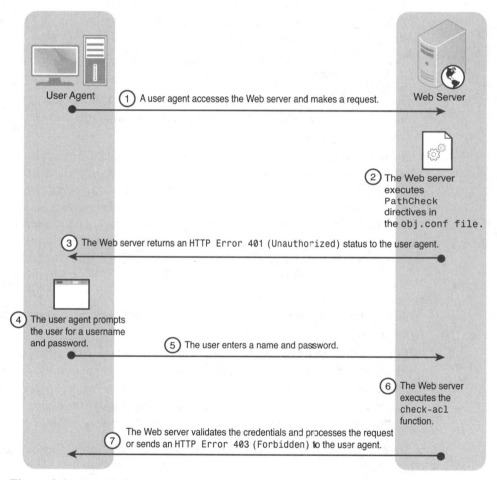

Figure 8.4 Access Control Flow

The communication between the user agent and Web Server in Figure 8.4 can be summarized as follows:

1. An HTTP user agent (i.e., a browser) accesses the Web Server and makes a request for a protected resource. The user's credentials are not sent as part of the HTTP header, so no authentication takes place.

2. The Web Server executes PathCheck directives as defined in the appropriate object configuration file.

3. The resource that the client is requesting is protected and the client has not yet authenticated to the Web Server. The Web Server returns an HTTP Error 401 (Unauthorized) status to the client.

4. The Error 401 status causes the browser to display a prompt for username and password entry.

5. The user enters a username and password. The client takes the information entered by the user and resends the original request, along with the authentication information.

   The username and password are validated against a data store. If the username and password do not match data found in the data store, the Web Server returns the HTTP Error 401 (Unauthorized) to the client, which again causes the browser to display a prompt for username and password entry (in which case you go back to Step 4). This process continues until either the user enters a valid username and password or selects the Cancel option on the prompt box. The Cancel option automatically produces a Forbidden message to the client (see Step 7).

6. The Web Server executes the check-acl function in the object configuration file to determine whether the user has the appropriate permissions to access this resource.

7. If the user has permissions to access the requested resource, then the Web Server obtains and returns the information. If the user has properly authenticated but is not allowed access to the requested resource, then the Web Server sends an HTTP Error 403 (Forbidden) message to the client, indicating that access is denied.

In this example, the user specified a username and password for authentication. It would have been just as easy to provide a trusted client certificate to the Web Server for authentication. This is called certificate-based authentication and provides a stronger level of encryption over standard username and password. Use of certificates to provide additional levels of security are discussed more in the next section.

8.2 Using SSL Certificates to Secure Data

Organizations use the Internet to conduct business with employees, customers, suppliers, and business partners on a daily basis. As such, the information exchanged between these entities users must be secure, unaltered, and the identity of both parties must be trusted.

For example, consider a web site that sells a product online. Customers wishing to purchase products from the site want to know with whom they are about to do business. They want to know that they can trust that vendors are who they say they are. Vendors, in turn, cannot look at a consumer's driver's license or employee badge to make sure the consumer is authorized to make a purchase or access information. In physical commerce transactions, there is a paper trail, including credit card slips and bills of sale, where both parties can provide proof that a transaction occurred. How can such proof be provided for electronic transactions where neither party may have ever met face to face?

The Internet uses shared broadcast media that can be completely unprotected at certain points during transmission. Using the analogy of a postal mail delivery system (where letters are sent in envelopes), information sent over the Internet is like sending a postcard. Postcards lack guarantee of delivery, can be read by anyone that handles the postcard, and can be altered without the knowledge of the sender or recipient. In fact, software is easily available that allows an unscrupulous party to intercept, read, and potentially alter electronic messages passed between a browser and a Web Server. So how can vendors and consumers keep information confidential and how do they keep information from being modified and forwarded? Fortunately, technology exists to protect the integrity of the transaction and ensure that it is private and both parties know and trust each other.

SSL (Secure Socket Layer) is a security protocol that provides privacy and authentication for network traffic to your server. To enable SSL, you must first install an X.509 digital certificate. The certificate provides a method of distributing various pieces of information (such as your public key) that is used to provide identification of your server to other entities. This enables those entities to trust your participation in the transaction after verifying certain components within the certificate (such as the issuer, subject, validity dates, and signature).

Netscape developed the Secure Sockets Layer Protocol (SSL) back in the mid 1990s to address issues surrounding Internet privacy. The SSL protocol and its successor, Transport Layer Security (TLS), established the trust necessary to conduct business on the Internet by securing online communications. Both protocols are widely used in all Web Servers today and are used by most encryption technologies as follows:

- Authentication and non-repudiation—X.509 certificates and digital signatures are used to verify identities. This is accomplished through asymmetric encryption using RSA (Rivest, Shamir, and Adleman) Security, Inc. public-key technology.

- Message privacy—Data Encryption Standard (DES), Rivest's Cipher 2 (RC2), or Rivest's Cipher 4 (RC4) symmetric encryption ensures that messages cannot be viewed by third parties.

- Message integrity—One-way hashes (or message digests) such as Message Digest (MD5) or Secure Hash Algorithm (SHA-1) are used to ensure messages are not altered in transit.

The SSL protocol supports the use of a variety of different cryptographic algorithms, or ciphers, for use in operations such as authenticating the server and client to each other, transmitting certificates, and establishing session keys. Clients and servers can support different cipher suites, or sets of ciphers, depending on factors such as the version of SSL they support, company policies regarding acceptable encryption strength, and government restrictions on the export of SSL-enabled software. These capabilities address fundamental concerns about communication over the Internet and other TCP/IP networks:

- SSL server authentication enables a user to confirm a server's identity. SSL-enabled client software can use standard techniques of public-key cryptography to check that a server's certificate and public ID are valid and have been issued by a certificate authority (CA) listed in the client's list of trusted CAs. This confirmation might be important if the user, for example, is sending a credit card number over the network and wants to check the receiving server's identity.

- SSL client authentication allows a server to confirm a user's identity. Using the same techniques as those used for server authentication, SSL-enabled server software can check that a client's certificate and public ID are valid and have been issued by a CA listed in the server's list of trusted CAs. This confirmation might be important if the server, for example, is a bank sending confidential financial information to a customer and the bank needs to check the recipient's identity.

- An encrypted SSL connection requires all information sent between a client and a server to be encrypted by the sending software and decrypted by the receiving software, thus providing a high degree of confidentiality. Confidentiality is important for both parties to any private transaction. In addition, all data sent over an encrypted SSL connection is protected with a mechanism for detecting tampering—that is, for automatically determining whether the data has been altered in transit.

The SSL 2.0 and SSL 3.0 protocols support overlapping sets of cipher suites. Administrators can enable or disable any of the supported cipher suites for both clients and servers. When a particular client and server exchange information during the SSL handshake, they identify the strongest cipher suites they have in common and use those for the SSL session.

Encryption strength is often described in terms of the size of the session keys used to perform the encryption. In general, longer keys provide stronger encryption. Key length is measured in bits. For example, 128-bit keys for use with the RC4 symmetric-key cipher supported by SSL provide significantly better cryptographic protection than 40-bit keys for use with the same cipher.

8.2.1 Symmetric-key Encryption

Computer applications are predictable and can do only what programmers program them to do. Logic contained within the application is processed over and over again with a certain level of predictability. As such, many of the algorithms used within computer programs can be easily determined with enough observation. The way that you introduce randomness into an algorithm is through the use of a random value or *key* that is not easily predictable. This allows the algorithm to utilize the key and produce data that does not lead back to the algorithm's logic without knowledge of the key value. The use of keys within programming can most notably be seen by random number generators that require the use of random seed values to make the output truly random.

Cryptography is the practice and study of hiding information and is used to facilitate secure Internet transactions. Cryptographic algorithms are used to convert ordinary information (plaintext) into what appears to be nonsensical information (ciphertext) and then back again. This allows two parties to communicate securely if they both share the same algorithms. To create an effective algorithm that is not easily breakable, cryptographic algorithms (or ciphers) must share a random key value. The simplest type cipher uses a trivially related, often identical, key for both decryption and encryption. The key is shared between both parties of the communication and as such is called a *symmetric key*. The process of using a symmetric key for the purpose of encrypting and decrypting data is called *symmetric key encryption*.

Figure 8.5 demonstrates the use of a shared symmetric key to allow William to send a message to Rachael.

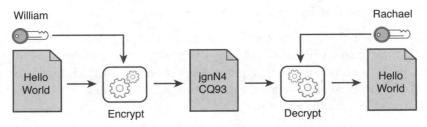

Figure 8.5   Message Sharing with a Shared (Symmetric) Key

Both parties agree to a cipher that will be used for encrypting and decrypting messages (for instance, Advanced Encryption Standard (AES)). Additionally, both parties share a secret key that will be used as a seed into the cipher. William creates a plaintext message that he would like to share with Rachael. He encrypts the message with the cipher and uses the symmetric key as an input. This produces a ciphertext message that cannot be read by anyone that does not have the symmetric key. When Rachael receives the message, she can decrypt and read it because she has a copy of the shared key.

Symmetric-key encryption is typically the fastest method of encrypting and decrypting messages, but the distribution of the symmetric key between both parties is its biggest drawback. You cannot send the key over an electronic medium for fear that it could be intercepted and used against you. So how can you share keys between two parties that may never have met? Public-key encryption provides a solution for this dilemma.

8.2.2 Public-key Encryption

Public-key encryption is called asymmetric because two different keys (a public key and a private key) are used to encode and decode the encrypted data. This is in contrast to symmetric-key encryption, which uses one key for both encryption and decryption. The algorithms used in public-key encryption are developed in such a way that data encrypted using one key can be decrypted only with the other key (and vice versa). The combination of these two tightly coupled keys is called the *key-pair*.

Entities that would like for others to communicate privately with them (for instance, commerce-enabled web sites) make one of the two keys available for general *public* use. They keep the other of the two keys *privately* locked away. Customers can then use the publicly available key to encrypt a message for the site that only the owner of the public key can read (because the owner has the corresponding key).

The private key is encrypted and stored in the Web Server's trust database using a password known only to the owner; it is never transmitted by any means. The other key, called the public key, is provided freely to anyone with whom the key-pair owner communicates. Because the public key is not secret, it can be sent to anyone in the clear (unencrypted).

After you have an entity's public key, you can generate a message for that entity and encrypt it with their public key. When you encrypt data with a public key, only the recipient can decrypt it with the corresponding private key. This allows the sender to feel confident that only the owner of the public key can decrypt them— because the owner has the corresponding private key.

The two parts of a key pair are inseparable; if the private key is lost or if the password is forgotten, a new key pair must be generated. Any messages encrypted with a public key can no longer be read if the private key is lost. This leads some companies to require backups of encryption keys.

Symmetric-key encryption is much faster than public-key encryption, but public-key encryption provides better authentication techniques. The SSL protocol uses a combination of public-key and symmetric-key encryption to provide the best of both worlds. Clients communicate with an SSL-enabled server over using public-key encryption where the public key is distributed through X.509 digital certificates. After the identity of the server is trusted, a symmetric key is generated by the client and passed to the server over public-key encryption methods. Both entities now share a secret key that can be used for encrypting and decrypting data. Communication between both parties now shifts to symmetric-key encryption using the shared key. For a detailed explanation of the SSL handshake, see Section 8.2.6.

8.2.3 X.509 Digital Certificates

Digital certificates are the electronic counterparts to driver's licenses, passports, and other forms of identification. You present your digital certificate electronically to prove your identity or your right to access information or services online.

Like any physical identification, digital certificates can be created, expired, renewed, revoked, or suspended.

Digital certificates bind an entity's identity to the key-pair that can be used to encrypt and sign information. Used with encryption, digital certificates provide a more complete security solution, ensuring the identity of all parties involved in electronic transactions.

Digital certificates normally contain the following information:

- Owner's public key
- Owner's name
- Expiration date of public key
- Name of the certificate issuer (Certificate Authority—CA)
- Serial number of the digital certificate
- Digital signature of the CA

The contents of certificates supported by Sun and many other companies are organized according to the X.509 v3 certificate specification, which has been recommended by the International Telecommunications Union, an international standards body, since 1988.

The following is an example of a decoded X.509 certificate for www.example.com:

```
Certificate:
   Data:
       Version: 1 (0x0)
       Serial Number: 7829 (0x1e95)
       Signature Algorithm: md5WithRSAEncryption
       Issuer: CN=VeriSign Class 3 Code Signing 2004 CA, OU=Terms of
   use at
https://www.verisign.com/rpa (c)04, OU=VeriSign Trust Network,
   O="VeriSign, Inc.",
C=US
       Validity:
           Not Before: Fri Oct 17 18:36:25 2008
           Not  After: Sat Oct 17 18:36:25 2009
       Subject: C=US, ST=Florida, L=Tampa, O=IT, OU=Internet, CN=www.
   example.com
       Subject Public Key Info:
           Public Key Algorithm: rsaEncryption
           RSA Public Key (1024 bit)
               Modulus (1024 bit):
```

```
00:ca:fa:79:98:8f:19:f8:d7:de:e4:49:80:48:e6:2a:2a:86:
ed:27:40:4d:86:b3:05:c0:01:bb:50:15:c9:de:dc:85:19:22:
43:7d:45:6d:71:4e:17:3d:f0:36:4b:5b:7f:a8:51:a3:a1:00:
98:ce:7f:47:50:2c:93:36:7c:01:6e:cb:89:06:41:72:b5:e9:
73:49:38:76:ef:b6:8f:ac:49:bb:63:0f:9b:ff:16:2a:e3:0e:
9d:3b:af:ce:9a:3e:48:65:de:96:61:d5:0a:11:2a:a2:80:b0:
7d:d8:99:cb:0c:99:34:c9:ab:25:06:a8:31:ad:8c:4b:aa:54: 91:f4:15
                Exponent: 65537 (0x10001)
Signature Algorithm: md5WithRSAEncryption
6d:23:af:f3:d3:b6:7a:df:90:df:cd:7e:18:6c:01:69:8e:54:65:fc:06:30:43
  :34:d1:63:1f:06
:7d:c3:40:a8:2a:82:c1:a4:83:2a:fb:2e:8f:fb:f0:6d:ff:75:a3:78:f7:52:4
  7:46:62:97:1d:d
9:c6:11:0a:02:a2:e0:cc:2a:75:6c:8b:b6:9b:87:00:7d:7c:84:76:79:ba:f8:
  b4:d2:62:58:c3:
c5:b6:c1:43:ac:63:44:42:fd:af:c8:0f:2f:38:85:6c:d6:59:e8:41:42:a5:4a
  :e5:26:38:ff:32
:78:a1:38:f1:ed:dc:0d:31:d1:b0:6d:67:e9:46:a8:dd:c4
```

The certificate follows the format specified in RFC 3280, commonly referred to as PKIX for Public Key Infrastructure (X.509). Although the certificate may contain quite a bit of information, you should pay particular attention to four main fields:

- The Issuer field contains the distinguished name of the certificate authority (CA), which is the entity that issued this certificate. Browsers look at this information and compare it to that found within their own list of trusted CAs. If the name is not found, a browser does not automatically trust this certificate.

- The Validity field contains the date that the certificate became valid and when it will expire. If a browser receives a certificate on a day that is outside those two dates, it does not automatically trust this certificate.

- The Subject field contains the distinguished name of the owner of the certificate. It may contain various attributes that help identify this certificate, but the most important attribute is the CN (or common name). The CN must match the hostname and domain name of the host the browser is trying to access. If the CN does not match this information, then the browser does not automatically trust this certificate.

- The certificate's signature immediately follows the Signature Algorithm field and contains an encoded bit stream signature. The browser computes this value by taking an MD5 hash of the first part of the certificate and encrypting it with CA's private key. Browsers can use the CA's public key to decrypt the digital signature to obtain the original hashed value of the certificate. They can then use the algorithm specified in the `Signature Algorithm` field and duplicate the hashing process. The two hashed values can then be compared to determine whether the certificate has been altered in any way.

Before you can enable SSL on the Web Server, you must first install a digital certificate. User Agents communicating with an SSL-enabled Web Server receive a copy of the digital certificate during the SSL handshake. User Agents extract the public key from the digital certificate and use it to initiate secure communication with the Web Server.

> **Note:** Digital certificates contain a copy of the owner's public key and are used as the primary mechanism for distributing the public key to those who would like to establish secure communication with the owner. Refer to Section 8.2.6 for more information on the SSL handshake and Section 8.2.2 for a description of public-key encryption.

Certificates are stored in the Web Server's trust database. By default, the Web Server stores security-based information in three Network Security Services (NSS) libdbm database files as follows:

- `cert8.db`—Stores publicly accessible objects (such as certificates, certificate revocation lists, and S/MIME records)
- `key3.db`—Stores the private keys generated by the Web Server. These keys were generated as part of the certificate request process.
- `secmod.db`—Stores Public Key Cryptography Standard (PKCS) #11 module configuration information. For example, the `secmod.db` file might contain configuration information for an external SSL hardware accelerator card.

These three files make up the *trust database*.

8.2.4 Types of Certificates

Three main types of algorithms are used for digital certificates: DSA (Digital Signature Algorithm), RSA (Rivest, Shamir, and Adleman—named after the three inventors of the algorithm), and ECDSA (Elliptic Curve Digital Signature Algorithm).

The Digital Signature Algorithm (DSA) is not an encryption algorithm in that it is used for digital signatures only. It was first proposed by the National Institute of Standards and Technology (NIST) for use in their Digital Signature Standard (DSS). DSA certificates are not used within the context of SSL-enabled Web Servers.

RSA was one of the first great advances in public key cryptography and achieved early success because of its capability to be used for both digital signatures and message encryption. RSA is still widely used, but longer key lengths are required to avoid being cracked by faster computers and distributed computing models. Today, RSA keys are typically 1024–2048 bits long and some experts believe that 1024-bit keys may become breakable in the near future. Others disagree with this, but experts recommend that key sizes be at least 2048 bits long to avoid being proven wrong. RSA is the most widely deployed type of certificate used today and until recently was the sole type of certificate used in Sun's Web Servers.

With the shift toward smaller, more mobile devices, the need for smaller and faster signatures has arisen and Elliptic Curve Cryptography (ECC) is now emerging as an attractive public-key cryptosystem for mobile and wireless environments.

Compared to traditional cryptosystems such as RSA, ECC offers equivalent security with smaller key sizes, which results in faster computations, lower power consumption, as well as memory and bandwidth savings. This is especially useful for mobile devices, which are typically limited in terms of their CPU, power, and network connectivity.

The fastest known algorithms to attack ECC run more slowly than the fastest known algorithms to attack RSA. ECC can therefore offer equivalent security with substantially smaller keys and much higher performance. For example, a 160-bit ECC key provides the same level of security as a 1024-bit RSA key at 4 times the RSA performance and a 224-bit ECC key provides the security equivalent to a 2048-bit RSA key at 14 times the RSA performance on large servers with 64-bit processors. For small 8-bit processors, ECC even offers a performance advantage of up to two orders of magnitude. Smaller keys result in faster computations, lower power consumption, and memory and bandwidth savings. These characteristics make ECC especially appealing for small client devices and alleviate the computational burden on secure web servers.

Moreover, the National Security Agency (NSA) requires that signatures used today last for the next 50 years. These requirements pave the way for digital certificates that use Elliptic Curve Cryptography (ECC)–based signatures.

> **Note:** Web Server 7.0 provides support for both RSA and ECC certificates. Refer to the Sun Labs Next Generation Crypto Project web site at http://research.sun.com/projects/crypto for more information on ECC certificates.

8.2.5 Certificate Authorities

A Certificate Authority (CA) creates and issues X.509 digital certificates for Web Servers (or other applications or devices) that would like to identify themselves over the Internet. This is most widely used to allow servers to provide content over SSL but may also be used for other identification purposes such as digital signatures or encrypted e-mail.

An administrator may request an X.509 digital certificate for a Web Server by submitting a request form to a Certificate Authority. The form may contain corporate information such as company name, web site address, physical address, phone number, city, state, and even a Dunn and Bradstreet number to help the CA perform due diligence on the company. The administrator may also submit a certificate signing request (or CSR) along with the request. The CSR is generated for a specific Web Server and consists of attributes to help identify the owner of the certificate; these may include characteristics such as the organization name, city, state, and country. Most importantly, the CSR also contains a public key generated by the Web Server. The corresponding private key is not included in the CSR, but is used to digitally sign the entire request.

You can use the Administration Console or the `create-cert-request` subcommand in the command line interface to create a CSR for Web Server 7.0. The following provides an example of how to use this command to generate a CSR for the certificate shown in section 8.2.3.

```
wadm> create-cert-request --key-type=rsa --key-size=1024  --org=IT
--org-unit=Internet --locality=Tampa --state=Florida --country=US
--config=www.example.com --token=internal --server-name=www.example.
com
```

The `key` option specifies the type of key being requested and the `key-size` option specifies the length of the key. The `token` option references the name of the PKCS token being used by the server, which is `internal` by default. The remaining options specify data to help identify the owner of the certificate. This subcommand produces an output similar to the following:

```
-----BEGIN NEW CERTIFICATE REQUEST-----
MIIB1jCCAT8CAQAwaTELMAkGA1UEBhMCVVMxEDAOBgNVBAgTBOZsb3JpZGExDjAM
BgNVBAcTBVRhbXBhMQswCQYDVQQKEwJJVDERMA8GA1UECxMISW5OZXJuZXQxGDAW
BgNVBAMTD3d3dy5leGFtcGxlLmNvbTCBnzANBgkqhkiG9w0BAQEFAAOBjQAwgYkC
gYEAt1r7KdP757Bi/dGmCq+V13Aa0PAewux7ixan5zW1herroM13zEYAmuEaZDda
BC2x6vKadv8C4xc06H1GaRab+pZg2TH+kbXG9r020HbGeviOGcf5AgRV4aGigb1I
jB0Xa016n10x0D133v1z9DJ45ibh6X4gI96p53dPIzDnDsECAwEAAaAtMCsGCSqG
SIb3DQEJDjEeMBwwGgYDVR0RBBMwEYIPd3d3LmV4YW1wbGUuY29tMA0GCSqGSIb3
DQEBBQUAA4GBAD0FpP0qnS0IIa46JbaoKyt1XYqnn0AkqMGJu0cbJPsb975zpoTq
bQ8+j0fXxYb5S8g+UYPyKZz0RK+TtLaYwiD7q9UTt5CgdCeE6pb2ho+0bHNkFvYB
t0Gmif9uIM0v7NcNNacpEHD0GFjPzjCrToDswr5dMFZqwffvr2H0vejN
-----END NEW CERTIFICATE REQUEST-----
```

The administrator submits the CSR (including the entire BEGIN and END lines) to the Certificate Authority along with the request form (if applicable). If the request is granted, the CA generates a certificate that contains, among other things, the public key that was included in the CSR. The certificate also contains the digital signature of the issuing Certificate Authority—in other words, the CA is vouching for the owner of the certificate. Therefore, a CA puts its reputation on the line each time it issues a new certificate. As such, the CA has the responsibility of identifying the owner of a specific public key before issuing a certificate to the entity. The method used by the CA to establish the identity of the owner is the most important part of CA security policy and the effectiveness of Internet security depends on the care taken when certificates are issued.

There is a cost associated with the certificate request process. CAs such as Veri-Sign and Entrust charge a fee for this service. There is a benefit, however, as browsers who encounter certificates signed by one of these *trusted* CAs do not generate security alerts for the end user.

A certificate obtained by a Certificate Authority takes the following form:

```
-----BEGIN CERTIFICATE-----
MIIDHTCCAoagAwIBAgIQb5xIuaHdBcOcnjXElsMspzANBgkqhkiG9w0BAQUFADCB
hzELMAkGA1UEBhMCWkExIjAgBgNVBAgTGUZPUiBURVNUSU5HIFBVU1BPU0VTIE90
```

lines deleted

```
YFGnDSHkGfcs+pAiFq6L1LKym2TCalrxyGMo+TalpnIfZkvfcIE4MkTmsroxBVLC
wD3JBp5EC8KKz0G8qGKCHYt+4GsNWyDExAmRY9LcCEqX
-----END CERTIFICATE-----
```

You can use the Administration Console or the install-cert subcommand in the command line interface to install the certificate in Web Server 7.0. The following provides an example of how to use the install-cert subcommand to install a certificate obtained from a Certificate Authority. The certificate is contained in the file, serverCert.fil.

```
wadm> install-cert --token=internal --cert-type=server
--nickname=exampleCert --config=www.example.com /serverCert.fil
```

The cert-type option specifies the type of certificate being installed and may be a CA certificate, a server certificate, or a certificate chain. The nickname option specifies how the certificate will be referenced in the Administration Server. Once again, the token option references the name of the PKCS token being used by the server, which is internal by default.

As indicated previously, there is a cost associated with certificates issued by CAs. If you do not want to incur the cost and you are not concerned with security alerts generated in the browser, then you may elect to generate or obtain a *self-signed certificate*. A self-signed certificate is a standard X.509 certificate that has been signed by its own creator. In other words, the person that created the certificate also signed off on its legitimacy. Self-signed certificates are widely used for internal or testing purposes, but most companies elect to purchase a certificate from a trusted CA for their customer-facing web sites.

Web Server 7.0 provides a mechanism for generating both RSA and ECC self-signed certificates. In fact, SSL has been enabled in the Administration Server through the use of a self-signed certificate that was created during the installation of the Web Server software. You can generate your own self-signed certificate with the Administration Console or by using the create-selfsigned-cert subcommand in the command line interface. The following provides an example of how to use this subcommand to create a self-signed certificate:

```
wadm> create-selfsigned-cert --key-type=rsa --key-size=1024 --org=IT
--org-unit=Internet --locality=Tampa --state=Florida --country=US
--config=www.example.com --token=internal
  --server-name=www.example.com
--nickname=exampleCert
```

The `create-selfsigned-cert` subcommand combines the CSR generation, certificate request, and certificate installation into a single step. With this subcommand, the Web Server generates the appropriate information necessary for the CSR and acts as its own CA. It automatically generates the self-signed certificate based on the internal CSR data and installs the certificate into the trust database.

Note: Previous versions of the Web Server included the NSS Certificate Database Tool (`certutil`) that could be used to generate, install, and manage self-signed certificates. The syntax for this command was difficult to understand and easily mistyped. The ability to generate and manage self-signed certificates in Web Server 7.0 has been dramatically improved.

8.2.6 SSL Handshake

A Web Server instance can be configured to communicate over SSL after a certificate has been installed. An SSL session always begins with an exchange of messages called the *SSL handshake*. The handshake allows the server to authenticate itself to the client using public-key techniques. It then allows the client and the server to cooperate in the creation of symmetric keys used for rapid encryption, decryption, and tamper detection during the session that follows. Optionally, the handshake also allows the client to authenticate itself to the server.

Figure 8.6 demonstrates the interaction between the client and the server during the SSL handshake.

The steps involved in the SSL handshake can be summarized as follows:

1. The User Agent (i.e., browser) makes a request to communicate with the Web Server over SSL. The User Agent sends the Web Server its SSL version number, cipher settings, randomly generated data, and other information that Web Server needs to communicate with the User Agent using SSL.

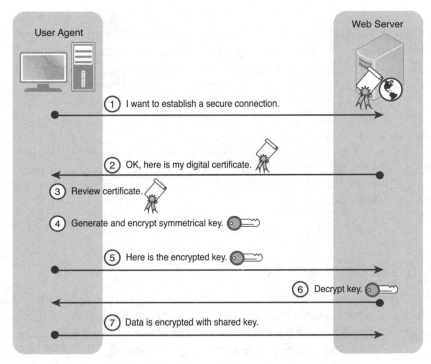

Figure 8.6   Client Interaction with an SSL-enabled Web Server

2. The Web Server responds to the User Agent by sending its own server's SSL version number, cipher settings, randomly generated data, and other information that the User Agent needs to communicate with the Web Server over SSL. The Web Server also sends its own digital certificate and, if the User Agent is requesting access to a resource that requires authentication, the Web Server may request that the User Agent provides its own certificate at this time.

3. The User Agent reviews the information contained in the Web Server's certificate to determine whether it should trust the Web Server. Specifically, the User Agent validates the following four items:

   • **Validity Period**—The current date and time must be within the range specified in the validity period. The certificate cannot be expired.

   • **Trusted CA**—Each SSL-enabled User Agent maintains a list of trusted CA certificates. This list determines which certificates the User Agent accepts. If the distinguished name (DN) of the issuing CA matches the DN of a CA on the User Agent's list of trusted CAs, then the User Agent automatically trusts the certificate.

- **Digital Signature**—The digital signature contained within the certificate is actually the certificate itself, hashed and encrypted with the CA's private key. The User Agent uses the public key from the CA's certificate to validate the digital signature on the Web Server certificate being presented. This method ensures that the certificate has not been altered in any way and the User Agent treats the Web Server's certificate as a valid letter of introduction from that CA.

- **Subject**—The subject of the certificate (i.e., www.example.com) is reviewed to determine whether it matches the host/domain requested by the User Agent. This step confirms that the Web Server from which the User Agent has received the certificate is actually the same one it was attempting to talk to.

4. Using all data generated in the handshake so far, the User Agent (with the cooperation of the Web Server, depending on the cipher being used) creates a secret message for the session, encrypts it with the Web Server's public key (obtained from the Web Server's certificate, sent in Step 2).

5. The User Agent sends the encrypted premaster secret message to the Web Server.

   Optional Steps:

   If the Web Server has requested User Agent authentication (an optional step in the handshake and not shown in Figure 8.6), the User Agent also signs another piece of data that is unique to this handshake and known only by the User Agent and Web Server. In this case, the User Agent sends both the signed data and the User Agent's own certificate to the Web Server, along with the encrypted premaster secret message.

   If the Web Server has requested User Agent authentication, the Web Server attempts to authenticate the User Agent. If the User Agent cannot be authenticated, the session is terminated. If the User Agent can be authenticated successfully, the handshake continues.

6. The Web Server uses its private key to decrypt the premaster secret message. It then performs a series of steps (which the User Agent also performs using the same premaster secret message) to generate the master secret message.

7. Both the User Agent and the Web Server use the shared master secret message to generate the session keys, which are symmetric keys used to encrypt and decrypt information exchanged during the SSL session and to verify its integrity—that is, to detect any changes in the data between the time it was sent and the time it is received over the SSL connection.

The User Agent sends a message to the Web Server, informing it that future messages from the User Agent are encrypted with the session key. It then sends a separate (encrypted) message indicating that the User Agent portion of the handshake is finished.

The Web Server sends a message to the User Agent informing it that future messages from the Web Server are encrypted with the session key. It then sends a separate (encrypted) message indicating that the Web Server portion of the handshake is finished.

The SSL handshake is now complete, and the SSL session has begun. The User Agent and the Web Server use the session keys to encrypt and decrypt the data they send to each other and to validate its integrity.

As indicated in step 5, the Web Server can be configured to request a User Agent's certificate to validate the identity of the User Agent. The Web Server can be configured to verify that the User Agent's certificate is present in the user's entry in an LDAP directory before continuing with the session. This configuration option provides one way of ensuring that the User Agent's certificate has not been revoked.

It is important to note that both User Agent and Web Server authentication involve encrypting some piece of data with one key of a public-private key pair and decrypting it with the other key.

In the case of server authentication, the User Agent encrypts the premaster secret message digest with the Web Server's public key. Only the corresponding private key can correctly decrypt the secret message digest, so the User Agent has some assurance that the identity associated with the public key is in fact the Web Server with which the User Agent is connected. Otherwise, the Web Server cannot decrypt the premaster secret message and cannot generate the symmetric keys required for the session, and the session is terminated.

In the case of client authentication, the User Agent encrypts some random data with the User Agent's private key—that is, it creates a digital signature. The public key in the User Agent's certificate can correctly validate the digital signature only if the corresponding private key was used. Otherwise, the Web Server cannot validate the digital signature, and the session is terminated.

8.3 Automating Maintenance of Certificate Revocation Lists (CRLs)

Applications that rely on Public Key Infrastructure (PKI) certificates as part of their security design generally implement some mechanism for ensuring that those certificates are valid. One common mechanism is obtaining a list of revoked certificates (called a CRL or certificate revocation list) from the Certificate Authority that issued them. Applications that rely on up-to-date certificate information generally obtain the latest versions of CRLs on a periodic basis and update their trust databases accordingly.

> **Note:** VeriSign maintains the crl.verisign.com web site where applications can obtain a list of current certificate revocation lists.

Previous versions of the Web Server allowed administrators to update the list of CRLs in the Administration Server through either the Administration GUI or with the `crlutil` command-line utility. The drawback to previous versions of the Web Server is that the instance had to be restarted after every CRL update.

Web Server 7.0 supports a dynamic CRL refresh that allows an administrator to configure the Web Server to check for updated CRLs in a particular file system directory and process any CRLs found in the directory. In Web Server 7.0 this does not require a server restart.

8.3.1 Automating CRL Processing

Two parameters must be configured to allow automated CRL processing; these include the directory in which to look for CRLs (this is specified by the PKCS property, `crl-path`, in the `server.xml`) and how often to look for files in this path (this is specified by the `event` element).

The CRL path can be configured using the `set-pkcs11-prop` subcommand, as follows:

```
wadm> set-pkcs11-prop --config=www.example.com crl-path=/crls
```

This causes the following elements to be created in the server.xml file:

```
<pkcs11>
  <crl-path>/crl</crl-path>
</pkcs11>
```

The Web Server will now look in the /crls directory for any updated certificate revocation lists. The Web Server assumes that all files found in the specified directory are CRLs.

To configure how often the Web Server looks in this directory for updated CRLs, use the create-event subcommand, as follows:

```
wadm> create-event --interval=60 --command=update-crl
--config=www.example.com
```

This causes the following elements to be created in the server.xml file:

```
<event>
  <interval>60</interval>
  <update-crl>true</update-crl>
</event>
```

This causes the Web Server to process CRLs every 60 seconds.

> **Note:** The Administration Console enables you to configure both parameters at the same time from the CRL Updates page. You can find this page by navigating as follows: Configurations, config_name, Certificates, CRL Updates.

Administrators that would like to take advantage of dynamic CRL refreshes must provide their own mechanism for downloading and placing the CRL files in the appropriate path. A typical way of performing this task is to use wget, curl, or a similar utility to connect to and obtain the appropriate CRLs from the CA. Once again, you do this by configuring a server event.

In addition to several predefined commands, the create-event subcommand also enables you to specify any script, executable, or operating system command that you would like to schedule. As such, you could schedule an event to run the wget command on a periodic basis to perform a download of one or more files from a CA. This can be demonstrated as follows:

```
wadm> create-event --interval=300 --command="path_to_wget/wget
wget_parameters" --config=www.example.com
```

You could also elect to use a UNIX cron job to run the wget command, but allowing the Web Server to perform this task has its advantages. Keeping Web Server events all in one place enables you to easily locate events applicable to your Web Server and makes debugging much easier.

For environments running clusters or otherwise multiple instances, you should obtain the CRL once from the CA and distribute it internally rather than connect to the CA multiple times.

8.3.2 CRL Processing

The Web Server is configured to look for updated CRLs in a particular directory on a periodic basis. When files are found in this directory the Web Server needs to know how to process them. The following items define how the Web Server processes files found in the CRL path:

- If the Web Server detects new files in the path (that is, they were not present during the previous check), then the new file is loaded into the Web Server as a CRL.

- If the Web Server detects that a file has changed (its modification timestamp has changed since the previous check), then the file is reloaded into the Web Server. The new file replaces the previous CRL loaded from the previous named file.

- If the Web Server determines that no changes have been made to a file (its modification timestamp has not changed), then no processing takes place.

- If the Web Server detects that a file has been deleted from the path, the corresponding CRL is unloaded from the Web Server.

Note: If you manually copy files into the crl-path directory, it is possible that the server might not recognize changes. This is most likely due to the timing of when you copied the file as compared to when the server was processing the update-crl command. If you find that CRL file changes are not being reflected in the Web Server properly, you can use file system commands like the UNIX touch command to update the timestamp on the file. This forces the update-crl command to process the file upon a subsequent execution.

8.4 Detecting and Responding to Denial-of-Service (DoS) Attacks

A denial-of-service (DoS) attack is an explicit attempt by a malicious person (or persons) to prevent legitimate access to a computer resource. Perpetrators of DoS attacks typically direct their efforts at high-profile web servers, but it is not uncommon for a company to instigate a DoS attack against one of its competitors.

A DoS attack can be perpetrated in a number of ways. Two of the most common methods are the following:

- A flood of requests by one or more clients that prevent legitimate business requests from getting through
- Multiple connections by one or more clients by which requests are made at an intentionally slow pace (thus monopolizing server resources)

Web Server 7.0 implements basic denial-of-service detection, which can be used to fend off attacks. This includes the capability to monitor requests that exceed a given configurable metric and limit responses accordingly. It also includes the capability to limit access of clients that open too many connections and request pages in an untimely manner (thus tying up server resources).

8.4.1 Request Flooding

A web server can process only a certain number of simultaneous requests; this is mainly because of system limitations, but may also be a factor of how the web server has been configured. A request flood occurs when one or more clients overload the server with so many requests that it cannot distinguish (nor can it process) legitimate requests from malicious ones.

To aid in the detection of request floods, Web Server 7.0 introduces a new server application function called `check-request-limits`. This SAF allows the Web Server to monitor client requests and refuse processing to those clients that exceed a particular configurable metric. For example, the Web Server can be configured to monitor the requests received from clients over a specific period of time. If the average number of requests per second exceeds those specified in the `check-request-limits` configurable threshold, then subsequent requests will not be serviced until the rate drops.

The check-request-limits SAF is used within the body of the PathCheck directive in the object configuration file. The syntax for this SAF can be summarized as follows:

```
PathCheck fn=check-request-limits [max-rps=x] [max-connections=x]
    [interval=i] [continue={silence|threshold}] [error=n] [monitor=attr]
```

The parameters defined for this SAF can be described as follows:

- The max-rps parameter is the threshold for the number of requests per second (RPS). If this value is exceeded, then subsequent connections are not serviced. As soon as the rate drops below this threshold, new requests are processed.

- The max-connections parameter is the maximum number of concurrent connections for this request. If a matching request is received while there are at least this many requests being processed, the request is rejected. As soon as the number of concurrent requests falls below this limit, new ones are processed.

Note: There are no default values for max-rps or max-connections with this SAF. You must specify at least one of these two parameters if you use the check-request-limits SAF.

- The interval parameter is the time interval in which the average requests per second is computed. The default value of the interval parameter is 30 seconds.

- The continue parameter determines what condition must be met for a blocked request type to become available again for servicing. There are two values for condition: silence (refused requests must fall to zero for service to resume) and threshold (refused request rate must fall below the RPS threshold for service to resume). The default value for continue is threshold.

- The error parameter contains the HTTP status code that is used to block requests. The default value for error is Error 503, Service Unavailable.

- The monitor parameter enables you to specify an optional request to monitor. Request rates are tracked in a receptacle (bucket) named by the value of this parameter. If the monitor parameter is not specified, requests are tracked in the anonymous (or general) bucket.

The following directive provides an example of how to use these parameters within the `check-request-limits` SAF to limit clients to a maximum of 10 requests per second:

```
PathCheck fn="check-request-limits" monitor="$ip" max-rps="10"
```

This is a general directive that can be used to keep track of requests from any client IP address; this is accomplished through the use of the `monitor` attribute. The `monitor` attribute specifies the name of the counter or bucket used to maintain the number of requests per second. Specifying a variable of `$ip` for this value enables you to maintain individual counters for each client IP address. The `interval`, `continue`, and `error` values are not explicitly stated; therefore the server will use the default values of `30`, `threshold`, and `503` for these attributes, respectively.

You can limit request tracking to a particular type of request through the use of conditional processing as follows:

```
<If path = "*.pl">
PathCheck fn="check-request-limits" monitor="$ip" max-rps="10"
</If>
```

This example demonstrates the use of the `<IF>` container to limit monitoring to PERL requests only. If a particular client attempts to process more than ten PERL requests (of any kind) within 30 seconds, then the next request is not serviced. Instead, the client is met with an error 503 (Service Unavailable). You see this error in the access log for any client requests where the limit has been exceeded.

You can use the command line interface to enable and configure request processing limits for a particular virtual server with the `enable-request-limits` subcommand as follows:

```
enable-request-limits --max-rps=10 --monitor-attribute="\$ip"
--config=www.example.com --vs=www.example.com
```

This adds the following directive to the object configuration file:

```
PathCheck fn="check-request-limits" max-rps="10" monitor="$ip"
```

Warning: You must use the backslash (\) character when configuring the `monitor` attribute to use a variable such as `$ip`. This is required to escape the dollar sign and tell the Web Server to use the next character as is.

The Administration Console also allows you to enable and configure request processing limits as well from the Virtual Server Request Limits page. You can find this page by navigating as follows: Configurations, *config_name*, Virtual Servers, *virtual_server_name*.

8.4.2 Monopolizing Server Connections

Clients utilize application threads during request processing. The Web Server maintains a pool of acceptor threads that accept the client request and worker threads that perform request processing. Threads are returned to the pool after the request has been completed and the server has provided a response to the client.

Note: See Chapter 2, "Web Server 7.0 Architecture," for more information on Web Server threads.

One client can open several connections to a Web Server and therefore take up multiple threads. That same client can provide requests in an intentionally slow manner and therefore hang on to threads longer than they should. Either of these two conditions can cause the thread pool to become depleted and additional requests cannot be processed. The `check-request-limits` SAF can be used to specify a maximum number of client connections, but it cannot be used to address intentionally slow request processing.

Previous versions of the Web Server enabled you to specify the number of seconds that the server waited for data to arrive from the client before closing the connection. This was configured with the `AcceptTimeout` directive in the `magnus.conf` file and was set to 30 seconds by default.

Note: The `AcceptTimeout` directive is now specified by the `io-timeout` element in the `server.xml` file and continues to have a default value of 30 seconds. You can observe the behavior of this element by using the TELNET command to connect to the Web Server on the appropriate port (for instance, TELNET `www.example.com 80`). The Web Server terminates the connection after 30 seconds if it does not see a request from the client.

This parameter is adequate in many cases, but it does not provide granular control throughout the entire request process. After the client makes an initial request of the server, the `io-timeout` setting no longer applies and the client is free to monopolize server connections.

To address the need for granularity, Web Server 7.0 now includes two additional timeout attributes:

1. `request-header-timeout`—Maximum time (in seconds) that the Web Server waits for the complete HTTP request header.
2. `request-body-timeout`—Maximum time (in seconds) that the Web Server waits for the complete HTTP request body.

Possible values for both attributes include 0–604800 seconds (which equates to 0–10,080 minutes or 0–168 days) and –1 (which disables the timer). The timers are disabled by default, but you can enable them as you determine necessary. For instance, if you want to ensure that all request headers are received within the first 10 minutes of the connection followed by all request body data within the next 60 minutes, you can set the `request-header-timeout` and `request-body-timeout` values to 600 and 3600, respectively. All connections that take longer than these two values are disconnected by the server automatically.

The CLI subcommand to accomplish this task is `set-http-prop` and can be used to specify these values as follows:

```
wadm> set-http-prop  --config=www.example.com request-header-
timeout=600
 request-body-timeout=3600
```

This subcommand causes the following two entries to be generated in the `server.xml` file:

```
<http>
  <request-body-timeout>3600</request-body-timeout>
  <request-header-timeout>600</request-header-timeout>
</http>
```

The Administration Console also allows you to enable and configure these timeout values from the HTTP Settings page. You can find this page by navigating as follows: Configurations, *config_name*, Performance, HTTP.

8.5 Using the Web Server as Reverse Proxy

A reverse proxy is a server that acts as a broker between two entities, validating and processing a transaction in such a way that the actual parties to the transaction do not directly communicate with one another. This means that the proxy acts on behalf of the content web server (also known as the *origin server*). A reverse proxy can represent one or several origin servers, as shown in Figure 8.7.

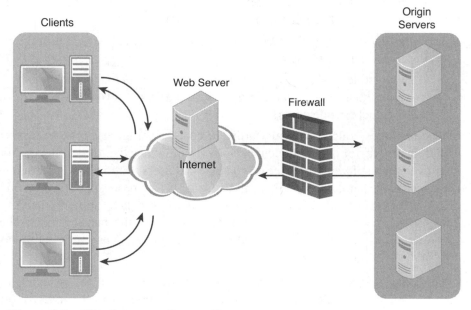

Figure 8.7   Web Server as a Reverse Proxy

When configured properly, random servers cannot be accessed through a reverse proxy and only a specific set of predetermined resources on the origin server can be accessed. A reverse proxy acts as a designated proxy for those servers, and it is used by all clients for access to the specific site that it is servicing.

Having a firewall working in tandem with a reverse proxy can greatly reduce the possibility of exposing back-end data resources. The firewall must be configured to allow only specific types of access (HTTP/HTTPS) from the reverse proxy to the back-end origin servers. This configuration ensures that requests coming from the proxy are valid and all other requests are seen as potential hackers. A properly configured firewall accepts requests from the proxy and routes them to the appropriate origin servers.

Benefits of implementing a reverse proxy for securing access to network resources include the following:

- Provide web clients with a single point of access to resources contained on origin servers.

  This obviously adds a second layer of security that enables you to track and contain an attack against your origin servers.

- Provide a single point of control where you can specify who can access the servers and what content they are allowed to access.

- Provide a layer of abstraction to mask or hide the actual names of the origin servers that are being proxied.

  This enables you to easily replace content servers or make hostname changes because the rules or *mappings* are handled by the reverse proxy. This does not affect outside clients.

For companies concerned with hardware costs, leveraging a reverse proxy can significantly lower hardware cost because it eliminates the need to have separate hardware and software for internal and external users. Internal and external users can access the same servers by using the same HTTP requests. This method also eliminates the need to have different hardware to store data for internal and external users. The reverse proxy is capable of securing the back-end data that is required to service an HTTP application without exposing any information to the outside world.

The idea of setting up an architecture with a single point of access also helps with load balancing and failover. In fact, configuring a reverse proxy to forward requests to multiple similarly configured origin servers allows the reverse proxy to operate as an application-level software load balancer. In a typical deployment, one or more reverse proxies are deployed between the browsers and the origin servers.

A secure platform is crucial when placing a reverse proxy in the demilitarized zone (DMZ). Web Server 7.0 rises to the occasion, however, and provides the most secure environment as compared to other web servers.

Warning: Although Apache, with its mod-proxy add-on, can also be used as a reverse proxy, customers should do so only under caution. Compared to Apache, the Java System Web Server has superior security, with ten times fewer vulnerabilities as reported by CERT (http://www.cert.org).

To configure Web Server 7.0 to act as a reverse proxy, you need to specify a mapping between a URI and one or more origin servers. You can perform this with the `create-reverse-proxy` subcommand in the CLI or by accessing the Reverse Proxy configuration page in the Administration Console.

Note: The Reverse Proxy configuration page can be found in the Administration Console by navigating as follows: Configurations, *config_name*, Virtual Servers, *virtual_server_name*, Content Handling, Reverse Proxy.

The syntax for the `create-reverse-proxy` subcommand is as follows:

```
create-reverse-proxy [--echo] [--no-prompt] [--verbose]
--config=config-name --vs=vs-name --uri-prefix=uri-prefix
--server=remote-server-url
```

The `uri-prefix` option specifies the URI by which the client is attempting to access content on the reverse proxy. This is forwarded or remapped to content on a particular origin server. The `server` option specifies the protocol and host for the origin server that is hosting the content. If the content may be found on multiple servers, then you can specify a comma-delimited list of servers as follows:

```
wadm> create-reverse-proxy --config=www.example.com
--vs=www.example.com
--uri-prefix="/" --server=http://www1.example.com,
http://www2.example.com
```

This subcommand generates a `NameTrans` directive that matches the specified URI. The `NameTrans` directive also specifies the name of a newly created object (`reverse-proxy-/`) that maps the URI to one or more origin servers. If you define multiple URLs, the server distributes the load among the specified servers in a round-robin fashion. Example 8.11 demonstrates the entries generated by this subcommand.

Example 8.11   Reverse Proxy Directives in the Object Configuration File

```
<Object name="default">
...
NameTrans fn="map" from="/" to="http:/" name="reverse-proxy-/"
...
</Object>
...
```

```
<Object name="reverse-proxy-/">
Route fn="set-origin-server" server="http://www1.example.com"
server="http://www2.example.com"
</Object>
```

Warning: The URI you are proxying must exist on the origin server as well; otherwise you will receive a status code of 404 (Not Found). The reverse proxy URI maps to the same URI on the origin server by default.

A reverse proxy can be configured to secure data by utilizing Secure Socket Layers (SSL). This type of configuration is known as a *secure reverse proxy*. A secure reverse proxy can provide an encrypted connection from a proxy server outside a firewall to a secure content server inside the firewall. It also enables clients to connect securely to the proxy server, facilitating the secure transmission of information (such as credit card numbers).

8.6 Summary

Web Server 7.0 provides an extensive security framework that makes it one of the most secure web servers available today. Access to resources can be secured through the use of access control lists, and users' identities are validated through multiple types of authentication databases. Data is secured across the network because Web Server 7.0 supports SSL v2 and v3, TLS 1.0, and Elliptic Curve Cryptography (all with key sizes of up to 4k). Administrators have the flexibility to use certificates signed by commercial Certificate Authorities such as VeriSign, or they can generate their own self-signed certificates through the easy-to-use Administration Console or command line interface. Dynamic updating of certificate revocation lists allows PKI management to be maintained while the requirements of high service availability are still met. Web Server 7.0 provides protection from denial of service attacks by allowing administrators to monitor requests and connections and refuse service to potential DoS threats. Finally, a fully integrated HTTP User Agent in Web Server 7.0 enables it to act as the HTTP endpoint between any User Agent and HTTP origin server. This provides companies with the peace of mind to provide indirect access to content while keeping the servers themselves safe and secure behind the corporate firewall.

8.7 Self-Paced Labs

Use the information contained in this chapter to perform the following exercises. These will help validate your understanding of the concepts described in this chapter.

8.7.1 Access Control

Use the Command Line Interface to validate your understanding of how to configure access control. Perform the following steps:

1. Create a file authentication database of type keyfile. Call the database `mykeyfile`. Do this for the default virtual server in the default configuration.

2. Create a file authentication database of type digestfile. Do this for the default virtual server in the default configuration.

3. (Optional) If you are performing these exercises on a Solaris server, create a file authentication database of type PAM. Do this for the default virtual server in the default configuration.

4. (Optional) If you have access to an LDAP directory server, create a file authentication database of type LDAP. Do this for the default virtual server in the default configuration.

5. List the authentication databases.

6. Add two users (i.e., user1 and user2) to the `mykeyfile` authentication database.

7. List the users in the `mykeyfile` authentication database.

8. Deploy the updated configuration to all nodes.

9. Verify that the user exists in the `mykeyfile` authentication file by using the UNIX `cat` command or the Windows `more` command.

10. Verify that the `server.xml` file contains entries for each of the newly created authentication databases.

11. Add an ACL that grants user1 permission to access the server, but does not allow anyone else access.

12. Verify that access control has been implemented properly in step 11. Ensure that user2 does not have access but user1 does.

13. Open the Access Log (`access`) and verify that you see entries for both user1 and user2.

14. Open the Server Log (`errors`) and review the entries that tell you why user2 was denied access to the server.

15. Remove the ACL entered in step 11 and verify that all users again have access to the server.

8.7.2 Digital Certificates

Use the Command Line Interface to validate your understanding of how to configure the Web Server for digital certificates. Perform the following steps:

1. Create a self-signed digital certificate for your server. Use the following parameters:

Key Type:	**RSA**
Key Size:	**1024**
Organization:	**My Company**
Organization Unit:	**Training**
City:	**Tampa**
State:	**Florida**
Country:	**U.S.**
Configuration:	*Use your default configuration*
Server:	**www.example.com**
Token:	**internal**
Nickname:	**exampleCertificate**

Note: The intent behind this step is to intentionally enter a server value that does not match your own hostname and domain name. If your server is configured to be www. example.com, then use a different value for the Server parameter.

2. Create a new HTTP listener on port 443 and configure it to use SSL. Use the exampleCertificate certificate to enable SSL. Use the following parameters:

Name:	**http-listener-ssl**
Port:	**443**
IP Address:	*
Server Name:	**www.example.com**
Default Virtual Server:	*Use your default configuration*
SSL:	**Enabled**
Certificate:	**exampleCertificate**

3. Deploy the configuration and restart the server when prompted to do so.

4. Connect to the server on port 443 and verify that you see an error message indicating that there is a subject mismatch. Review the message and review the certificate.

5. Accept the certificate for this session only. You should see the main web page for your Web Server instance.

6. Delete the exampleCertificate certificate and create a new certificate with the correct server name (i.e., your real hostname and domain name). Deploy the configuration, access the site once again, and verify that you do not see the subject mismatch error.

7. Accept the certificate for this session only. You should see the main web page for your Web Server instance.

Note: Previous versions of the Web Server required that you provide the password to the trust database before starting the server instance. This is no longer a requirement of Web Server 7.0. You can, however, configure the server to require the password if your security policy deems it necessary.

8. Configure the server to require a password during instance startup.

   You first need to associate a password with the internal token. You can do this by accessing the PKCS11 Tokens page in the Administration Console at the following location: Configurations, *config_name*, Certificates, PKCS11 Tokens, internal.

   After you have associated a password with the internal token, you will not be able to see any certificate-related data without first providing the password. You can see certificate-related data once again by clicking the Set Password button and providing the password. This password will be valid for this session of the Administration Server only. You need to re-enter the password if you log out and log back in again.

9. Stop and start the instance from either the Administration Console or from the command line. Enter the password configured in step 8 when prompted to do so and verify that the server process starts properly.

10. Disable the token state for the `internal` token. This removes the password from the `internal` token.

8.7.3 Certificate Revocation Lists

Use the Command Line Interface to validate your understanding of how to configure dynamic certificate revocation lists. Perform the following steps:

1. Download one or more CRLs from crl.verisign.com into a directory on your local host. Examples of CRLs found on this site include the following: `BTClass1Individual.crl`, `Class1Individual.crl`, and `RSASecureServer. crl`.

2. Open another window and run the UNIX `tail -f` command on the Server Log (`errors`). This enables you to monitor the status of the server reading in these files.

3. Configure the server to update the CRLs found in the directory from step 1 every 60 seconds.

Note: You are required to restart the server when the event is configured, but you are not required to restart the server every time the CRL is read.

4. Restart the server to start the process of automatic updates.

5. Return to the window that is running the `tail -f` command. You should see entries generated in the Server Log. The entries should indicate that the files could not be read.

Note: If you do not see CRL-specific entries generated in the Server Log, it is most likely because the Web Server has not yet attempted to read these files. You can force the reading of the files with the UNIX `touch` command as follows: `touch *.crl`. Wait 60 seconds and you should see the expected CRL entries.

6. Determine the file permissions on the CRLs. Why can't the server read the files?

7. Modify the file permissions to correct the problem and use the UNIX `touch` command to modify the file's timestamp.

8. Modify the timestamp of one file, wait 60 seconds, and observe the entries generated in the Server Log.

9. Delete one of the CRLs, wait 60 seconds, and observe the entries generated in the Server Log.

10. Configure a server event to automatically download CRLs from crl.verisign. com into the CRL directory on a periodic basis. Verify that the Web Server reads these files properly.

8.7.4 Denial of Service Attacks

Use the command line interface to validate your understanding of how to configure the Web Server against DoS attacks. Perform the following steps:

1. Create a script or obtain an application that is able to flood the Web Server with requests. You should place this script on another server or workstation in your environment. This enables you to execute the script without introducing a performance hit based on the script, itself.

Note: You can find a script on http://www.sunwebserver.com that provides this capability. It has been written for a Solaris installation that has the `wget` command available beneath the `/usr/sfw/bin` directory.

---

2. Execute the script with an iteration of 1000 requests for the `/index.html` page on your Web Server. While the script is running, open a browser window and attempt to access the same page with the browser. Verify that you see an impact in performance. If you do not see an impact, run multiple instances of the script from the same server until you do.

3. Configure the instance for a maximum RPS of 10.

4. Repeat step 2 and verify that the response time has increased. You should also notice the throttling of the requests in the script itself as the server stops responding until it has gone below the threshold.

8.7.5 Reverse Proxy Configuration

Use the Command Line Interface to validate your understanding of how to configure the Web Server as a reverse proxy. Perform the following steps:

1. Create a new configuration. Call the new configuration proxy and associate it with an available listen socket on your Web Server.

2. Modify the configuration to act as a reverse proxy for www.google.com. Specify / as the URI.

3. Test the proxy configuration by attempting to access content on your Web Server. Make sure that you are trying to access the port configured in step 1. You should see Google's web site appear in your browser window, but the URL line should reflect your server's name.

4. Perform a search and observe the URL in your browser. You should see it change to reflect Google's hostname and domain. Why did this occur?

5. Update the proxy configuration to correct this.

Note: Go to http://www.sunwebserver.com for detailed instructions on how to perform each of these exercises.

9

Providing Dynamic Content Through Scripting

IN addition to providing support for hosting static content, web servers also include support for creating dynamic web pages using server-side scripting languages. A number of popular server-side scripting languages are used to generate dynamic responses in a web server. These languages enable the content developer to customize the response generated by the web server based on information in the request.

Web Server supports a variety of programming technologies and Application Programming Interfaces (APIs) to generate dynamic content in response to client requests.

This chapter explains how Web Server 7.0 provides support for generating dynamic content using popular server-side scripting technologies such as CGI, SHTML, FastCGI, ASP, and PHP. Specifically, this chapter discusses each of these technologies and describes the administration support included in Web Server for enabling and configuring these technologies. One other language that is very popular among dynamic content developers is Java. Chapter 10 describes using server-side Java technologies with Web Server 7.0 for dynamic content generation.

9.1 Common Gateway Interface (CGI)

The Common Gateway Interface (CGI) is a standard interface for external programs to interface with a web server. You can implement Common Gateway Interface (CGI) programs by using a number of programming languages. On UNIX computers, CGI programs are typically written in scripting languages such as Perl and Bourne shell or in C/C++. On Windows platforms, CGI programs can be written in languages such as Perl or C/C++ or in a Windows-specific language such as Visual Basic. Web Server 7.0 includes support for the Common Gateway Interface Specification Version 1.1.

CGI specifies an interface for a server to pass data to and receive data from an external program. Figure 9.1 illustrates how a web server passes HTTP request data to the CGI program and then passes the response from the CGI program back to the HTTP client.

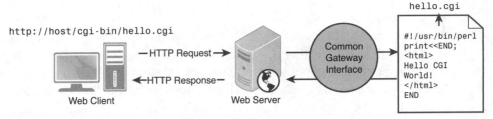

Figure 9.1   Common Gateway Interface overview

On UNIX/Linux systems, Web Server 7.0 creates `Cgistub` processes to help in executing CGI programs. These processes are created when a CGI is first accessed, and their number varies depending on the CGI load on the server.

On computers running Windows, Web Server 7.0 can be configured to use Windows file associations to run CGI programs or to run files as a Windows CGI program.

The following section describes the configuration of the CGI subsystem in Web Server 7.0.

9.1.1 CGI Configuration

Configuring the server to recognize and execute CGI programs includes the following:

- Specifying a directory as one containing CGI programs
- Specifying that files with certain extensions are CGI programs
- Specifying additional CGI security settings on UNIX
- Specifying global settings for the CGI subsystem

Table 9.1 identifies Web Server 7.0's configuration files that contain CGI subsystem configuration.

Table 9.1 CGI Configuration Files

Filename	Description
`obj.conf`	Contains SAFs that implement request processing for CGI programs. Virtual server–specific configuration of the CGI subsystem is specified in the virtual server's object file.
`server.xml`	The `cgi` element in the main instance configuration file configures the global settings of the CGI subsystem.

`mime.types`	Specifies file extensions that are to be considered as CGI programs. Web Server assigns one of the following MIME types when processing requests for CGI programs:
	`magnus-internal/cgi`
	`magnus-internal/shellcgi`
	`magnus-internal/wincgi`
	You can configure MIME type associations on a per-virtual-server basis by using the mime-file subelement of the virtual-sever element in the `server.xml` file.

The redesigned task-oriented Administration Console and the new command line tool (`wadm`) for administration in Web Server 7.0 include support for configuring all aspects of the CGI subsystem.

Figure 9.2 illustrates how the CGI subsystem can be enabled when creating a new configuration with the Administration Console.

The page that configures the CGI subsystem in a virtual server is readily accessible from the home page of the Administration Console. Figure 9.3 demonstrates this.

Figure 9.4 shows the Administration Console page that configures the CGI settings of a virtual server.

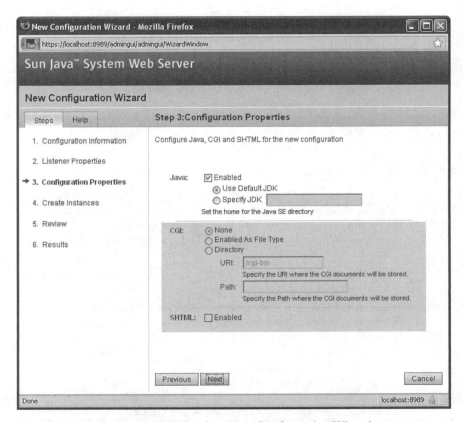

Figure 9.2   Administration Console—New Configuration Wizard

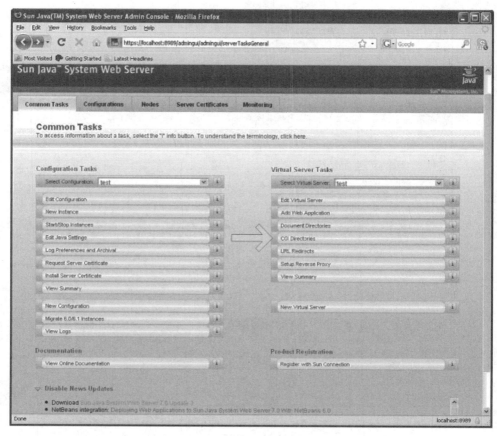

Figure 9.3 Administration Console—Common Tasks

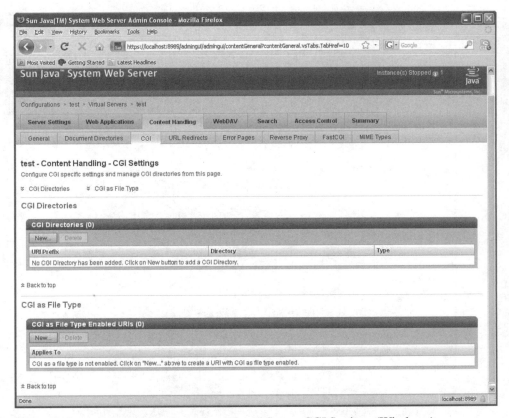

Figure 9.4   Administration Console—Virtual Server CGI Settings (Windows)

The rest of this section describes the different options for configuring CGI in Web Server.

9.1.1.1 CGI Configuration by Directory

To specify CGI configuration by directory, you map a URI prefix in a virtual server to a directory containing CGI programs. All files in the directory are executed as CGI programs, regardless of their extension. A virtual server may specify several URI prefixes that map to directories containing CGI programs.

Figure 9.5 illustrates creating a directory mapping for CGI using the Administration Console.

Figure 9.6 shows the CGI Settings tab after a CGI directory mapping has been added. You can delete individual entries in the CGI Directories table by enabling the corresponding check box in the table and then clicking on the Delete button.

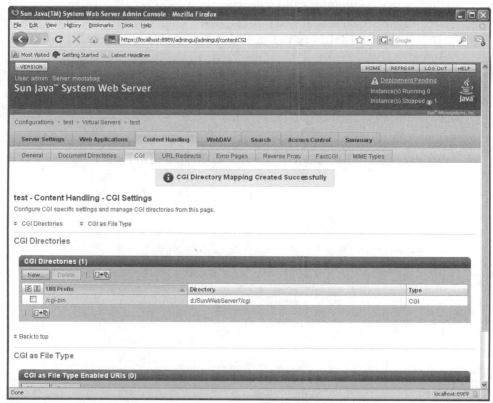

Figure 9.5 Administration Console—Add CGI Directory

Figure 9.6 Administration Console—Virtual Server CGI Settings

The create-cgi-dir and delete-cgi-dir subcommands of wadm may also be used to create and delete CGI directory mappings. The list-cgi-dirs subcommand of wadm may be used to enumerate the CGI directory mappings in a server, as demonstrated in the following example:

```
wadm> list-cgi-dirs --verbose --config=test --vs=test --all
uri-prefix     directory      type
-----------------------------------
/cgi-bin       d:/Sun/WebServer7/cgi cgi
```

Refer to the *Sun Java System Web Server 7.0 CLI Reference Manual* for more information on these subcommands.

9.1.1.2 CGI Configuration by File Extension

Web Server can be configured to treat files with specific extensions as CGI programs. Requests for such files result in CGI program execution, regardless of the directory in which they are. Specifying CGI programs by file extension is useful when both CGI programs and other content such as HTML files reside in the same directory. Web Server can be configured to recognize CGI programs based on file extension for all URIs in the virtual server or for specific URIs in the virtual server.

The file extensions that are associated with CGI programs are specified in the server's mime.types file. The default file extensions for CGI programs are .exe, .bat, and .cgi, as illustrated in Figure 9.7.

You can customize the CGI MIME types for a virtual server from the MIME Types subtab of the Administration Console, as illustrated in Figure 9.8.

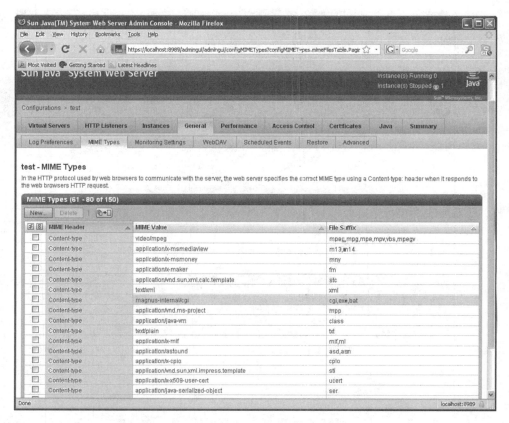

Figure 9.7 Administration Console—Global MIME Types

Figure 9.9 demonstrates how an administrator might configure CGI programs based on the file's extension.

Figure 9.10 shows the CGI Settings tab after a CGI File Type URI has been added. You can delete individual entries in the CGI as File Type table by enabling the corresponding check box in the table and then clicking on the Delete button.

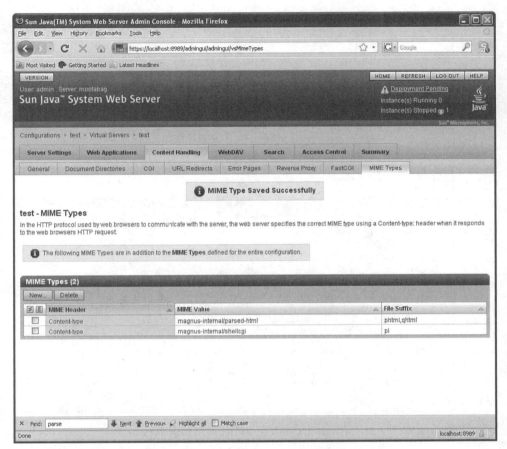

Figure 9.8 Administration Console—Virtual Server MIME Types

The `enable-cgi-file-type`, `disable-cgi-file-type`, and `get-cgi-file-type-prop` subcommands of `wadm` may also be used to manage URI mappings that recognize CGI programs based on their extension. Refer to the *Sun Java System Web Server 7.0 CLI Reference Manual* for more information on these subcommands.

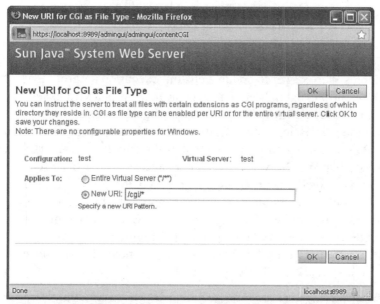

Figure 9.9   Administration Console—New URI for CGI as File Type

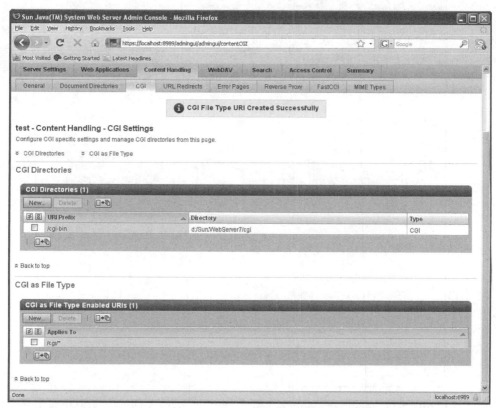

Figure 9.10   Administration Console—Virtual Server CGI Settings

9.1.1.3 CGI Security Configuration (UNIX only)

On UNIX/Linux systems, Web Server creates and uses a pool of Cgistub processes to execute CGI programs. The use of a Cgistub process to execute CGI
programs enables Web Server to create a custom execution environment for CGI
programs. For example, using Web Server you can prevent a virtual server's CGI
programs from interfering with other users by configuring the CGI programs to be
executed with the permissions of a unique UNIX user and group. The additional
security restrictions enforced by Cgistub makes it difficult for hackers to exploit
the CGI subsystem in Web Server 7.0 to get root access. Refer to the section titled
"Creating Custom Execution Environments for CGI Programs" in the *Sun Java
System Web Server 7.0 Developer's Guide* for more information on configuring
the execution environment for CGI programs in Web Server 7.0. Figure 9.11 demonstrates the additional fields (when compared to Figure 9.10) in the Administration Console to configure the CGI execution environment of a virtual server in a
Web Server 7.0 installed on a UNIX system.

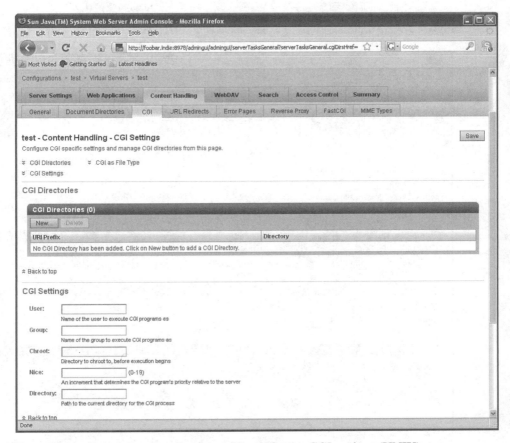

Figure 9.11   Administration Console—Virtual Server CGI settings (UNIX)

These settings can also be manipulated if you use the `get-cgi-prop` and `set-cgi-prop` subcommands of `wadm`. Refer to the *Sun Java System Web Server 7.0 CLI Reference Manual* for more information on these subcommands.

9.1.1.4 Global CGI Configuration

Global CGI settings apply to all virtual servers and include the following:

- Timeouts after which idle or non-responsive CGI programs are terminated
- Timeout after which an unused CGI stub process may be terminated (UNIX only)
- CGI environment variables
- Minimum and maximum number of CGI stub processes that the server uses for executing CGI programs (UNIX only)

Example 9.1 provides an excerpt from the `server.xml` file that demonstrates how the `cgi` element is used to configure the CGI subsystem's global settings.

Example 9.1   Excerpt from the `server.xml` File

```
<cgi>
  <cgistub-idle-timeout>60</cgistub-idle-timeout>
  <max-cgistubs>10</max-cgistubs>
  <env-variable>
    <name>MYVAR</name>
    <value>foo</value>
    <description>A custom CGI environment variable</description>
  </env-variable>
</cgi>
```

The server must be restarted to propagate changes made to global CGI settings. The global CGI settings are configured from the CGI subtab of the Performance tab of a configuration, as shown in Figure 9.12.

These settings can also be manipulated if you use the `create-cgi-envvar`, `delete-cgi-envvar`, `list-cgi-envvars`, `get-cgi-prop`, and `set-cgi-prop` subcommands of `wadm`. Refer to the *Sun Java System Web Server 7.0 CLI Reference Manual* for more information on these subcommands.

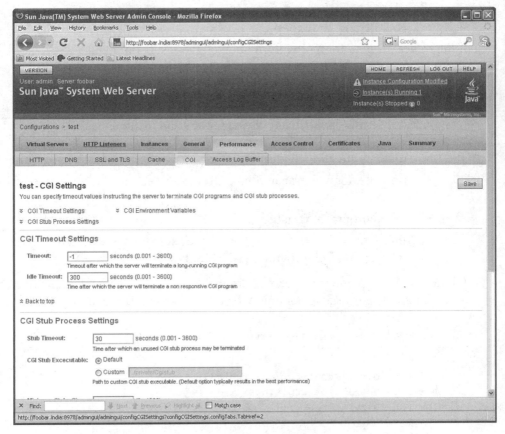

Figure 9.12   Administration Console—Global CGI Settings

9.1.2 CGI Server Application Functions (SAFs)

The CGI engine in Web Server participates in request processing by using Server Application Functions. Chapter 6, "Web Server 7.0 Request Processing," describes the different stages of request processing that the Web Server goes through on every request. Table 9.2 describes the Server Application Functions (SAFs) that implement support for executing CGI programs in Web Server.

Table 9.2 CGI Server Application Functions

Request Processing Stage	SAF	Description
Init	`init-cgi`	Configures the CGI subsystem. This SAF is deprecated and is superseded by the `cgi` element in the `server.xml` file.
Service	`send-cgi` `send-wincgi` `send-shellcgi` `query-handler`	The `send-cgi` function sets up the CGI environment variables that are used to pass data to the CGI program, executes the CGI program in a separate process, and sends the results to the client. Parameters to this SAF are used to configure the custom execution environment for CGI programs on UNIX/Linux systems. You can configure Web Server to execute a file as a CGI program by associating the file extension with the `magnus-internal/cgi` MIME type. The `send-wincgi` SAF executes the file as a Windows CGI program and sends the results to the client. You can configure Web Server to execute a file as a Windows CGI program by associating the file extension with the `magnus-internal/wincgi` MIME type. The `send-shellcgi` SAF executes the file as a CGI program, using the file associations set in Windows. The `query-handler` SAF runs a CGI program and is used to support the obsolete `ISINDEX` tag. Query handlers are no longer used. Web browsers use HTML forms to submit data to the server.

Example 9.2 demonstrates the `obj.conf` file for a server configuration on Windows that can execute CGI programs. CGI subsystem-related directives and objects are marked with bold font in Example 9.2.

Example 9.2 `obj.conf` File (in a CGI-enabled Server)

```
#
# Copyright 2008 Sun Microsystems, Inc.  All rights reserved.
# Use is subject to license terms.
#

# You can edit this file, but comments and formatting changes
# might be lost when you use the administration GUI or CLI.

# Use only forward slashes in pathnames as backslashes can cause
# problems.  Refer to the documentation for more information.

<Object name="default">
AuthTrans fn="match-browser" browser="*MSIE*" ssl-unclean-
shutdown="true"
NameTrans fn="ntrans-j2ee" name="j2ee"
```

```
NameTrans fn="pfx2dir" from="/mc-icons"
dir="D:/Sun/WebServer7/lib/icons" name="es-internal"
NameTrans fn="pfx2dir" from="/cgi-bin" dir="d:/Sun/WebServer7/cgi"
    name="cgi"
PathCheck fn="uri-clean"
PathCheck fn="check-acl" acl="default"
PathCheck fn="find-pathinfo"
PathCheck fn="find-index-j2ee"
PathCheck fn="find-index" index-names="index.html,home.html,index.jsp"
ObjectType fn="type-j2ee"
ObjectType fn="type-by-extension"
ObjectType fn="force-type" type="text/plain"
Service method="(GET|HEAD)" type="magnus-internal/directory" fn="
    index-common"
Service fn="send-shellcgi" type="magnus-internal/shellcgi"
Service fn="send-cgi" type="magnus-internal/cgi"
Service method="(GET|HEAD|POST)" type="*~magnus-internal/*" fn="
    send-file"
Service method="TRACE" fn="service-trace"
Error fn="error-j2ee"
AddLog fn="flex-log"
</Object>

<Object name="j2ee">
Service fn="service-j2ee" method="*"
</Object>

<Object name="es-internal">
PathCheck fn="check-acl" acl="es-internal"
</Object>

<Object name="cgi">
ObjectType fn="force-type" type="magnus-internal/cgi"
Service fn="send-cgi"
</Object>

<Object name="send-precompressed">
PathCheck fn="find-compressed"
</Object>

<Object name="compress-on-demand">
Output fn="insert-filter" filter="http-compression"
</Object>

<Object name="shellcgi">
ObjectType fn="force-type" type="magnus-internal/shellcgi"
Service fn="send-shellcgi" type="magnus-internal/shellcgi"
</Object>
```

Refer to the chapter titled "Managing Server Content" in the *Sun Java System Web Server 7.0 Administrator's Guide*, and to the chapter titled "Using Common Gateway Interface" in the *Sun Java System Web Server 7.0 Developer's Guide* for more information on the support for CGI in Web Server 7.0.

9.2 Server-Parsed HTML (SHTML)

Server-Parsed HTML (SHTML) or Server-Side HTML (SHTML) or Server Side Includes (SSI) is a basic server-side scripting language that for the most part is HTML, but it also has a limited set of dynamic directives for including other files, printing HTTP environment variables, executing programs on the server, displaying when a file was last modified, and so on.

When processing requests for HTML files, a web server normally does not parse the contents of these files. The server simply sends the contents of the files exactly as they exist on disk to the client. However, Web Server can be configured to parse HTML files and include the output of any SHTML commands in the files in the response that is sent to the client. SHTML directives are placed in HTML comments so that users don't see the directives when server-side HTML parsing has not been enabled. The SHTML subsystem in Web Server has been optimized for performance without negatively impacting the scalability of the server.

Example 9.3 demonstrates a file containing SHTML commands intermixed with HTML content.

Example 9.3   Server-Parsed HTML Example—`sample.shtml`

```
<html>
<head>
    <title>Sample Server-Parsed HTML Page</title>
</head>
<body>
    <!--#config sizefmt="bytes" -->
    <h1>Server Side Directives in HTML Pages</h1>
    This document (<b><!--#echo var="DOCUMENT_NAME" --></b>) was served
    by <b><!--#echo var="SERVER_SOFTWARE" --></b>.
    <br>
    This document was last modified on
    <b><!--#flastmod file="sample.shtml" --></b> and the file size is
    <b><!--#fsize file="sample.shtml" --></b> bytes.
    <br>
```

```
    The current time is <b><!--#echo var="DATE_LOCAL" --></b>.
    <br>
    The contents of text.html are included below:
    <br>
    <b><!--#include file="text.html" --></b>
</body>
</html>
```

Figure 9.13 illustrates the content served by Web Server in response to a request for the server-parsed HTML file shown in Example 9.3.

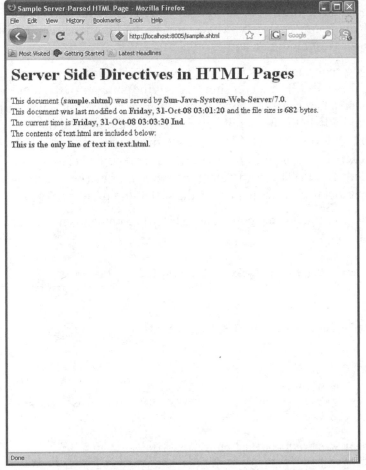

Figure 9.13 Sample Response Generated by an SHTML-enabled Web Server

The next section briefly describes the various SHTML commands that can be used with Web Server 7.0.

9.2.1 SHTML Commands

SHTML commands are embedded in HTML comments. This enables the use of SHTML commands in HTML files even when Server-Parsed HTML is not enabled because browsers do not display the contents of HTML comments.

The format for a SHTML command is as follows:

```
<!--#command name="value" name="value" . .  -->
```

Each `name="value"` pair denotes an attribute. Commands and attribute names are specified in lowercase.

Table 9.3 briefly describes the standard SHTML commands that Web Server 7.0 recognizes. You can also extend the functionality of Web Server's SHTML subsystem by defining custom SHTML tags. Please refer to the section titled "Defining Custom Server-Parsed HTML Tags" in the *Sun Java System Web Server 7.0 Developer's Guide* for more information on implementing custom SHTML tags.

Table 9.3   SHTML Commands

SHTML Command	Description
config	Initializes the format used by other commands to represent times, sizes, and error messages.
echo	Inserts the value of an environment variable or inserts (none) if the variable is not found. You can use the echo command to print any of the standard CGI environment variables. The following additional variables are also available to the echo command: DOCUMENT_NAME, DOCUMENT_URI, QUERY_STRING_UNESCAPED, DATE_LOCAL, DATE_GMT, and LAST_MODIFIED Refer to the sections titled "Environment Variables in Server-side HTML Commands" and "CGI Variables" in the *Sun Java System Web Server 7.0 Developer's Guide* for more information on the environment variables that can be used in SHTML.
exec	Includes the output of executing a shell command or a CGI program.
flastmod	Prints the date a file was last modified. The date format is controlled by the config command.
fsize	Prints the size of a file. The size format is controlled by the config command.
include	Includes the contents of a file. If the file being included is itself an SHTML file, then Web Server recursively parses and executes any SHTML commands in the file.

In a Java-enabled Web Server that also has SHTML enabled, you can include SHTML files from Java web application content such as servlets and JavaServer Pages (JSP) scripts. Web Server's SHTML subsystem also includes support for the `<servlet>` tag. This enables content developers to embed output from a Java servlet in an SHTML file. Please refer to the section titled "Embedding Servlets" in the *Sun Java System Web Server 7.0 Developer's Guide* for more information on the `<servlet>` tag.

9.2.2 SHTML Configuration

Configuring Web Server to enable SHTML parsing includes the following:

- Specifying a virtual server or a directory containing SHTML files
- Specifying the files that the server will parse for SHTML commands

Table 9.4 identifies Web Server 7.0's configuration files that contain SHTML subsystem configuration.

Table 9.4   SHTML Configuration Files

Filename	Description
`obj.conf`	Contains SAFs that implement request processing for SHTML parsing. Virtual server–specific configuration of the SHTML subsystem is specified in the virtual server's object file.
`mime.types`	Specifies file extensions that are to be considered as SHTML files. Web Server assigns the following MIME type when processing requests for SHTML files: `magnus-internal/parsed-html` MIME type associations can be configured on a per-virtual-server basis if you use the mime-file subelement of the virtual-sever element in the `server.xml` file.

Web Server 7.0's administration framework includes support for enabling and configuring SHTML parsing for virtual servers.

Figure 9.2 in the section titled "CGI Configuration" also illustrates how SHTML parsing can be enabled when using the Administration Console to create a new configuration.

Figure 9.14 shows the General subtab of the Content Handling tab on the Administration Console page that configures the SHTML-enabled URIs of a virtual server.

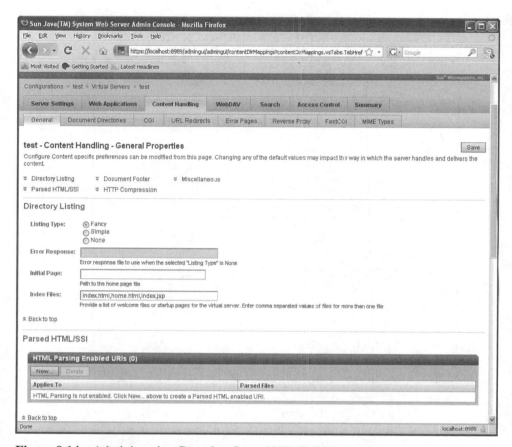

Figure 9.14 Administration Console—Parsed HTML/SSI

Figure 9.15 illustrates enabling SHTML parsing for all files that have an `.shtml` extension in the virtual server named `test`.

The HTML Parsing Enabled URIs table in Figure 9.16 illustrates a configuration where SHTML parsing has been enabled for all files having an `.shtml` extension in the virtual server and also for all files having an `.html` or `.shtml` extension in the `shtml` subdirectory of the virtual server's document root directory. You can delete individual entries in the table by enabling the corresponding check box in the table and then clicking on the Delete button.

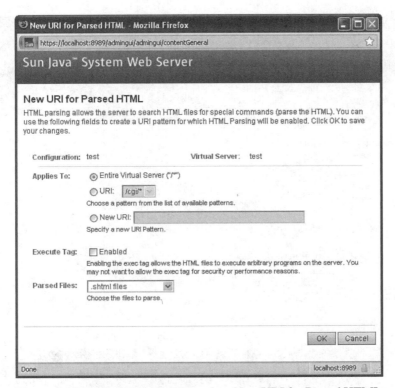

Figure 9.15   Administration Console—New URI for Parsed HTML

The extensions that are associated with files containing SHTML commands are specified in the server's `mime.types` file. The default file extension for Server-Parsed HTML files is `.shtml`, as illustrated in Figure 9.17.

You can customize the SHTML MIME types for a virtual server from the MIME Types sub-tab of the Administration Console, as previously demonstrated in Figure 9.8.

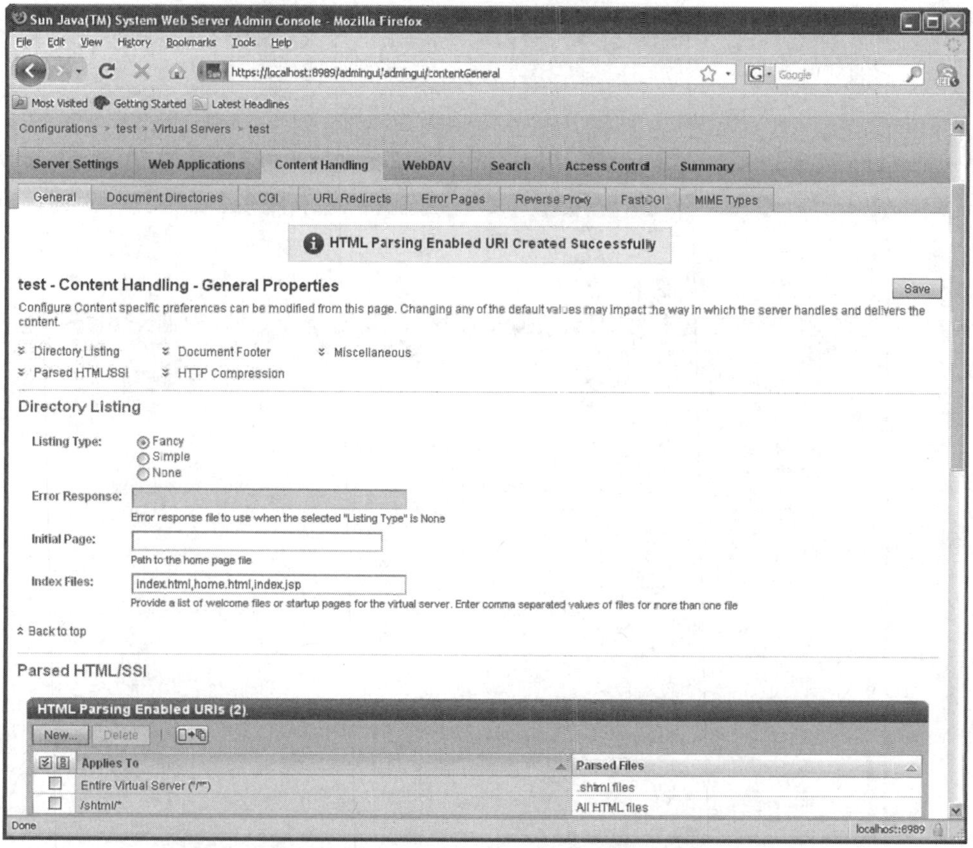

Figure 9.16 Administration Console—Parsed HTML/SSI

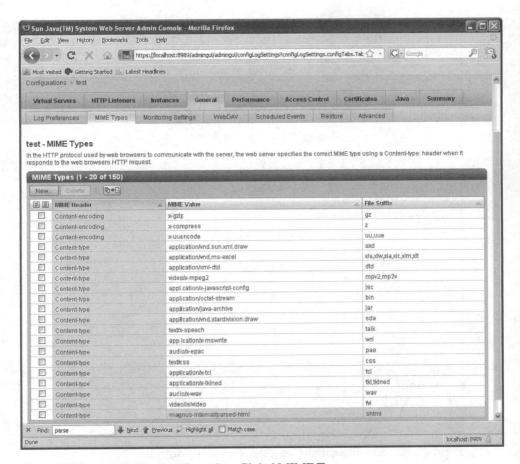

Figure 9.17   Administration Console—Global MIME Types

The `enable-parsed-html`, `disable-parsed-html`, and `get-parsed-html-prop` sub-commands of wadm may also be used to manage URI mappings that recognize and parse HTML files. The command-line tool offers the same functionality as the web-based interface, as illustrated by the following:

```
wadm> enable-parsed-html
Usage: enable-parsed-html --help|-?
  or   enable-parsed-html [--echo] [--no-prompt] [--verbose] [--no-
exec-tag] [--files-to-parse=shtml|exec-html|html] [--uri-
pattern=pattern] --config=config-name --vs=vs-name
CLI014 vs is a required option.
wadm>
wadm> disable-parsed-html
Usage: disable-parsed-html --help|-?
```

```
  or  disable-parsed-html [--echo] [--no-prompt] [--verbose] [--uri-
pattern=pattern] --config=config-name --vs=vs-name
CLI014 vs is a required option.
wadm>
wadm> get-parsed-html-prop
Usage: get-parsed-html-prop --help|-?
  or  get-parsed-html-prop [--echo] [--no-prompt] [--verbose] [--uri-
pattern=pattern] --config=config-name --vs=vs-name (property-name)*
CLI014 vs is a required option.
```

Refer to the *Sun Java System Web Server 7.0 CLI Reference Manual* for more information on these subcommands.

9.2.3 SHTML Server Application Functions (SAFs)

The SHTML engine in Web Server participates in request processing by using Server Application Functions. Chapter 6 describes the different stages of request processing that the Web Server goes through on every request. Table 9.5 describes the Server Application Functions (SAFs) that implement support for parsing SHTML commands embedded in HTML files.

Table 9.5 SHTML Server Application Functions

Request Processing Stage	SAF	Description
Init	shtml-init	Initializes the SHTML subsystem in Web Server. It is no longer necessary to invoke this SAF from an Init directive in the magnus. conf file to enable SHTML parsing. The SHTML subsystem is always initialized during server startup. This SAF is deprecated.
ObjectType	shtml-hacktype	Enables SHTML parsing for files with an .html or .htm extensions. Normally the server assigns text/html as the Content-Type for files with an .html or .htm extension. The sthml-hacktype SAF changes the Content-Type for .html/.htm files to magnus-internal/parsed-html so that the file is processed by the shtml-send SAF instead of the send-file SAF.
Service	shtml-send	Processes HTML files containing SHTML commands.

Example 9.4 demonstrates the obj.conf file for a server configuration with Server-Parsed HTML processing enabled. SHTML-related directives and objects are marked with bold font in Example 9.4.

Example 9.4   `obj.conf` File (in an SHTML-enabled Server)

```
#
# Copyright 2008 Sun Microsystems, Inc.  All rights reserved.
# Use is subject to license terms.
#

# You can edit this file, but comments and formatting changes
# might be lost when you use the administration GUI or CLI.

# Use only forward slashes in pathnames as backslashes can cause
# problems.  Refer to the documentation for more information.

<Object name="default">
AuthTrans fn="match-browser" browser="*MSIE*" ssl-unclean-shutdown="true"
NameTrans fn="assign-name" from="/shtml/*" name="/shtml/*"
NameTrans fn="ntrans-j2ee" name="j2ee"
NameTrans fn="pfx2dir" from="/mc-icons" dir="D:/Sun/WebServer7/lib/icons"
    name="es-internal"
PathCheck fn="uri-clean"
PathCheck fn="check-acl" acl="default"
PathCheck fn="find-pathinfo"
PathCheck fn="find-index-j2ee"
PathCheck fn="find-index" index-names="index.html,home.html,index.jsp"
ObjectType fn="type-j2ee"
ObjectType fn="type-by-extension"
ObjectType fn="force-type" type="text/plain"
Service method="(GET|HEAD)" type="magnus-internal/directory" fn="index-
    common"
Service fn="shtml-send" type="magnus-internal/parsed-html"
    method="(GET|HEAD)" opts="noexec"
Service method="(GET|HEAD|POST)" type="*~magnus-internal/*" fn="send-file"
Service method="TRACE" fn="service-trace"
Error fn="error-j2ee"
AddLog fn="flex-log"
</Object>

<Object name="j2ee">
Service fn="service-j2ee" method="*"
</Object>

<Object name="es-internal">
PathCheck fn="check-acl" acl="es-internal"
</Object>

<Object name="cgi">
ObjectType fn="force-type" type="magnus-internal/cgi"
Service fn="send-cgi"
</Object>
```

```
<Object name="send-precompressed">
PathCheck fn="find-compressed"
</Object>

<Object name="compress-on-demand">
Output fn="insert-filter" filter="http-compression"
</Object>

<Object name="/shtml/*">
ObjectType fn="shtml-hacktype"
Service fn="shtml-send" type="magnus-internal/parsed-html"
   method="(GET|HEAD)" opts="noexec"
</Object>
```

Refer to the chapter titled "Managing Server Content" in the *Sun Java System Web Server 7.0 Administrator's Guide* and to the chapter titled "Server-Parsed HTML Tags" in the *Sun Java System Web Server 7.0 Developer's Guide* for more information on the support for Server-Parsed HTML in Web Server 7.0.

9.3 FastCGI

FastCGI is an extension to the Common Gateway Interface that provides the versatility of CGI while reducing the overhead of web server interactions. Using FastCGI provides high performance and scalability for applications that interoperate with web servers.

The following describes the main aspects of FastCGI:

- FastCGI eliminates the process creation/termination overhead incurred by CGI for every request. FastCGI applications are persistent and handle multiple requests. The process creation/termination overhead is the main reason for the poor scalability of CGI.

- FastCGI applications run in a separate process from the web server. The FastCGI application can be restarted independently of the web server. Abnormal termination of the FastCGI application does not impact the web server process. This process separation also enables system administrators to configure different execution environments for different applications.

- FastCGI may be used to run applications written in any language such as Perl, Python, PHP, and so on.
- FastCGI applications can maintain state such as content caches and connection pools across requests.
- FastCGI uses a client/server protocol that enables hosting of FastCGI applications on remote computers. The web server and the FastCGI application communicate using either TCP sockets or UNIX sockets. The protocol multiplexes a single transport connection between several independent FastCGI requests. Data can be exchanged between the web server and the FastCGI application in both directions using a single transport connection rather than separate pipes (for `stdin`, `stdout` and `stderr`), as with CGI.
- FastCGI applications can be categorized into three well-defined roles, namely *Responder*, *Authorizer*, and *Filter*. A Responder FastCGI application behaves just like a CGI program: It receives an HTTP request and generates an HTTP response. An Authorizer FastCGI application generates an HTTP authorization response based on information in the HTTP request. A Filter FastCGI application uses the information in the HTTP request as well as data from a file stored on the web server, and generates a filtered version of the data as an HTTP response.
- FastCGI is designed to support application servers and web servers and is a stable protocol.

Refer to *FastCGI Specification Version 1.0* for more information about FastCGI.

9.3.1 FastCGI Configuration

Support for FastCGI in Web Server 7.0 is implemented as an NSAPI plug-in. The FastCGI plug-in is located in the `plugins/fastcgi` directory of your Web Server 7.0 installation. This directory also contains an executable named `Fastcgistub` that the plug-in uses to manage the lifecycle of FastCGI applications. Configuring Web Server's FastCGI plug-in includes the following:

- Configuring Web Server to load the plug-in
- Specifying the file extensions associated with FastCGI applications
- Configuring the virtual server's URI space to enable request processing for FastCGI applications

Table 9.6 identifies Web Server 7.0's configuration files that specify FastCGI configuration.

Table 9.6 FastCGI Configuration Files

Filename	Description
`magnus.conf`	Loads the FastCGI plug-in and initializes the FastCGI subsystem in Web Server.
`obj.conf`	Contains SAFs that implement request processing for FastCGI applications. Virtual server–specific FastCGI configuration is specified in the virtual server's object file.
`mime.types`	Specifies file extensions that are to be considered as FastCGI programs. The following MIME type is typically used for FastCGI applications in Web Server: `magnus-internal/fastcgi` You can configure MIME type associations on a per-virtual-server basis by using the mime-file subelement of the virtual-server element in the `server.xml` file.

Web Server 7.0's administration framework includes support for enabling and configuring FastCGI request processing for virtual servers.

Figure 9.18 shows the FastCGI sub-tab of the Content Handling tab on the Administration Console page that configures the SHTML-enabled URIs of a virtual server.

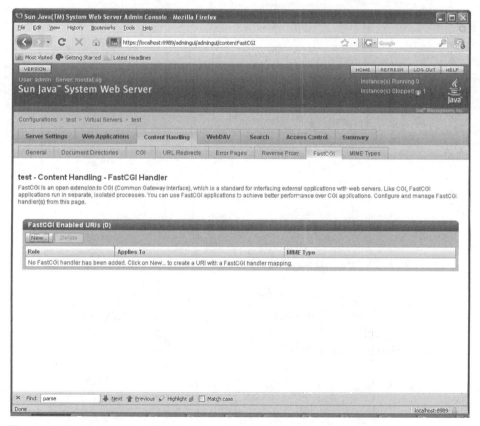

Figure 9.18 Administration Console—FastCGI

Figure 9.19 illustrates the Administration Console dialog used for configuring FastCGI URIs in a virtual server.

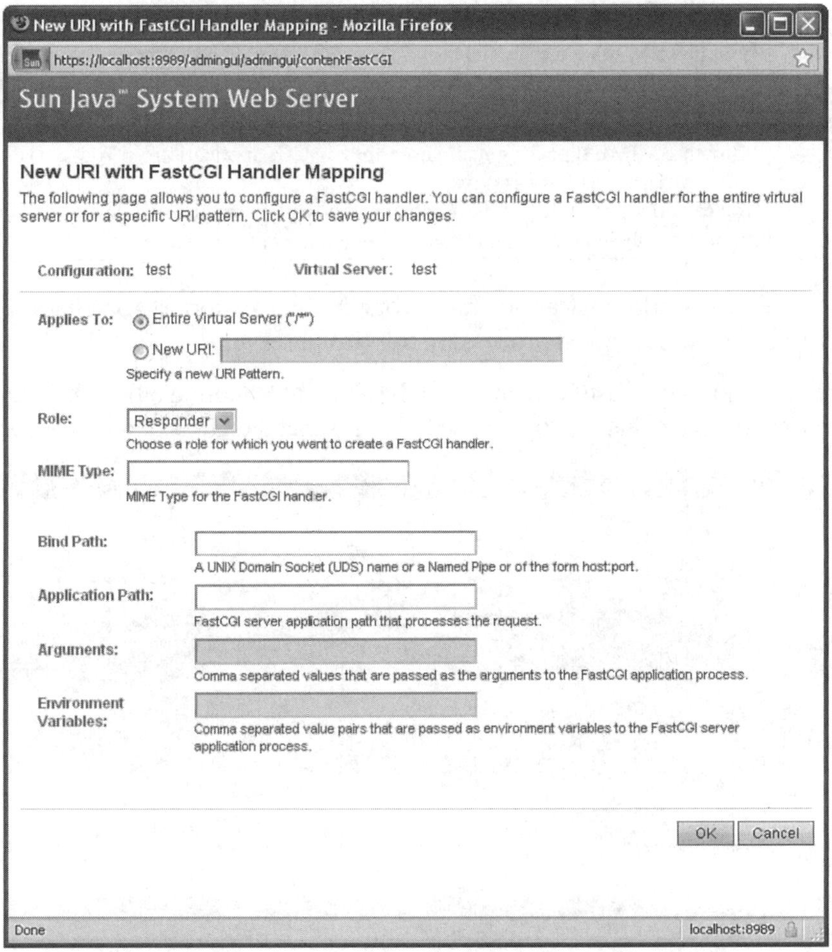

Figure 9.19   Administration Console—New URI with FastCGI Handler Mapping

You can customize the FastCGI MIME types for a virtual server from the MIME Types sub-tab of the Administration Console, as previously demonstrated in Figure 9.8. The following entry in the mime.types file of a virtual server can be used to enable PHP script execution, using the FastCGI implementation of PHP:

```
type=magnus-internal/fastcgi exts=php
```

The following wadm subcommands facilitate FastCGI plug-in configuration in Web Server:

- create-fastcgi-handler
- delete-fastcgi-handler
- list-fastcgi-handlers
- get-fastcgi-handler-prop
- set-fastcgi-handler-prop

The *Sun Java System Web Server 7.0 CLI Reference Manual* contains more information on these subcommands.

9.3.2 FastCGI Server Application Functions (SAFs)

The FastCGI subsystem in Web Server 7.0 is implemented as an NSAPI plug-in. The FastCGI SAFs implemented in the plug-in participate in the various stages of request processing that were previously described in Chapter 6. Table 9.7 describes the Server Application Functions (SAFs) that implement support for FastCGI applications in Web Server.

Table 9.7 FastCGI Server Application Functions

Request Processing Stage	SAF	Description
Init	init-fastcgi	Initializes the FastCGI subsystem. This SAF is deprecated and it is no longer necessary to explicitly specify this SAF using an Init directive in magnus.conf. The init-fastcgi SAF is automatically invoked when the FastCGI shared library is loaded during server startup.
PathCheck	auth-fastcgi	Forwards the request to a FastCGI application that performs the role of an Authorizer and returns the response from the Authorizer application to the client.
Service	responder-fastcgi, filter-fastcgi	The responder-fastcgi SAF is used to process requests to FastCGI applications that perform the role of a Responder. The filter-fastcgi SAF is used to process requests to FastCGI applications that perform the role of a Filter.
Error	error-fastcgi	Handles errors that occur during FastCGI request processing. System administrators may use this SAF to customize the error response that is returned to the client after an error occurs during FastCGI processing.

Example 9.5 lists the contents of the `magnus.conf` file of a FastCGI-enabled Web Server 7.0 configuration. Deleting or disabling (by prefixing the line with #) the `Init` directive marked in bold font in Example 9.5 disables the FastCGI subsystem throughout the server.

Example 9.5   `magnus.conf` File (in a FastCGI-enabled Server)

```
#
# Copyright 2006 Sun Microsystems, Inc.  All rights reserved.
# Use is subject to license terms.
#

Init fn="load-modules" shlib="libfastcgi.so"
```

Looking at the messages that the server logs during startup is an easy way to determine whether the FastCGI plug-in is enabled or not. Starting a server that has the FastCGI plug-in enabled provides a response similar to the following:

```
# bin/startserv
Sun Java System Web Server 7.0U3 B06/16/2008 12:00
info: FCGI1000: Sun Java System Web Server 7.0U3 FastCGI NSAPI Plugin
B06/16/2008 12:00
info: HTTP3072: http-listener-1: http://test:9000 ready to accept
requests
info: CORE3274: successful server startup
```

The message marked in bold font is logged during FastCGI plug-in initialization. This indicates that Web Server's FastCGI plug-in has been loaded.

Example 9.6 demonstrates the `obj.conf` file for a server configuration that runs PHP scripts using FastCGI. FastCGI related directives and objects are marked in bold font in Example 9.6.

Example 9.6   `obj.conf` File (in an FastCGI-enabled Server)

```
#
# Copyright 2008 Sun Microsystems, Inc.  All rights reserved.
# Use is subject to license terms.
#

# You can edit this file, but comments and formatting changes
# might be lost when you use the administration GUI or CLI.
```

```
# Use only forward slashes in pathnames as backslashes can cause
# problems.  Refer to the documentation for more information.

<Object name="default">
AuthTrans fn="match-browser" browser="*MSIE*" ssl-unclean-shutdown="true"
NameTrans fn="pfx2dir" from="/mc-icons" dir="D:/Sun/WebServer7/lib/icons"
    name="es-internal"
NameTrans fn="assign-name" from="/php/*" name="/php/*"
PathCheck fn="uri-clean"
PathCheck fn="check-acl" acl="default"
PathCheck fn="find-pathinfo"
PathCheck fn="find-index" index-names="index.html,home.html,index.jsp"
ObjectType fn="type-by-extension"
ObjectType fn="force-type" type="text/plain"
Service method="(GET|HEAD)" type="magnus-internal/directory" fn="index-
    common"
Service method="(GET|HEAD|POST)" type="*~magnus-internal/*" fn="send-file"
Service method="TRACE" fn="service-trace"
AddLog fn="flex-log"
</Object>

<Object name="es-internal">
PathCheck fn="check-acl" acl="es-internal"
</Object>

<Object name="send-precompressed">
PathCheck fn="find-compressed"
</Object>

<Object name="compress-on-demand">
Output fn="insert-filter" filter="http-compression"
</Object>

<Object name="/php/*">
Service fn="responder-fastcgi" app-path="d:/programs/php/php-cgi.exe"
</Object>
```

Please refer to the appendix titled "FastCGI Plug-in" in the *Sun Java System Web Server 7.0 Administrator's Guide* for more information on the support for FastCGI in Web Server 7.0.

9.4 PHP: Hypertext Processor (PHP)

PHP is a very popular scripting language that is especially suited to creating dynamic web pages and can be embedded into HTML. PHP's popularity for web development can be attributed to its simplicity, accessibility, cost (it's free!), and the large number of available modules. PHP can be run on most web servers and is freely available on a large number of platforms and operating systems. PHP scripts are typically compiled at runtime by the PHP engine. The overhead of parsing and compiling the script on every request can be reduced by using PHP accelerators that cache the compiled form of a PHP script in shared memory.

PHP commands are typically embedded within <?php?> tags, as illustrated in Example 9.7.

Example 9.7   Sample PHP Script

```
<html>
<head>
<title>PHP Example</title>
</head>
<body>
<h1>PHP Example</h1>
This page displays information about the PHP engine.
<?php
phpinfo();
?>
</body>
</html>
```

9.4.1 PHP Configuration

The different interfaces that Web Server can use to run PHP scripts are the following:

- CGI (the PHP engine runs in a separate process from Web Server)
- FastCGI (the PHP engine runs in a separate process from Web Server)
- NSAPI (the PHP engine runs in Web Server)

Use of these interfaces to run PHP scripts is described in detail in the online article titled "Using PHP on Sun Java System Web Server" on the Sun Developer Network web site (http://developers.sun.com). The rest of this section briefly describes each of these alternatives.

9.4.1.1 Running PHP as a CGI Program

Running PHP scripts in Web Server using the PHP engine as a CGI includes the following:

- Using a PHP engine that has been compiled to run as a CGI.
- Configuring Web Server to recognize and execute CGI programs as described previously in the section titled "CGI Configuration."
- On UNIX/Linux platforms, specifying the location of the PHP engine on the first line of each PHP script using the magic string (#!). For example, `#!/usr/bin/php-cgi`.
- On Windows platforms, associating the file extensions for PHP scripts with the `php-cgi.exe` executable.
- Accessing the PHP script with a browser.

Note: The CGI/FastCGI version of the PHP engine is named `php-cgi` (on UNIX/Linux) or `php-cgi.exe` (on Windows). Instructions for compiling the PHP engine are available on the PHP web site http://www.php.net/. The Web Server 7.0 PHP Add-On 1.0 download that is available from Sun Microsystems Inc. provides a pre-built PHP engine for use with Web Server 7.0. Many operating systems also provide pre-built binaries of PHP that you can use with Web Server.

9.4.1.2 Running PHP as a FastCGI Program

Running PHP scripts in Web Server using the PHP engine as a FastCGI application includes the following:

- Using a PHP engine that has been compiled to run as a FastCGI application.
- Configuring FastCGI support in Web Server as described previously in the section titled "FastCGI Configuration."
- Associating PHP file extensions (`.php`, `.php3`, `.php4`, `.php5`) with the `magnus-internal/fastcgi` MIME type.
- Accessing the PHP script with a browser.

Note: The `samples/fastcgi` directory of your Web Server installation contains some sample PHP scripts and instructions for running the scripts in Web Server using the FastCGI interface.

Figure 9.20 shows the output of the sample PHP script in Example 9.7 when run in Web Server 7.0, using FastCGI.

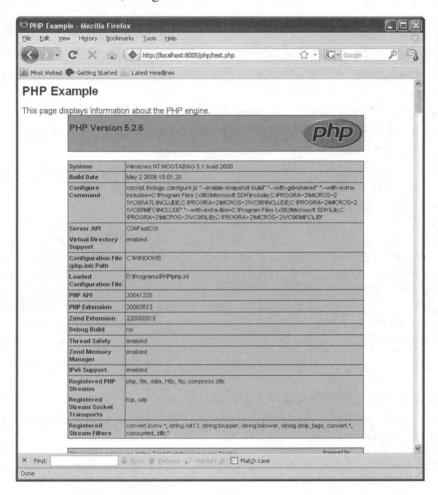

Figure 9.20 Sample PHP output

9.4.1.3 Running PHP as an NSAPI Plug-in

Running PHP scripts using the NSAPI plug-in for Web Server includes the following:

- Installing the NSAPI plug-in for PHP and configuring Web Server to load the plug-in by manually editing the magnus.conf file.

- Configuring a virtual server's object file (obj.conf) to specify URIs that will be handled by the Server Application Functions (SAFs) in the PHP NSAPI plug-in.
- Associating PHP file extensions (.php, .php3, .php4, .php5) with the magnus-internal/x-httpd-php MIME type.
- Accessing the PHP script using a browser.

Note: More information on the NSAPI plug-in for PHP can be found in the "NSAPI" section of the PHP manual at http://www.php.net.

Please refer to the *PHP for Sun Java System Web Server 7.0* web page (http://www.sun.com/software/products/web_srvr/php.xml) for more information on the support for PHP in Web Server 7.0.

9.5 Active Server Pages

Active Server Pages (ASP) is a server-side scripting environment first developed by Microsoft for Internet Information Services (IIS). An ASP script is an HTML page that embeds server-side scripting commands and can contain Common Object Model (COM) components. ASP scripts are usually implemented through the use of VBScript. Example 9.8 shows an example of an ASP script.

Example 9.8   Sample ASP Script

```
<%
Response.ContentType="text/html"
%>
<html>
<body>
<%
Response.Write("Hello World!")
%>
Today's date is: <%Response.Write(Date())%>.
</body>
</html>
```

Sun Java System Active Server Pages (also known as Sun Java System ASP Server) is an implementation of ASP technology that is available on a number of

UNIX/Linux platforms and also on Windows. You can use Sun Java System ASP Server to run ASP scripts on platforms other than Windows.

Sun Java System ASP Server provides an NSAPI plug-in that can be used to configure Web Server to process requests for ASP scripts.

Figure 9.21 illustrates how Web Server uses the ASP NSAPI plug-in to interact with the ASP Server to process requests for ASP content.

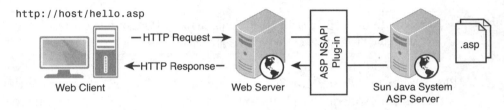

Figure 9.21   Overview of Web Server and Sun Java System ASP Server

Running ASP scripts using the NSAPI plug-in for Web Server includes the following:

- Installing the NSAPI plug-in for Sun Java System ASP Server and configuring Web Server to load the plug-in by manually editing the `magnus.conf` file.
- Configuring a virtual server's object file (`obj.conf`) to specify URIs that will be handled by the Server Application Functions (SAFs) in the ASP NSAPI plug-in.
- Associating ASP file extensions (`.asp`, `.asa`) with the `chilisoft-internal/ active-server-page` MIME type.
- Using a browser to access the ASP script.

Web Server 7.0's administration framework does not include support for configuring the ASP plug-in. Please refer to the *Sun Java System Active Server Pages Release Notes* for more information about the support for ASP in Web Server 7.0.

9.6 Summary

In this chapter you have learned about the support in Web Server for hosting dynamic web pages implemented in a number of scripting languages. A single server can host different types of dynamic content. Web Server can be configured to process different types of content based on either the MIME type or the URI used to access the content. Web Server's access control capabilities can be used to protect dynamic content as well as static content. Web Server includes web-based and command-line support for most of the scripting technologies described in this chapter. Web Server's inherent extensibility, stability, and scalability makes it an ideal platform for hosting large-scale applications that use both established and emerging server-side scripting technologies.

9.7 Self-Paced Labs

Use the information contained in this chapter to perform the following exercises. These will help validate your understanding of the concepts described in this chapter.

1. Configure your server to use CGI to execute all Perl programs.
2. Configure your server to parse only .shtml files in the ssi subdirectory of the document root directory as Server-Parsed HTML files.
3. Create a Server-Parsed HTML file that invokes a CGI program. Access this in Web Server and verify that it produces the expected output.
4. How many Cgistub processes are created when Web Server is started? When are Cgistub processes created?
5. Use multiple clients to access a CGI program in Web Server. Check the number of Cgistub processes that are created.
6. Create a CGI program that appears to hang by executing an infinite loop. Access the program using a browser. What does Web Server do?
7. Create a CGI program that lists all its environment variables and run it in Web Server 7.0.
8. Execute a PHP script on Windows by using the FastCGI PHP engine with Web Server 7.0.
9. Configure Web Server so that all files with a .pp extension are executed as PHP CGI programs.
10. Is it possible to change the CGI/FastCGI/SHTML configuration of Web Server without restarting the server?
11. List the pros and cons of CGI versus FastCGI versus NSAPI in the context of Web Server.

Note: Go to www.sunwebserver.com for detailed instructions on how to perform each of these exercises.

10

Providing Dynamic Content Through Java

THE content base of most web sites usually contains a mix of static content (HTML files, images, etc.) and dynamic content (generated by server-side scripting languages). These server-side scripting languages are used to generate web pages that consist of static content (such as text and images) interspersed with dynamic content (such as tabular data retrieved from a database).

In Chapter 9, "Providing Dynamic Content Through Scripting," we described how you can use some of today's popular server-side scripting languages (to generate dynamic content) in Web Server 7.0. One other language that is very popular among dynamic content developers is Java. Technologies based on the Java programming language are used to generate a lot of the dynamic content that we see today on web sites across the Internet.

This chapter explains how Web Server 7.0 provides support for generating dynamic content with Java-based technologies to implement server-side scripting. Specifically, this chapter discusses the support included in Web Server 7.0 for the various Java technologies that are commonly used in web applications. This chapter describes the main configuration files associated with the Java subsystem in Web Server and the administration support for configuring, deploying, and managing web applications in the server. Finally, the chapter describes the support for Web Server 7.0 in the NetBeans Integrated Development Environment (IDE).

10.1 Server-side Java Technologies

The Java Platform, Enterprise Edition (Java EE, previously known as J2EE) is an industry standard for implementing portable, secure, and scalable server-side applications. Java EE builds on the solid foundation of the Java Platform, Standard Edition (Java SE, previously known as J2SE), and simplifies the process of writing distributed, enterprise-class business applications.

Figure 10.1 illustrates the server-side Java-related technologies in Web Server's Java web container plug-in.

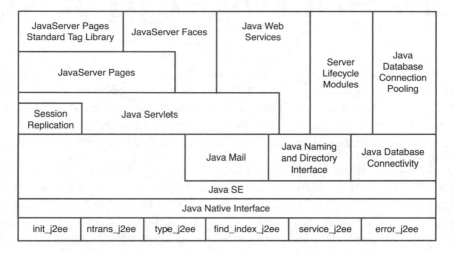

Figure 10.1   Web Server's Java Technologies

The rest of this section introduces these web-related technologies that are part of the Java EE platform and are included with Web Server 7.0.

10.1.1 Java Servlets

The Java Servlet API provides developers with a portable programmatic interface to extend the functionality of a web server. A servlet can be thought of as a FastCGI program written in the Java programming language. Servlets are platform-independent, server-side objects that receive requests and generate responses based on the data in the requests. In addition to the servlet object, the Java Servlet API defines Java objects that represent servlet requests and responses and also objects that are used to configure the servlet's runtime environment.

Although servlets can be used to process requests in any protocol, they are most commonly used to extend the functionality of web servers. The servlet programming model follows the request-response model of HTTP (Hyper Text Transfer Protocol). An application that uses servlets can maintain state across requests by using Java web application sessions. Web application sessions are described later in this chapter in Section 10.5.5, "Session Management in Java Web Applications."

Before it can be executed, a servlet must be compiled and deployed to the web server. The Servlet API is fully backward compatible with earlier releases. Therefore, any servlets that have been written for an older version of the API will continue to work without any changes or recompilation.

The integrated Java runtime environment (within a web/application server process) that runs servlets is referred to as the *Java web container*.

The current release of Web Server 7.0 includes support for the Java Servlet Specification Version 2.5.

10.1.2 JavaServer Pages

JavaServer Pages (JSP) technology is an extension to Java servlets that enables rapid development of dynamic web pages. Typically, a JSP page consists of HTML content that contains XML-like tags and embedded Java code that together encapsulate the logic for generating the dynamic portions of the response.

The main components of a JSP page consist of the following:

- Static content such as text, HTML, XML
- Scripting elements
- Standard directives (static tags)
- Standard actions (dynamic tags)
- Tag extensions (custom tags)

JSP technology enables separation of the model from the view, thus allowing web page designers to change the look of the page without having to change how the content for the page is generated. Like Java servlets, JSP technology also is platform independent. This means that you can run your JSP-based application on any Java web container that implements the JSP standard. The Expression Language (EL) feature of JSP makes it easier for JSP page authors to access and manipulate data using a simplified expression language instead of having to deal with the complexity associated with the Java programming language.

Unlike servlets, JSP pages do not have to be compiled before they are deployed. The JSP compiler within the Java web container in the server automatically compiles the JSP page as needed. The JSP compiler compiles the JSP page into a servlet and this servlet is then dynamically added to the server. Web Server also includes a command-line tool—jspc—to precompile JSPs into servlets. Refer to the "Developing JavaServer Pages" chapter of the *Sun Java System Web Server 7.0 Developer's Guide to Java Web Applications* for more information on the JSP command-line compiler. The JSPs included in a Java web application can also be precompiled using Web Server's administration interfaces to deploy the Java web application. Section 10.5.4, "Deploying Java Web Applications into Web Server," describes the administration support in Web Server for deploying Java web applications.

The current release of Web Server 7.0 includes support for the JavaServer Pages Specification Version 2.1.

10.1.3 JavaServer Pages Standard Tag Library

The JavaServer Pages Standard Tag Library (JSTL) extends the JSP specification and consists of a standard set of tags that JSP programmers can use (in lieu of Java code scriptlets) in JSP pages. These tags implement functionality that is commonly used in JSP pages. Examples of tags in the JSTL include loops/iterators, tags for accessing data in databases, tags for implementing conditional logic, internationalization tags, and tags for manipulating XML data.

Table 10.1 summarizes the four separate tag libraries that comprise the JSTL, each of which contains tags for a specific functional area. The table also lists the URIs used to reference the libraries and the tag prefixes (although the JSP developer is free to assign a different prefix).

Table 10.1　JSTL Libraries

Functional Area	URI	Prefix	Description
Core	http://java.sun.com/jstl/core	c	Contains tags that are commonly used by all web applications such as iterators, conditionals, and URL manipulation.
XML Processing	http://java.sun.com/jstl/xml	x	Contains tags for parsing, processing, and transforming XML data.

Functional Area	URI	Prefix	Description
Internationalization/ Formatting	http://java.sun.com/jstl/fmt	`fmt`	Contains tags for parsing and formatting data such as numbers, times, and dates in a locale-sensitive manner.
Relational Database Access	http://java.sun.com/jstl/sql	`sql`	Contains tags for accessing and modifying data stored in a relational database.

The current release of Web Server 7.0 includes support for the JavaServer Pages Standard Tag Library Specification Version 1.2.

10.1.4 Java Database Connectivity

The Java Database Connectivity (JDBC) API is a standard that defines how a Java program can access, query, and update data in a database. Database connections are expensive to create in that this usually involves time-consuming operations such as user authentication and transactional context creation. Creating too many connections from a Java application to the database can affect the application's scalability. Sharing a pool of JDBC connections among all the applications running in a server can greatly improve the scalability and resource utilization of the overall system. Applications that use the JDBC API to access a database do so using a `java.sql.DataSource` object. The application using the `DataSource` object is unaware of implementation specifics such as connection pooling.

Web Server 7.0 implements connection pooling for JDBC resources and enables the administrator to configure the connection pool when defining a JDBC resource either via the command-line administration tool or via the graphical user interface. Section 10.4.4, "Global Java Settings," enumerates the administration support in Web Server for configuring JDBC resources.

10.1.5 Java Naming and Directory Interface

The Java Naming and Directory Interface (JNDI) provides Java-based applications with a portable, unified interface to naming and directory services. A naming service enables you to associate a name with an object and also to find an object given its name. An example of a naming service is the Domain Name Service (DNS), which maps hostnames (such as www.google.com) to IP addresses (such as 209.85.153.104). A directory service associates names with objects and also makes it possible for objects to contain attributes. Objects can be located by name or by specifying criteria to match the object's attributes. An example of a directory service is a company's employee database, where one can find employee records by either searching for names or by searching for other attributes such as employee identification numbers, department codes, and so on.

JNDI support in Web Server 7.0's Java web container enables system administrators and web application developers to create, locate, and access Java resources such as database sources, database connection pools, Java mail sessions, and external JNDI resources, using a standard naming syntax and a portable programmatic interface. Refer to Section 10.4.4, "Global Java Settings," for more information on the administration support in Web Server for configuring server resources.

10.1.6 JavaServer Faces

JavaServer Faces (JSF) technology is a standard for building server-side user interfaces. It is a web application framework that simplifies the process of building user interfaces for server-side Java applications. JavaServer Faces technology includes

- A set of APIs for representing user interface components, managing their state, input validation, event handling, error handling, defining page navigation, and supporting accessibility and internationalization
- Two JavaServer Pages (JSP) tag libraries for implementing a JavaServer Faces user interface within a JSP page.

Applications implemented using JavaServer Faces technology run the user interface code on the server, responding to events from the client. JSF enables development of reusable components for web-based user interfaces.

To run a Java web application that uses JSF technology, simply deploy the application using any of the methods described in Section 10.5.4, "Deploying Java Web Applications into Web Server," and access the application using a browser. Figure 10.2 demonstrates the `carstore` JSF sample application that is included in Web Server.

The current release of Web Server 7.0 includes support for the JavaServer Faces Specification Version 1.2.

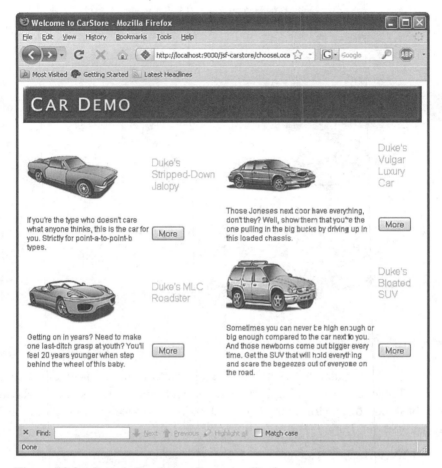

Figure 10.2   Sample JavaServer Faces Application

10.1.7 Java Web Services

Web Services provide a standard way for software applications running on a variety of platforms to interoperate. SOAP is a lightweight protocol for exchanging structured data between distributed software applications. Web services use the Web Services Description Language (WSDL) standard, an XML-based language, to describe themselves. Clients discover web services by looking them up in a registry. Clients and servers that comprise a web service communicate using SOAP to exchange XML messages. Figure 10.3 illustrates how web services are described and discovered.

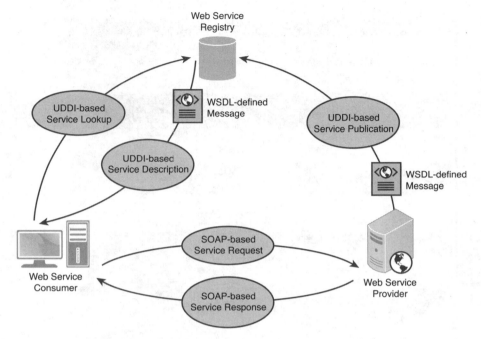

Figure 10.3   Web Services Technologies

Web Server 7.0's integrated Java web services runtime and tools enable it to host portable Java web services implementations. Web Server also supports the WS-Security standard. The following lists the Java Web Service technologies included with Web Server 7.0:

- JAX-WS 2.0
- JAXB 2.0
- JAXP 1.3.1
- SOAP 1.2
- WSDL 1.1
- SAAJ 1.3
- XWSS-XML
- Fast Infoset
- Message Security

A web service is packaged as a web application and then deployed into Web Server. Using the Web Server's administration tools, a system administrator can configure and deploy Java web applications that include web services. Web Server 7.0's support for Java web applications is described in more detail in Section 10.5, "Java Web Applications."

10.1.8 Lifecycle Modules

Web Server 7.0 includes support for executing custom logic (written in the Java programming language) during different phases of the server's lifecycle. Such logic is implemented within a Java class that implements the server's lifecycle interface. The following list summarizes the different stages of the server's lifecycle at which the server can invoke custom logic in a user-defined lifecycle module class:

- **Initialization**—Invoked when the server is creating its built-in subsystems.
- **Startup**—Invoked when the server is loading its applications.
- **Service**—Invoked to indicate that the server is ready to process requests.
- **Termination**—Invoked when the server is being shut down.
- **Reconfiguration**—Invoked when the server's configuration is dynamically reconfigured. This is the only state that can occur several times during the life of a server process.

The section titled "Global Java Settings" enumerates the administration support in Web Server for configuring lifecycle modules. Refer to the "Developing Lifecycle Listeners" chapter of the *Sun Java System Web Server 7.0 Developer's Guide to Java Web Applications* for more information on implementing lifecycle listeners in Web Server 7.0.

10.1.9 Java Web Application Session Replication

The Servlet specification defines several approaches by which a Java web container can track and maintain session state across Java web application requests. The session replication feature in Web Server provides a limited level of high availability for Java web application session data.

This feature applies only to Java web applications that have been deployed to a Web Server 7.0 cluster. As described in Chapter 4, "Web Server 7.0 Administration," a cluster is a set of web server instances, spanning across one or more nodes and running identical configurations. When the session replication feature is enabled in a cluster, each instance in the cluster replicates its in-memory representation of its Java web application sessions to another instance in the cluster. In the event of a failure where an instance in the cluster is unavailable, the cluster continues to have access to the backup copy of the failed instance's session data.

10.1.10 Java Native Interface

Java Native Interface (JNI) is a standard programming interface that enables integration of Java code with code written in other languages. JNI provides a standard way for Java methods running in a Java Virtual Machine (JVM) to invoke or be invoked by native applications written in other languages such as C and C++. This interface also enables native applications to embed the Java Virtual Machine (JVM). Web Server 7.0, being a C/C++ application, uses the Java Native Interface to integrate the server-side Java technologies described earlier in this section. As illustrated in Figure 10.1, Web Server's Java web container Server Application Functions (SAFs, written in the C/C++ programming languages)—`init_j2ee`, `ntrans_j2ee`, `find_index_j2ee`, `type_j2ee`, `service_j2ee`, and `error_j2ee`—use JNI to interact with the server-side Java technologies (written in the Java programming language).

10.2 Server-side Java Process Model

Server-side Java technologies in a web/application server execute within the context of the Java Virtual Machine (JVM). The subsystem within a web/application server that handles requests for dynamic Java content is referred to as the Java web container or simply web container.

Some servers, such as Tomcat, GlassFish Application Server, WebSphere Application Server, and WebLogic Application Server, are implemented as Java applications, whereas others such as Apache HTTP Server and Sun Java System Web Server are implemented as C/C++ applications.

Application/web servers implemented in Java (such as GlassFish and Tomcat) typically execute as a single Java process that processes requests for both static and dynamic content.

The Apache HTTP Server, however, does not provide a Java web container that can process requests for dynamic Java content. A widely used deployment scenario for hosting a web site that contains both static content and dynamic Java content is to run one or more Apache HTTP servers that are configured to proxy requests for Java content to one or more Java application/web servers. The Apache HTTP server is configured so that it processes requests for static content and delegates requests for content hosted in Java web applications to another process (such as Tomcat) that runs a Java web container. The `mod_jk`, `mod_proxy` and mod_proxy_ajp modules are the most commonly used to integrate Tomcat with Apache. Although the Apache/Tomcat model enables separation of content and server processes between the web tier and the application tier, it includes unnecessary processing overheads when there is a need to serve both static and dynamic Java content in the web tier itself.

Web Server 7.0 includes an integrated Java web container that is implemented as an NSAPI plug-in. When the Java plug-in is enabled, the worker process creates an embedded Java Virtual Machine that hosts the Java web container. A single Java-enabled Web Server worker process can efficiently service requests for both static content and dynamic Java content. This single process model eliminates the overheads of inter-process communication and uses fewer system resources than the Apache/Tomcat multi-process model. Using the integrated reverse-proxy features of Web Server, a web server instance can also be configured to emulate the Apache/Tomcat model and serve only static content while delegating processing of requests for Java web application resources to a back-end server.

The Java web container configuration in Web Server is specified in the same configuration files (such as obj.conf, server.xml) as is the configuration for the other sub-systems in the server. The formats of the configuration files for Apache and Tomcat are very different, and this increases the complexity of Apache/Tomcat's configuration. Web sites that have no Java content can choose to disable Web Server's Java plug-in, thus leading to much improved startup times and reduced consumption of system resources such as memory and threads.

10.3 Java Request Processing Behavior

As mentioned earlier in this chapter, the Web Server's Java web container is implemented as an NSAPI plug-in, and it participates in the various stages of request processing. Chapter 6, "Web Server 7.0 Request Processing," describes the different stages of request processing that the Web Server goes through on every request. Table 10.2 describes the Server Application Functions (SAFs) that are implemented in Web Server's Java web container plug-in.

Table 10.2   Java Server Application Functions

Request Processing Stage	SAF	Description
Init	init-j2ee	Creates the embedded Java Virtual Machine (JVM) and initializes the Java web container NSAPI plug-in. The NSAPI plug-in participates in the various phases of server initialization (such as virtual server creation) to properly configure the Java subsystem.
NameTrans	ntrans-j2ee	Determines whether the requested resource (as identified by the URI in the request) maps to content that is hosted in a Java web application.
PathCheck	find-index-j2ee	Implements welcome file processing for Java web applications. Java web application developers may specify an ordered list of partial URIs (containing neither a leading nor a trailing /) called welcome files in the web application's deployment descriptor file—web.xml. The list of welcome files in web.xml is used by the Java web container when the request corresponds to a directory within a Java web application. The find-index-j2ee SAF appends each of the partial URIs that specify a welcome file (in the order in which they are specified in web.xml) to the request URI and sends the request to the first resource that matches this concatenated URI.
		This SAF acts upon only those URIs that map to directories within the Java web application and even then takes no action when no welcome files are specified in web.xml or when none of the welcome files match a resource. When no action is taken by this SAF, the next PathCheck SAF (usually find-index) specified in obj.conf is executed.
		This SAF must be positioned above the find-index SAF in obj.conf to ensure that the welcome file order specified in a web application's web.xml file takes precedence over the index file order configured for the find-index SAF.
ObjectType	type-j2ee	May set the value of the Content-Type request header field when the request URI maps to a resource in a Java web application. The Content-Type request header field indicates the media type of the request body.
		Java web application developers may specify mappings between extensions and Multipurpose Internet Mail Extension (MIME) types in web.xml. If the last segment in the request URI contains an extension (such as .jsp) the type-j2ee SAF checks whether there is a MIME mapping in web.xml that matches the extension. If a match is found, the type-j2ee SAF sets the Content-Type value to the corresponding MIME type. This SAF must be the first ObjectType SAF in obj.conf to ensure that web.xml MIME type mappings take precedence over the default MIME type mappings when the request is for a resource in a Java web application.
		Use of the Content-Type value during request processing is described in the section titled "Object Type (ObjectType) Stage" in Chapter 6.

Request Processing Stage	SAF	Description
Service	`service-j2ee`	Processes requests for resources in Java web applications and returns a response (upon success) to the client.
Error	`error-j2ee`	Handles errors that occur during servicing of a request for a resource within a Java web application. Web application developers may customize the response that is generated when an error condition is detected while processing a request for a resource within a Java web application. You define such customization by defining a list of error page descriptions in `web.xml`. `error-j2ee` applies any error page customizations specified in `web.xml` when generating an error response for a request to a resource within a Java web application.

Example 10.1 lists the contents of the `magnus.conf` file of a Java-enabled Web Server 7.0 configuration. Deleting or disabling (by prefixing the line with #) the `Init` directive marked in bold font in Example 10.1 disables the Java web container throughout the server.

Example 10.1 `magnus.conf` File (in a Java-enabled Server)

```
#
# Copyright 2006 Sun Microsystems, Inc.  All rights reserved.
# Use is subject to license terms.
#

Init fn="load-modules" shlib="libj2eeplugin.so"
```

Previous releases of Web Server explicitly listed the Server Application Functions (SAFs) by using `Init` directives in `magnus.conf`. The following demonstrates the `Init` directives in `magnus.conf` in Web Server 6.1:

```
Init fn="load-modules" shlib="install_dir/lib/libj2eeplugin.so"
    funcs="init-j2ee,ntrans-j2ee,service-j2ee,error-j2ee" shlib_
    flags="(global|now)"
Init fn="init-j2ee" LateInit=yes
```

The simple, compact form of `Init` directives in Web Server 7.0's `magnus.conf` are the result of some subtle innovations by the engineers at Sun that designed and developed Web Server 7.0. The server knows to load NSAPI plug-ins from certain well-known directories (such as `install_dir/lib`) and therefore doesn't hardwire paths (that may change from one machine to another) to its shared libraries (such as libj2eeplugin.so on UNIX and j2eeplugin.dll on Windows) in magnus.conf. The Init directive illustrated in Example 10.1 doesn't explicitly enumerate each SAF because Web Server 7.0's Java web container plug-in uses the NSAPI function nsapi_module_init() to register its SAFs.

Note: The nsapi_module_init() function is documented in the section titled "NSAPI Function and Macro Reference" in the *Sun Java System Web Server 7.0 NSAPI Developer's Guide*.

The rest of this section builds on the information described in "Default Request Processing Behavior" in Chapter 6 by tracing the path through the different request processing stages using sample client requests for content in Java web applications.

Example 10.2 demonstrates the obj.conf file for a server configuration that has enabled the Java web container. This information will be used to help describe request processing for Java content in Java web applications. Usage of the Java web container's request processing SAFs (described in Table 10.2) is marked in bold in Example 10.2.

Example 10.2   obj.conf File (in a Java-enabled Server)

```
 1 #
 2 # Copyright 2006 Sun Microsystems, Inc.  All rights reserved.
 3 # Use is subject to license terms.
 4 #
 5
 6 # You can edit this file, but comments and formatting changes
 7 # might be lost when you use the administration GUI or CLI.
 8
 9 <Object name="default">
10 AuthTrans fn="match-browser" browser="*MSIE*" ssl-unclean-
   shutdown="true"
11 NameTrans fn="ntrans-j2ee" name="j2ee"
12 NameTrans fn="pfx2dir" from="/mc-icons" dir="/opt/webserver7/lib/
   icons" name="es-internal"
13 PathCheck fn="uri-clean"
14 PathCheck fn="check-acl" acl="default"
15 PathCheck fn="find-pathinfo"
16 PathCheck fn="find-index-j2ee"
17 PathCheck fn="find-index" index-names="index.html,home.html,index.jsp"
18 ObjectType fn="type-j2ee"
19 ObjectType fn="type-by-extension"
```

```
20 ObjectType fn="force-type" type="text/plain"
21 Service method="(GET|HEAD)" type="magnus-internal/directory"
   fn="index-common"
22 Service method="(GET|HEAD|POST)" type="*~magnus-internal/*" fn="send-
   file"
23 Service method="TRACE" fn="service-trace"
24 Error fn="error-j2ee"
25 AddLog fn="flex-log"
26 </Object>
27
28 <Object name="j2ee">
29 Service fn="service-j2ee" method="*"
30 </Object>
31
32 <Object name="es-internal">
33 PathCheck fn="check-acl" acl="es-internal"
34 </Object>
35
36 <Object name="cgi">
37 ObjectType fn="force-type" type="magnus-internal/cgi"
38 Service fn="send-cgi"
39 </Object>
40
41 <Object name="send-precompressed">
42 PathCheck fn="find-compressed"
43 </Object>
44
45 <Object name="compress-on-demand">
46 Output fn="insert-filter" filter="http-compression"
47 </Object>
```

10.3.1 Request for Java Content

Referring to the obj.conf file specified in Example 10.2, the server would process the following directives (in this order) when a client makes a request for Java content (such as http://www.example.com/index.jsp or http://www.example.com/book-store/CatalogueServlet) other than directories in Java web applications:

```
10 AuthTrans fn="match-browser" browser="*MSIE*" ssl-unclean-
   shutdown="true"
11 NameTrans fn="ntrans-j2ee" name="j2ee"
13 PathCheck fn="uri-clean"
14 PathCheck fn="check-acl" acl="default"
15 PathCheck fn="find-pathinfo"
16 PathCheck fn="find-index-j2ee"
```

```
17 PathCheck fn="find-index" index-names="index.html,home.html,
   index.jsp"
18 ObjectType fn="type-j2ee"
19 ObjectType fn="type-by-extension"
29 Service fn="service-j2ee" method="*"
25 AddLog fn="flex-log"
```

Although they are executed, the find-index-j2ee and find-index SAFs do nothing; they act only on requests for directories.

> **Note:** The section titled "Name Translation (name) Attributes" in Chapter 6 describes how the name attribute of NameTrans affects request processing.

10.3.2 Request for Java Content that Does Not Exist

Referring to the obj.conf file specified in Example 10.2, the server would process the following directives (in this order) when a client makes a request for Java content that does not exist (such as http://www.example.com/abcdef.jsp):

```
10 AuthTrans fn="match-browser" browser="*MSIE*" ssl-unclean-
   shutdown="true"
11 NameTrans fn="ntrans-j2ee" name="j2ee"
13 PathCheck fn="uri-clean"
14 PathCheck fn="check-acl" acl="default"
15 PathCheck fn="find-pathinfo"
16 PathCheck fn="find-index-j2ee"
17 PathCheck fn="find-index" index-names="index.html,home.html,
   index.jsp"
18 ObjectType fn="type-j2ee"
19 ObjectType fn="type-by-extension"
29 Service fn="service-j2ee" method="*"
24 Error fn="error-j2ee"
25 AddLog fn="flex-log"
```

The directives are similar to those found when processing requests for Java content (refer to Section 10.3.1, "Request for Java Content"), with the exception that an additional directive (line 24) has been processed to handle the fact that the Java resource does not exist.

10.3.3 Request for a Directory in a Java Web Application

Assuming that there is a Java web application deployed at the URI /bookstore and also assuming that the web application's web.xml file does not specify any welcome files, which directives in the obj.conf file would be executed to process a request for http://www.example.com/bookstore? Referring to the obj.conf file specified in Example 10.2, the server would process the following directives (in this order):

```
10 AuthTrans fn="match-browser" browser="*MSIE*" ssl-unclean-
   shutdown="true"
11 NameTrans fn="ntrans-j2ee" name="j2ee"
13 PathCheck fn="uri-clean"
14 PathCheck fn="check-acl" acl="default"
15 PathCheck fn="find-pathinfo"
16 PathCheck fn="find-index-j2ee"
17 PathCheck fn="find-index" index-names="index.html,home.html,
   index.jsp"
18 ObjectType fn="type-j2ee"
19 ObjectType fn="type-by-extension"
29 Service fn="service-j2ee" method="*"
25 AddLog fn="flex-log"
```

10.3.4 Request for a Directory in a Java Web Application with Welcome Files

Example 10.3 provides an excerpt from a web.xml file that demonstrates how Java web applications specify welcome files in their deployment descriptor.

Example 10.3   Excerpt from the web.xml File

```
<welcome-file-list>
    <welcome-file>home.jsp</welcome-file>
    <welcome-file>home.html</welcome-file>
</welcome-file-list>
```

If the /bookstore application did specify welcome files as shown in Example 10.3 and if the root directory of the application did contain a file named home.jsp, which directives in the obj.conf file would be executed to process a request for http://www.example.com/bookstore? Referring to the obj.conf file specified in Example 10.2, the server would process the following directives (in this order):

```
10 AuthTrans fn="match-browser" browser="*MSIE*" ssl-unclean-
   shutdown="true"
11 NameTrans fn="ntrans-j2ee" name="j2ee"
13 PathCheck fn="uri-clean"
14 PathCheck fn="check-acl" acl="default"
15 PathCheck fn="find-pathinfo"
16 PathCheck fn="find-index-j2ee"
17 PathCheck fn="find-index" index-names="index.html,home.html,
   index.jsp"
18 ObjectType fn="type-j2ee"
19 ObjectType fn="type-by-extension"
29 Service fn="service-j2ee" method="*"
25 AddLog fn="flex-log"
```

The directives are similar to those found when processing requests for directories in Java web applications without welcome files (see the section titled "Request for a Directory in a Java Web Application"), with the exception that during execution find-index-j2ee (line 16) successfully maps the requested URI to the welcome file in the web application's document root and therefore find-index (line 17) does nothing because it acts only upon requests for directories.

10.3.5 Request for MIME-Mapped Content in a Java Web Application

Example 10.4 provides an excerpt from a web.xml file that demonstrates how Java web applications specify mappings between extensions and Multipurpose Internet Mail Extension (MIME) types.

Example 10.4   Excerpt from the web.xml File

```
<mime-mapping>
   <extension>pdf</extension>
   <mime-type>application/pdf</mime-type>
</mime-mapping>
```

If the /bookstore application introduced in the previous section did specify MIME mappings as shown in Example 10.4 and if the root directory of the application did contain a file named book.pdf, which directives in the obj.conf file would be executed to process a request for http://www.example.com/bookstore/book.pdf? Referring to the obj.conf file specified in Example 10.2, the server would process the following directives (in this order):

```
10 AuthTrans fn="match-browser" browser="*MSIE*" ssl-unclean-
   shutdown="true"
11 NameTrans fn="ntrans-j2ee" name="j2ee"
13 PathCheck fn="uri-clean"
14 PathCheck fn="check-acl" acl="default"
15 PathCheck fn="find-pathinfo"
16 PathCheck fn="find-index-j2ee"
17 PathCheck fn="find-index" index-names="index.html,home.html,
   index.jsp"
18 ObjectType fn="type-j2ee"
29 Service fn="service-j2ee" method="*"
25 AddLog fn="flex-log"
```

The directives are similar to those found when processing a request for Java content (refer to Section 10.3.1, "Request for Java Content"), with the exception that one less directive (line 19 in Example 10.2) was processed because `type-j2ee` (line 18) found a MIME-type mapping for the requested resource.

10.4 Java Configuration

Java configuration in Web Server is specified in configuration files and includes the following:

- Enabling the Java web container
- Configuring the Java Virtual Machine (JVM)
- Configuring global Java web container settings
- Configuring and deploying Java web applications

Typically, web application developers specify configuration information for web applications, whereas system administrators specify the deployment and execution environment for Java web applications in the server.

Web Server's Administration Console and Command Line Interface (`wadm`) include support for configuring a server's Java web container and Java web applications. You can also edit the configuration files manually to effect changes to the Java configuration of a server instance.

10.4.1 Java Configuration Files

Table 10.3 describes the various configuration files in which a system administrator would configure the server's Java execution and web application deployment environment. These configuration settings include

- Process-wide settings such as JVM configuration, JDBC resources, and so on
- Virtual-server-specific settings such as Java request processing configuration in obj.conf

Table 10.3 Java Web Container Configuration Files

Filename	Description
login.conf	Contains configuration information for use by the Java Authentication and Authorization Service (JAAS).
magnus.conf	Contains the Java plug-in initialization directive (if Java has been enabled for the server instance).
obj.conf	Contains SAFs that implement request processing for Java content (if Java has been enabled for the virtual server corresponding to the obj.conf file).
server.policy	Java Security Manager policy file that controls the access that Java web applications have to resources.
server.xml	The main instance configuration file, containing configuration information about the Java web container, the Java Virtual Machine (JVM), global Java resources, and other Java-related settings.

Java web application configuration is specified in the files shown in Table 10.4. These configuration settings include

- Configuration information that is private to each of the Java web applications that are deployed on the server
- Configuration information that is shared by all the Java web applications that are deployed on the server

Table 10.4 Java Web Application Configuration Files

Filename	Description
default-web.xml	Global web deployment descriptor that is shared by all the web applications in the instance. Individual web applications can override the settings specified in this file.
server.xml	Specifies deployment information about the Java web applications in each virtual server.

Filename	Description
sun-web.xml	Contains web application deployment descriptor configuration specific to Sun Java System Web Server and Sun Java System Application Server (now known as Glass-Fish Application Server). Complements web.xml.
web.xml	Standard web application deployment descriptor as defined by the Java Servlet Specification Version 2.5.

Note: This chapter contains examples of Java configuration in Web Server's configuration files. Documenting each of the Java-related settings in these configuration files is beyond the scope of this book. This information is already available in the *Sun Java System Web Server 7.0 Administrator's Configuration File Reference* and in the *Sun Java System Web Server 7.0 Developer's Guide to Java Web Applications*.

10.4.2 Globally Enabling/Disabling Java

The Java web container is enabled by default when you create a new server configuration, as shown in the highlighted section in Figure 10.4.

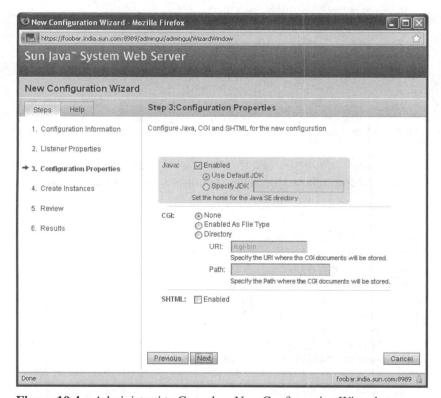

Figure 10.4 Administration Console—New Configuration Wizard

You can also enable or disable the Java web container in existing server configurations by using the server's administration interfaces. Figure 10.5 highlights the check box on the screen used for enabling or disabling the Java web container for a configuration.

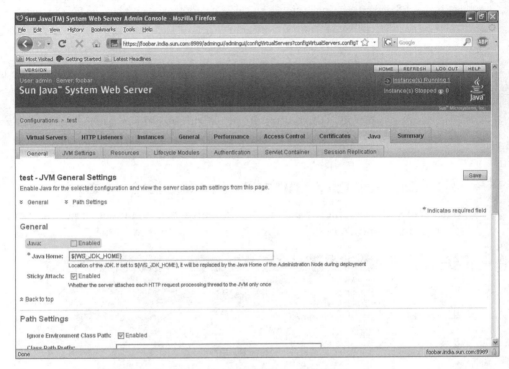

Figure 10.5   Administration Console—JVM General Settings

The following shell-mode example shows how the wadm script's enable-java and disable-java subcommands are used to configure the state of the Java web container:

```
wadm> disable-java --config=test
CLI201 Command 'disable-java' ran successfully
wadm> deploy-config --restart test
CLI201 Command 'deploy-config' ran successfully
wadm>
wadm> enable-java --config=test
CLI201 Command 'enable-java' ran successfully
wadm> deploy-config --restart test
CLI201 Command 'deploy-config' ran successfully
```

> **Note:** Refer to the section titled "Command Line Interface (CLI)" in Chapter 4 and to the *Sun Java System Web Server 7.0 CLI Reference Manual* for more information about the wadm script.

Looking at the messages that the server logs during startup is an easy way to determine whether the Java web container is enabled or not. Starting a server that has the Java web container enabled provides a response similar to the following:

```
# bin/startserv
Sun Java System Web Server 7.0U3 B06/16/2008 12:00
info: CORE5076: Using [Java HotSpot(TM) Server VM, Version 1.5.0_15]
    from [Sun Microsystems Inc.]
info: HTTP3072: http-listener-1: http://test:9000 ready to accept
    requests
info: CORE3274: successful server startup
```

The message marked in bold is logged during Java web container initialization. This indicates that the web server is Java enabled.

Starting the server after disabling the Java web container provides a response similar to the following:

```
% bin/startserv
Sun Java System Web Server 7.0U3 B06/16/2008 12:00
info: HTTP3072: http-listener-1: http://test:9000 ready to accept
    requests
info: CORE3274: successful server startup
```

Absence of the message identified as CORE5076 is an indication that the Java web container has not been enabled in this server.

10.4.3 Enabling/Disabling Java for a Virtual Server

The previous section described how you can enable or disable Java content processing for the entire server. What do you do if your server configuration has multiple virtual servers and you want to disable Java content processing in only one of the virtual servers? Manually editing the configuration files is currently the only way to accomplish this. The rest of this section describes how to do so.

Disabling Java for a virtual server involves editing the virtual server's obj.conf file and removing all the directives that reference the Java web container Server Application Functions described earlier in Table 10.2.

Virtual servers are defined in server.xml. The object-file subelement of a virtual server's definition in server.xml specifies the file to use to determine how to process requests for that virtual server. To disable Java for a virtual server, find the virtual server's object-file definition in server.xml, as demonstrated in Example 10.5.

Example 10.5   Object Configuration File Definition for a Virtual Server

```
<virtual-server>
  <name>www.example.com</name>
  <http-listener-name>http-listener-1</http-listener-name>
  <host>www.example.com</host>
  <object-file>www.example.com-obj.conf</object-file>
  <document-root>/export/home/example.com/public_html</document-root>
  <access-log>
      <file>/export/home/example.com/logs/access</file>
  </access-log>
</virtual-server>
```

Using an editor, edit the named object file (found in the instance's config subdirectory) and using Example 10.2 as a reference; delete all the lines marked in bold and save these changes to the file.

> **Note:** This assumes that there are no other virtual servers using this object file for which you want to continue using Java.

Dynamically reconfigure your server instance to disable Java processing for a specific virtual server.

To verify whether you have disabled Java processing for the virtual server, you can install/create a simple JavaServer Pages (JSP) script in the document root of the virtual server and then send a request for the JSP script that you just installed. A virtual server that does not have Java processing enabled generates a response that includes the source code of the JSP script.

10.4.4 Global Java Settings

Figure 10.5 is a screen capture of Web Server's Administration Console that shows various tabs that specify Java-related configuration in Web Server. The administration framework in Web Server also includes command-line support to configure the Java subsystem in the server. Changes in many of these settings require that the server be restarted. Table 10.5 enumerates the command-line support and configuration file elements for each of the Java configuration tabs shown in Figure 10.5.

Table 10.5 Java Administration

Console Tab Name	wadm Subcommands	server.xml Elements	Server restart required?	Description

General	`enable-java`
	`disable-java`
	`set-jvm-prop`
	`get-jvm-prop`
		`jvm`	Yes	Manage core configuration for the Java Virtual Machine (JVM).

JVM Settings	`create-jvm-options`
	`create-jvm-profiler`
	`delete-jvm-options`
	`delete-jvm-profiler`
	`list-jvm-options`
	`list-jvm-profilers`
		`jvm-options`
		`debug`
		`debug-jvm-options`
		`profiler`
			Yes	Manage optional JVM configuration and Java profiler configuration.

Resources	`create-custom-resource`
	`create-custom-resource-userprop`
	`create-external-jndi-resource`
	`create-external-jndi-resource-`
	`  userprop`
	`create-jdbc-resource`
	`create-jdbc-resource-userprop`
	`create-mail-resource`
	`create-mail-resource-userprop`
	`delete-custom-resource`
	`delete-custom-resource-userprop`
	`delete-external-jndi-resource`
	`delete-external-jndi-resource-`
	`  userprop`
	`delete-jdbc-resource`
	`delete-jdbc-resource-userprop`
	`delete-mail-resource`
	`delete-mail-resource-userprop`
	`get-custom-resource-prop`
	`get-external-jndi-resource-prop`
	`get-jdbc-resource-prop`
	`get-mail-resource-prop`
	`list-custom-resources`
	`list-custom-resource-userprops`
	`list -external-jndi-resources`
	`list-external-jndi-resource-`
	`  userprops`
	`list-jdbc-resources`
	`list-jdbc-resource-userprops`
	`list-mail-resources`
	`list-mail-resource-userprops`
	`set-custom-resource-prop`
	`set-external-jndi-resource-prop`
	`set-jdbc-resource-prop`
	`set-mail-resource-prop`
		`custom-resource`
		`external-jndi-resource`
		`jdbc-resource`
		`mail-resource`
			Yes	Manage JDBC, JNDI, JavaMail, and Custom resource configuration.

Table 10.5   Java Administration *continued*

Console Tab Name	wadm Subcommands	server.xml Elements	Server restart required?	Description

Lifecycle Modules	`create-lifecycle-module`
	`create-lifecycle-module-userprop`
	`delete-lifecycle-module`
	`delete-lifecycle-module-userprop`
	`get-lifecycle-module-prop`
	`list-lifecycle-module-userprops`
	`list-lifecycle-modules`
	`set-lifecycle-module-prop`
		Lifecycle-module	Yes	Manage server lifecycle listener classes.

Authentication	`create-auth-realm`
	`create-auth-realm-userprop`
	`delete-auth-realm`
	`delete-auth-realm-userprop`
	`get-auth-realm-prop`
	`list-auth-realm-userprops`
	`list-auth-realms`
	`set-auth-realm-prop`
	`create-soap-auth-provider`
	`create-soap-auth-provider-`
	`  userprop`
	`delete-soap-auth-provider`
	`delete-soap-auth-provider-`
	`  userprop`
	`get-soap-auth-provider-prop`
	`list-soap-auth-provider-`
	`  userprops`
	`list-soap-auth-providers`
	`set-soap-auth-provider-prop`
		`auth-realm`
		`default-auth-`
		`realm-name`
		`soap-auth-`
		`provider`
		`default-`
		`soap-auth-`
		`provider-name`
			Yes	Manage Java authentication realms and SOAP authentication providers.

Servlet Container	`get-servlet-container-prop` `set-servlet-container-prop`	`servlet-` `container`	No	Manage Java web container runtime settings.
Session Replication	`get-session-replication-prop` `set-session-replication-prop`	`session-` `replication`	Yes	Manage web application session replication settings.

10.5 Java Web Applications

A Java web application is a collection of Java resources (such as Servlets, JavaServer Pages, and utility classes), static content (such as images, HTML files, and XML files), deployment descriptors (such as web.xml), and other web resources that together make up a complete application on a web server. The Java web container associates each Java web application with a ServletContext object. The Servlet-Context provides Java components within the application (such as servlets and JSPs) with a view of the application as well as access to resources in the application.

10.5.1 Java Web Application Lifecycle

The lifecycle of a Java web application in the context of Web Server can be summarized as follows:

- Develop the web application content and code
- Create the runtime deployment descriptor(s)
- Package the web application
- Deploy the packaged contents into Web Server 7.0's Java web container
- Access the web application via a web browser
- Debug problems in the web application
- Undeploy the web application

Web Server's administration framework includes support for deploying, debugging, and undeploying Java web applications. Most web application developers prefer developing and packaging web applications (including creating the web application deployment descriptors) using a Java IDE (integrated development environment) such as NetBeans or Eclipse. The section titled "Web Server and NetBeans" describes developing, managing, and debugging Java web applications in Web Server 7.0 using NetBeans.

10.5.2 Java Web Application Contents

A Java web application consists of a structured hierarchy of directories as shown in Figure 10.6.

The top level of the directory hierarchy serves as the application's document root. The document root is where HTML files, images, JSP scripts, CGI programs, and other types of content are stored in application-specific subdirectories.

The document root may contain special subdirectories named WEB-INF and META-INF. As specified in the Java Servlet Specification Version 2.5, the Java web container protects the contents of these directories from direct client access. The contents of these directories are visible to servlet code within the web application via the getResource and getResourceAsStream methods of the ServletContext. Table 10.6 describes the contents of the WEB-INF directory.

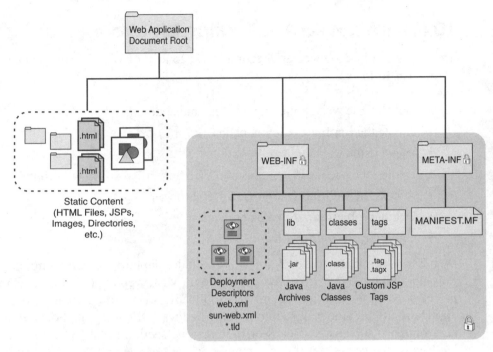

Figure 10.6   Java Web Application Structure

Table 10.6   WEB-INF Contents

File/Directory	Optional?	Description
web.xml	Yes	The web application deployment descriptor. Defined by the Java Servlet Specification Version 2.5.
sun-web.xml	Yes	Web application deployment descriptor specific to Web Server (and also Sun's Application Server). Defined by the *Sun Java System Web Server 7.0 Developer's Guide to Java Web Applications*.
*.tld	Yes	Tag library descriptors. Defined by the JavaServer Pages Specification Version 2.1.
classes	Yes	A directory containing the application's server-side Java classes such as servlets, utility classes, and JavaBeans. Java package names must be reflected in this directory hierarchy. For example, a class named `com.example.TestServlet` would need to be stored in a file named `TestServlet.class` under `WEB-INF/classes/com/example/`. The web application's class loader loads all the classes under the `WEB-INF/classes` directory before loading the JAR files from the `WEB-NIF/lib` directory.
lib	Yes	A directory containing the application's server-side classes packaged as Java Archive (JAR) files.
tags	Yes	A directory containing the application's JSP tag files.

A Web application can be packaged into a Web ARchive format (WAR) file if you simply archive the directory hierarchy by using the standard jar tool. The META-INF directory is created when the web application is packaged into a Web Archive (WAR) file format. It contains manifest information useful to Java archiving tools.

In addition to supporting "unpackaged" Java web applications where the files and directories exist on the file system, Web Server 7.0 includes support for deploying Java web applications packaged as WAR files.

The next section describes how Web Server uses the deployment descriptors that specify web application configuration.

10.5.3 Java Web Application Configuration in Web Server

The different aspects of Java web application configuration are specified in the following configuration files:

- `server.xml`
- `default-web.xml`
- `web.xml`
- `sun-web.xml`

Figure 10.7 demonstrates how Web Server uses the information in these files to initialize and load Java web applications.

The rest of this section describes these files in more detail.

10.5.3.1 The server.xml File

The `server.xml` file is the main configuration file for Web Server and is found in the `config` subdirectory of every server instance. The information it contains includes the Java web applications deployed in each virtual server. The `web-app` element in `server.xml` configures a Java web application mapping within a virtual server. The `web-app` element is a subelement of the `virtual-server` element and may appear 0 or more times within the `virtual-server` element. Table 10.7 enumerates the child elements of the `web-app` element in the `server.xml` file.

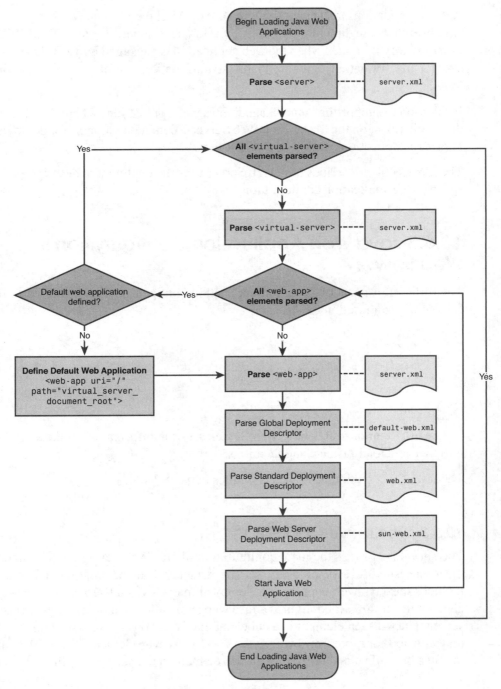

Figure 10.7   Java Web Application Initialization

Table 10.7 web-app Child Elements in server.xml

Element	Required?	Description
description	No	Textual description of the web application. Intended to serve as a reference for the web site administrator.
enabled	No	A Boolean value that controls whether the web application is enabled at runtime. Can be used to temporarily disable the web application at runtime without need to remove the web-app element. The default value is true.
path	Yes	A file system path to the web application's contents. This can be an absolute path or a relative one. The relative path is specified relative to the server's config directory.
uri	Yes	The context path for accessing the web application.

Section 10.5.4, "Deploying Java Web Applications into Web Server," contains more information about Web Server 7.0's administrative interfaces for managing web-app elements in server.xml.

10.5.3.2 The default-web.xml File

The default-web.xml file contains web application configuration that is shared by all the Java web applications deployed to the server. This file is found in the config subdirectory of every server instance.

This file is an XML-formatted file whose contents are validated against the standard XML data type definition (DTD) that validates the web.xml file as follows:

```
<!DOCTYPE web-app
    PUBLIC "-//Sun Microsystems, Inc.//DTD Web Application 2.3//EN"
    "http://java.sun.com/dtd/web-app_2_3.dtd">
```

As Figure 10.7 indicates, this file can be used to specify common configurations for all web applications that would otherwise need to be duplicated in each web application's deployment descriptor file—web.xml. Individual web applications can always override any of the settings specified in this file.

The rest of this section describes the contents of the default-web.xml file that is created for each configuration and also describes the support included in Web Server's administration framework for managing this file. The order and grouping of the elements has been changed to explain related configuration together.

As described earlier, Web Server 7.0's Java web container includes support for JavaServer Pages. The JSP engine in Web Server 7.0 includes a JSP compiler that compiles JSP scripts to servlets and a JSP runtime that executes these compiled scripts. By default, all web applications in Web Server 7.0 use Web Server's JSP engine for processing requests for JavaServer Pages. Web Server's JSP engine is made available to web applications via the `jsp` servlet and its mappings, which are defined in `default-web.xml` as follows:

```
<servlet>
  <servlet-name>jsp</servlet-name>
  <servlet-class>org.apache.jasper.servlet.JspServlet</servlet-class>

  <init-param>
    <param-name>httpMethods</param-name>
    <param-value>GET,HEAD,POST</param-value>
  </init-param>
  <init-param>
    <param-name>fork</param-name>
    <param-value>false</param-value>
  </init-param>
  <init-param>
    <param-name>mappedfile</param-name>
    <param-value>false</param-value>
  </init-param>
  <load-on-startup>3</load-on-startup>
</servlet>

<servlet-mapping>
  <servlet-name>jsp</servlet-name>
  <url-pattern>*.jsp</url-pattern>
</servlet-mapping>

<servlet-mapping>
  <servlet-name>jsp</servlet-name>
  <url-pattern>*.jspx</url-pattern>
</servlet-mapping>
```

The `default` servlet processes requests for content that do not map to any other servlets in the web application, such as requests for static content (HTML files, images, etc.). Web Server's `default` servlet is tightly integrated with the server's NSAPI engine and enables the Java web container to use the server's file cache to efficiently serve static content. The default servlet implementation in Web Server 7.0 also facilitates seamless integration of Java and non-Java dynamic content such as JSPs, including CGI programs, Servlets including SHTML files, and so on. The default servlet and its mappings are specified in `default-web.xml` as follows:

```
<servlet>
  <servlet-name>default</servlet-name>
  <servlet-class>com.sun.webserver.servlets.DefaultServlet</servlet-
    class>
  <load-on-startup>1</load-on-startup>
</servlet>

<servlet-mapping>
  <servlet-name>default</servlet-name>
  <url-pattern>/</url-pattern>
</servlet-mapping>
```

Clients access a servlet by specifying a URI pattern that maps to the servlet. These servlet mappings are specified in web.xml, the web application's deployment descriptor. Example 10.6 is an excerpt from a sample web.xml file that illustrates two servlet mappings for the HelloServlet.

Example 10.6   Excerpt from the web.xml File

```
<servlet-mapping>
  <servlet-name>HelloServlet</servlet-name>
  <url-pattern>/helloworld</url-pattern>
</servlet-mapping>
<servlet-mapping>
  <servlet-name>HelloServlet</servlet-name>
  <url-pattern>/hello/*</url-pattern>
</servlet-mapping>
```

By specifying these mappings in web.xml, a web application developer enables access to the HelloServlet to client requests such as */context_path/*helloworld, */context_path/*hello/foo, */context_path/*hello/bar, and so on. Similarly, to enable access to each servlet in the application, a servlet definition and one or more servlet mappings must be defined in web.xml for each servlet.

The invoker servlet enables a web application to dynamically register servlet definitions and also enables client access to such servlets. This facilitates rapid application development by removing the need to specify servlet definitions and servlet mappings when prototyping servlets. It is recommended that the invoker servlet be disabled when using Web Server in production. The following defines the invoker servlet and its mappings in default-web.xml:

```
<servlet>
  <servlet-name>invoker</servlet-name>
  <servlet-class>org.apache.catalina.servlets.InvokerServlet</
    servlet-class>
```

```
    <init-param>
      <param-name>debug</param-name>
      <param-value>0</param-value>
    </init-param>
    <load-on-startup>2</load-on-startup>
  </servlet>

  <servlet-mapping>
    <servlet-name>invoker</servlet-name>
    <url-pattern>/servlet/*</url-pattern>
  </servlet-mapping>
```

The invoker servlet mapping defined in `default-web.xml` enables access to any servlet in a web application, using requests of the form */context_path/*`servlet/` *servlet_name* where *context_path* is the URI at which the web application is deployed and *servlet_name* is either a `<servlet-name>` value from `web.xml` or the fully qualified name of the servlet's Java class file. The following URI examples illustrate use of the invoker servlet to access individual servlets in a web application deployed at `/test`:

- `/test/servlet/HelloWorld` (accessed using `servlet-name` value in `web.xml`)
- `/test/servlet/foo.bar.HelloServlet` (accessed using Java classname)

Table 10.8 includes examples that illustrate how the servlet mappings specified in the `default-web.xml` file control the servlet that is invoked.

Table 10.8   `default-web.xml` Servlet Mapping Examples

URL	Servlet Invoked
`http://host:port/webapp/index.jsp`	`jsp`
`http://host:port/webapp/index.html`	`default`
`http://host:port/webapp/subdir/catalog.jspx`	`jsp`
`http://host:port/webapp/banner.jpg`	`default`
`http://host:port/webapp/servlet/ShoppingCart`	`invoker`
`http://host:port/webapp/servlet/index.html`	`invoker`

The `default-web.xml` file can also be used to specify session configuration for all Java web applications in Web Server. The `default-web.xml` file included in Web Server 7.0 specifies only the default timeout for Java web application sessions as follows:

```
<session-config>
  <session-timeout>30</session-timeout>
</session-config>
```

Although Web Server's administration framework does not include support for editing individual elements within the `default-web.xml` file, the command line interface—`wadm`—does provide support for managing the file via the `get-config-file` and `set-config-file` subcommands. Figure 10.8 illustrates the use of `get-config-file` and `set-config-file` to modify the `default-web.xml` file.

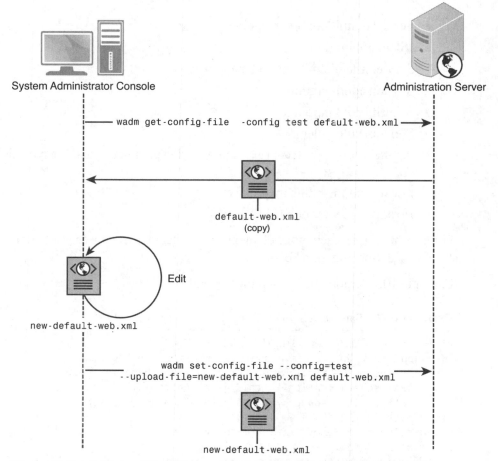

Figure 10.8   Command Line Support for Managing the `default-web.xml` File

Configuration settings specified in the web application's deployment descriptor can be used to override settings specified in the `default-web.xml` file. The following section describes the `web.xml` file.

10.5.3.3 The web.xml File

The web.xml file is a J2EE-standard XML document that describes the content of a Java web application. This deployment descriptor includes both deployment and configuration information for the Java web application. The format and contents of the web.xml file are defined in the Java Servlet Specification Version 2.5. If present, the web.xml file must reside in the WEB-INF subdirectory of the application. A web application is NOT required to contain a web.xml file.

The types of information specified in an application's web.xml file include

- Servlet definitions and mappings
- JSP configuration
- Servlet filter definitions and mappings
- Session configuration
- Security configuration
- Welcome file order
- Application (ServletContext) initialization parameters and lifecycle listeners
- Locale and Encoding mappings
- Error page declarations

For information on each of the elements in this deployment descriptor, refer to the Java Servlet Specification Version 2.5.

Example 10.7 demonstrates a sample web.xml file.

Example 10.7   Sample web.xml File

```
<?xml version="1.0" encoding="ISO-8859-1"?>
<web-app xmlns="http://java.sun.com/xml/ns/javaee"
      xmlns:xsi="http://www.w3.org/2001/XMLSchema-instance"
      xsi:schemaLocation="http://java.sun.com/xml/ns/javaee
      http://java.sun.com/xml/ns/javaee/web-app_2_5.xsd"
      version="2.5">
   <display-name>Yummy Pizzas</display-name>
   <context-param>
      <param-name>Owner</param-name>
      <param-value>raj@yummypizzas.com</param-value>
   </context-param>
   <servlet>
      <servlet-name>MenuServlet</servlet-name>
```

```
            <servlet-class>yummypizzas.MenuServlet</servlet-class>
            <init-param>
                <param-name>specials</param-name>
                <param-value>true</param-value>
            </init-param>
        </servlet>
        <servlet-mapping>
            <servlet-name>MenuServlet</servlet-name>
            <url-pattern>/menu/*</url-pattern>
        </servlet-mapping>
        <session-config>
            <session-timeout>10</session-timeout>
        </session-config>
        <welcome-file-list>
            <welcome-file>menu.jsp</welcome-file>
            <welcome-file>index.jsp</welcome-file>
            <welcome-file>index.html</welcome-file>
        </welcome-file-list>
        <error-page>
            <error-code>404</error-code>
            <location>/nosuchpizza.html</location>
        </error-page>
        <resource-ref>
            <description>Pizza Database</description>
            <res-ref-name>jdbc/pizzas</res-ref-name>
            <res-type>javax.sql.DataSource</res-type>
            <res-auth>Container</res-auth>
        </resource-ref>
</web-app>
```

To enable rapid development, Web Server's Java web container can automatically redeploy the application without restarting the server or affecting other applications when it detects that an application's web.xml file has been modified. More information on this is described in Section 10.5.9, "Dynamically Reconfiguring Java Web Applications."

Figure 10.7 illustrates how the server uses the information in web.xml to initialize Java web applications. Web Server does not include tools for creating or editing the web.xml file. Popular Java Integrated Development Environments (IDEs) such as NetBeans and Eclipse include support for creating and packaging web applications and their associated deployment descriptors. Figure 10.9 illustrates editing the sample web.xml file from Example 10.7, using the NetBeans IDE.

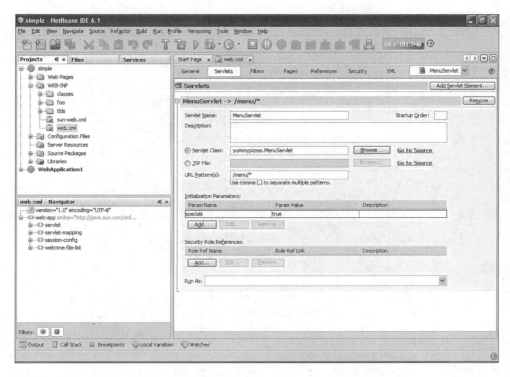

Figure 10.9   web.xml Editor in NetBeans 6.1

10.5.3.4 The sun-web.xml File

The sun-web.xml file is an optional deployment descriptor that is specific to Sun's web tier servers, namely Web Server and Application Server. This file is also an XML-formatted document that specifies web application deployment and configuration information specific to features included in Web Server 7.0. The format and contents of the sun-web.xml file are defined in Appendix A of the *Sun Java System Web Server 7.0 Developer's Guide to Java Web Applications*. If present, the sun-web.xml file must reside in the WEB-INF subdirectory of the application. A web application is NOT required to contain a sun-web.xml file.

All entries in this file are validated against the XML data type definition (DTD) for the sun-web.xml deployment descriptor as follows:

```
<!DOCTYPE sun-web-app PUBLIC
"-//Sun Microsystems, Inc.//DTD Application Server 9.0 Servlet 2.5//
  EN"
"http://www.sun.com/software/appserver/dtds/sun-web-app_2_5-0.dtd">
```

In addition to the URL referenced in the DOCTYPE declaration, the data type definition file (`sun-web-app_2_5-0.dtd`) can also be found in the `install_dir/lib/dtds` directory.

The `sun-web.xml` deployment descriptor is a companion descriptor to `web.xml` that specifies the web application configuration specific to the runtime environment provided by Web Server 7.0. The types of information specified in the `sun-web.xml` file of an application include

- Session manager configuration
- Session configuration
- Servlet/JSP caching configuration
- Security role mappings (between a security role and users/groups in the realm)
- Web Services runtime settings
- Classloader configuration
- JSP configuration
- Internationalization settings
- JNDI name mappings between resource references in `web.xml` and server resources configured in `server.xml`

Example 10.8 demonstrates a sample `sun-web.xml` file that configures some of the Sun-specific features of Java web applications that run in Web Server.

Example 10.8   Sample `sun-web.xml` File

```
<!DOCTYPE sun-web-app PUBLIC
"-//Sun Microsystems, Inc.//DTD Application Server 9.0 Servlet 2.5//EN"
"http://www.sun.com/software/appserver/dtds/sun-web-app_2_5-0.dtd">
<sun-web-app>
   <session-config>
      <session-manager persistence-type='file'>
         <manager-properties>
            <property name='reapIntervalSeconds' value='30'/>
            <property name='maxSessions' value='1000'/>
         </manager-properties>
      </session-manager>

      <cookie-properties>
         <property name='cookieMaxAgeSeconds' value='300'/>
      </cookie-properties>
   </session-config>
```

```
    <resource-ref>
        <res-ref-name>jdbc/pizzas</res-ref-name>
        <jndi-name>jdbc/pizzadb</jndi-name>
    </resource-ref>

    <class-loader delegate='true'/>

    <jsp-config>
        <property name="reload-interval" value="-1"/>
    </jsp-config>
    <property name='singleThreadedServletPoolSize' value='15'/>
    <property name='encodeCookies' value='false'/>
</sun-web-app>
```

Figure 10.7 illustrates how the server uses `sun-web.xml` to initialize Java web applications. Web Server does not include tools for creating or editing the `sun-web.xml` file. Popular Java Integrated Development Environments (IDEs) such as NetBeans include support for creating and editing `sun-web.xml` when developing Java web applications. Figure 10.10 demonstrates editing the sample `sun-web.xml` file from Example 10.8, using the NetBeans IDE.

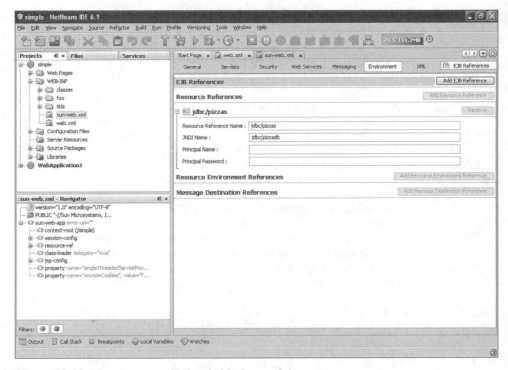

Figure 10.10   `sun-web.xml` Editor in NetBeans 6.1

10.5.4 Deploying Java Web Applications into Web Server

A Java web application must be deployed into the server before it can be accessed by clients. Each Java web application is rooted at a specific path (known as the context path) within the Web Server's URI space. You access the Java web application by specifying the context path in the URI of the requested resource. The context path is specified when the Java web application is deployed into the server. Web Server maps each Java web application's context path to the document root directory of the application and uses this information to translate request URIs to pathnames on the file system. For example, if a bookstore application is deployed to the context path /bookstore, then a request URI referring to /bookstore/index. jsp maps to the index.jsp file in the document root directory of the bookstore application.

Each virtual server in a Web Server configuration can host zero or more Java web applications. You specify web application deployment into a virtual server by using the web-app subelement of the virtual-server element in server.xml. The following sections describe Web Server's administration interfaces for deploying and managing a virtual server's Java web applications.

10.5.4.1 Web-based Deployment

This section describes Web Server 7.0's web-based Administration Console support for deploying and managing Java web applications. Using the web-based console, you can easily add, remove, list, enable, disable, and configure Java web applications.

Figure 10.11 illustrates how the graphical user interface screen for adding a Java web application to a specific virtual server is readily accessible on the home page of the Administration Console—the Common Tasks screen.

Figure 10.12 illustrates how you can also access this functionality from the Virtual Servers Web Application screen of a specific virtual server.

Selecting the Add Web Application task (Figure 10.11) from the Common Tasks screen or clicking on the New button (Figure 10.12) on the Virtual Server Web Applications screen results in the Add Web Application dialog shown in Figure 10.13.

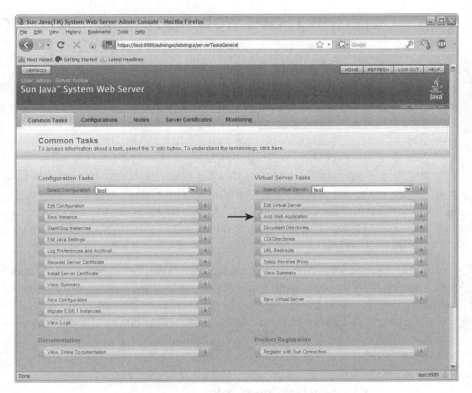

Figure 10.11   Administration Console—Common Tasks

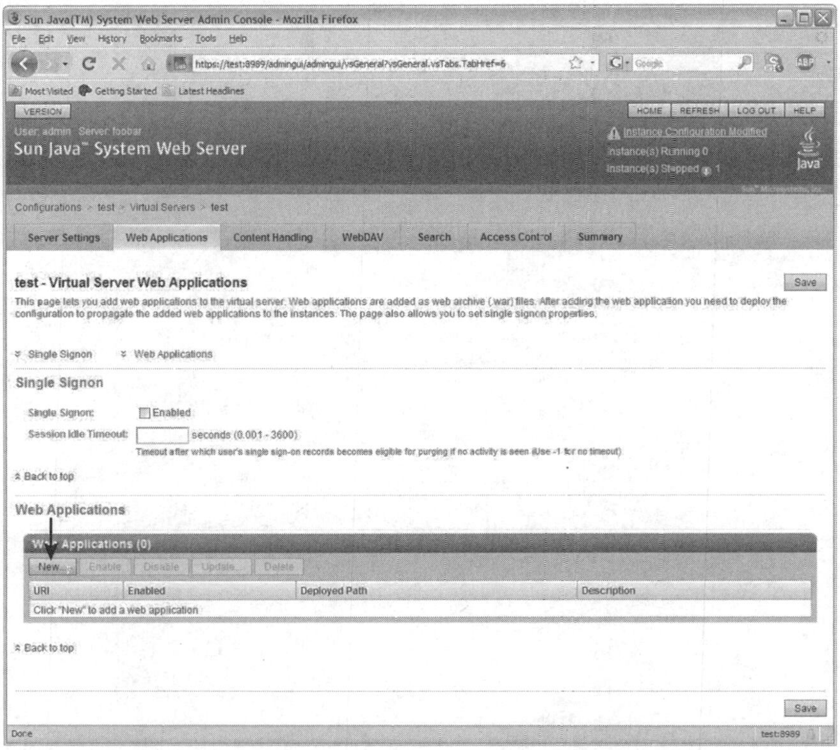

Figure 10.12   Administration Console—Virtual Server Web Applications

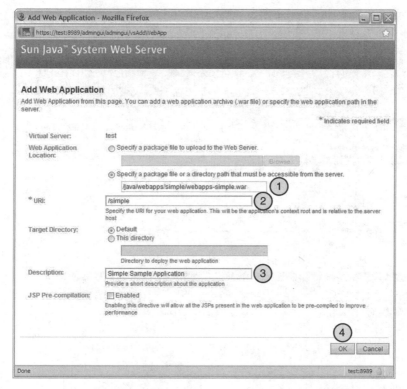

Figure 10.13   Administration Console—Add Web Application

Figure 10.13 demonstrates adding a web application at a context path of /simple into the virtual server named test by identifying the user interactions on the dialog box. Figure 10.14 illustrates how Web Server's administration framework deploys .war files by extracting their contents into the web-app subdirectory of the instance.

A new web-app subelement is added to the corresponding virtual-server element in server.xml. when a Java web application is deployed into that virtual server. Example 10.9 lists the relevant portion of server.xml that corresponds to the sample web application that was added earlier in Figure 10.13.

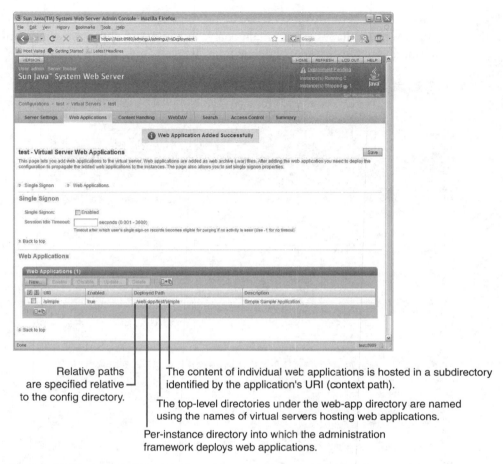

Relative paths are specified relative to the config directory.

The content of individual web applications is hosted in a subdirectory identified by the application's URI (context path).

The top-level directories under the web-app directory are named using the names of virtual servers hosting web applications.

Per-instance directory into which the administration framework deploys web applications.

Figure 10.14   Administration Console—Virtual Server Web Applications

Example 10.9   Excerpt from the `server.xml` file

```
<virtual-server>
  <name>test</name>
  <host>test</host>
  <http-listener-name>http-listener-1</http-listener-name>
  <document-root>../docs</document-root>
  <web-app>
    <uri>/simple</uri>
    <path>../web-app/test/simple</path>
    <description>Simple Sample Application</description>
  </web-app>
</virtual-server>
```

The web-based administration console also enables the administrator to manage multiple web applications simultaneously. Figure 10.15 shows how an administrator might enable, disable, or delete multiple web applications together.

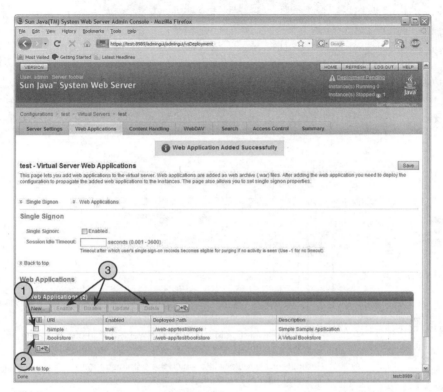

Figure 10.15   Administration Console—Group Operations on Web Applications

10.5.4.2 Command-Line Deployment

Web Server's primary administrative command line interface—the wadm script—provides the following subcommands to support Java web application administration:

- add-webapp
- disable-webapp
- enable-webapp
- list-webapps
- remove-webapp

The following shell-mode example shows how some of these commands are used to deploy and undeploy Java web applications using the command line interface:

```
wadm> list-webapps --verbose --all --config=test --vs=test
uri          enabled
----------------------
/simple       true
wadm>
wadm> add-webapp --description="JSTL Sample Application" --config=test
  --vs=test --uri=/jstl c:/sun/webserver7/samples/java/webapps/jstl/
  webapps-jstl.war
CLI201 Command 'add-webapp' ran successfully
wadm>
wadm> list-webapps --verbose --all --config=test --vs=test
uri          enabled
----------------------
/simple       true
/jstl         true
wadm>
wadm> remove-webapp --config=test --vs=test --uri=/simple
CLI201 Command 'remove-webapp' ran successfully
wadm>
wadm> list-webapps --config=test --vs=test --verbose --all
uri          enabled
----------------------
/jstl         true
wadm>

wadm> deploy-config test
CLI201 Command 'deploy-config' ran successfully
```

Unlike the web-based interface, the wadm subcommands do not support group operations for enabling, disabling, and removing multiple web applications with a single command.

Note: When using wadm in shell mode, file paths are always (even when using wadm on Windows) specified with UNIX-style forward slashes (/) rather than backslashes (\).

10.5.4.3 Automatic Deployment

Web Server includes support for rapid, iterative deployment of web applications from a designated directory. Both "packaged" Java web applications (in the form of WAR files) and "unpackaged" web applications (where the files and directories exist on the file system) can be automatically deployed into the server from the designated directory. This feature is intended for use during web application development. Sun Java System Web Server 7.0 Update 3 was the first release of Web Server to include support for automatic deployment of Java web applications.

The designated directory for a server instance from which web applications are automatically deployed is *instance_dir*/https-*instance*/auto-deploy. Adding a Java web application to this directory causes the application to be deployed into all the active virtual servers in the instance. Removing a previously auto-deployed application from this directory causes the application to be undeployed from all the active virtual servers in the instance.

Automatic deployment does not involve adding or deleting web-app elements in server.xml. During auto-deployment, Web Server uses the file or directory name of the application to dynamically determine the context path into which to deploy the application. Table 10.9 demonstrates the correlation between the web application's WAR file or directory (in *instance_dir*/https-*instance*/auto-deploy) and the context path used during auto-deployment.

Table 10.9   Context Path Examples for Auto-Deployed Web Applications

File/Directory Name	Format	Dynamic Context Path
simple	Unpackaged (Directory)	/simple
hello_world.war	Packaged (Web Archive)	/hello_world
tax-planner	Unpackaged (Directory)	/tax-planner
100examples.war	Packaged (Web Archive)	/100examples

Automatic deployment of Java web applications from the *instance_dir*/https-*instance*/auto-deploy directory occurs at the following phases in the server life-cycle:

- Server startup
- Dynamic reconfiguration

A Web Server instance can be configured to periodically check its auto-deploy directory for additions/deletions and automatically reflect these changes in the running instance. The dynamic-reload-interval attribute (described in Section 10.5.9, "Dynamically Reconfiguring Java Web Applications") controls how often the server checks the auto-deploy directory for changes.

Unlike the two methods of deployment described earlier (in the sections titled "Web-based Deployment" and "Command Line Deployment"), automatic deployment (or auto-deployment) does not require that the administration server be running. Java web applications that are auto-deployed are accessible on all active virtual servers that have been configured in the server.

The rest of this section describes the mechanics of adding and removing auto-deployed Java web applications, using a couple of the sample Java web applications included with Web Server 7.0.

To automatically deploy a Java web application packaged as a Web Archive file (.war file), simply copy the .war file to the server instance's auto-deploy directory, as demonstrated in the following:

```
C:\Sun\WebServer7>copy samples\java\webapps\jstl\webapps-jstl.war
   https-test\auto-deploy\
       1 file(s) copied.
C:\Sun\WebServer7>
C:\Sun\WebServer7>https-test\bin\startserv.bat
Sun Java System Web Server 7.0U3 B06/16/2008 11:32
info: CORE5076: Using [Java HotSpot(TM) Server VM, Version 1.5.0_15]
   from [Sun Microsystems Inc.]
info: WEB0100: Loading web module in virtual server [test] at [/
   webapps-jstl]
info: HTTP3072: http-listener-1: http://test:9C00 ready to accept
   requests
info: CORE3274: successful server startup
```

Note: Bold font is used to illustrate how the Web Server uses the name of the .war file for the context path into which to deploy the application.

The auto-deployed application can now be accessed from a browser, as illustrated in Figure 10.16.

The previous example demonstrated how Web Server automatically deployed a .war file during *startup*. The following illustrates how to auto-deploy a Java web application by *dynamically reconfiguring* a running server after unpacking the contents of the web application into a subdirectory of the instance's auto-deploy directory:

```
C:\Sun\WebServer7\https-test\auto-deploy>mkdir simple
C:\Sun\WebServer7\https-test\auto-deploy>cd simple
```

```
C:\Sun\WebServer7\https-test\auto-deploy\simple>jar xf C:\Sun\
    WebServer7\samples\java\webapps\simple\webapps-simple.war
C:\Sun\WebServer7>https-test\bin\reconfig.bat
info ( 4092): CORE3276: Installing a new configuration
info ( 4092): WEB0100: Loading web module in virtual server [test] at
    [/simple]
info ( 4092): PWC3031: Security role name tomcat used in an <auth-con-
    straint> without being defined in a <security-role> in context [/
    simple]
info ( 4092): PWC3031: Security role name role1 used in an <auth-con-
    straint> without being defined in a <security-role> in context [/
    simple]
```

Note: Bold font is used to illustrate how the Web Server uses the name of the directory for the context path into which to deploy the application.

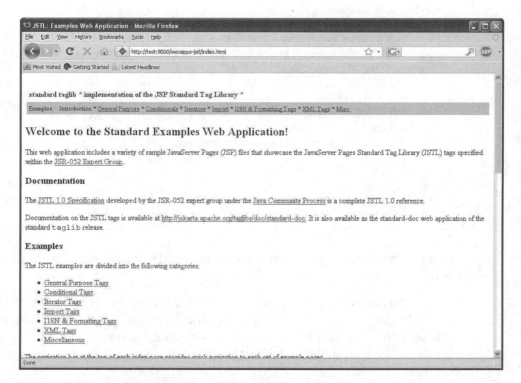

Figure 10.16   Auto-Deployed Java Web Application

Removing the .war file or the directory corresponding to an auto-deployed web application results in undeployment of the application. On UNIX platforms, this delete operation can be performed even when the server is running. However, on Windows platforms, you must stop the server before deleting the file/directory as attempts to delete the file or directory of an auto-deployed application while the server is running result in an error message similar to the following:

```
C:\Sun\WebServer7>del https-test\auto-deploy\webapps-jstl.war
C:\Sun\WebServer7\https-test\auto-deploy\webapps-jstl.war
The process cannot access the file because it is being used by another
    process.
```

Undeploying an auto-deployed application simply involves deleting the corresponding file/directory, as illustrated in the following (on UNIX platforms, reconfig.bat can be used instead of startserv.bat to undeploy the application from a running server):

```
C:\Sun\WebServer7>del https-test\auto-deploy\webapps-jstl.war
C:\Sun\WebServer7>https-test\bin\startserv.bat
Sun Java System Web Server 7.0U3 B06/16/2008 11:32
info: CORE5076: Using [Java HotSpot(TM) Server VM, Version 1.5.0_15]
    from [Sun Microsystems Inc.]
info: WEB0100: Loading web module in virtual server [test] at [/
    simple]
info: PWC3031: Security role name tomcat used in an <auth-constraint>
    without being defined in a <security-role> in context [/simple]
info: PWC3031: Security role name role1 used in an <auth-constraint>
    without being defined in a <security-role> in context [/simple]
info: HTTP3072: http-listener-1: http://test:9000 ready to accept
    requests
info: CORE3274: successful server startup
```

The Administration framework in Web Server currently provides no support for managing applications in the auto-deploy directory. Neither the list-webapps subcommand of wadm nor the Virtual Server Web Applications screen in Figure 10.17 include the Java web applications in the server's auto-deploy directory.

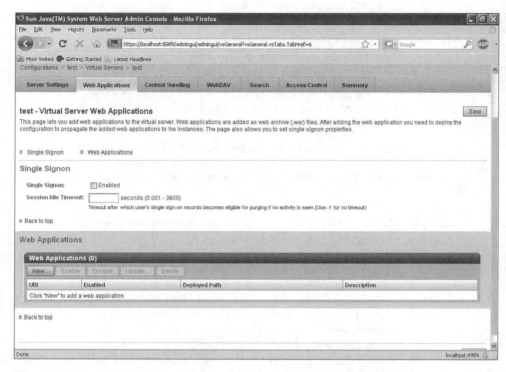

Figure 10.17   Administration Console—Virtual Server Web Applications

10.5.4.4 Manual Deployment

To manually deploy a Java web application to a specific virtual server, simply extract the contents of the web application into a directory on the file system. Then edit the server instance's `server.xml` file and add a `web-app` subelement with the relevant information about the web application you extracted onto the file system within the correct `virtual-server` element. Example 10.9 shows an example of what the `virtual-server` would look like after these changes. The web application's `path` subelement specifies the path on the file system to the directory containing the web application's files. Starting, restarting, or dynamically reconfiguring the server deploys the newly added web application into the specified virtual server.

To manually undeploy a web application, simply delete the corresponding `web-app` element from `server.xml` and dynamically reconfigure or restart the server.

Note: When making manual changes to the configuration of an instance, it is recommended that the `pull-config` subcommand of `wadm` or the Administration Console be used to synchronize the manual changes with configuration maintained by Web Server's administration framework.

10.5.4.5 Default Web Application

A Java web application that is deployed using "/" as the context path is known as the default web application (for the virtual server into which it has been deployed). The default web application processes requests for resources that are not part of any of the other web applications hosted by the virtual server. In a Java-enabled Web Server, every virtual server has its own default web application.

Default web application configuration is either explicit (user-assigned) or implicit (system assigned). Any Java web application can be configured as the default web application for a virtual server simply by assigning "/" as its context path (URI), as illustrated in Example 10.10.

Example 10.10   Default Web Application Excerpt from the `server.xml` File

```
<virtual-server>
  <name>test</name>
  <host>test</host>
  <http-listener-name>http-listener-1</http-listener-name>
  <document-root>../docs</document-root>
  <web-app>
    <uri>/</uri>
    <path>../web-app/test/simple</path>
    <description>Simple Sample Application</description>
  </web-app>
</virtual-server>
```

A virtual server that is configured as is shown in Example 10.10 displays the Simple Sample Application's index page for client requests that do not specify a partial URI or specify "/" as the URI.

If a default web application is not explicitly configured for a virtual server, then Web Server implicitly creates a default web application, using the virtual server's document root directory as the base directory of the web application. Unlike a user-assigned default web application, an implicit default web application is not represented by a corresponding `web-app` element in `server.xml`.

10.5.5 Session Management in Java Web Applications

A session is defined as a series of related requests from a client to the server. Either a specific HTTP cookie or a specific parameter in the URL is used to track Java web application sessions. The Java web container creates and maintains Java objects that represent user sessions. These session objects reside on the server and are identified by a unique identifier. The client and the server use this session identifier to track sessions across multiple requests. Web applications may store application-specific data in a session object. A session object persists for a specified period of time, after which it is deemed to have expired. Session objects and any attributes that may be stored in them are not shared between web applications. Each Java web application in Web Server has a session manager that maintains and manages any sessions that the application may create.

Web Server 7.0 includes support for Java web application sessions and provides several configuration options for session management. Because session objects consume system resources, configuring how Web Server manages sessions becomes important for busy web sites. Configuring session management for a web application in Web Server involves

- Deciding where sessions are stored (i.e., in memory, on disk, in a database, or replicated)
- Choosing an optimum timeout value that controls session expiration (choosing a very large timeout could lead to unnecessary waste of memory caused by idle sessions; choosing a short timeout could lead to frequent session creation caused by frequent session expiration)
- Determining the total size of attributes stored in each session
- Deciding the maximum number of active sessions to allow
- Configuring the Java heap size

The default storage area for sessions in Web Server is in memory. This means that all session information is lost when the server is stopped or restarted. Web Server also includes other types of session managers that maintain sessions in persistent storage such as on the file system or in databases.

10.5.5.1 Session Managers

A web application session is deemed to have expired after a period of inactivity. The session timeout value controls when the session is deemed to have expired. Every web application's session manager executes a thread that periodically examines all the sessions in the application to determine whether any have expired, and if so the manager purges the session from storage. The frequency at which a session manager processes sessions for expiry is controlled by the `reapIntervalSeconds` property configured in `sun-web.xml`. Proper configuration of the session timeout (usually specified by the `session-timeout` element in `web.xml`) and the session manager reap interval contribute to efficient resource utilization. For example, to ensure that expired sessions don't waste storage, the session manager should be configured to purge sessions more frequently when the session timeout is set to a small value. In an application with long-lived sessions, the session manager can be configured to run less frequently, thus saving computing resources.

To specify session manager configuration, use the `session-manager` element in a web application's `sun-web.xml` file. The *Sun Java System Web Server 7.0 Developer's Guide to Java Web Applications* contains a complete chapter that describes each of the session managers included with Web Server 7.0 in more detail.

10.5.5.2 Session Replication

The session replication feature introduced in Web Server 7.0 provides a limited level of high availability for session data in Java web applications running in a Web Server 7.0 cluster that is accessed via a load balancer. When session replication is enabled in a Web Server 7.0 cluster, each Web Server instance in the cluster replicates all its Java web application sessions on another instance in the cluster. In the event of failure in one of the nodes in the cluster, the load balancer directs the request to another node, which then retrieves the session data from the backup node on which the data was replicated. Session replication encodes the location of every session's backup node (in the cluster) in a cookie and hence requires that the browser used for accessing the application accept HTTP cookies.

Enabling session replication in a cluster involves enabling this feature in the web application as well as in the server in each node of the cluster.

Enabling session replication in a Java web application involves specifying the following in the application's `sun-web.xml` file:

```
<session-manager persistence-type="replicated"/>
```

The `session-replication` element in the `server.xml` file configures Java web application session replication within a server cluster. Figure 10.18 demonstrates the screen in Web Server 7.0's administration console that configures values for this element.

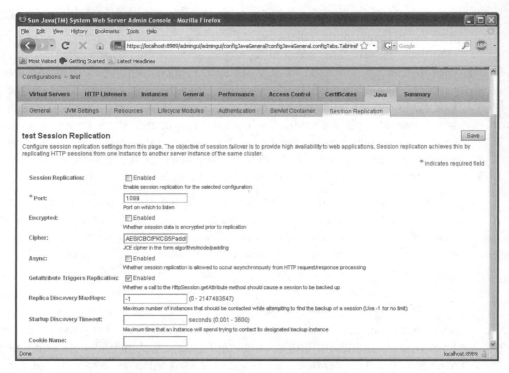

Figure 10.18 Administration Console—Session Replication

The get-session-replication-prop and set-session-replication-prop subcommands of wadm may also be used to configure session replication in a server cluster.

10.5.6 Java Web Application Security

Web Server 7.0's Java web container provides a highly secure environment based on the Java EE security model. The security aspects of Web Server's Java web container include the following:

- Full compliance with the security model specified in the Java Servlet Specification Version 2.5
- Support for the Access Control List (ACL)–based security model, in addition to the Java Servlet security model
- Support for Java Security Manager. For performance reasons, the Java Security Manager is disabled by default. It is recommended that the Java Security Manager be enabled during development.

- Support for single sign-on across all Java web applications within a single security domain. This feature enables sharing of user authentication information among applications and thereby avoids requiring the user to authenticate to each application.

- Support for Programmatic Login. Programmatic Login enables a Java web application to invoke a login method.

- Support for several underlying authentication realms, such as file and LDAP

- Support for SSL client certificate authentication

- Support for Solaris PAM

- Support for Web Services Message Security

- Support for declarative security through Web Server–specific XML-based role mapping

You specify security configuration in Web Server by using several different directives across various configuration files such as `server.xml`, `server.policy`, `login.conf`, `obj.conf`, `web.xml`, and `sub-web.xml`. Refer to the "Securing Web Applications" chapter in the *Sun Java System Web Server 7.0 Developer's Guide to Java Web Applications* and to the "Controlling Access to Your Server" chapter in the *Sun Java System Web Server 7.0 Administrator's Guide* for more information on the security features of Web Server 7.0.

10.5.7 Caching in Java Web Applications

Execution of a servlet or JSP dynamically generates the response for a servlet or JSP request. Caching dynamic responses or caching portions of dynamic responses contributes to faster response times and better usage of computing resources. Java web applications deployed in Web Server 7.0 can be configured to enable response caching for requests to servlets, JSPs, and other resources within the Java web application. Web Server 7.0 also includes a custom tag library that web application developers can use to cache JSP page fragments.

Web Server leverages its file cache when processing requests for static content within Java web applications. Enable caching of dynamic content in Java web applications by configuring the `cache` element in the application's `sun-web.xml` deployment descriptor as follows:

```
<cache enabled="true">
```

10.5.7.1 Caching Entire Responses

Caching configuration for responses is specified in the cache element of the sun-web.xml file and includes support for the following:

- Caching the response from a servlet identified by the servlet name
- Caching the response from a servlet identified by a URL pattern
- Caching responses from requests that use the web application's Request Dispatcher interface
- Caching criteria configuration using constraints such as HTTP methods, context attributes, request headers, request parameters, request cookies, session IDs, and session attributes
- Custom cache key generation
- Configuration of cache size, timeout, and other parameters

Refer to Appendix A of the *Sun Java System Web Server 7.0 Developer's Guide to Java Web Applications* for more information about the cache element in sun-web.xml.

Example 10.11 illustrates an example of cache configuration that caches one- and two-topping pizza menus for two minutes.

Example 10.11   Cache Configuration in the sun-web.xml File

```
<?xml version="1.0" encoding="UTF-8"?>
<!DOCTYPE sun-web-app PUBLIC
"-//Sun Microsystems, Inc.//DTD Application Server 8.1 Servlet 2.4//EN"
"http://www.sun.com/software/sunone/appserver/dtds/sun-web-app_2_4-1.
  dtd">

<sun-web-app>
   <cache enabled="true" timeout-in-seconds="120" >
      <cache-mapping>
         <servlet-name>YummyPizzasMenuServlet</servlet-name>
         <key-field name="toppings" scope="request.parameter"/>
         <constraint-field name="toppings" scope="request.parameter">
            <value>one</value>
            <value>two</value>
         </constraint-field>
      </cache-mapping>
   </cache>
</sun-web-app>
```

10.5.7.2 Caching Page Fragments

Web Server includes custom tags that enable JSP developers to cache JSP page fragments. These tags are specified in the *install_dir*/lib/tlds/sun-web-cache. tld tag library descriptor file. The JSP cache tags included with Web Server are as follows:

- cache—Caches the body between its begin and end tags
- flush—Flushes the entire cache or flushes a specified entry in the cache

To use these tags, copy the tag library descriptor (sun-web-cache.tld) to the WEB-INF directory of your Java web application and reference the tag library in your JSP. Example 10.12 demonstrates use of the cache tag in a JSP.

Example 10.12 Cache Tag Usage in a JSP

```
<%@ taglib prefix="suncache" uri="/com/sun/web/taglibs/cache" %>
<h1>Pizza Menu</h1>
<suncache:cache timeout="1h">
<b>Hourly Specials</b>
<br/>
<%
// Get the hourly specials
%>
</suncache:cache>
<b>Available toppings</b>
<%
// Get the list of pizza toppings
%>
```

Refer to the "Developing JavaServer Pages" chapter of the *Sun Java System Web Server 7.0 Developer's Guide to Java Web Applications* for more information about the cache tags included in Web Server.

10.5.8 Classloaders

Classloaders in a Java Virtual Machine (JVM) are responsible for finding and loading Java classes at runtime. Classloaders are organized into a hierarchy of parent classloaders and children classloaders. Classloaders follow a delegation model when loading a class. Classloaders first request the parent classloader to load the class and only if the parent classloader cannot load the class does the classloader attempt to load the class. If a class exists in a classloader as well as in its parent, the parent version is preferred. A parent classloader does not delegate classloading to any of its child classloaders. The Java classloader delegation model avoids `ClassCastExceptions` caused by the presence of multiple versions of the same class.

Figure 10.19 illustrates the delegation model between the various classloaders that are created by Web Server.

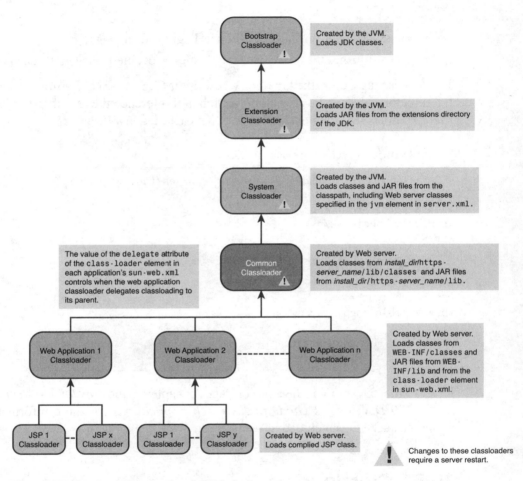

Figure 10.19   Java Classloaders in Web Server

The web application classloader follows the classloader delegation model recommended in "SRV.9.7.2 Web Application Class Loader" in the Java Servlet Specification Version 2.5 and attempts to load classes and resources within the Java web application before delegating to its parent classloader. You override this behavior by specifying the following in the web application's `sun-web.xml` file:

```
<class-loader delegate="true"/>
```

Understanding the role that each classloader plays in Web Server can help troubleshoot classloading problems. Additional information about Web Server's classloaders is available in the *Sun Java System Web Server 7.0 Developer's Guide to Java Web Applications*.

10.5.9 Dynamically Reconfiguring Java Web Applications

The dynamic reconfiguration feature in Web Server 7.0 includes support for Java web applications. During dynamic reconfiguration, only Java web applications that are determined to have changed are reloaded. Existing web applications that are unchanged continue to run without interruption. Existing session data (in applications that are unchanged) remains unchanged before, during, and after dynamic reconfiguration. Not requiring a server restart enables rapid deployment of changes during the application development cycle. The section titled "Global Java Settings" includes information about changing Java settings that require a server restart.

The types of changes that do not require that Web Server be restarted include the following:

- Adding and removing Java web applications
- Adding, removing, and updating Java web applications packaged as WAR files
- Adding, removing, and updating static content in the web application
- Adding, removing, and updating Java Servlet classes and JSPs in the web application
- Adding, removing, and updating Java archive (JAR) files in the web application
- Adding, removing, and updating Java web application deployment descriptors including `web.xml`, `sun-web.xml`, and tag library descriptors
- Changing web application configuration specified in the `web-app` element in `server.xml`
- Changing Java web container configuration specified in the `servlet-container` element in `server.xml`
- Changing the global deployment descriptor (`default-web.xml`) shared by all Java web applications
- Changing the contents of the `META-INF` and `WEB-INF` directories of the web application

Changes related to static content do not require dynamic reconfiguration for the changes to take effect. The file cache in Web Server automatically serves new static content when it detects that the content on disk is newer than the copy in the cache.

By default, the JSP engine in the Java web container in Web Server detects JSP changes and automatically recompiles the JSP when processing the request. You can change the default behavior of detecting JSP changes at request time by configuring the `reload-interval` property of the `jsp-config` element in the `sun-web.xml` file of the web application. Appendix A of the *Sun Java System Web Server 7.0 Developer's Guide to Java Web Applications* contains more information about this property.

During dynamic reconfiguration, the Java web container in Web Server 7.0 uses several heuristics to automatically determine whether a Java web application has "changed" and needs to be reloaded. Figure 10.20 illustrates how the Java web container determines whether a web application has to be reloaded or not when the server is dynamically reconfigured.

Web Server 7.0 includes support for enabling a web application developer or web site administrator to forcibly reload a web application. When this functionality is enabled, the Java web container looks for a file named `.reload` in the document root directory of each web application. The server reloads any web application that contains a `.reload` file that has been updated since the last time the server checked the web application. This feature is disabled by default and can be enabled by configuring a non-zero value for the dynamic reload interval property of the Java web container. The dynamic reload interval specifies the frequency at which the Java web container checks web applications for changes to the `.reload` file. Figure 10.21 shows the Administration Console screen that configures this property.

The following demonstrates using the `wadm` script to configure the Java web container to check for web application changes every 5 seconds:

```
wadm> set-servlet-container-prop --config=test dynamic-reload-
    interval=5
CLI201 Command 'set-servlet-container-prop' ran successfully
wadm> deploy-config test
CLI201 Command 'deploy-config' ran successfully
```

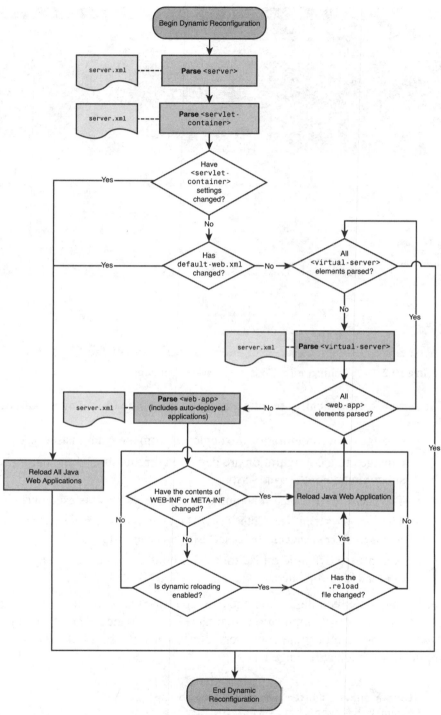

Figure 10.20 Dynamic Reconfiguration—Java Web Applications

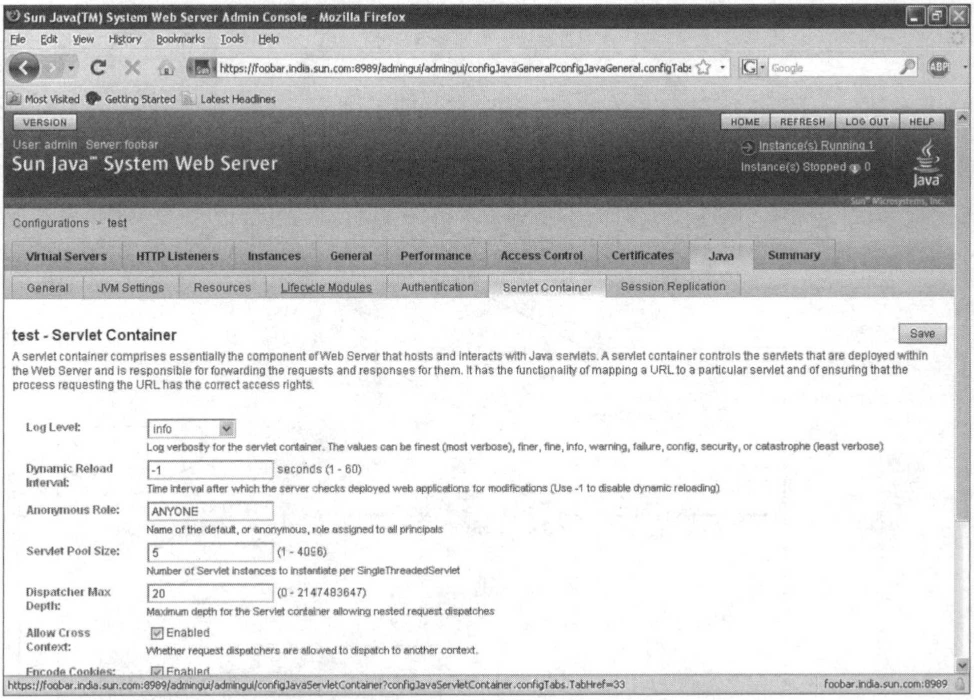

Figure 10.21   Administration Console—Servlet Container

The server is dynamically reconfigured when any of the following actions occur:

- Changes to a configuration are deployed from the Administration console.
- Changes to a configuration are deployed through use of the `deploy-config` subcommand of the `wadm` script.
- The `reconfig-instance` subcommand of the `wadm` script is executed.
- The `reconfig` script is executed (*install_root*/https-*instance*/bin/reconfig or *install_root*\https-*instance*\bin\reconfig.bat).
- A non-zero dynamic reload interval is configured and a web application's `.reload` file is updated.

During dynamic reconfiguration, the messages that the server logs to its error file indicate the Java web applications that have been reloaded. The following annotated example demonstrates how server messages can be used to identify web applications that have changed:

```
Start a server containing two Java web applications
C:\Sun\WebServer7>https-test\bin\startserv.bat
```

```
Sun Java System Web Server 7.0U3 B06/16/2008 11:32
info: CORE5076: Using [Java HotSpot(TM) Server VM, Version 1.5.0_15]
    from [Sun Microsystems Inc.]
info: WEB0100: Loading web module in virtual server [test] at [/
    simple]
info: WEB0100: Loading web module in virtual server [test] at [/
    WebApplication1]
info: HTTP3072: http-listener-1: http://test:9000 ready to accept
    requests
info: CORE3274: successful server startup
```

Reconfigure the server without changing anything and note the absence of messages related to web application loading

```
C:\Sun\WebServer7>https-test\bin\reconfig.bat
info: CORE3276: Installing a new configuration
info: CORE3280: A new configuration was successfully installed
```

Modify the deployment descriptor of one of the applications

```
C:\Sun\WebServer7>notepad https-test\web-app\test\simple\WEB-INF\
    web.xml
```

Reconfigure the server and note the message indicating that the application that was modified was reloaded

```
C:\Sun\WebServer7>https-test\bin\reconfig.bat
info: CORE3276: Installing a new configuration
info: WEB0100: Loading web module in virtual server [test] at [/
    simple]
info: CORE3280: A new configuration was successfully installed
```

10.6 Web Server and NetBeans

NetBeans is a free, open-source Integrated Development Environment (IDE) that can be used to create professional web applications. NetBeans IDE is easy to install and use and runs on many platforms including Solaris, Linux, Windows, and Mac.

The Sun Java System Web Server plugin for NetBeans IDE enables developers to easily develop, debug, and deploy Java web applications to Web Server 7.0. The plugin also enables developers to perform basic administration tasks on Web Server instances. The rest of this section uses screenshots to walk you through using NetBeans to develop, debug, and deploy Java web applications to Web Server 7.0.

10.6.1 Installing the Web Server 7.0 Plugin for the NetBeans IDE

This section briefly describes installing the NetBeans IDE itself and the IDE support modules (plugins) for Java web applications and Web Server 7.0.

Download and install NetBeans IDE from the NetBeans home page, http://www.netbeans.org, shown in Figure 10.22.

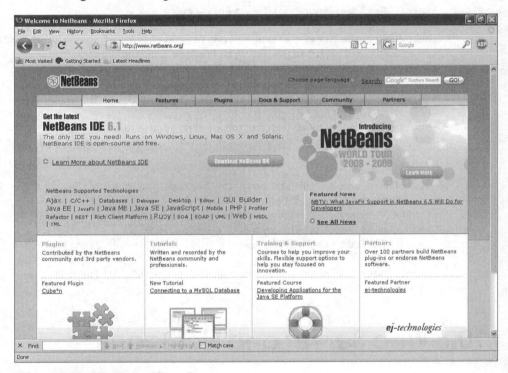

Figure 10.22   NetBeans Home Page

Start the NetBeans IDE and select the Plugins menu item of the Tools menu, as demonstrated in Figure 10.23.

Select and install the Sun Java System Web Server 7.0 plugin and the Web Applications plugin from the Available Plugins tab of the Plugins dialog box, as illustrated in Figure 10.24.

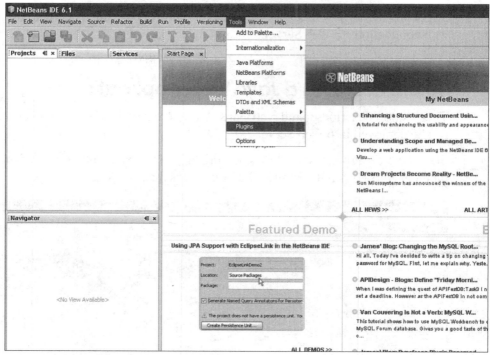

Figure 10.23   NetBeans IDE—Tools Menu

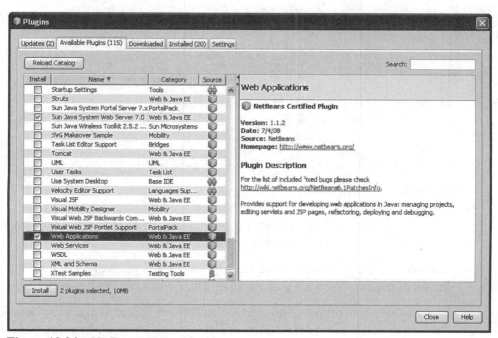

Figure 10.24   NetBeans IDE—Plugins

NetBeans IDE is now ready for use in developing, debugging, and deploying Java web applications to Web Server.

10.6.2 Creating a Java Web Application

This section describes using NetBeans IDE to create a Java web application that can be deployed into Web Server 7.0.

Start the New Project wizard by selecting the New Project menu item of the File menu in NetBeans IDE. Figure 10.25 illustrates this.

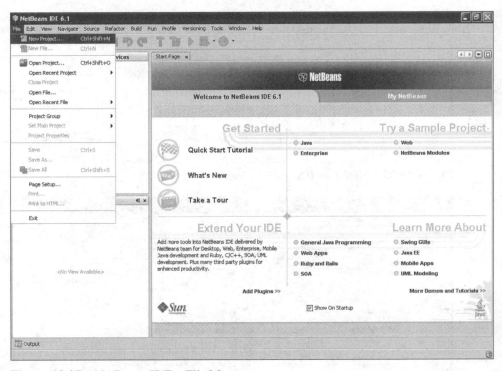

Figure 10.25   NetBeans IDE—File Menu

Choose to create a Web Application project and click on the Next button in the New Project wizard, shown in Figure 10.26.

Specify a name and location for the new web application and click on the Next button of the New Web Application dialog box, illustrated in Figure 10.27.

The next step is to register the target server for web application deployment. Click Add, as shown in Figure 10.28. You can also register a server by using the Servers menu item of the Tools menu.

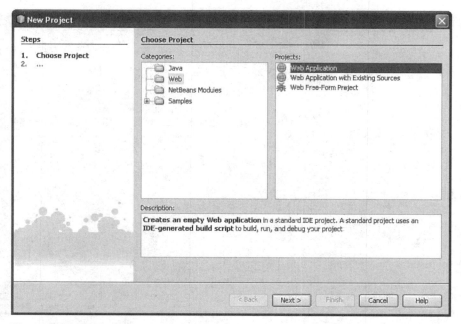

Figure 10.26 NetBeans IDE—New Project Wizard

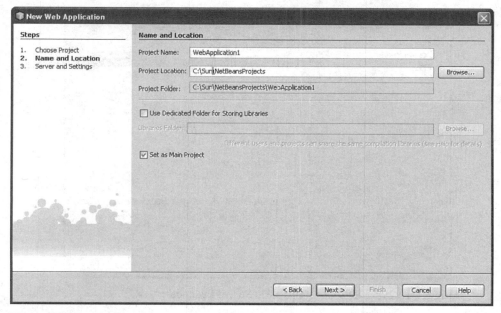

Figure 10.27 NetBeans IDE—New Web Application

Select Sun Java System Web Server 7.0 and click on the Next button in the Add Server Instance dialog box depicted in Figure 10.29.

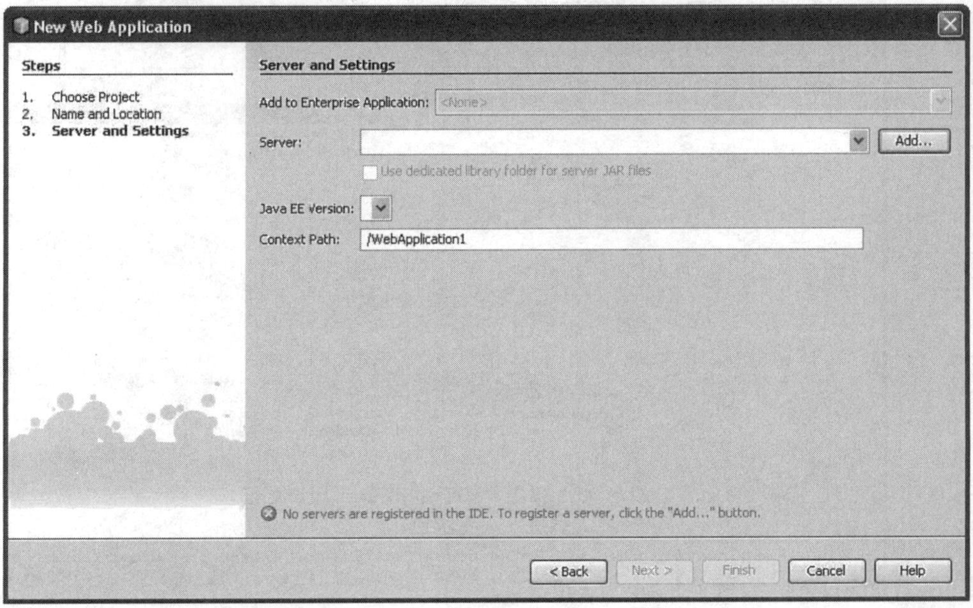

Figure 10.28   NetBeans IDE—Register Server

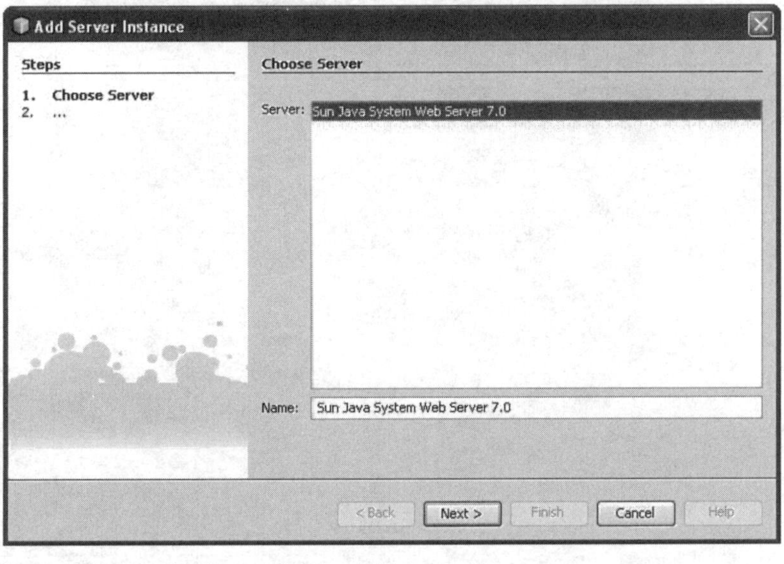

Figure 10.29   NetBeans IDE—Add Server Instance

Similar to what Figure 10.30 demonstrates, specify the location and configuration of your Web Server 7.0 installation and click the Finish button to complete registering your Web Server with NetBeans IDE.

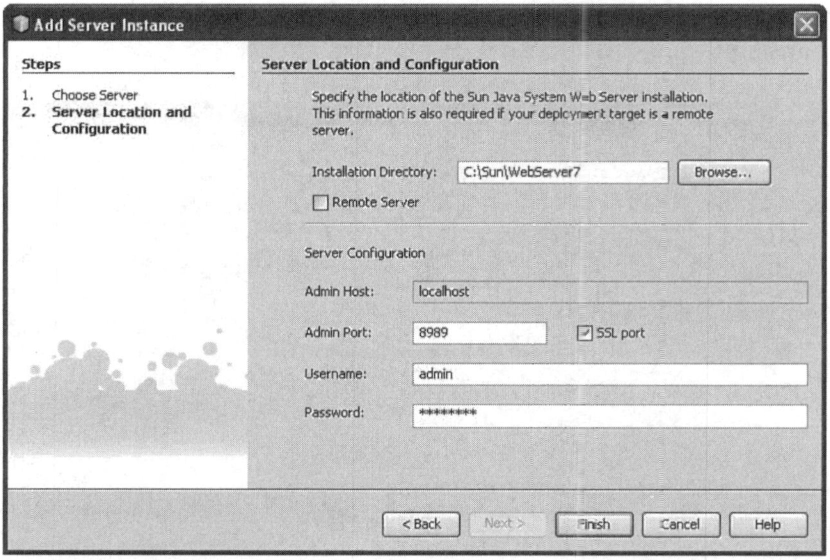

Figure 10.30 NetBeans IDE—Server Location and Configuration

Figure 10.31 illustrates the final step in creating a new web application. When compared to Figure 10.28, note that the server field now shows "Sun Java System Web Server 7.0." Click the Finish button to complete web application creation.

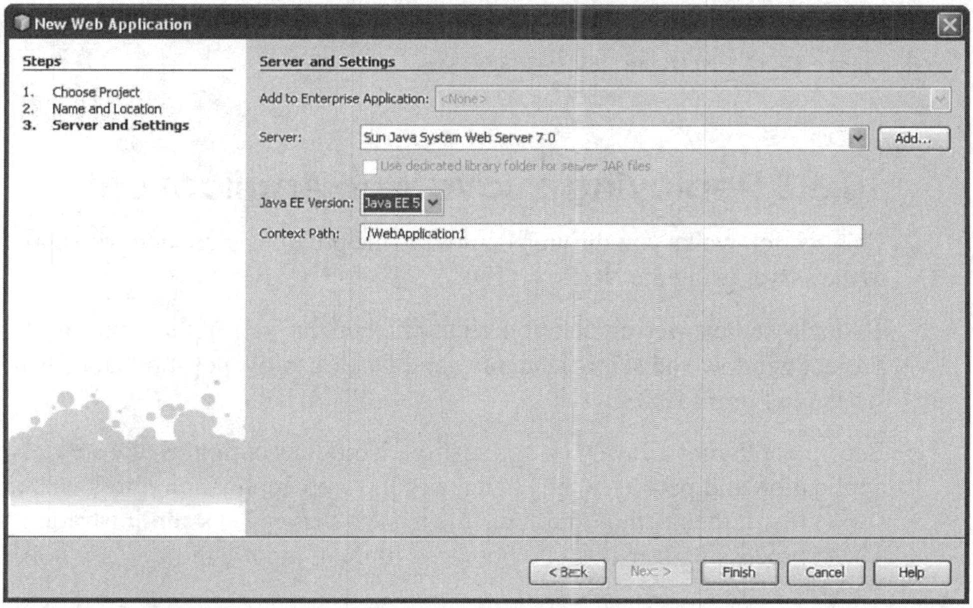

Figure 10.31 NetBeans IDE—New Web Application

Figure 10.32 displays the default `index.jsp` file that NetBeans IDE created in the new web application.

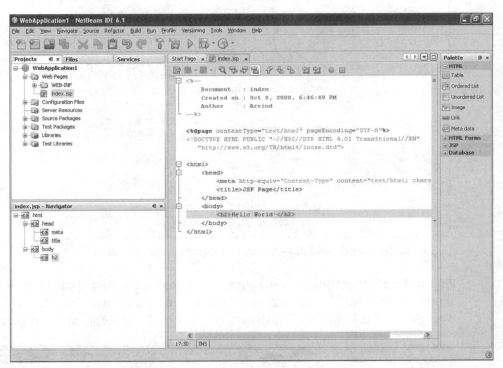

Figure 10.32   NetBeans IDE—`index.jsp`

10.6.3 Deploying a Java Web Application

This section walks you through deploying the previously created web application to the server using the NetBeans IDE.

To deploy a Java web application, right-click on the web application's name in the Project window and select Undeploy and Deploy in the pop-up menu, as demonstrated in Figure 10.33.

Before deploying a Java web application, NetBeans compiles any servlets in the application and packages the contents of the web application into a web archive (`.war`) file. It then deploys the `.war` file to Web Server 7.0's administration server. These processing steps can be observed in the Output window shown in Figure 10.34.

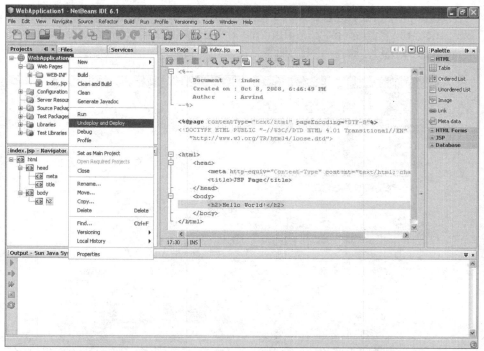

Figure 10.33 NetBeans IDE—Deploy web application

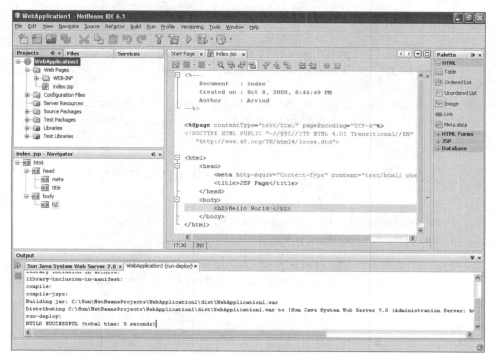

Figure 10.34 NetBeans IDE—Deploy Output Window

To deploy and run the web application that was just deployed from NetBeans, select the Run menu item from the web application's pop-up menu, as shown in Figure 10.35.

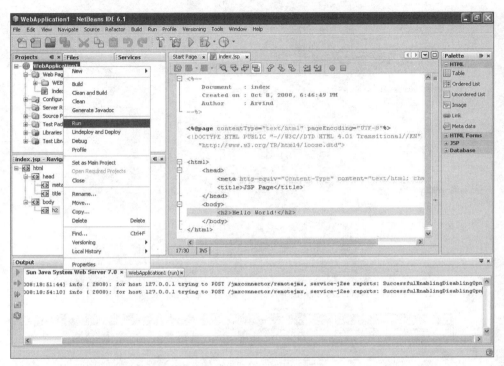

Figure 10.35   NetBeans IDE—Run a Web Application

To run the application, the NetBeans IDE starts a web browser and accesses the web application from the browser, as Figure 10.36 demonstrates.

10.6.4 Basic Web Server Administration

The Web Server plug-in for NetBeans also enables developers to perform some basic administration operations on a Web Server installation from within the NetBeans IDE.

Figure 10.37 identifies the administration tasks that are available by right-clicking on the Sun Java System Web Server 7.0 server in the Services tab of the IDE.

Figure 10.36   Sample Web Application Accessed Through a Browser

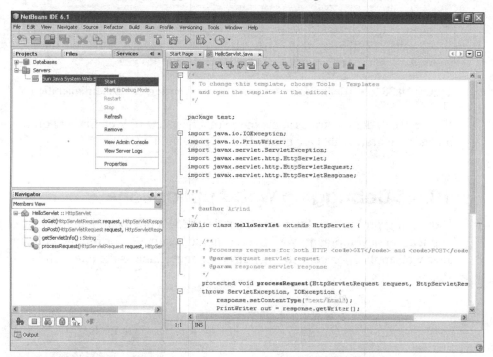

Figure 10.37   NetBeans IDE—Services—Basic Web Server 7.0 Administration

When Web Server 7.0 is managed from NetBeans, a new tab in the Output window contains the server's log messages. The Sun Java System Web Server 7.0 tab also contains buttons that enable developers to perform common tasks such as starting and stopping the server. Figure 10.38 shows an example of such a tab.

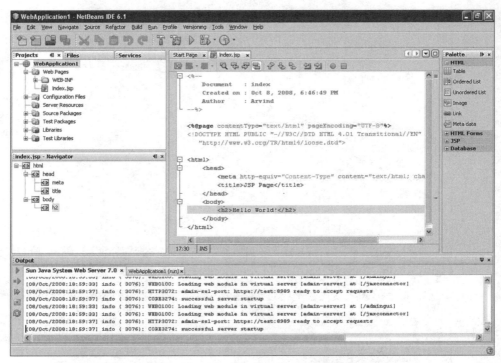

Figure 10.38   NetBeans IDE—Output—Basic Web Server 7.0 Administration

Figure 10.39 demonstrates some of the other aspects of Web Server configuration and administration that are exposed via NetBeans.

10.6.5 Debugging Web Applications

Debugging problems within servlet code or JSP code is an integral part of web application development. Web Server includes support for remote debugging of Java web application code, using a Java debugger such as the one included in NetBeans.

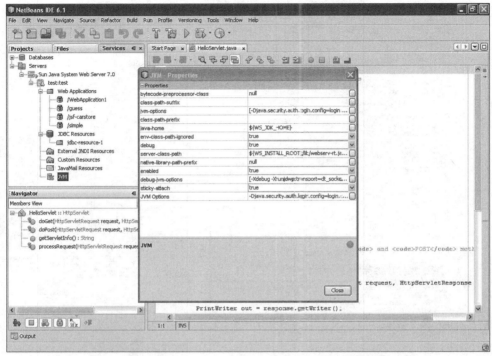

Figure 10.39   NetBeans IDE—Services—Web Server 7.0 Configuration

For the purposes of this exercise, we shall add a sample servlet to the web application created previously and then proceed to demonstrate setting a breakpoint in the servlet's Java code.

To add a servlet to the web application, right-click the name of the web application in the Projects window to bring up the pop-up menu and then select the Servlet menu item in the New menu, as demonstrated in Figure 10.40.

Enter a class and package name for the servlet and then click on the Next button in the New Servlet wizard, as shown in Figure 10.41.

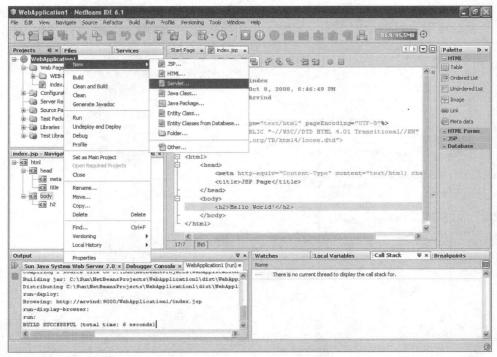

Figure 10.40   NetBeans IDE—Add Servlet

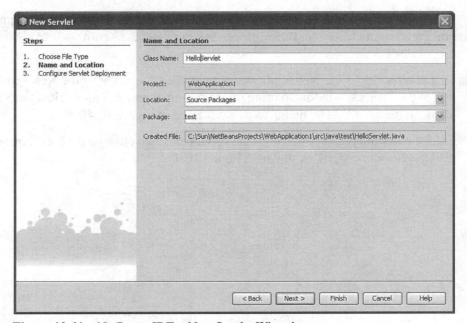

Figure 10.41   NetBeans IDE—New Servlet Wizard

Configure the servlet deployment parameters by specifying a URL pattern to access the servlet and check the Add Information to Deployment Descriptor (web. xml) check box so that NetBeans automatically creates and populates a web application deployment descriptor. Figure 10.42 demonstrates this.

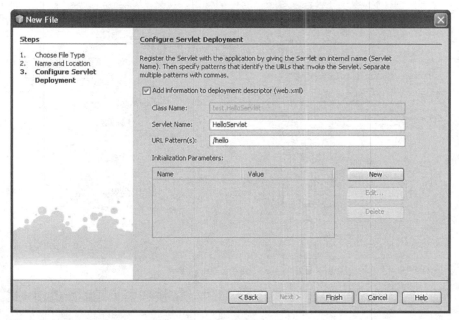

Figure 10.42   NetBeans IDE—New File Wizard

Clicking on the Finish button in Figure 10.42 creates the `HelloServlet.java` servlet shown in Figure 10.43.

Figure 10.44 demonstrates `HelloServlet` in action when deployed to Web Server and then accessed from a browser.

To set a breakpoint in the servlet, simply click on the left margin of the source display window. Execution stops at the breakpoint the next time the servlet is executed and the developer can control execution through the rest of the servlet by using the NetBeans IDE. A highlighted red line identifies a breakpoint. Figure 10.45 shows a breakpoint at the highlighted code statement `out.println("<html>");`.

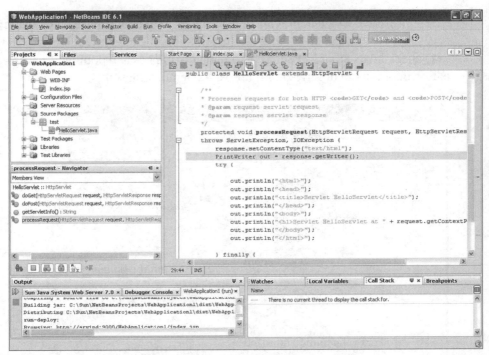

Figure 10.43   NetBeans IDE—HelloServlet.java

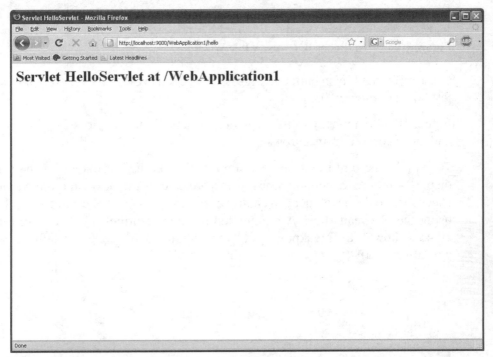

Figure 10.44   NetBeans IDE—HelloServlet

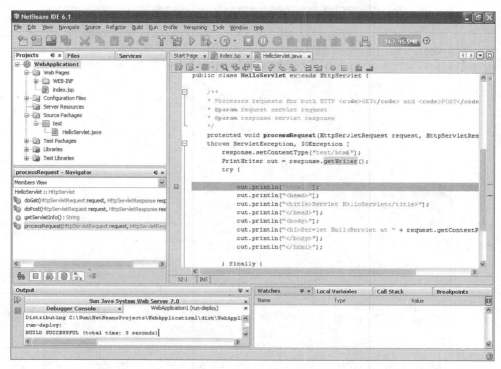

Figure 10.45   NetBeans IDE—Java Debugger Breakpoint

A highlighted green line identifies the line of code where execution has stopped. The Java debugger in the NetBeans IDE enables developers to easily examine and debug application code running in Web Server.

To debug a web application in which breakpoints have been set, simply right-click the application in the Projects window and select the Debug menu item from the pop-up menu, as shown in Figure 10.46.

Figure 10.47 illustrates a debugging session where servlet execution has stopped at the breakpoint set at the `out.println("<html>");` statement on line 32 in `HelloServlet.java`.

To end a debugging session, select Finish Debugger Session from the Run menu, as shown in Figure 10.48.

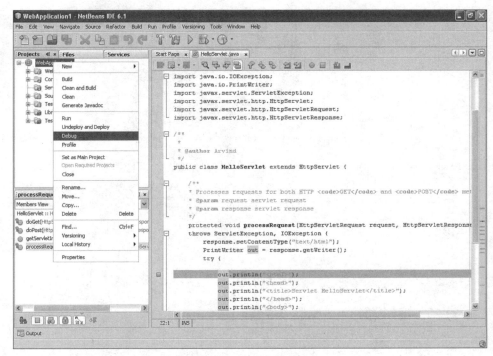

Figure 10.46   NetBeans IDE—Start Java Debugging Session

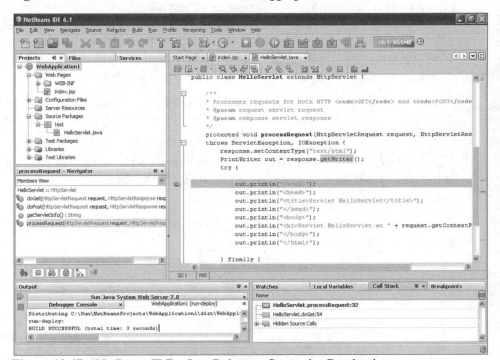

Figure 10.47   NetBeans IDE—Java Debugger Stopped at Breakpoint

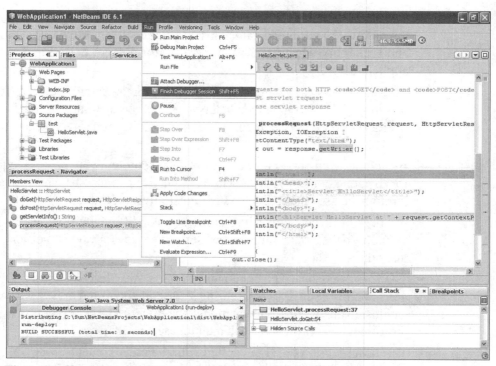

Figure 10.48 NetBeans IDE—Finish Debugger Session

10.7 Summary

Web Server's multi-threaded, multi-process architecture provides a secure, scalable platform for hosting both static and dynamic content on a variety of operating systems. All aspects of the server can be configured and managed by using the Administration Server either via the graphical user interface or the command line interface.

The following summarizes some of the features and benefits of the integrated Java web container in Web Server 7.0:

- Web Server's Java web container includes support for the following Java technologies: Servlet 2.5, JSP 2.1, JSTL 1.2, JavaMail, JDBC, JDBC connection-pools, JSF 1.2, JNDI, JAX-WS 2.0, JAXB 2.0, JAXP 1.3.1, SOAP 1.2, WSDL 1.1, SAAJ 1.3, XWSS-XML, Fast Infoset, Message Security, Java web application session replication, and server Lifecycle modules.

- The Java web container is implemented as an NSAPI plug-in that is both thread-aware and thread-safe. This contributes to improved performance and scalability when processing requests for content hosted in Java web applications.

- The single-process, multi-threaded architecture wherein the Java Virtual Machine (JVM) is embedded in the worker process eliminates much of the overhead and latency incurred by the multi-process Apache/Tomcat model.

- By default, Web Server instances are already configured to process requests for dynamic content in Java. The Java plug-in can also be easily disabled through the use of Web Server's administrative interfaces.

- It is possible to customize the configuration of different virtual servers individually so that some of the virtual servers are Java-aware at the same time that others are not.

- The in-process Java web container leverages Web Server's highly efficient and scalable file cache when serving static content hosted in Java web applications. In the Apache/Tomcat model, the Apache HTTP server process and the Tomcat server process each maintain separate file caches.

- The Java plug-in is well integrated with the other content-processing subsystems (such as CGI, SHTML) in the server. This gives content developers the flexibility to mix Java and non-Java content in the same page.

- Web Server's administrative graphical (web) interface and robust command-line tool includes support for configuring all aspects of the integrated Java web container.

- Many of the files (such as `obj.conf`, `server.xml` and `magnus.conf`) that specify the configuration of other components in the server also specify Java web container configuration. The XML schema that describes the contents of `server.xml` also includes validation rules for Java web container configuration. Web Server's robust configuration validation protects web site users from server misconfigurations.

- The Administration Server's graphical user interface is implemented through the use of Java web application technologies.

- Almost all the Java web container's configuration settings can be changed even when the server is running. This contributes to an improved developer experience because deploying changes to the Java components in the server doesn't require that the developer restart the server.

- Web Server can automatically deploy and run web applications packaged as web application archives (.war files) and doesn't require that the contents of the archive be extracted to a directory.

- The NetBeans plug-in for Web Server 7.0 provides NetBeans users with basic web server administration facilities.

- Web Server's Java web container includes full support for debugging and profiling Java web applications with a Java IDE such as NetBeans.

10.8 Self-Paced Labs

Use the information contained in this chapter to perform the following exercises. These will help validate your understanding of the concepts described in this chapter.

1. Start your Administration Server. Identify and access the Java web applications in the Administration Server.

2. Identify the version of the Java Virtual Machine (JVM) that the Administration Server uses.

3. Identify the Java heap configuration of a Java-enabled server, using the Administration console or the command line interface (wadm). What are the default values used to specify the minimum heap size and the maximum heap size of the Java Virtual Machine (JVM)?

4. Examine and build the sample Java web applicatons included with Web Server.

5. Deploy a Java web application archive to the server and access the web application, using a browser.

6. Deploy and access a Java web application, using the automatic deployment feature in Web Server.

7. Configure a Java web application to be the default web application of a virtual server. Access the default web application to ensure that it has been configured correctly. Now disable the Java web application, using either the administration console or the command line interface and deploy the changes. What happens when you access the default web application of the virtual server?

8. Do you have to restart the server for the server to detect changes made to JSP files in a Java web application?

9. Does the `.reload` file need to be updated for the server to detect changes made to JSP files in a Java web application?

10. Does the `.reload` file need to be updated for the server to detect changes made to Java classes and deployment descriptors in a Java web application?

11. Create and deploy a Java web application to Web Server, using the NetBeans IDE.

12. Make changes to the Java web application and re-deploy it to Web Server.

13. Using NetBeans IDE, set a breakpoint within a servlet in your Java web application and then access the servlet with a browser. Use the Java debugger in NetBeans to trace execution through the servlet.

14. Enable and configure caching in a Java web application. Does caching help improve your application's response times?

Note: Go to www.sunwebserver.com for detailed instructions on how to perform each of these exercises.

11

Troubleshooting Web Server 7.0

WEB Server is a complex piece of software that fulfills the requirements of an enterprise-quality web server and is also developer-friendly. Web Server 7.0 provides a highly scalable, secure, extensible multi-threaded, multi-process platform for hosting web-based applications on a number of UNIX/Linux platforms as well as on Windows. Web Server includes support for a number of dynamic technologies such as CGI, FastCGI, SHTML, JSP, Servlets and Web Services. You can extend the functionality of the server by using NSAPI plug-ins. You can use an Integrated Development Environment (IDE) such as NetBeans IDE to develop and deploy Java web applications to Web Server. Web Server contains built-in support for using a Lightweight Directory Access Protocol (LDAP) server for authenticating users. Web Server can be configured as a reverse-proxy server that distributes requests to other web and application servers. Web Server 7.0 includes a well designed web-based graphical interface and a robust command-line tool for managing Web Server instances. The administrative framework includes functionality to deploy, manage, and monitor a web server or a cluster of web servers.

Problems encountered when using Web Server may be attributed to a number of factors including, but not limited to, configuration errors, insufficient memory, errors in third-party NSAPI plug-ins, errors in other servers that Web Server interacts with, and faults in the server itself. Knowledge of how Hypertext Transfer Protocol (HTTP) works, understanding operating system concepts and client-server computing, and understanding how Web Server works and having a logical, systematic approach to problem-solving are great assets for diagnosing and fixing Web Server problems.

This chapter provides useful information for troubleshooting problems in Web Server 7.0. Specifically, this chapter describes guidelines, methodologies, and tools for identifying, analyzing, and finding solutions to problems encountered when using Web Server 7.0. The information in this chapter is intended to supplement the information found in the *Sun Java System Web Server 7.0 Troubleshooting Guide*.

11.1 The Crimes

Errors encountered with Web Server 7.0 can be broadly categorized into the following:

- Installation problems
- Startup problems
- Crashes
- Hangs
- Runtime errors
- Performance/Scalability problems
- Administration problems
- Migration errors
- Uninstallation problems

The remainder of this section briefly describes each of these categories.

11.1.1 Installation Problems

Problems encountered while installing Web Server 7.0 are typically caused by a lack of resources such as memory, disk space, or insufficient permissions to install the server in the specified directory. Installation errors may also occur when you try to install Web Server 7.0 on a platform that does not meet the minimum system requirements for Web Server 7.0. Installation errors are reported to the user console and are also recorded in the installer's log files.

11.1.2 Startup Problems

Errors that occur during server startup typically prevent the server from being started from either the command line or the Administration Console. Common causes for startup failures include errors in one or more of the configuration files, file ownership/permissions problem, lack of system resources such as memory, errors in third-party NSAPI plug-ins, and port conflicts with other processes on the system. Startup errors are reported to the user console and are also recorded in the server's error logs. On Windows, startup errors are also reported to the Windows Event Log service.

11.1.3 Crashes

A crash is an abnormal termination of a process. Web Server crashes result in disruption of service to end-users. Examples of catastrophic errors that can cause Web Server to crash include an acute shortage of key system resources such as memory, buffer overflow errors in NSAPI plug-ins, fatal errors in the Java Virtual Machine (JVM), hardware errors, errors in the operating system, and memory corruption errors in any of the processes that comprise Web Server 7.0. Evidence of server crashes is usually recorded in error messages in the server's log files. Additionally, a core file that contains the memory image of the process when it crashed may be found on UNIX/Linux systems.

11.1.4 Hangs

A server is said to be hanging when it stops responding to client requests. Hangs may also occur intermittently and only cause temporary disruption of service to end-users. A server hang may be caused by resource contention within Web Server, lack of system resources, synchronization issues in NSAPI plug-ins, synchronization issues in the Java Virtual Machine (JVM), or problems in a back-end server such as an application server or directory server or database server from which Web Server has requested a resource. You can detect server hangs by using Web Server's monitoring facilities in conjunction with other operating system commands.

11.1.5 Runtime Errors

Runtime errors are those that occur while the server is running but do not result in abnormal program termination. Examples of runtime errors include those that occur while processing requests for dynamic content such as CGI/FastCGI programs, SHTML files, and Java web applications. Application configuration errors, user authentication and authorization errors, and errors related to Secure Sockets Layer (SSL) configuration are other examples of runtime errors.

11.1.6 Performance/Scalability Problems

If Web Server appears to be slow in responding to client requests or if Web Server cannot handle a large number of simultaneous client requests, then this might indicate that one or more of the subsystems in the server are not functioning optimally. Causes of performance/scalability limitations include poorly configured systems, poorly configured servers, network issues such as low bandwidth or high latency, other resource-hungry processes that are running on the same system as Web Server, multi-threading issues in NSAPI plug-ins, time-intensive operations such as complex database queries, and compute-intensive operations such as encryption and compression that may be executed when processing client requests.

11.1.7 Administration Problems

This category includes errors that occur when managing Web Server instances using either the web-based Administration Console or the command-line tool. Causes of errors encountered when using Web Server 7.0's administrative framework can include lack of system resources, configuration errors caused by manual edits, user error, JVM errors, and problems in the administrative framework itself. These errors are logged in the Administration Server's/Node's error log files and are also reported to the administrator via the Administration Console or the command-line tool.

11.1.8 Migration Errors

Errors can occur when you migrate server instances from earlier versions of Web Server to Web Server 7.0. Web Server 7.0 enables you to perform your migration using either a graphical user interface or an administrative command-line interface. Migration errors can be caused by incorrect file ownerships/permissions, configuration errors in the server being migrated, and a lack of system resources such as disk space. Detailed migration information, including errors, is recorded in the migration log file.

11.1.9 Uninstallation Problems

Causes of uninstallation errors include insufficient user privileges and file access issues such as trying to delete a Web Server file that is being used by some other process on the system. Errors that occur during uninstallation may require manual intervention before the server can be re-installed on the system. Uninstallation errors are reported to the user console and are also recorded in the uninstaller's log files.

11.2 Canvassing the Neighborhood

To comprehensively describe the problem, you must gather details about the hardware, operating system, Web Server environment, and the browser. The rest of this section calls attention to details you should consider when gathering this information.

11.2.1 Hardware Information

Gathering information about the system on which you are running can be as valuable, if not more so, than simply stating the problem. Some problems can be attributed to hardware, operating systems (or patches), software release levels of your Web Server, or how the Web Server interacts with other third-party applications.

The first step in gathering system information is to document your hardware environment. Pay particular attention to RAM, disk space, and the number and type of your CPUs. Document how much of each you have installed by default, and then determine how much of each is being used and how much is available.

In addition, determine how you are connected to the network and if you are using any other devices such as hardware accelerator cards.

11.2.2 Operating System Information

The next step in gathering information is to look at the operating system. What operating system are you running? What is the revision level? Have you installed any patches? What are the limitations on system resources available to Web Server? How much free disk space is available for use by Web Server? How much free memory is available? What other processes are running on the system?

11.2.3 Web Server Environment

The next step in gathering system information is to understand your Web Server environment.

Is your Web Server serving static and/or dynamic content? For what kinds of dynamic content (JSP, Servlets, FastCGI, SHTML, PHP, etc.) can the server process requests?

Have you enabled the Java plug-in? What is the version number of the Java Virtual Machine (JVM)? What JVM options have been configured? Have you specified additional Java Archive (JAR) files in the server's classpath? Is the Java Security Manager enabled? Have you configured additional Java resources such as database connection pools? Have you changed any settings in your server instance's `default-web.xml` file?

What type of NSAPI or third-party plug-ins are you running on this server? Is there a version number associated with the plug-in and has it been certified to run with this version of the Web Server?

Are you running SSL? If so, are you using a hardware accelerator card?

Are you having problems working with a specific web browser? Does the problem occur only when there are multiple simultaneous requests? Can you consistently reproduce the problem? What is the severity of the problem? Does the server start? Does the server crash? Does the server sporadically hang?

What is your network topology? How many Web Servers are you running? Where are they located? Are you performing any load balancing? Are you front-ending an application server? Is a proxy server or a load balancer routing requests to Web Server? Is there a firewall?

You need to know what other applications running on this server might be causing problems. For instance, is the Web Server machine also acting as an e-mail server or as an enterprise-wide directory server? If so, these applications might affect your Web Server's performance.

11.2.4 Environment on Other Servers

The next step in gathering system information is to understand the environment on other servers with which your Web Server might be interacting. If the Web Server is communicating with application servers, web service providers, or simply acting as a proxy to other web servers, then the environment on those servers might be an issue.

What are the versions of the servers with which Web Server interacts? Have there been any changes and/or upgrades to those servers? Are those versions supported by Web Server 7.0? Are there any known issues with these servers?

What protocol is used to communicate with the other servers? Are other applications also communicating with those servers over the same protocol? Are they having problems doing so?

Is the Web Server communicating with those servers over SSL? If so, has the communication been previously tested? What version of SSL is being used? What level of encryption is being used? Does the Web Server trust the certificate being used by the other server? Has anything changed on either server as it pertains to SSL?

Are there plug-ins or other special configuration settings that might have recently changed on the other server that might have affected Web Server? Are the plug-ins supported by Web Server 7.0?

Do you see the same problem when connecting to the other servers directly? If so, you should be able to rule out the possibility of the problem being in Web Server altogether.

11.2.5 HTTP Client Environment

The final step is to gather information regarding the HTTP client.

What kind of browser are you using? What's the browser's version number? Is the browser supported by Web Server 7.0? What version of HTTP is being used on the browser? Is the browser communicating with Web Server over SSL?

Is the problem localized to a particular browser, vendor, or version? Does the problem occur with older versions of the browser? Is the problem specific to a particular area of your network? Is the problem specific to requests for a specific type of content?

The next section describes the various areas in which problems are likely to occur.

11.3 The Usual Suspects

Figure 11.1 demonstrates the various areas in the Web Server environment where you are likely to troubleshoot problems. The HTTP Client, the Web Server, other Web or Application Servers, directory servers, database servers, or even the network can all be suspect when problems arise.

The number of possible subsystems that may need to be investigated can complicate the process of diagnosing errors. Figure 11.2 shows examples of components or subsystems that can cause Web Server errors.

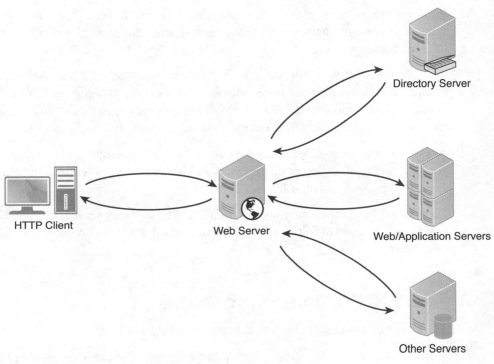

Figure 11.1   Web Server Environment

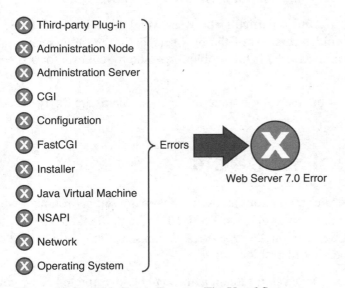

Figure 11.2   Web Server Errors—The Usual Suspects

When investigating Web Server problems, knowing where to look can greatly reduce the time taken to identify the cause of the problem. The next section describes the various sources of information that you can use to troubleshoot problems.

11.4 The Informants

The main sources of information that can be used to diagnose and troubleshoot Web Server problems include the following:

- Error messages recorded in log files
- HTTP access logs
- Core files
- Web Server statistics
- Network traffic
- Product documentation

The rest of this section describes how these "informants" can help in the trouble-shooting process.

11.4.1 Log Files

The following are the general types of log messages that are recorded in log files:

- **Error messages** mark critical failures and generally provide detailed context information about the problem that occurred. Java exceptions fall under this category of messages.
- **Warning messages** call attention to non-critical failures and generally contain information about the nature of the failure.
- **Informational messages** are used to convey information about the normal functioning of the server such as server status or completion of particular tasks.
- **Debug messages** provide additional information to assist in troubleshooting problems.

A problem is usually accompanied by a descriptive error message that is recorded in a log file. Apart from recording the fact that an error has occurred, one of the main purposes of the error message is to provide troubleshooting information. Diagnosing Web Server problems usually involves evaluating the information in error messages that are recorded in log files.

A logged message for an event/action usually provides the following information:

- Date/time of the event/action
- Message type/level such as warning, catastrophe, debug
- Message text

Information contained in the text of some messages can be very clear about what is wrong and what needs to be done. For example, stack traces of Java exceptions identify exactly where the problem lies. Other messages may give only general information about the problem or solution. In this case, the problem is not obvious, or there might be multiple things wrong.

Error messages recorded in the errors log file of a Web Server instance include the following additional pieces of information:

- Process identifier (PID) of the Web Server process that generated the message
- Message identifier that includes a four-digit integer prefixed with a short name that identifies the subsystem that generated the message
- An optional identifier that identifies the virtual server that generated the message

Figure 11.3 shows the various error message fields recorded in the logs/errors file of a Web Server instance.

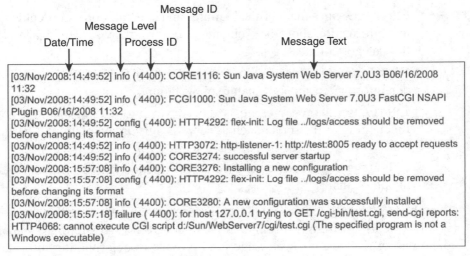

Figure 11.3   Web Server Error Message Fields

Log files other than a Web Server instance's Server Log file contain valuable information for diagnosing errors. Table 11.1 identifies the various log files that contain useful information for troubleshooting Web Server problems. For convenience purposes, the file system paths for all platforms in Table 11.1 use the UNIX forward slash (/) character.

Table 11.1   Log Files that Help Troubleshoot Errors

Component	Logs	Comments
Web Server 7.0—Server Instance	`install_dir/https-instance/logs/errors` `install_dir/https-instance/logs/access`	The server's error log file is the primary source of information about server problems.
Web Server 7.0—Administration Server/ Node	`install_dir/admin-server/logs/errors` `install_dir/admin-server/logs/access`	The Administration Server/Node writes error messages and records HTTP accesses to files in its `logs` directory.
Web Server 7.0 - Installer	`install_dir/setup/Sun_Java_System_Web_Server_install.log` `/var/sadm/install/logs/Sun_Java_Sytem_Web_Server_install.`*AmmddHHMM*(Solaris) `/var/sadm/install/logs/Sun_Java_System_Web_Server_install.`*BmmddHHMM*(Solaris) `/var/tmp/Sun_Java_System_Web_Server_install.`*AmmddHHMM*(Solaris/Linux/AIX/HP-UX) `/var/tmp/Sun_Java_System_Web_Server_install.`*BmmddHHMM*(Solaris/Linux/AIX/HP-UX) `%TMP%/Sun_Java_System_Web_Server_install.`*AmmddHHMM*(Windows) `%TMP%/Sun_Java_System_Web_Server_install.`*BmmddHHMM*(Windows)	Refer to the section titled "Installation Log Files" in Chapter 3, "Web Server 7.0 Installation and Migration," for more information on these files.
Web Server 7.0 - Uninstaller	`install_dir/setup/Sun_Java_System_Web_Server_uninstall.log` `/var/sadm/install/logs/Sun_Java_System_Web_Server_install.`*mmddHHMM*(Solaris) `/var/tmp/Sun_Java_System_Web_Server_install.`*mmddHHMM* (Solaris/Linux/AIX/HP-UX) `%TMP%/Sun_Java_System_Web_Server_install.`*mmddHHMM* (Windows)	Errors that occur during the uninstallation process are logged here. Before running the uninstaller on Windows, make sure that other applications such as editors or command shells are not referencing files hosted under Web Server's installation root directory.

Table 11.1   Log Files that Help Troubleshoot Errors   *continued*

Component	Logs	Comments
Web Server 7.0 - Migration	*install_dir*/admin-server/logs/ MIGRATION_yyyymmddhhmmss.log	Errors encountered when migrating an instance of an older version of Web Server to Web Server 7.0 are recorded in this file.
Java Virtual Machine	*install_dir*/https-*instance*/logs/errors	JVM errors are logged to the server instance's error log.
FastCGI	*install_dir*/https-*instance*/logs/ https-*instance*-Fastcgistub.log (Windows) *install_dir*/https-*instance*/logs/ Fastcgistub.log (UNIX/Linux)	This log file is written to by the Fastcgistub process.
Operating System (Solaris)	/var/adm/messages	Operating system error messages are logged in this file.
Operating System (Linux)	/var/log/messages	Operating system error messages are logged in this file.
Operating System (Windows)	Event Viewer	Event Viewer is an application to view Windows Event Logs. This tool can be launched from the Administrative Tools subfolder of the Windows Control Panel.

11.4.2 HTTP Access Log Files

Information about requests that clients send to the server and responses that the server sends back to clients is recorded in a server instance's Access Log file. The following specifies some of the components of information that may be recorded in an HTTP Access Log file:

- Client hostname
- Date
- HTTP request line
- HTTP response status code
- Response content length

- Name of authorized user
- Any header value
- Value of a cookie
- Virtual Server ID
- Time that the server spent handling the request

Please refer to the appendix titled "Using the Custom Log File Format" in the *Sun Java System Web Server 7.0 Configuration File Reference* for a more complete list of the types of information that can be recorded in Web Server 7.0's HTTP Access Log file. Example 11.1 shows an excerpt from an Access Log file of a Web Server 7.0 instance.

Example 11.1   Access Log File

```
format=%Ses->client.ip% - %Req->vars.auth-user% [%SYSDATE%]
   "%Req->reqpb.clf-request%" %Req->srvhdrs.clf-status%
   %Req->srvhdrs.content-length%
127.0.0.1 - - [03/Nov/2008:14:50:56 +0530] "GET / HTTP/1.1" 200 12370
127.0.0.1 - - [03/Nov/2008:14:50:56 +0530] "GET /img/gradation_header_
   R.gif HTTP/1.1" 200 403
127.0.0.1 - - [03/Nov/2008:14:50:56 +0530] "GET /img/sjsws_title_text.gif
   HTTP/1.1" 200 1906
127.0.0.1 - - [03/Nov/2008:14:50:56 +0530] "GET /img/gradation_header_
   L.gif HTTP/1.1" 200 365
127.0.0.1 - - [03/Nov/2008:14:50:56 +0530] "GET /img/sun_logo.gif
   HTTP/1.1" 200 2349
127.0.0.1 - - [03/Nov/2008:14:50:56 +0530] "GET /img/footer_R.gif
   HTTP/1.1" 200 254
127.0.0.1 - - [03/Nov/2008:14:50:56 +0530] "GET /img/footer_L.gif
   HTTP/1.1" 200 257
127.0.0.1 - - [03/Nov/2008:14:57:59 +0530] "GET /php/test.
   php?=PHPE9568F34-D428-11d2-A769-00AA001ACF42 HTTP/1.1" 200 2524
127.0.0.1 - - [03/Nov/2008:14:57:59 +0530] "GET /php/test.
   php?=PHPE9568F35-D428-11d2-A769-00AA001ACF42 HTTP/1.1" 200 2146
127.0.0.1 - - [03/Nov/2008:15:57:18 +0530] "GET /cgi-bin/test.cgi
   HTTP/1.1" 500 305
```

HTTP access logging is enabled by default; the default name of the Access Log file in Web Server is access and it is located in the server instance's logs directory. You can also configure Web Server to create and use a separate Access Log file for each virtual server. You can access and modify log file settings for the Access Log at either the server or virtual server level, using Web Server 7.0's administrative framework. More information about the support in Web Server 7.0 for managing Access Log files can be found in the section titled "Web Server Log Files" in Chapter 7, "Monitoring Web Server 7.0."

Web Server uses HTTP response status codes to notify clients of errors that may have occurred during request processing. The response status code is a three-digit integer whose first digit defines the class of response, as shown in Table 11.2.

Table 11.2   HTTP Response Status Codes

Status Code	Class of Response	Description
1xx	Informational	This class of response indicates that the server has received the request and is continuing to process it. An example of this class of responses would be "100 Continue."
2xx	Success	This class of response indicates that the server has successfully received, understood, and accepted the request from the client. Examples of this class of responses include "200 OK" and "204 No Content."
3xx	Redirection	This class of response indicates that further action by the client is required to complete the request. Examples of this class of responses include "301 Moved Permanently" and "304 Not Modified."
4xx	Client Error	The server sends a 4xx response to notify the client of errors in the request or requests that cannot be fulfilled. Examples of this class of responses include "401 Unauthorized," "404 Not Found," and "405 Method Not Allowed."
5xx	Server Error	The server sends a 5xx response to the client to indicate that the server failed to fulfill an apparently valid request. "500 Internal Server Error" is the most commonly encountered example of this class of responses.

Access Log file entries that contain a 5xx response status codes indicate requests that caused problems for the server. You can use the information in the *install_dir*/https-*instance*/logs/access file to identify information about requests that the server failed to fulfill.

11.4.3 Core Files

Core files are very useful for debugging Web Server crashes and hangs on UNIX/Linux systems. A core file contains the memory image of the process when it crashed. Core files generally contain sufficient information to determine what the process was doing when it crashed. The contents of a core file include information about the following:

- Process stack
- Threads
- Program register values
- Data structures and their contents

A core file is generally named core and is created in the directory where the application was running before it crashed. Examples of errors that can result in core file creation include buffer overflows, bus errors, and user-requested core generation.

You can use a number of tools to analyze the information in a core file. These tools can help you identify what the server was doing when it crashed or when it hung. Many of these tools also enable you to inspect parameter values to functions that the server was executing when it crashed/hung.

Core files corresponding to server process (webservd or webservd-wdog) crashes can be found in the config directory of the server instance that crashed.

11.4.4 Web Server Statistics

Effective monitoring of your Web Server can help you identify performance bottlenecks, which in turn can enable you to tune the system for optimal performance. Statistical data that is maintained for each request can also be used to troubleshoot an instance that has either stopped responding or has been restarted.

The following are a few examples of statistical data that Web Server 7.0 maintains:

- Connection queue information
- Response times
- HTTP error counts
- Request counts
- Java Virtual Machine statistics
- Java Web Application statistics
- File cache information

Web Server 7.0's monitoring subsystem exposes this statistical data for consumption by various clients. Statistical data can be viewed at different levels of granularity. Using Web Server 7.0, you can view statistical data for individual virtual servers, server instances, or configurations. Statistical data is available in a variety of formats that include XML, plain text, and Simple Network Management Protocol (SNMP). Interpreting the statistical data that Web Server provides can help you identify and tune under-performing servers. Statistical data can also give you useful insight when troubleshooting server hangs.

Please refer to Chapter 7 for a detailed description of the various methods you can use to monitor your Web Server.

11.4.5 Network Traffic

Web Server 7.0 is designed to use Transport Communication Protocol (TCP) connections to receive HTTP requests and send HTTP responses. HTTP request and response data is sent on the network over Transport Communication Protocol (TCP) connections. All the arrows illustrated in Figure 11.1 indicate data transfer over a network connection. You can also configure Web Server to use secure/ encrypted communication channels when interacting with HTTP clients or other servers.

When troubleshooting Web Server problems it is sometimes necessary to inspect the data on the network itself. Examining the raw data on the network can help you identify problems such as Secure Sockets Layer (SSL) errors, formatting errors in the request, invalid characters, and incorrect content lengths for responses.

11.4.6 Product Documentation

The sections titled "Known Issues" and "Resolved Issues" in the *Release Notes* for the version of Web Server 7.0 that you are troubleshooting can help you determine whether the problems you are encountering are ones that the Web Server development team is aware of. Information in the *Release Notes* for the *most recent* update to Web Server 7.0 can tell you whether the problems you are encountering have been fixed.

Refer to the sections titled "Supported Platforms," "Required Patches," and "Supported Browsers" in the *Release Notes* for the version of Web Server 7.0 that you are troubleshooting for the most up-to-date system requirements and dependencies.

11.5 Interrogation Methods

To troubleshoot Web Server problems, you may need to collect information from several different sources. This section describes the different tools and methodologies you can use to get a better understanding of the problem.

11.5.1 Diagnostic Commands and Tools

You can use a number of freely available tools and commands to diagnose Web Server problems. Some of these tools are included in Web Server; some are available on the Internet and others are included in the operating system. Table 11.3 briefly describes many of these tools.

Table 11.3 Troubleshooting Tools

Command/ Tool	Location	Description
certutil	*install_dir/* bin/certutil *install_dir* bin\certutil. bat	You can use the `certutil` command to inspect and repair Web Server's certificate and key databases. `certutil` usage is documented in the web page titled "Using the Certificate Database Tool," located at the following URL: http://www.mozilla.org/ projects/security/pki/nss/tools/certutil.html.
df	/bin/df	`df` is a standard UNIX/Linux command that is used to display the amount of free/available disk space for filesystems.
DTrace	/usr/sbin/ dtrace	`DTrace` is a dynamic tracing framework created by Sun Microsystems to troubleshoot problems in the operating system and in applications.
free	/usr/bin/free	`free` is a Linux command that displays the amount of used and free physical and swap memory in the system.
gcore	/usr/bin/ gcore	`gcore` is a standard UNIX/Linux command that is used to generate a `core` file for a running process. To generate a core file for a process you must supply the process ID (PID) as an argument to the `gcore` command. `gcore` is commonly used to generate core files of a server process that has hung.
kill	/bin/kill	`kill` is a standard UNIX/Linux command that terminates or signals processes. You can use `kill` to forcibly terminate hung processes. When debugging problems in Web Server's Java web container, you can also use `kill` to generate stack traces for all threads in the Java Virtual Machine (JVM) of a Java-enabled Web Server instance.

Table 11.3   Troubleshooting Tools   *continued*

Command/Tool	Location	Description
Live HTTP Headers	http://livehttp-headers.mozdev.org	Live HTTP Headers is a browser add-on that enables you to easily view the HTTP headers in browser requests and in Web Server responses.
modutil	*install_dir*/bin/modutil *install_dir*\bin\modutil.bat	The Security Module Database tool—modutil—is used to manage Web Server's database of PKCS#11 modules. modutil usage is documented in the web page titled "Using the Security Module Database (modutil)" located at the following URL: http://www.mozilla.org/projects/security/pki/nss/tools/modutil.html.
netstat	/bin/netstat	netstat is a standard UNIX/Linux command that shows network status. netstat is generally used to troubleshoot server failures caused by port conflicts.
pfiles	/usr/bin/pfiles	pfiles is a Solaris utility that lists all open files in a specified process. You can use pfiles to troubleshoot file-related problems such as when Web Server is unable to open files because it has run out of file descriptors.
prstat	/usr/bin/prstat	prstat is a Solaris utility (similar to top) that continuously reports statistics such as CPU usage, process run priority, and process execution team for each active process on the system.
ps	/bin/ps	ps is a standard UNIX/Linux command that reports process status. You generally use ps to check whether a process is running or not.
pstack	/usr/bin/pstack	pstack is a command found on both Solaris and Linux that is used to print a stack trace for each light-weight process (LWP) in a specified process. pstack can also be used to print stack traces of each LWP in a core file.
ptree	/usr/bin/ptree	ptree is a Solaris utility that prints a process tree containing the parent processes and child processes of a specified process identified by its process identifier (PID). The ptree command is useful for identifying the parent-child relationship between a webservd-wdog process and a webservd process.
pwdx	/usr/bin/pwdx	pwdx is a Solaris command that prints a process's current directory. You can use this to determine the directory in which you may find any core files.
showrev	/usr/bin/showrev	showrev is a Solaris utility that displays revision information about the hardware, the operating system, and any patches that may have been installed. This command is used to verify that the computer meets the minimum supported requirements for running Web Server 7.0.

Command/ Tool	Location	Description
snoop	`/usr/sbin/ snoop`	snoop is a Solaris command similar to the `tcpdump` utility on Linux, which can capture and inspect network packets. Captured packets can be displayed as they are received, or saved to a file for later inspection.
ssltap	`http://www. mozilla.org/ projects/ security/pki/ nss/tools/ ssltap.html`	ssltap is used to capture HTTP traffic and to capture information exchanged during Secure Sockets Layer (SSL) handshakes.
startserv	*install_dir/* `https-` *instance/bin/* `startserv` *install_dir* `https-` *instance\bin* `startserv.bat`	The startserv command can be used to verify the validity of the information in the server configuration files without actually starting the server. To verify configuration files, run the startserv command with the `--configtest` option.
strace	`/usr/bin/ strace`	strace is a Linux command similar to the `truss` utility on Solaris, which can trace system calls and signals in an active process. strace is used to trace a process's execution path and is a useful tool for troubleshooting Web Server errors such as server hangs and startup errors.
swap	`/usr/sbin/ swap`	swap is a Solaris command that can be used to display swap usage information when troubleshooting Web Server errors caused by insufficient free memory.
swapon	`/sbin/swapon`	swapon is a Linux command that can be used to display swap usage information when troubleshooting Web Server errors caused by insufficient free memory.
tcpdump	`/usr/sbin/ tcpdump`	tcpdump is a Linux utility (similar to snoop) that can capture network traffic. tcpdump can be used to save network packet data to a file for later analysis. Reading packets from a network interface may require that you have super-user privileges.
top	`/usr/bin/top`	top is a UNIX/Linux utility that displays a dynamic real-time view of the active processes in a system. You can use top to identify processes that consume the most CPU or processes that occupy a lot of memory.
truss	`/usr/bin/ truss`	truss is a Solaris command similar to the `strace` utility on Linux, which can trace system calls and signals in an active process. truss is used to trace the execution path of a process and is a useful tool for troubleshooting Web Server errors such as server hangs and startup errors.

Table 11.3   Troubleshooting Tools   *continued*

Command/ Tool	Location	Description
ulimit	/bin/ulimit	ulimit is an UNIX/Linux command that configures system resource limitations for the current shell and any processes that may be executed from the shell. Run the command ulimit -a in a shell to list all its resource limits.
uname	/bin/uname	uname is a standard UNIX/Linux command that prints information about the current system. The information that uname prints includes the name of the operating system, operating system release level, network nodename, machine hardware class, and processor type.
vmstat	/usr/bin/ vmstat	vmstat is a standard UNIX/Linux utility that reports information about processes, kernel threads, memory, paging, disks, traps, and CPU activity. vmstat is useful for analyzing Web Server performance issues.
Wireshark	http://www. wireshark.org	Wireshark is an open-source, multi-platform network protocol analyzer that can analyze hundreds of protocols (including LDAP, HTTP, HTTPS, TCP). Network data can be captured live or saved to a file for later analysis. Wireshark can read and write in several different capture file formats, including tcpdump and snoop.

The rest of this section describes the most frequently employed tools in more detail.

11.5.1.1 Live HTTP Headers

Live HTTP Headers is a browser add-on that enables you to easily view HTTP headers in requests that the browser sends to the server and in responses that the server sends back to the browser. Using Live HTTP Headers you can view HTTP headers that are sent over SSL connections between the server and the browser. You can use regular expressions to configure Live HTTP Headers to enable/suppress HTTP header capture for specific URLs. You can also modify the headers of previous requests and replay them to test various scenarios.

Live HTTP Headers can be configured as a sidebar, a new tab, or a new window depending on your browser.

Figure 11.4 demonstrates Live HTTP Headers in action in the Firefox browser.

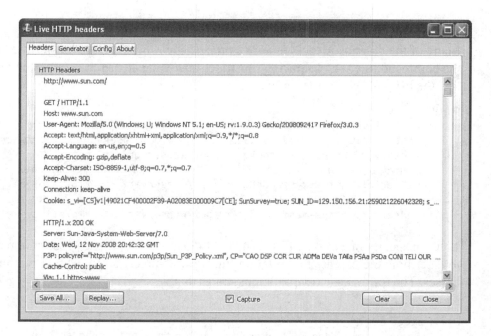

Figure 11.4   HTTP Headers for http://www.sun.com, Captured in the Live HTTP Headers Window

11.5.1.2 netstat

The netstat command is generally used to check whether a port is in use. The following shows how you can use netstat to determine that port 8080 is not in use:

```
# netstat -an | grep 8080
#
```

The following example demonstrates that some process is listening for connections on port 1894:

```
# netstat -an | grep 1894
    *.1894              *.*             0    0 49152    0 LISTEN
#
```

11.5.1.3 prstat, ps, ptree, and pwdx

Many of the diagnostic tools require a process identifier (PID) to be specified on the command line. The following illustrates how you can use the ps command to find the PIDs of Web Server processes.

```
# ps -ef | grep webservd
    root 14431    1  0 23:23:23 ?           0:00 webservd-wdog -d /opt/
    webserver7/https-test/config -r /opt/webserver7 -t /tmp/h
webservd 14433 14432   0 23:23:25 ?          0:43 webservd -d /opt/
    webserver7/https-test/config -r /opt/webserver7 -t /tmp/https-
    root 14432 14431   0 23:23:23 ?          0:11 webservd -d /opt/
    webserver7/https-test/config -r /opt/webserver7 -t /tmp/https-
```

You can specify one of the PIDs (14431, 14433, or 14432) to the ptree command to determine the parent-child relationships between the various Web Server processes. The following example demonstrates this:

```
# ptree 14432
14431 webservd-wdog -d /opt/webserver7/https-test/config -r /opt/
    webserver7 -t
 14432 webservd -d /opt/webserver7/https-test/config -r /opt/
    webserver7 -t /tm
  14433 webservd -d /opt/webserver7/https-test/config -r /opt/
    webserver7 -t /
```

Using the output of the ptree command and correlating that to how the various processes in Web Server are started you can determine that the webservd process with a PID of 14433 is the worker process.

Having identified the PID of the worker process, you can use the prstat command to look at LWP statistics within the worker process. This is illustrated in Example 11.2.

Example 11.2 Worker Process LWP Statistics

```
# prstat -L -p 14433
   PID USERNAME  SIZE  RSS STATE  PRI NICE      TIME  CPU PROCESS/LWPID
 14433 webservd  388M 202M sleep   59    0   0:00:13 0.1% webservd/30
 14433 webservd  388M 202M sleep   59    0   0:00:05 0.0% webservd/19
 14433 webservd  388M 202M sleep   59    0   0:00:09 0.0% webservd/1
```

```
14433 webservd  388M  202M sleep  59   0   0:00:02 0.0% webservd/25
14433 webservd  388M  202M sleep  59   0   0:00:01 0.0% webservd/9
14433 webservd  388M  202M sleep   0  19   0:00:01 0.0% webservd/20
14433 webservd  388M  202M sleep  59   0   0:00:00 0.0% webservd/28
14433 webservd  388M  202M sleep  59   0   0:00:00 0.0% webservd/23
14433 webservd  388M  202M sleep  59   0   0:00:00 0.0% webservd/22
14433 webservd  388M  202M sleep  59   0   0:00:00 0.0% webservd/21
14433 webservd  388M  202M sleep  59   0   0:00:00 0.0% webservd/18
14433 webservd  388M  202M sleep  59   0   0:00:03 0.0% webservd/17
14433 webservd  388M  202M sleep  59   0   0:00:03 0.0% webservd/16
14433 webservd  388M  202M sleep  59   0   0:00:00 0.0% webservd/15
14433 webservd  388M  202M sleep  59   0   0:00:00 0.0% webservd/14
14433 webservd  388M  202M sleep  59   0   0:00:00 0.0% webservd/13
14433 webservd  388M  202M sleep  59   0   0:00:00 0.0% webservd/12
14433 webservd  388M  202M sleep  59   0   0:00:00 0.0% webservd/11
14433 webservd  388M  202M sleep  59   0   0:00:00 0.0% webservd/10
14433 webservd  388M  202M sleep  59   0   0:00:00 0.0% webservd/8
14433 webservd  388M  202M sleep  59   0   0:00:00 0.0% webservd/7
Total: 1 processes, 36 lwps, load averages: 0.19, 0.19, 0.18
```

11.5.1.4 ssltap

The SSL Debugging Tool (ssltap) is an SSL-aware command-line proxy that can display data exchanged over TCP connections, including SSL streams. ssltap opens a socket and listens for incoming requests from a client and passes those requests on to a server. When the response is received from the server, ssltap then passes that information back to the client. ssltap displays both the request and the response data, including SSL records and handshaking in the window from which it was invoked. You can use the -f option to the ssltap command to redirect this information to an HTML file.

Example 11.3 demonstrates the data (including the HTTP request line and headers), as captured by ssltap, that the browser sent to Web Server for loading the http://blogs.sun.com/ URL.

Example 11.3   ssltap Request Data Capture

```
--> [
GET http://blogs.sun.com/ HTTP/1.1
Host: blogs.sun.com
User-Agent: Mozilla/5.0 (Windows; U; Windows NT 5.1; en-US; rv:1.9.0.3)
   Gecko/2008092417 Firefox/3.0.3
Accept: text/html,application/xhtml+xml,application/xml;q=0.9,*/*;q=0.8
Accept-Language: en-us,en;q=0.5
Accept-Encoding: gzip,deflate
Accept-Charset: ISO-8859-1,utf-8;q=0.7,*;q=0.7
Keep-Alive: 300
Proxy-Connection: keep-alive

]
```

A request from the client is denoted by an arrow pointing to the right. The content of the request is displayed between an opening square bracket and a closing square bracket.

Example 11.4 demonstrates the first portion of the server response (as captured by ssltap) for the request shown in Example 11.3. The response data captured by ssltap includes the HTTP status line and HTTP response headers such as Server and Content-length. The response from the server is signified by an arrow pointing to the left. The content of the response is once again enclosed between an opening square bracket and a closing square bracket.

Example 11.4   ssltap Response Data Capture

```
<-- [
HTTP/1.1 200 OK
Server: Sun-Java-System-Web-Server/7.0
Date: Wed, 12 Nov 2008 21:09:46 GMT
X-robots-tag: noindex,follow
Last-modified: Wed, 12 Nov 2008 21:05:54 GMT
Expires: Thu, 01 Jan 1970 00:00:00 GMT
Content-type: text/html;charset=utf-8
Content-length: 31579

<!DOCTYPE html PUBLIC "-//W3C//DTD XHTML 1.0 Transitional//EN" "http://
   www.w3.org/TR/xhtml1/DTD/xhtml1-transitional.dtd">
<html xmlns="http://www.w3.org/1999/xhtml">
<head>
```

The `ssltap` tool does not interpret the raw data stream in any way. This can result in peculiar effects, such as sounds, flashes, and even crashes of the command shell window. Use the `-h` option to substitute non-printable characters with dots.

To capture data over an SSL connection you must use the `-s` option to enable SSL parsing and decoding.

The page you retrieved may look incomplete in the browser. By default the tool terminates after the first HTTP request/response exchange has been completed. As such, the browser is unable to request subsequent resources that may be part of the overall page (such as images). To force the tool to continue to accept connections, run `ssltap` in looping mode with the `-l` option.

Refer to the section titled "Analyzing SSL Requests" in the *Sun Java System Web Server 7.0 Troubleshooting Guide* for another example that demonstrates using `ssltap` to analyze SSL requests. Please refer to http://www.mozilla.org/projects/security/pki/nss/tools/ssltap.html for more information on `ssltap`.

11.5.1.5 snoop

You can use the `snoop` command to capture network packets and display their contents in a format that you specify. Packets can be displayed in real time, or saved to a file for later analysis. RFC 1761 specifies the format of the packet capture file. The `snoop` command, itself, can be used to interpret the captured file and placed into a human readable format. Other tools such as Wireshark can also read and analyze Snoop Version 2 packet capture files.

Example 11.5 demonstrates a portion of data captured and interpreted by the `snoop` command.

Example 11.5 snoop Data Sample

```
HTTP: ----- HyperText Transfer Protocol -----
HTTP:
HTTP: GET /index.html HTTP/1.1
HTTP: Host: www.sun.com
HTTP: [...]
```

```
HTTP:

ETHER:  ----- Ether Header -----
ETHER:
ETHER:  Packet 5 arrived at 12:47:30.33
ETHER:  Packet size = 60 bytes
ETHER:  Destination = 8:0:20:a3:24:7d, Sun
ETHER:  Source      = 0:20:78:db:3f:43,
ETHER:  Ethertype = 0800 (IP)
ETHER:
```

You may require super-user privileges to capture packets to and from the default interface in promiscuous mode. Refer to the snoop(1M) man page for more information about its usage.

11.5.1.6 Wireshark

Wireshark is an open-source, multi-platform network protocol analyzer that can analyze hundreds of protocols (including LDAP, HTTP, HTTPS, TCP). Network data can be captured live or saved to a file for later analysis. Wireshark can read and write several different capture file formats, including tcpdump and snoop. Wireshark includes an easy-to-use graphical user interface for analyzing network traffic.

Figure 11.5 demonstrates live network data capture and analysis using Wireshark's graphical user interface.

This tool provides several advantages over snoop, such as ease of use and search, but it must be installed separately. The Wireshark home page—http://www.wireshark.org—contains more information about its usage.

11.5.1.7 DTrace

DTrace is a dynamic tracing framework that is built into Solaris and can be used by system administrators and developers to examine the behavior both of applications (such as Web Server) and of the operating system itself. DTrace enables you to record additional data at specific locations in the execution path of an application or from the operating system itself. These data-gathering sensors are called *probes*. DTrace has the combined capabilities of many of the tools described in Table 11.3. The following are some of the common uses of the DTrace framework in Solaris:

- Dynamically enable and manage thousands of probes
- Implement new DTrace probes
- Dynamically associate actions with probes
- Examine trace data from a running system or from a system crash dump

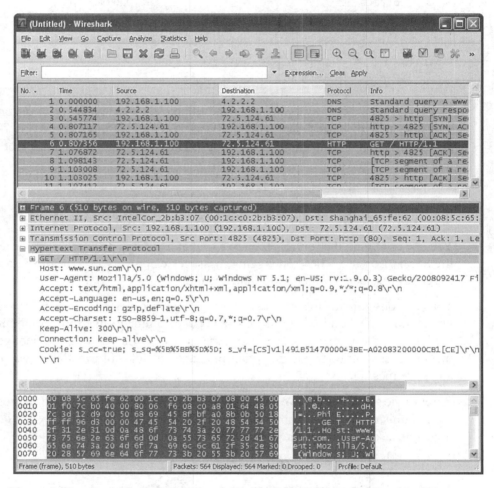

Figure 11.5 Analyzing HTTP Network Traffic Using Wireshark's Graphical User Interface

The current release of Web Server 7.0 does not have any built-in DTrace probes. However, you can use the various probes that are included in the Solaris operating system to troubleshoot problems in Web Server. Example 11.6 demonstrates how you can use the dtrace command to list all the probes in Solaris.

Example 11.6   DTrace Probes in Solaris

```
# dtrace -l
  ID   PROVIDER          MODULE              FUNCTION NAME
   1    dtrace                                BEGIN
   2    dtrace                                END
   3    dtrace                                ERROR
   4 Xserver721          Xsun             AddResource resource-alloc
   5 Xserver721          Xsun      WriteEventsToClient send-event
^C
# dtrace -l | wc -l
   50570
```

Using DTrace you can examine, tune and troubleshoot the behavior of the entire software stack on your Solaris system. Please refer to the *Solaris Dynamic Tracing Guide* for more information on using DTrace to examine, troubleshoot and tune system behavior.

11.5.2 Increasing Server Log Message Verbosity

You can configure the server's log level so that it records debugging messages to the Server Log file. These debugging messages can give you useful insight into the conditions under which a problem occurs.

You can configure the log level used for logging error messages in Web Server by using either the Administration Console or the command-line tool. Configuring the server log level to one of fine, finer, or finest causes the server to log debugging messages in addition to logging other messages such as informational, warning, and error messages.

Refer to the section titled "Web Server Log Files" in Chapter 7 for information on the administrative support in Web Server 7.0 for configuring the level of detail logged in a server instance's Server Log file.

11.5.3 Correlating Access and Server Log Entries

Each entry in the HTTP Access Log file and in the Server Log file usually contains a timestamp. You can search the HTTP Access Log file for requests that the server failed to process successfully (because of server errors) by simply searching for HTTP response status codes in the 5xx class of responses. Use the timestamp value from the Access Log file for each request that returned a 5xx status code and search the Server Log file for error messages that also contain the same timestamp. You may need to search for a range of timestamp values because error messages and Access Log entries may not be recorded at exactly the same time.

This methodology enables you to find error messages corresponding to requests that caused server problems.

11.5.4 Generating Stack Trace Information for Java Threads

Examining stack traces of Java threads can help you troubleshoot thread-related hangs in the Java Virtual Machine (JVM) in Web Server 7.0. In a Java-enabled Web Server instance, the JVM is embedded in the worker process.

On UNIX/Linux platforms, you must use the `kill` command to send a `SIGQUIT` signal to the worker process (`kill -QUIT` *pid* or `kill -3` *pid*) to cause the embedded JVM to print Java thread stack trace information. Java thread stack trace information generated by the JVM is recorded in the instance's Server Log file (`logs/errors`).

On Windows, you must press Ctrl+\ in the console window from which the server was started.

Warning: Do not configure the JVM's `-Xrs` option because this option causes the JVM to ignore signals.

11.5.5 Effective Monitoring

Web Server 7.0 includes support for gathering and reporting statistics about the various components that comprise Web Server. You can monitor data for all nodes that share a particular configuration, narrow down on a particular instance within the configuration, or even on a particular virtual server within a single instance. You can keep track of information at the process level or even look within the Java Web container to monitor a Web application or a specific servlet. You can view the data either as an XML stream or as a plaintext report or by using the `perfdump` SAF or via the Administration Console. Example 11.7 illustrates the use of `wadm` and `perfdump` to report monitoring data.

Example 11.7   Sample perfdump Report

```
wadm> get-perfdump --config=test --node=foobar

Sun Java System Web Server 7.0U3 B06/16/2008 12:00 (SunOS DOMESTIC)

Server started Wed Nov 12 23:23:24 2008
Process 14433 started Wed Nov 12 23:23:24 2008

ConnectionQueue:
------------------------------------------
Current/Peak/Limit Queue Length          0/2/16384
Total Connections Queued                 43
Average Queue Length (1, 5, 15 minutes)  0.00, 0.00, 0.00
Average Queueing Delay                   0.48 milliseconds

ListenSocket http-listener-1:
------------------------
Address                 http://0.0.0.0:9000
Acceptor Threads        1
Default Virtual Server  test

KeepAliveInfo:
--------------------
KeepAliveCount       0/32768
KeepAliveHits        102
KeepAliveFlushes     0
KeepAliveRefusals    0
KeepAliveTimeouts    30
KeepAliveTimeout     30 seconds

SessionCreationInfo:
------------------------
Active Sessions        0
Keep-Alive Sessions    0
Total Sessions Created  8/129

CacheInfo:
-----------------------
File Cache Enabled      yes
File Cache Entries      15/1024
File Cache Hit Ratio    257/278 ( 92.45%)
Maximum Age             30
Accelerator Entries     12/1024
Acceleratable Requests  15/132 ( 11.36%)
Acceleratable Responses 12/15 ( 80.00%)
Accelerator Hit Ratio   0/9 (  0.00%)
```

```
Native pools:
----------------------------
NativePool:
Idle/Peak/Limit              1/1/128
Work Queue Length/Peak/Limit 0/0/0

DNSCacheInfo:
------------------
enabled           yes
CacheEntries      0/1024
HitRatio          0/0 ( 0.00%)

Async DNS disabled

Performance Counters:
--------------------------------------------------
                              Average     Total       Percent

Total number of requests:                 132
Request processing time:      0.0006      0.0798

default-bucket (Default bucket)
Number of Requests:                       132         (100.00%)
Number of Invocations:                    1665        (100.00%)
Latency:                      0.0002      0.0290      ( 36.26%)
Function Processing Time:      0.0004      0.0509      ( 63.74%)
Total Response Time:          0.0006      0.0798      (100.00%)

Sessions:
---------------------------------------------------------
Process Status Client Age VS Method URI Function
```

By analyzing the monitoring data you can identify subsystems in the server that are poorly configured. For example, an application that invokes long-running database queries may require additional worker threads to keep up with the incoming request rate. In such a scenario, the information in the "Native pools" section of the `perfdump` report can be used to determine whether the worker threads are being used efficiently.

The *Sun Java System Web Server 7.0 Performance Tuning, Sizing, and Scaling Guide* contains detailed information on how you can use Web Server monitoring data to troubleshoot performance problems.

11.5.6 Tracing Server Hangs and Infinite Loops

The pstack command records stack traces of all the LWPs in a process. Web Server's worker process may contain many LWPs, and pstack may generate a large amount of data for such a process.

When troubleshooting a runaway server process that is unnecessarily wasting CPU cycles, you can use the prstat command to identify the LWP in the worker process that is consuming the most CPU cycles. You can then search the pstack output for the LWP number to view the stack trace of the thread that is wasting CPU cycles.

When troubleshooting server processes that have hung, you can use the pstack command to generate stack traces of all the threads in the process and save the output to a file. Repeat this a few times over a period of time. Comparing the files containing pstack output generated at different points of time using a tool such as diff helps you identify threads that are active and those that are stuck/hung or waiting for an event to occur. Comparing the pstack output of a server that has hung to the pstack output of the same server immediately after it started can also help you identify where the problem is.

You can also use the gcore command to cause a server process that has hung to generate a core file. You can then investigate the problem further, using debugging tools that understand core files.

> **Note:** For security reasons, SSL-enabled Web Server instances do not generate core files by default. If you want to generate a core file for an SSL-enabled server, you must explicitly set the SSL_DUMP environment variable in the startserv script of the corresponding server. You can set the SSL_DUMP environment variable by adding the following in the startserv script of the server: SSL_DUMP=1; export SSL_DUMP.

11.5.7 Editing the Correct Virtual Server Object File

You can configure Web Server 7.0 to use a different object file (obj.conf) for each virtual server. When you create a server instance, Web Server's administrative framework creates a default object file named obj.conf in the config directory of the instance. Subsequent administrative actions may result in the creation of additional object files named *virtual_server*-obj.conf. In such a scenario, the original obj.conf file may not be referenced by any of the virtual servers in the configuration. When making manual changes to the request processing behavior of a virtual server, always check the main server configuration file—`server.xml`—for the correct object file name corresponding to the virtual server. The object file is specified by the `object-file` element in the `server.xml` file.

11.5.8 Making Incremental Configuration Changes

Web Server errors caused by errors in the server's configuration files can be difficult to troubleshoot when you deploy many configuration changes together. In such scenarios, adopting a systematic approach and incrementally making, deploying, and testing configuration changes can help you isolate the change that causes the problem. This is especially true when modifying the request processing directives in a virtual server's object file (`obj.conf`) and when modifying Access Control Lists (ACLs).

11.6 Other Investigating Agencies

The "Sun Java System Web Server" online forum at http //forums.sun.com/ contains discussions about Web Server by web application developers, system administrators, and web server users. Past and present members of Web Server 7.0's product and development team also actively participate in this forum. You can search for information related to your Web Server problem in the "Sun Java System Web Server" online forum. You can also seek help from other users on the forum regarding any Web Server problems that you are facing. Remember to describe the problem clearly and concisely.

The "Web Tier" home page of the Sun Developer Network at http://developers. sun.com/webtier/ contains many useful articles, including screencasts that demonstrate Web Server 7.0 features. You can search the web site to check whether what you are trying to do has already been documented. The development engineers on the Web Server product team at Sun Microsystems periodically contribute new content for upload onto this web site.

If you have a support contract with Sun, you can contact the technical support team to report the problem. Use the information in this chapter to clearly describe the problem and the problem environment. You can also search the knowledgebase on the Sun Support Center web site, which is located online at http://www.sun.com/support/ for information about Web Server problems you have encountered.

11.7 Summary

In this chapter you have learned about the different kinds of problems that one might encounter when using Web Server 7.0. This chapter also described the areas where problems are most likely to occur and the diagnostic tools and procedures you can use to troubleshoot Web Server problems. Using the troubleshooting concepts described in this chapter can help you find and fix Web Server errors quickly, thus minimizing the amount of time that your web site is unavailable to users.

11.8 Self-Paced Labs

Use the information contained in this chapter to perform the following exercises. These will help validate your understanding of the concepts described in this chapter.

1. Configure the Server Log level to finest and use a browser to request /index. html. Use the log messages in the Server Log file to trace the Server Application Functions (SAFs) that the server executes to process this request.

2. How many system calls does Web Server invoke when processing a request for /index.html?

3. Generate a Java stack trace for a Java-enabled Web Server running on Windows.

4. Install Wireshark and use it to capture HTTP traffic on the network.

5. Capture the HTTP request and response headers corresponding to a request for http://www.sun.com/.

 Note: Go to http://www.sunwebserver.com for more troubleshooting exercises and for detailed instructions on how to perform each of these exercises.

Building Secure, Dynamic Web 2.0 Sites with Web Server 7.0

WEB 1.0 sites are somewhat static in nature, with content being maintained by the company itself. Webmasters of Web 1.0 sites are constantly being burdened with the need to update the site's content in an effort to keep visitors informed and engaged. Sites built in the Web 1.0 framework are typically characterized as read-only and are analogous to online billboards with downloadable technical documents. Figure 12.1 demonstrates the interaction between the site and its visitors in a Web 1.0 framework.

These types of sites fit users' needs during the early days of the Web, but today users are looking for more than just information; they are looking for an *interactive experience*.

Web 2.0 sites such as YouTube, MySpace, Wikipedia, and Flickr are characterized by a community of users who share the responsibility of content creation, management, and distribution with the webmaster. Web 2.0 sites provide the platform where users are more than just visitors—they are active participants. They may accomplish this by tagging content, contributing to wikis, or performing podcasts or blogging. In essence the end user is an integral part of the creation of information for the site and is constantly interacting both with the site and with other users. Figure 12.2 demonstrates user interaction in today's Web 2.0 sites.

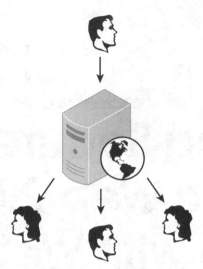

Figure 12.1   User Interaction on a Web 1.0 Site

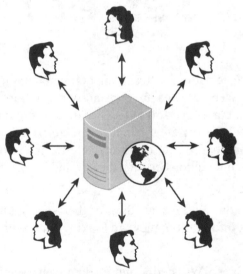

Figure 12.2   User Interaction on a Web 2.0 Site

Web 2.0 sites are social in nature, interactive, and are easy to use. The guiding motto behind these sites is that users add value, and the overall goal of such sites is to create an environment where the data provided by the end user increases the site's value.

Communication is constant with Web 2.0 sites in that information is passed back and forth through a multitude of clients (web browsers, mobile phones, feeds, or APIs). As such, the traffic in and out of Web 2.0 sites necessitates a platform that can meet today's needs and yet be dynamic enough to scale to a greater number of transactions as the site's popularity increases.

The most innovative companies today are taking advantage of the next-generation, collaborative Web 2.0 capabilities to reach out to new prospects, enhance the sense of loyalty among existing customers, and run their operations more efficiently. Whether they are startups or established companies, if they are attempting to go beyond the limits of traditional HTML, they will want to construct new, dynamic Web capabilities built upon a dynamic, scalable, stable, and proven platform. They will want to build their sites on Sun Web Server 7.0.

The traditional web site, comprising HTML pages and database-backed web applications, may be fine for Web 1.0 sites, but newer Web 2.0 sites demand a more robust architecture comprising a scalable HTTP server coupled with a dynamic scripting engine and a database with a caching layer for optimal performance. As such, customers wishing to take advantage of the dynamic nature of Web 2.0 sites should consider the scalable architecture; ease of configuration, monitoring, and tuning; and security-related features contained in Web Server 7.0.

In addition to its customers, Sun Microsystems is a client of its own software products and has battle-tested Web Server 7.0 in its own production environment. The next three sections take a closer look at three Web 2.0 sites that have been implemented with Web Server 7.0.

12.1 Site: Sun Blogs

Sun Blogs (blogs.sun.com) is a secure blogging service for thousands of Sun employees worldwide. The site serves 4 million hits a day on average and represents one of the busiest blogging sites with over 30GB of data transferred per day—all while utilizing only 3% of the CPU and maintaining 97% idle time!

Sun Blogs uses a custom version of the open source blogging server, Apache Roller Weblogger, that has been deployed to Web Server 7.0. Figure 12.3 provides an overview of the architecture used for Sun Blogs.

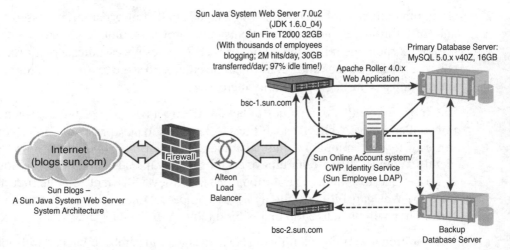

Figure 12.3   Sun Blogs System Architecture

The Web Server configuration consists of two instances installed on two Sun Fire T2000 servers with 32GB of RAM, negligible disk space utilized, and a shared file system (NFS from a sun cluster). Both servers sit behind a hardware load balancer that splits traffic evenly. All data is stored in a MySQL database server and utilizes memcached to provide an additional increase in performance. Finally, the entire service is integrated with Sun's secure single-sign-on identity system, backed by a worldwide employee LDAP directory for authentication and authorization.

The Web Server required minimal configuration to support this application, with the majority of changes being made to tuning parameters. Example 12.1 demonstrates the configuration changes required to obtain the desired site performance. The entire `server.xml` file is not listed; rather only relevant sections are provided and inline comments shown.

Example 12.1   Server Configuration for Sun Blogs

```
<server>

  <log>
    <log-file>../logs/errors</log-file>
    <archive-suffix>.%Y%m%d</archive-suffix>
    <log-level>info</log-level>
  </log>

  <!-- Increase output buffer size for each thread.  This allows the Web
  Server to receive data from the j2ee-module SAF and buffer it for slow
  clients.  This in turn allows the j2ee-module to return system resources
  in a timelier manner.  -->
```

```
<http>
  <output-buffer-size>40960</output-buffer-size>
</http>

<!-- Typical worker thread pool with higher stack size not uncommon for
Java web applications with deeper invocation stack depths -->
<thread-pool>
  <max-threads>250</max-threads>
  <stack-size>256000</stack-size>
</thread-pool>

<!-- Java VM settings  -->
<jvm>
  <java-home>.../jdk</java-home>
  <server-class-path>...</server-class-path>
  <debug>false</debug>
  <debug-jvm-options>-Xdebug -Xrunjdwp:transport=dt_socket,server=y,
    suspend=n,address=7896</debug-jvm-options>
  <jvm-options>-Djava.security.auth.login.config=lcgin.conf</jvm-
    options>

  <!-- Increased ms and mx, by default it was -Xms128m -Xmx256m -->
  <jvm-options>-Xms3g -Xmx3g -XX:NewSize=1g</jvm-options>
  <jvm-options>-server -Xsqnopause</jvm-options>
  <jvm-options>-XX:+UseParallelGC -XX:+UseParallelOldGC
    -XX:ParallelGCThreads=20</jvm-options>

  <!-- Added java keystore locations -->
  <jvm-options>-Dcom.sun.management.jmxremote -Djavax.net.ssl.key-
 Store=...keystore -Djavax.net.ssl.keyStorePassword=...</jvm-options>
</jvm>

<!-- Configure MySQL data source as a JDBC resource -->
<jdbc-resource>
  <jndi-name>jdbc/rollerdb</jndi-name>
  <datasource-class>com.mysql.jdbc.jdbc2.optional.MysqlDataSource</
    datasource-class>
  <property>
    <name>Password</name>
    <value>...</value>
    <description/>
  </property>
  <property>
    <name>User</name>
    <value>...</value>
    <description/>
  </property>
  <property>
```

```xml
      <name>URL</name>
      <value>jdbc:mysql://somedburl:3306/database?relaxAutoCommit=
        true&amp;useUnicode=true&amp;characterEncoding=utf-8</value>
      <description/>
    </property>
    <description>roller datasource</description>
    <min-connections>15</min-connections>
    <max-connections>250</max-connections>
    <idle-timeout>180</idle-timeout>
    <connection-validation>meta-data</connection-validation>
  </jdbc-resource>

  <mail-resource>
    <jndi-name>mail/Session</jndi-name>
    <description>roller mail session</description>
    <property>
      <name>mail.smtp.host</name>
      <value>mailhost</value>
      <description>Mail server hostname</description>
    </property>
  </mail-resource>

  <!-- The blogs web application is configured within the virtual server.
   All traffic with a URI of '/' executes the web application -->
  <virtual-server>
    <name>blogs</name>
    <host>blogs</host>
    <http-listener-name>http-listener-1</http-listener-name>
    <web-app>
      <uri>/</uri>
      <path>../web-app/blogs/_default</path>
      <description/>
    </web-app>
  </virtual-server>

  <!-- Logs are rotated once a day. -->
  <event>
    <time>
      <time-of-day>00:00</time-of-day>
    </time>
    <rotate-access-log>true</rotate-access-log>
  </event>

  <event>
    <time>
      <time-of-day>00:00</time-of-day>
```

```
    </time>
    <rotate-log>true</rotate-log>
  </event>

</server>
```

Web Server 7.0 seems to be living up to expectations and has made one system administrator quite happy. In the words of Allen Gilliland, the blogs.sun.com site administrator,

> "As far as my experience with Sun Java System Web Server 7, I love it. We used Tomcat for the first couple years of the site when only Sun Java System Web Server 6.1 was available, and quite frankly, Sun Java System Web Server 6.1 lacked some features and ease of use. At that time, we preferred Tomcat, even though it lacked a lot of cool features.
>
> Shortly after Sun Java System Web Server 7.0 came out, we switched and since then I've been a big fan. In my opinion, Web Server 7 offers way more features than Tomcat does, and has been very stable and nice to work with. Also, we are using Web Server because we like some of the benefits the native Web Server 7 code gives us.
>
> One of the interesting problems we solved using Web Server 7 was an issue caused by slow clients that were tying up Web Server threads in j2ee-module. Basically, if a client was slow and the thread got stuck in j2ee-module, it would continue to tie up limited resources, such as database connections, and at one point, this became a real problem.
>
> To resolve the problem, we utilized the ability of Web Server to set a larger output-buffer-size for each thread so that the response data for a slow client could be effectively buffered by Web Server and the thread wouldn't be stuck in j2ee-module.
>
> In my experience, this ability is something you don't get from other web servers. I have found that Web Server 7 provides better integration between a native web server and a Java 2 Platform, Enterprise Edition (J2EE) container than other solutions such as Apache Tomcat.
>
> I've also been a big fan of the Web Server perfdump and stats.xml data, which can be retrieved from the Web Server at runtime, even when the site appears to be hanging from the Web. That data has been immensely valuable in debugging Web Server issues, such as the one described previously.

Apart from that, our use of Web Server 7 has been pretty much clear sailing. We've actually been running our current installations for about a year with almost no tweaks necessary. The application just sits there and runs."

12.2 Site: Sun Forums

Sun Forums (forums.sun.com) is one of the busiest Sun.com sites after www.sun.com and the Sun download centers. This site utilizes the Jive forum web application by Jive Software to provide interactive forums for hundreds of thousands of visitors.

Deployed on Sun Java System Web Server 7.0, Sun Forums offers Web 2.0-style forum services for all Sun products and technologies, and features RSS feeds and a rich-text editor for forum posts and responses.

Sun Forums traffic is increasing at the rate of over 3 percent year over year. In 2007, this web site had over 60 million hits. In 2008, it far surpassed that number. In March 2008, the site had 6.6 million page views and 3.8 million visits (not including RSS feeds). Typically, over 60 users are logged in to the site at all times, and the site reaches a maximum of 1,200 users online during high-traffic times.

Figure 12.4 demonstrates the Sun Forums system architecture.

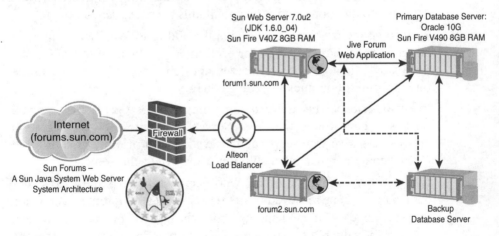

Figure 12.4   Sun Forums System Architecture

This is a typical web tier deployment with a farm of web servers that are secured by a firewall, front-ended by a load balancer, and supported by a database server with redundancy in the back end.

Sun Forums is based on Jive Forums, a Java web application that is deployed as a simple WAR file on the web server running on Java Platform, Standard Edition (Java SE) 6. Jive is deployed on Web Server 7.0 and runs on two Sun Fire V40Z servers with 8GB of RAM. The servers interface to an Oracle 10g database server running on a Sun Fire V490 server that uses the Solaris 10 operating system.

Similar to Sun Blogs (see Section 12.1), the Web Server required minimal configuration to support this application. Example 12.2 demonstrates the configuration changes required to obtain the desired site performance. The entire server.xml file is not listed; rather only relevant sections are provided with inline comments being shown.

Example 12.2   Server Configuration for Sun Forum

```
<server>
  <!-- Java VM settings, max out available Java heap size for a 32-bit
  server, aggressive, parallel GC options and Tangosol coherence session
  backup. -->
  <jvm>
  <jvm-options>-Xms2048m -Xmx2748m -server -XX:+UseParallelGC -XX
   :+UseParallelOldGC -XX:ParallelGCThreads=4 -XX:+AggressiveOpts</
  jvm-options>
  <jvm-options>-Dtangosol.coherence.localhost=72.5.126.82</jvm-options>
  </jvm>

  <!-- Slightly higher keep-alive threads setting, indicating higher
  anticipated concurrent HTTP connections -->
  <keep-alive>
  <threads>8</threads>
  </keep-alive>

  <!-- Typical worker thread pool with higher stack size not uncommon for
  Java web applications with deeper invocation stack depths -->
  <thread-pool>
  <min-threads>128</min-threads>
  <max-threads>256</max-threads>
  <stack-size>262144</stack-size>
  </thread-pool>

  <!-- Oracle data source configured as a JDBC resource -->
  <jdbc-resource>
  <jndi-name>jdbc/jdcforum</jndi-name>
  <datasource-class>oracle.jdbc.pool.OracleDataSource</datasource-
    class>
  <min-connections>130</min-connections>
  <max-connections>200</max-connections>
  <idle-timeout>0</idle-timeout>
```

```
<isolation-level>read-committed</isolation-level>
<property>
<name>MaxStatements</name>
<value>200</value>
</property>
<property>
<name>ImplicitCachingEnabled</name>
<value>true</value>
</property>
</jdbc-resource>

<!-- HTTP listener is configured to serve the forums virtual server; the
acceptor threads count of 8 is tuned for a 4x dual core AMD Opteron
server. -->
<http-listener>
<name>http-listener-1</name>
<acceptor-threads>8</acceptor-threads>
</http-listener>

<!-- A single forums web app with document root '/' runs the virtual
server -->
<virtual-server>
<name>forum</name>
<host>forum</host>
<http-listener-name>http-listener-1</http-listener-name>
<web-app>
<uri>/</uri>
<path>../web-app/forum/_default</path>
</web-app>
</virtual-server>

<!-- Logs are rotated once a day. -->
<event>
  <time>
    <time-of-day>23:55</time-of-day>
  </time>
      <rotate-access-log>true</rotate-access-log>
</event>

<event>
  <time>
    <time-of-day>23:55</time-of-day>
  </time>
      <rotate-log>true</rotate-log>
</event>
</server>
```

The parameters configured for forums.sun.com are quite similar to those configured for Sun Blogs (see Section 12.1). One exception should be noted, however, and that is with the number of acceptor threads configured for the HTTP listener. Chapter 2 introduced the concept of acceptor threads and indicated that a good rule of thumb is to configure the number of acceptor threads to be equal to the number of CPUs.

Note: Acceptor threads are threads that wait for client connections. When a request is received, the acceptor thread places it in a queue where it is then picked up by a worker thread for processing. Ideally, you want to have enough acceptor threads so that one is always available when a user needs one, but few enough so that they do not provide too much of a burden on the system. A good rule is to have one acceptor thread per CPU on your system.

In today's multi-core systems, where a single processor may contain many *virtual* CPUs, the rule of thumb can be modified as follows:

A good rule is to have one acceptor thread per CPU, but you can safely scale to one acceptor thread per virtual CPU, if necessary.

In the case of the Sun Forums site, Sun is using a Sun Fire V40Z with four dual-core AMD Opteron processors. That means there are 4×2 (or 8) *virtual* processors that can be leveraged as needed. The number of requests actually experienced on Sun Forums warranted the use of additional acceptor threads.

The key portion of the modified rule of thumb is "if necessary." You do not necessarily need to set the acceptor threads equal to the number of virtual CPUs right out of the box, but it is good to know that you can use them if necessary.

Note: Sun has created an article entitled, "Sun Forums: A Sun Java System Web Server 7.0 Reference Deployment." This article contains additional information on the Sun Forums site, including problems experienced during the deployment, how the problems were debugged, and finally how the site was tuned for optimal performance. This document can be found on the Sun BigAdmin System Administration Portal at http://www.sun.com/bigadmin/features/articles/sun_forums_ref.jsp.

12.3 Major League Baseball Advanced Media LP

Major League Baseball Advanced Media (MLBAM) is the interactive media and Internet company of Major League Baseball. Established in June 2000, MLBAM manages MLB.com as well as sites for all 30 individual major league clubs, baseball's minor leagues, the Major League Baseball Players Association, and the National Baseball Hall of Fame and Museum. MLBAM has recently announced a significant move into the non-baseball entertainment area.

Baseball fans from around the world are flocking to MLB.com, the official web site of Major League Baseball. There, visitors can listen to and watch live games and highlights, check scores, buy game tickets, purchase team merchandise, and even manage a virtual team. MLB.com is the Internet's most successful broadband web portal devoted to professional sports, offering more than one billion minutes of streaming media and over 2,430 full-length games per season to over one billion visitors.

Behind this success is a strategic technology alliance between Major League Baseball Advanced Media (MLBAM) and Sun Microsystems. Sun had worked with MLBAM to design and implement the original infrastructure for MLB.com, all to MLBAM's satisfaction. When the time came to extend the capabilities of the existing site to the new frontier of video and audio content, MLBAM sought a technology partner who could provide the necessary system design, deployment, and sustaining services. MLBAM chose Sun to deliver an advanced media platform featuring unparalleled flexibility, sophistication, and reliability.

Sun managed the project to build new data centers in New York and Chicago. Sun consultants assisted with the design and implementation of a wide range of Sun servers, storage, and software. MLBAM brought in Sun Advantage Partner AT&T to provide hosting services for Internet connectivity, vital to ensure broadband connectivity to all 30 ballparks.

The New York data center features more than a hundred Sun Fire servers running the Solaris 9 operating system. The Chicago data center mirrors the New York site to provide enhanced business continuity. After the data center infrastructures were built, MLB.com engineers installed software applications, including Oracle 9i database, which serves as the data repository for all of MLB.com's information— from player profiles to team histories—and an SAS customer relationship management solution.

To create web services and software applications such as live Internet broadcasts, digital downloads of all playoff games, live pre-game shows, and other expanded broadband capabilities, MLBAM developers rely on components of the Sun Java Enterprise System. Sun Java System Web Server receives and routes requests from web site visitors, using JavaServer Pages (JSP) components. In fact, MLBAM is one of the Internet's largest dynamic JSP content providers with hundreds of thousands of JSP files active on any given day. MLB.com also uses Sun Cluster 3.0 software for high availability, with good results: The site has experienced no downtime in two years of operation.

Needing to archive every game, MLB.com requires massive storage capabilities. It meets those needs with a digital asset management system based on Sun StorageTek storage systems and tape libraries, and the Sun Digital Asset Management Reference Architecture. Sun StorageTek SAM-FS and QFS software manages shared file and archiving capabilities, whereas Artesia Technologies' TEAMS asset management software provides a more efficient and intuitive interface for MLB.com video producers and Z Microsystems' TEAMS Video Adapter helps MLBAM import, encode, and manage audio and video content. The MLB.com digital asset management archive enables users to access and view in real time any media stored in the MLB.com archive.

To maintain the required levels of availability, MLB.com relies on SunSpectrum Platinum and Gold service plans, and uses SunSolve Online to manage patch releases and noncritical support requests. To enhance efficiency and maintain skills, the MLBAM IT team takes Sun training courses in Sun Fire server and Solaris administration.

Already, MLB.com is averaging six million visitors daily with a record-breaking 15 million visitors in a single day. And the web site typically serves up 10 million page views per day with a record-breaking 90 million views delivered during Game Seven of the 2004 American League playoffs. Going forward, MLB.com will feature as many as 15 live games daily and more than 6,000 audio-streamed games over the course of the year.

The alliance with Sun is helping MLBAM to realize its bold initiative for reaching more fans and generating more excitement while producing additional revenue. And that can only be good news for the growth of America's national pastime.

12.4 Summary

Web Server 7.0 provides a proven, stable, secure, and scalable environment for deploying mission critical sites. Its connection-handling architecture is uniquely suited to handle the massive number of transactions experienced by dynamic Web 2.0 sites. Its support for dynamic programming technologies such as Ruby, PHP, Java, and even ASP allows developers the choice to build next-generation web sites on whatever platform they choose. Web Server 7.0's ability to manage a complete server farm as easily as a single server makes it a natural choice for building secure, dynamic, Web 2.0 web sites.

12.5 Self-Paced Labs

Previous chapters in this book provided self-paced labs that allowed you to validate your understanding for configuring and administering Web Server 7.0. With the knowledge gained from these chapters, you should now be able to create your own Web 2.0 sites and feel confident that they are both secure and able to provide the performance requirements necessary to support an extensive user community.

If you feel like you would like more practice, however, you can find additional exercises at http://www.sunwebserver.com. New Web 2.0 sites are being developed all the time, and much of the infrastructure is provided by open source implementations of forums, blogging software, chat, and other interactive products. In fact, there are far too many for us to list here. So instead, go to http://www.sunwebserver.com for instructions on how to install applications such as MediaWiki, Joomla, Moodle, Roller, and more. Although Web Server 7.0 technologies may not change all that frequently, the applications that can be supported by the product will change all the time. As such, the site will be updated with instructions for new applications as they become available. By installing many of these applications and seeing how to configure Web Server 7.0 to support them, you should feel more comfortable customizing the Web Server. Who knows—you might build the next Facebook or YouTube application on top of Web Server 7.0!

As an added benefit, the site also contains self-assessment questions, frequently asked questions, and self-paced labs not found in the book. The purpose of this information is to create a community of like-minded developers and administrators who are interested in building on top of Web Server 7.0. Here you will be able to interact with others to see how they are addressing issues and using the product to develop their own Web 2.0 applications.

A Detailed Look at the server.xml File

AT first glance, the server.xml file might seem a little intimidating. You will find, however, that its format is straightforward and easy to modify after you understand the names of elements and their possible values.

The following example demonstrates a sample server.xml file. Line numbers have been added for reference purposes.

```
1.   <?xml version="1.0" encoding="UTF-8"?>
2.
3.   <!--
4.   Copyright 2006 Sun Microsystems, Inc.  All rights reserved.
5.   Use is subject to license terms.
6.   -->
7.
8.   <server>
9.     <cluster>
10.      <local-host>boulder.example.com</local-host>
11.      <instance>
12.        <host>boulder.example.com</host>
13.      </instance>
14.    </cluster>
15.
16.    <log>
17.      <log-file>../logs/errors</log-file>
18.      <log-level>info</log-level>
19.    </log>
20.
21.    <platform>64</platform>
22.
```

```
23.   <temp-path>/tmp/https-boulder.example.com-6accbd0a</temp-path>
24.
25.   <user>webservd</user>
26.
27.   <jvm>
28.     <java-home>/sun/webserver7/jdk</java-home>
29.     <server-class-path>/sun/webserver7/lib/webserv-rt.jar:/sun/
          webserver7/
          lib/pwc.jar:/sun/webserver7/lib/ant.jar:${java.home}/lib/
            tools.jar:/sun/
          webserver7/lib/ktsearch.jar:/sun/webserver7/lib/webserv-
            jstl.jar:
          /sun/webserver7/lib/jsf-impl.jar:/sun/webserver7/lib/jsf-
          api.jar: /sun/webserver7/lib/webserv-jwsdp.jar:/sun/
            webserver7
          /lib/container-auth.jar:/sun/webserver7/lib/mail.jar:
          /sun/webserver7/lib/activation.jar</server-class-path>
30.     <debug>false</debug>
31.     <debug-jvm-options>-Xdebug -Xrunjdwp:transport=dt_
          socket,server=y,
          suspend=n, address=7896</debug-jvm-options>
32.     <jvm-options>-Djava.security.auth.login.config=login.conf</
          jvm-options>
33.     <jvm-options>-Xms128m -Xmx256m</jvm-options>
34.   </jvm>
35.
36.   <thread-pool>
37.     <max-threads>128</max-threads>
38.     <stack-size>131072</stack-size>
39.   </thread-pool>
40.
41.   <default-auth-db-name>keyfile</default-auth-db-name>
42.
43.   <auth-db>
44.     <name>keyfile</name>
45.     <url>file</url>
46.     <property>
47.       <name>syntax</name>
48.       <value>keyfile</value>
49.     </property>
50.     <property>
51.       <name>keyfile</name>
52.       <value>keyfile</value>
53.     </property>
54.   </auth-db>
55.
56.   <acl-file>default.acl</acl-file>
57.
```

```
58.    <mime-file>mime.types</mime-file>
59.
60.    <access-log>
61.      <file>../logs/access</file>
62.    </access-log>
63.
64.    <http-listener>
65.      <name>http-listener-1</name>
66.      <port>80</port>
67.      <server-name>boulder.example.com</server-name>
68.      <default-virtual-server-name>boulder.example.com</default-
            virtual-
              server-name>
69.    </http-listener>
70.
71.    <virtual-server>
72.      <name>boulder.example.com</name>
73.      <host>boulder.example.com</host>
74.      <http-listener-name>http-listener-1</http-listener-name>
75.      <document-root>/sun/webserver7/https-boulder.example.com/
            docs</document-root>
76.    </virtual-server>
77.  </server>
```

The following is a detailed explanation for each element shown in the `server.xml` file:

Line Number	Description
Line 1	This is the XML declaration, which specifies the version of XML being used in this file. The version declaration can also contain other information, such as an encoding declaration or standalone declarations. The encoding is UTF-8 to maintain compatibility with regular UNIX text editors.
Line 2	This line is empty. Spacing is ignored in the `server.xml` file. (Subsequent empty lines are not discussed in this explanation.)
Lines 3–6	These lines contain comments. Comments begin with a character string of `<!--` and end with a character string of `-->`. Comments cannot exist within the body of attribute definitions.
Line 8	The `<server>` element is the topmost element in the `server.xml` file. This line designates the start of the definition (or opening *tag*) for this element. There is a corresponding closing tag for the `<server>` element found on Line 77. Closing tags are noted by the forward slash usage associated with the element name (that is,. `</server>`).
	All elements defined between lines 8 and 77 are considered *child* elements of the `<server>` element. Allowable child elements and element values are specified by the Web Server 7.0 XML schema file (`sun-web-server_7_0.xsd`).

Line Number	Description
Lines 9–14	A *cluster* is a set of instances that can span one or more nodes. Each instance in the cluster must have an identical configuration and offer an identical set of runtime services. These lines contain the cluster definition for this server. The `<cluster>` element in this example contains two child elements: `<local-host>` and `<instance>`. The `<local-host>` element contains the network address of this server's instance. You will have one `<local-host>` element defined within a cluster. The value of the `<local-host>` element reflects the name (or IP address) of the local server to which the configuration has been deployed. The `<instance>` element defines the cluster's members. You will have at least one member (that is, the local server) but you can have additional instances defined as well. The `<instance>` element in this example contains one child element. The `<host>` element specifies the network address of the instance. This value of the `<host>` element can be either a DNS resolvable hostname or an IP address of this instance. In this example, one instance is defined as part of this cluster, and that is simply the name of the local server. This demonstrates what you would see when you perform an installation where you configure the Administration Server and Administration Node, both on the same physical server (that is, a standalone installation).
Lines 16–19	Errors detected by the server can be stored in a file located on the file system. This file is called the *Server Log*. The details for the Server Log are specified by the `<log>` element. In this example, there are two child elements to the `<log>` element. The `<log-file>` element specifies the path to the Server Log. (Note: This path is relative to the config directory for this instance.) The `<log-level>` attribute specifies the verbosity for the Server Log. This element has a direct effect on both the number of messages and the detail for each message that appears in the Server Log. The value can be finest (most verbose), finer, fine, info, warning, failure, config, security, or catastrophe (least verbose).
Line 21	The `<platform>` element specifies whether the server is running as a 32-bit or 64-bit process. If the `<platform>` element is absent from the `server.xml` file, the server is running in 32-bit mode.
Line 23	The `<temp-path>` element specifies the location where the server stores its temporary files (that is, process identifier—pid—and socket files). If a relative path is used, it is relative to the server's config directory.
Line 25	The `<user>` element specifies the account the server runs as (UNIX only).
Lines 27–34	The `<jvm>` element configures the Java Virtual Machine (JVM). Examples of configuration settings (child elements) for this element include the path to the Java Development Kit (`<jdk>`), the class path (`<server-class-path>`), and various options, such as the minimum and maximum memory allocation for the JVM.

Line Number	Description
Lines 36–39	The `<thread-pool>` element configures the threads used to process HTTP requests. In this example, there are two child elements for `<thread-pool>`: `<max-threads>` and `<stack-size>`. The `<max-threads>` element specifies the maximum number of worker threads that have been allocated for HTTP request processing. The value can be from 1 to 4096. The `<stack-size>` element specifies the size (in bytes) of the thread's stack when a new worker thread is created. The value can be from 8192 to 67108864.
Line 41	The `<default-auth-db-name>` element specifies the name of the default authentication database used for access control processing. The value of this element must be defined elsewhere in the `server.xml` file within the context of an existing `<auth-db>` element. In this example, the `<default-auth-db-name>` value corresponds to the authentication database defined on line 43 and named on line 44.
Lines 43–54	The `<auth-db>` element provides the definition for an authentication database that may be used during access control processing. Several child elements can be defined within the `<auth-db>` element. They specify the name of the authentication database (`<name>`), the type of authentication database (`<url>`), and various properties (`<property>`) that are used within the context of the authentication database (such as the format and syntax of the authentication database). In this example, a file-based authentication database (line 45) has been defined and is referenced by the name, `keyfile` (line 44). The name of the actual file is also called `keyfile` (lines 50–53), and it might be found directly beneath this instance's `config` directory. The syntax of any entries found in the file follows a `keyfile` format (lines 46–49).
Line 56	The `<acl-file>` element defines a file that is used to specify the rules for controlling access to various server resources. In this example, the `<acl-file>` element defines a file called `default.acl` that may be used for access control processing. If the fully qualified file name is not specified, the name of the file is relative to the `config` directory for this server instance.
Line 58	The `<mime-file>` element defines a file that is used to configure Multipurpose Internet Mail Extensions (MIME)–type mappings for the Web Server. This file is used during HTTP request processing to map file types to the appropriate service for processing. In this example, the `<mime-file>` element defines a file called `mime.types` that may be used for this purpose. The file may be found beneath the `config` directory for this server instance.
Lines 60–62	All HTTP requests are stored in the server's Access Log. The `<access-log>` element can have several child elements that are used to define the name, format, location, and status of the Access Log. In this example, the `<access-log>` element specifies that the Access Log may be found beneath the `logs` directory. The name of the file is simply `access`. The default format of this file is the CLF (common log file) format.

Line Number	Description
Lines 64–69	Client requests are received on a particular port or *HTTP listener*. The `<http-listener>` element is used to configure the HTTP listener. The `<http-listener>` element in this example contains four child elements: `<name>`, `<port>`, `<server-name>`, and `<default-virtual-server-name>`.
	The `<name>` element specifies the name that is used to reference the listener.
	The `<port>` element specifies the port number for which the listener is configured. The `<port>` element may be associated with the `<ip>` element to produce various combinations of virtual servers. If the `<ip>` element is missing from the `<http-listener>` definition, the `<port>` element applies to all IP addresses for which this server has been configured.
	The `<server-name>` element specifies the default server name used for this listener. The value can include a scheme prefix (for example, `http://`) and port suffix (for example, `:80`).
	The `<default-virtual-server-name>` element specifies the name of the virtual server that will be used for request processing if the server is not able to determine the virtual server from programmatic methods. This element is likely to be used when multiple web sites map to the same IP address in DNS, but no virtual server has been configured within the Web Server for that web site.
Lines 71–76	Virtual servers enable you to host multiple web sites within a single installed server. The `<virtual-server>` element is used to configure an HTTP virtual server for your instance. Each server typically has at least one virtual server configured, and all virtual servers have an HTTP Listener specified.
	The `<virtual-server>` element in this example contains four child elements: `<name>`, `<host>`, `<http-listener-name>`, and `<document-root>`.
	The `<name>` element specifies the name that is used to reference the virtual server.
	The `<host>` element specifies the name of the host(s) for which the virtual server services requests. Host comparisons are not case sensitive, and the value of the `<host>` element can be a hostname or a wildcard pattern (for example, `*.example.com`).
	The `<http-listener-name>` element specifies the name of an HTTP listener associated with one or more of the virtual server's hostnames. The value of the `<http-listener-name>` is the name from an `<http-listener>` element. The server will flag an error if the virtual server that is called upon to process the request does not have an `<http-listener-name>` configured for the listener that received the original request.
	The `<document-root>` element specifies the directory path on the Web Server's file system where documents (or content) are generally available.
Line 77	This is the corresponding closing tag for the `<server>` element found on Line 8.

Sample XML Report Data

AFTER a Web Server instance is started, it begins gathering statistical data that is useful for monitoring purposes and is accessible through an XML data report. The Administration Console and certain text reports extract information from the XML data to provide you with a user friendly interface. There are times, however, when you might need to review the raw XML data because it contains much more detailed information than a formatted web page or report.

The entirety of the Web Server's statistical data can be accessed by default using the `get-stats-xml` subcommand in the CLI. Additionally, you can enable Web Server to provide this data when prompted with a specific URI.

Note: See section 7.3.2, "XML Report," in Chapter 7 for more information.

The following example demonstrates a nonfiltered output of the XML data:

```
<?xml version="1.0" encoding="utf-8"?>

<!DOCTYPE stats SYSTEM "sun-web-server-stats_7_0_1.dtd">

<stats versionMajor="1" versionMinor="3" enabled="1">
    <server id="https-www.example.com" versionServer="Sun Java System
    Web Server
 7.0U2 B12/12/2007 08:48 (WINNT DOMESTIC)" timeStarted="1211245262"
secondsRunning="88460" ticksPerSecond="1000" maxProcs="1" max-
   Threads="128"
flagProfilingEnabled="1">
        <connection-queue id="cq1"/>
```

```
        <thread-pool id="thread-pool-0" name="NativePool"/>
        <profile id="profile-0" name="all-requests" description="All
    requests"/>
        <profile id="profile-1" name="default-bucket"
    description="Default
bucket"/>
        <profile id="profile-2" name="cache-bucket" description="Cached
            responses"/>
        <process pid="2192" mode="active" timeStarted="1211245262"
            countConfigurations="3">
            <connection-queue-bucket connection-queue="cq1"
countTotalConnections="2" countQueued="0" peakQueued="1" max-
    Queued="16384"
countOverflows="0" countTotalQueued="2" ticksTotalQueued="0"
countQueued1MinuteAverage="0.000000" countQueued5MinuteAver-
    age="0.000000"
countQueued15MinuteAverage="0.000000"/>
            <thread-pool-bucket thread-pool="thread-pool-0" count
                ThreadsIdle="1"
countThreads="1" maxThreads="128" countQueued="0" peakQueued="1"
    maxQueued="0"/>
            <dns-bucket flagCacheEnabled="1" countCacheEntries="0"
maxCacheEntries="1024" countCacheHits="0" countCacheMisses="0"
    flagAsyncEnabled="0"
countAsyncNameLookups="0" countAsyncAddrLookups="0"
countAsyncLookupsInProgress="0"/>
            <keepalive-bucket countConnections="0"
                maxConnections="65536"
countHits="1" countFlushes="0" countRefusals="0" countTimeouts="2"
secondsTimeout="30"/>
            <cache-bucket flagEnabled="1" secondsMaxAge="30"
                countEntries="3"
maxEntries="1024" countOpenEntries="0" maxOpenEntries="1024" size-
    HeapCache="8944"
maxHeapCacheSize="10739732" sizeMmapCache="0" maxMmapCacheSize="0"
    countHits="2"
countMisses="9" countInfoHits="1" countInfoMisses="7" countConten-
    tHits="0"
countContentMisses="0" countAcceleratorEntries="0" countAccelerat-
    ableRequests="3"
countUnacceleratableRequests="0" countAcceleratableResponses="0"
countUnacceleratableResponses="3" countAcceleratorHits="0"
countAcceleratorMisses="0"/>
            <thread mode="idle" timeStarted="1211245269"
                connection-queue="cq1">
```

```xml
                <request-bucket countRequests="0" countBytesReceived="0"
countBytesTransmitted="0" rateBytesTransmitted="0" maxByteTransmis-
    sionRate="0"
countOpenConnections="0" maxOpenConnections="0" count2xx="0"
    count3xx="0"
count4xx="0" count5xx="0" countOther="0" count200="0" count302="0"
    count304="0"
count400="0" count401="0" count403="0" count404="0" count503="0"/>
                <profile-bucket profile="profile-0" countCalls="0"
countRequests="0" ticksDispatch="0" ticksFunction="0"/>
                <profile-bucket profile="profile-1" countCalls="0"
countRequests="0" ticksDispatch="0" ticksFunction="0"/>
                <profile-bucket profile="profile-2" countCalls="0"
countRequests="0" ticksDispatch="0" ticksFunction="0"/>
            </thread>
            <thread mode="idle" timeStarted="1211245269"
              connection-queue="cq1"
addressClient="127.0.0.1">
                <request-bucket countRequests="3" countBytes
                  Received="1394"
countBytesTransmitted="4290" rateBytesTransmitted="0" maxByteTrans-
    missionRate="0"
countOpenConnections="0" maxOpenConnections="0" count2xx="1"
    count3xx="1"
count4xx="1" count5xx="0" countOther="0" count200="1" count302="0"
    count304="1"
count400="0" count401="0" count403="0" count404="1" count503="0"/>
                <profile-bucket profile="profile-0" countCalls="48"
countRequests="3" ticksDispatch="9" ticksFunction="1"/>
                <profile-bucket profile="profile-1" countCalls="48"
countRequests="3" ticksDispatch="9" ticksFunction="1"/>
                <profile-bucket profile="profile-2" countCalls="0"
countRequests="0" ticksDispatch="0" ticksFunction="0"/>
            </thread>
            <thread mode="idle" timeStarted="1211245300"
              connection-queue="cq1">

                <request-bucket countRequests="0" countBytesReceived="0"
countBytesTransmitted="0" rateBytesTransmitted="0" maxByteTransmis-
    sionRate="0"
countOpenConnections="0" maxOpenConnections="0" count2xx="0"
    count3xx="0"
count4xx="0" count5xx="0" countOther="0" count200="0" count302="0"
    count304="0"
count400="0" count401="0" count403="0" count404="0" count503="0"/>
                <profile-bucket profile="profile-0" countCalls="0"
countRequests="0" ticksDispatch="0" ticksFunction="0"/>
                <profile-bucket profile="profile-1" countCalls="0"
```

```
countRequests="0" ticksDispatch="0" ticksFunction="0"/>
                <profile-bucket profile="profile-2" countCalls="0"
countRequests="0" ticksDispatch="0" ticksFunction="0"/>
            </thread>
            <jvm countClassesLoaded="1944" countTotalClasses
            Loaded="1944"
countTotalClassesUnloaded="0" sizeHeap="9338152" peakThreads="7"
countTotalThreadsStarted="8" countThreads="7" version="1.5.0_12-b04"
  name="Java
HotSpot(TM) Server VM" vendor="Sun Microsystems Inc." countGarbage-
  Collections="4"
millisecondsGarbageCollection="37"/>
        </process>
        <virtual-server id="www.example.com" mode="active" hosts=
          "www.example.com"
interfaces="*:8080">
            <request-bucket method="GET" uri="/favicon.ico" count
                Requests="3"
countBytesReceived="1394" countBytesTransmitted="4290" rateBytes-
  Transmitted="0"
maxByteTransmissionRate="0" countOpenConnections="0" maxOpenConnec-
  tions="0"
count2xx="1" count3xx="1" count4xx="1" count5xx="0" countOther="0"
  count200="1"
count3
02="0" count304="1" count400="0" count401="0" count403="0"
  count404="1"
count503="0"/>
            <profile-bucket profile="profile-0" countCalls="48" count
                Requests="3"
ticksDispatch="9" ticksFunction="1"/>
            <profile-bucket profile="profile-1" countCalls="48" count
                Requests="3"
ticksDispatch="9" ticksFunction="1"/>
            <profile-bucket profile="profile-2" countCalls="0" count
                Requests="0"
ticksDispatch="0" ticksFunction="0"/>
            <web-app-bucket uri="/" mode="enabled" countJsps="0"
countReloadedJsps="0" countSessions="0" countActiveSessions="0"
peakActiveSessions="0" countRejectedSessions="0" countExpiredSes-
  sions="0"
secondsSessionAliveMax="0" secondsSessionAliveAverage="0">
                <servlet-bucket name="jsp" countRequests="0"
                    countErrors="0"
millisecondsProcessing="0" millisecondsPeakProcessing="0"/>
                <servlet-bucket name="invoker" countRequests="0"
                    countErrors="0"
 millisecondsProcessing="0" millisecondsPeakProcessing="0"/>
```

```
            <servlet-bucket name="default" countRequests="0"
                countErrors="0"
millisecondsProcessing="0" millisecondsPeakProcessing="0"/>
            </web-app-bucket>
          </virtual-server>
        </server>
      </stats>
```

Most (but not all) elements within the XML Report can be accessed through various areas of the Administration GUI or the CLI. See Chapter 7, "Monitoring Web Server 7.0," for more information.

Sample Plain Text Report Data

`service-dump` is a Server Application Function (SAF) built in to the Web Server that collects various pieces of performance data from internal Web Server statistics (`stats-xml`) and displays them in an ASCII-formatted text report.

Note: You might see references to `service-dump`, `perfdump`, or a Plain Text Report in the Sun documentation. They all refer to the same functionality.

Plain Text Report data does not display all the statistics available through the CLI or the Administration Console, but it can still be a useful tool for monitoring your Web Server. You can obtain a Plain Text Report by using the `get-perfdump` sub-command in the CLI or by defining a URI to intercept and obtain the data.

A Plain Text Report provides statistics in the following categories:

- Connection Queue Information
- HTTP Listener (Listen Socket) Information
- Keep-Alive Information
- Session Creation (Thread) Information
- File Cache Information (Static Content)
- Thread Pool Information
- DNS Cache Information

Note: See section 7.3.3, "Performance Monitoring Tool (`perfdump`)," in Chapter 7 for more information.

The remainder of this appendix demonstrates information contained in a typical Plain Text Report. Notes have been inserted at various points within the report to provide an explanation of the data being displayed, as well as possible options for tuning your Web Server. See the *Sun Java System Web Server 7.0 Performance Tuning, Sizing and Scaling Guide* for more information on tuning your Web Server based on this data.

Warning: Before making any changes to any of these parameters, you should establish (and possibly automate) test cases that can be used to create a performance benchmark on a controlled system. After you have gathered your data you can then modify the parameters discussed in this appendix and execute the tests once again to ensure that the changes you made actually had a positive effect on system performance.

```
Sun Java System Web Server 7.0U2 B12/12/2007 08:48 (WINNT DOMESTIC)

Server started Mon May 19 21:01:01 2008
Process 2192 started Mon May 19 21:01:01 2008
```

Note: The first portion of the report provides information pertaining to the Web Server version and the operating system on which it is running. It also contains information detailing the time the server process was started and the process identifier associated with the currently running Web Server instance.

```
ConnectionQueue:
-------------------------------------------
Current/Peak/Limit Queue Length        0/1/16384
Total Connections Queued               23
Average Queue Length (1, 5, 15 minutes) 0.00, 0.00, 0.00
Average Queueing Delay                 0.00 milliseconds
```

Note: When a client makes a request from the Web Server, the connection is first accepted by an *acceptor thread* that is associated with the HTTP listener. The acceptor thread places the connection on the *Connection Queue* and returns to wait for the next client request. Request processing threads (called *worker threads*) then take the connection from the Connection Queue and process the request. In a typical Web Server instance, you will have several requests queued and waiting to be processed. Too many queued requests, however, can be an indication that the server is not responding to requests in a timely manner.

Connection Queue information in the `perfdump` data shows the number of sessions in the Connection Queue and the average delay before the connection is accepted by the request processing thread.

The Connection Queue information provided in this example demonstrates a server that has a minimal load on it. If you find that the Peak Queue Length is close to the Limit Queue Length (maximum queue size), you should consider increasing the maximum Connection Queue size to avoid dropping connections under heavy load.

```
ListenSocket http-listener-1:
------------------------
Address                 http://0.0.0.0:8080
Acceptor Threads        1
Default Virtual Server  www.example.com

ListenSocket http-listener-2:
------------------------
Address                 https://0.0.0.0:443
Acceptor Threads        1
Default Virtual Server  www.example.com
```

Note: The ListenSocket (HTTP listener) information includes the IP address, port number, number of acceptor threads, and the default virtual server. You can have many HTTP listeners enabled for virtual servers, but at least one is enabled for your default server instance (usually http://0.0.0.0:80).

Although it is convenient to use an IP address of 0.0.0.0 (which represents any IP address), doing so causes one additional system call to be made for each connection. You can cut down the number of system calls (and therefore increase performance) by specifying an actual IP address when you create or modify your HTTP listener.

The most important field in the HTTP listener information, however, is the number of acceptor threads. Ideally, you want to have enough acceptor threads so that one is always available when a client makes a request of the Web Server, but few enough so that they do not place too much of a burden on the system.

A good rule is to have one acceptor thread per CPU on your system. You can increase this value to about double the number of CPUs if you find indications of TCP/IP listen queue overruns.

```
KeepAliveInfo:
--------------------
KeepAliveCount        1/65536
KeepAliveHits         117
KeepAliveFlushes      0
KeepAliveRefusals     0
KeepAliveTimeouts     7
KeepAliveTimeout      30 seconds
```

Note: In Web Server terminology, a Keep-Alive connection refers to a client's request (and subsequent agreement by the Web Server) to keep the current connection *alive* (or active) so that multiple requests can be made without having to open, close, and reopen connections for each request. This dramatically reduces the overhead associated with opening and closing connections, especially when a single web page may require several requests before it is completely transferred. Older versions of the HTTP standard used the terminology of *keep-alive* to describe this capability, but HTTP version 1.1 now refers to this concept as a PersistentConnection. The Sun Web Server, however, continues to refer to this by the previous reference of Keep-Alive connections.

The Web Server maintains a counter for the maximum number of waiting Keep-Alive connections. In Example 7.1, this is represented by the 65536 value contained in the KeepAliveCount value and indicates the maximum number of Keep-Alive connections that the Web Server will maintain at any one time.

The keep-alive subsystem in Web Server is designed to be massively scalable. The out-of-the-box configuration can be less than optimal, however, if the workload is not persistent (for example, if the client is using HTTP 1.0 and does not provide the KeepAlive header) or for a lightly loaded system that's primarily servicing Keep-Alive connections.

```
SessionCreationInfo:
------------------------
Active Sessions         0
Keep-Alive Sessions     1
Total Sessions Created  4/128
```

Note: Session (thread) creation statistics include the current number of threads being used to process requests (Active Sessions), the number of threads being used to process keep-alive sessions (Keep-Alive Sessions) and the total number of sessions that have been created compared to the maximum number of threads (Total Sessions Created).

The Web Server can service certain type of requests, such as cached static content, from the keep-alive threads. Therefore, the maximum threads in the Total Sessions Created value is the sum of the maximum threads configured in the thread-pool element in the server.xml file plus the number of keep-alive threads. In Example 7.1, this is represented by the number 128 in the Total Sessions Created field and is referred to as the Maximum Threads setting.

The Maximum Threads setting specifies the maximum number of simultaneous transactions that the Web Server can handle at any given time. The default value is 128. Changes to this value can be used to throttle the server, minimizing latencies for the transactions that are performed. The Maximum Threads value acts across multiple virtual servers but does not attempt to load balance. It is set for each configuration.

Reaching the maximum number of configured threads is not necessarily undesirable, and you do not need to automatically increase the number of threads in the server if you reach the Maximum Threads value. Reaching this limit means that the server needed this many threads at peak load, but as long as it was able to serve requests in a timely manner, the server is adequately tuned. You should, however, monitor the Total Sessions Created value because requests are queued once you reach the Maximum Threads value. If requests continue to queue up, you could potentially overflow the Connection Queue and stop servicing requests. If you monitor your server's performance regularly and notice that the total number of sessions created is often near the maximum number of threads, you should consider increasing your thread limits.

```
CacheInfo:
-----------------------
File Cache Enabled        yes
File Cache Entries        4/1024
File Cache Hit Ratio      325/466 ( 69.74%)
Maximum Age               30
Accelerator Entries       0/1024
Acceleratable Requests    45/140 ( 32.14%)
Acceleratable Responses   0/45 (  0.00%)
Accelerator Hit Ratio     0/0 (  0.00%)
```

Note: Retrieving content from the file system can be an extremely expensive operation in terms of performance. As such, the Web Server employs a file caching mechanism that enables you to store and serve content directly from memory. Effective configuration of the file cache can have a dramatic increase in performance for files that are primarily static in nature.

The optimal file cache heap size depends on how much system memory is free. A larger heap size means that the Web Server can cache more content and therefore obtain a better hit ratio. However, the heap size should not be so large that the operating system starts paging cached files.

The `CacheInfo` section of the `perfdump` data provides information on how your file cache has been configured and statistics on how effectively your file cache is being utilized. File caching is enabled by default; this can be seen in Example 7.1 in the `File Cache Enabled` value. If you decide to disable the file cache, the remaining fields in this section are not displayed.

For sites with scheduled updates to content, consider shutting down the cache while the content is being updated and starting it again after the update is complete. Although performance slows down, the server operates normally when the cache is off.

The `File Cache Entries` value provides information on the current number of cached entries as well as the maximum number of cache entries possible. Keep in mind that these values are based on the entries, not on how much file cache has been consumed by the file. The amount of file cache (or RAM) consumed by entries can vary based on the size of the entry being cached. The Web Server attempts to keep this as manageable as possible by caching small files in their entirety in memory but caching only open file descriptors for larger files.

You can increase the maximum number of cached entries up to a value of 1,048,576. However, if you set the value to be too large, the server could potentially cache files that are not referenced all that often (this might actually waste memory). If the value is too small, the benefit of using the file cache is lost. You should monitor the `File Cache Hit Ratio` to find the optimal solution for your environment.

The `File Cache Hit Ratio` value provides you with the number of files served out of cache (`Total Cache Hits`) compared to the number of cache lookups (`Total Cache Hits + Total Cache Misses`). A ratio that approaches 100% indicates that the file cache is operating effectively, while numbers approaching 0% could indicate that the file cache is not serving many requests.

The `Maximum Age` field displays the maximum age (in seconds) of a valid cache entry. This parameter controls how long a file remains cached after it has been placed in the file cache. An entry older than the `Maximum Age` setting will be replaced by a new entry for the same file.

Set the `Maximum Age` setting based on whether your static content is updated on a regular schedule. For example, if content is updated four times a day at regular intervals, you could set the maximum age to 21600 seconds (6 hours). Otherwise, consider setting the maximum age to the longest time you are willing to serve the previous version of a file after it has been modified. If your web site's content changes infrequently, you might want to increase this value for improved performance.

Web Server 7.0 provides a new accelerator cache technology that speeds the delivery of small files. The `Accelerator Entries` field in the `perfdump` data specifies the number of files that have been cached in the accelerator cache, as well as the maximum number of files that can be cached. The accelerator cache is automatically enabled and is tightly coupled with the `File Cache Entries` setting. It does not have any particular settings of its own, but it can be affected when you modify the `File Cache Entries` setting. For example, the maximum number of accelerator cache entries is increased when you increase the number of `File Cache Entries`. The actual files served from the accelerator cache will typically be smaller than the `File Cache Entries` number, however, because the accelerator cache caches information about only files and not directories.

The `Acceleratable Requests` setting specifies the number of client requests that were *eligible* for processing by the accelerator cache. This includes simple `GET` requests but does not include requests that explicitly disable caching (such as a forced reload of a web page) or requests that include query strings included in the URI. To maximize the number of requests served out of the accelerator cache, you should structure your web sites to use static files if/when possible and avoid using query strings in requests for static files.

When the server serves a static file from the file cache, the accelerator cache might be able to cache the response for faster processing on subsequent requests. The `Acceleratable Responses` value specifies the number of times the response to an acceleratable request was eligible for addition to the accelerator cache. To effectively utilize the accelerator cache, you should maximize the number of responses that are acceleratable. In the default configuration, all responses to requests for static files can be cached in the accelerator cache. The following configuration changes might prevent a response from being acceleratable:

- ACLs that deny read access
- Additional directives in the default object of the `obj.conf` file, including third-party plug-ins
- Using `<Client>` or `<If>` containers in an object configuration file's `default` object
- Custom access log formats
- Java servlet filters

To maximize the number of responses that are acceleratable, you should avoid such configurations.

The `Accelerator Hit Ratio` contains the number of times the response for an acceleratable request was found in the accelerator cache. The Web Server can serve requests from the accelerator cache asynchronously directly from the keep-alive threads, thereby bypassing the Connection Queue altogether. This leads to improved performance for these requests and at the same time reduces contention on the Connection Queue. Higher hit ratios result in better performance, but this can be achieved only if your site is serving content that is relatively static in nature and follows the guidelines specified for `Acceleratable Requests` or `Acceleratable Responses`.

```
Native pools:
----------------------------
NativePool:
Idle/Peak/Limit                    2/2/128
Work Queue Length/Peak/Limit       0/1/0

my-custom-pool:
Idle/Peak/Limit                    1/1/128
Work Queue Length/Peak/Limit       0/0/0
```

Note: If you are using the default settings, worker threads from the default thread pool are used to process client requests. You can, however, create your own custom thread pools and use them to process custom NSAPI functions. Additionally, the Web Server creates one additional pool, named NativePool, that can be also be used for this purpose. The perfdump report provides insight into how effectively the Native-Pool thread pool is being used. If you have defined additional custom thread pools, they are found beneath the NativePool section, as shown by the my-custom-pool section shown in Example 7.1.

Each native pool defined in this section contains information that specifies the number of threads that are currently idle (Idle), the number of threads utilized during peak processing (Peak), and the maximum number of native threads allowed in the pool (Limit).

Information pertaining to the Work Queue provides insight into the number of queued server requests that are waiting for the use of a native thread from the pool. The Work Queue Length is the current number of requests waiting for a native thread. Peak refers to the highest number of requests that were ever queued up simultaneously for the use of a native thread since the server was started. This value can be viewed as the maximum concurrency for requests requiring a native thread. Limit is the maximum number of requests that can be queued at one time to wait for a native thread and is determined by the NativePoolQueueSize setting in the magnus.conf file.

You can increase the pool size or queue length if you find that you are frequently reaching the Peak value for either the NativePool threads or the Work Queue Length. Care should be taken, however, because increasing these values consumes additional RAM from your server and might not address the actual problem. You might often find other causes for reaching the Peak values, such as a Web application that does not properly release database connections. You should look in other areas before simply modifying these settings.

```
DNSCacheInfo:
------------------
enabled           yes
CacheEntries      0/1024
HitRatio          0/0 (  0.00%)

Async DNS disabled
```

Note: The Web Server uses a DNS caching mechanism to reduce the number of DNS lookups performed while it resolves DNS hostnames into IP addresses. The DNS cache stores IP addresses to DNS name mappings and is used to increase performance for logging and access control rules that refer to DNS names. DNS cache is enabled by default, but if you do not perform operations that require a DNS lookup, the DNS cache is not utilized.

The CacheEntries values in the perfdump report show the current number of cached entries compared to the maximum possible number of cache entries. A single cache entry represents a single IP address or DNS name lookup. When tuning the DNS cache you should attempt to configure it to be as large as the maximum number of clients that will access your web site concurrently. This can realistically be performed only by monitoring the CacheEntries values and should not be modified without first doing so. Setting the DNS cache size too high can actually waste memory and degrade server performance.

The HitRatio value is simply a comparison of the number of cache hits compared to the number of cache lookups.

The Web Server can be configured to use its own asynchronous DNS resolver or use the synchronous resolver provided by the operating system. To save time on lookups, it uses the operating system's resolver by default. This is indicated by the Async DNS disabled reference in the perfdump report.

```
Performance Counters:
---------------------------------------------------
                              Average    Total      Percent

Total number of requests:                139
Request processing time:      0.0872     12.1250

default-bucket (Default bucket)
Number of Requests:                      139       (100.00%)
Number of Invocations:                   2650      (100.00%)
Latency:                      0.0064     0.8850    (  7.30%)
Function Processing Time:     0.0809     11.2400   ( 92.70%)
Total Response Time:          0.0872     12.1250   (100.00%)
```

```
Sessions:
-------------------------------------------------------------
Process  Status      Client      Age  VS  Method  URI  Function

2192     keep-alive  127.0.0.1
```

 Note: The remaining information contained in the `perfdump` report provides insight into how well your Web Server is performing overall. This information can be found in the `Performance Counters` section in Example 7.1. This section contains the average, total, and percentage values for various metrics that enable you to determine how your changes might be affecting server performance.

You can isolate certain requests or categories of requests by using performance *buckets*. Performance buckets enable you to define monitoring containers and link them to various server functions. Every time one of these functions is invoked, the server collects statistical data and adds it to the bucket. For example, `send-cgi` and `service-j2ee` are functions used to serve the CGI and Java servlet requests, respectively. You can either define two buckets to maintain separate counters for CGI and servlet requests, or create one bucket that counts requests for both types of dynamic content. The cost of collecting this information is minimal, and the impact on the server performance is usually negligible.

Performance bucket data contains the following information:

- Average, Total, and Percent columns give data for each requested statistic.

- `Request processing time` is the total time required by the server to process all requests it has received so far.

- `Number of Requests` is the total number of requests for the function.

- `Number of Invocations` is the total number of times that the function was invoked. This differs from the number of requests in that a function could be called multiple times during the processing of a single request. The percentage column for this row is calculated in reference to the total number of invocations for all the buckets.

- `Latency` is the time in seconds that Web Server takes to prepare for calling the function.

- `Function Processing Time` is the time in seconds that Web Server spent inside the function. The percentage of `Function Processing Time` and `Total Response Time` is calculated with reference to the total `Request Processing Time`.

- `Total Response Time` is the sum in seconds of `Function Processing Time` and `Latency`.

Data contained in the `perfdump` report can provide valuable insight into how well your server is processing requests. `stats-xml` data provides a comprehensive view of all available statistical data and is quite useful for diving deeper into the data, but it might actually contain too much information. As an alternative, a `perfdump` report provides a formatted subset of the `stats-xml` data and gives you a dashboard view of your Web Server's overall performance.

Index